From Treason to Runaway Slaves

THE FAIRLEIGH DICKINSON UNIVERSITY PRESS

Series in Law, Culture, and the Humanities

Series Editor: Caroline Joan "Kay" S. Picart, MPhil (Cantab), PhD, JD, Esquire

Attorney at Law; Adjunct Professor, FAMU College of Law; former English & HUM professor, FSU

The Fairleigh Dickinson University Press Series in Law, Culture, and the Humanities publishes scholarly works in which the field of Law intersects with, among others, Film, Criminology, Sociology, Communication, Critical/Cultural Studies, Literature, History, Philosophy, and the Humanities.

On the Web at http://www.fdu.edu/fdupress

Publications

Linda Myrsiades, *From Treason to Runaway Slaves: Legal Culture in New Republic Trials, 1783–1808* (2024)

Eamon P. H. Keane and Peter Robson, *The Ian Willock Collection on Law and Justice in the Twenty-First Century* (2023)

Peter Robson and Ferdinando Spina, *Vigilante Justice in Society and Popular Culture: A Global Perspective* (2022)

Joel Silverman, *The Legal Exhibitionist: Morris Ernst, Jewish Identity, and the Modern Celebrity Lawyer* (2022)

Matthew Sorrento and David Ryan, *David Fincher's* Zodiac*: Cinema of Investigation and (Mis)Interpretation* (2021)

T. Patrick Hill, *No Place for Ethics: Judicial Review, Legal Positivism, and the Supreme Court of the United States* (2021)

Caroline Joan "Kay" S. Picart, *Monsters, Law, Crime: Explorations in Gothic Criminology* (2020)

Elaine Wood, *Gender Justice and the Law: Theoretical Practices of Intersectional Identity* (2020)

Orit Kamir, *Betraying Dignity: The Toxic Seduction of Social Media, Shaming, and Radicalization* (2019)

Marouf A. Hasian Jr., *Lawfare and the Ovaherero and Nama Pursuit of Restorative Justice, 1918–2018* (2019)

George Pate, *Enter the Undead Author: Intellectual Property, the Ideology of Authorship, and Performance Practices since the 1960s* (2019)

From Treason to Runaway Slaves

Legal Culture in New Republic Trials, 1783–1808

Linda Myrsiades

FAIRLEIGH DICKINSON UNIVERSITY PRESS
Vancouver • Madison • Teaneck • Wroxton

Published by Fairleigh Dickinson University Press
Copublished by The Rowman & Littlefield Publishing Group, Inc.
4501 Forbes Boulevard, Suite 200, Lanham, Maryland 20706
www.rowman.com

86-90 Paul Street, London EC2A 4NE, United Kingdom

Fairleigh Dickinson University Press gratefully acknowledges the support received for scholarly publishing from the Friends of FDU Press.

British Library Cataloguing in Publication Information Available

Library of Congress Cataloging-in-Publication Data

Names: Myrsiades, Linda, 1941– author.
Title: From treason to runaway slaves : legal culture in new Republic trials, 1783-1808 / Linda Myrsiades.
Description: Vancouver ; Lanham, Maryland : Fairleigh Dickinson University Press, 2023. | Series: The fairleigh dickinson university press series in law, culture, and the humanities | Includes bibliographical references and index. | Summary: "From Treason to Runaway Slaves provides case studies of high-profile trials from the early Republic examined in terms of the period's history, law, and culture. It focuses on a historical period and place crucial to identity formation in the new nation and the survival of the U.S. as a democratic experiment"—Provided by publisher.
Identifiers: LCCN 2023032329 (print) | LCCN 2023032330 (ebook) | ISBN 9781683933847 (cloth) | ISBN 9781683933854 (epub)
Subjects: LCSH: Trials—United States—History. | Treason—Law and legislation—United States—History. | Slavery—Law and legislation—United States—History. | Fugitive slaves—Legal status, laws, etc.—United States—History. | Antislavery movements—United States—History. | Riots—United States—History.
Classification: LCC KF220 .M97 2023 (print) | LCC KF220 (ebook) | DDC 345/.730231—dc23/eng/20230919
LC record available at https://lccn.loc.gov/2023032329
LC ebook record available at https://lccn.loc.gov/2023032330

For Dean

"O brave new world, that has such people in it!"

Contents

Acknowledgments

My very first acknowledgment goes to Ron McColl, West Chester University's incredibly astute research librarian and head of Special Collections whose expert assistance was essential to the successful completion of a book with considerable sourcing needs. Interlibrary loan librarian Jennifer O'Leary's assistance was, as always, irreplaceable, generously offered, and gratefully accepted. I am indebted to the state and federal archives, private collections, historical societies, college and university libraries, bar associations, and history centers that have helped with locating documents. These include the Special Collections Library at West Chester University, Chester County Archives and its archivist Laurie Rofini, Christopher Densmore and the Friends Historical Library at Swarthmore College, the Paterson Papers at William Paterson College, the Gilder Lehrman Institute of American History, the C. P. Humrich Collection, the Western Historical Society, the Washington County Courts of Pennsylvania, Dartmouth College, the University of Georgia, the Pennsylvania History and Museum Commission, the Pennsylvania State Archives, the Library Company, the Massachusetts Historical Society, the Virginia State Archives, the Pennsylvania Bar Association, the University of Pennsylvania Biddle Law Library, Dickinson College, Rutgers University, the Cumberland County Historical Society, Washington and Jefferson College, the Western Bar Association, and the Heinz History Center. Of the many libraries upon whose resources this study relied, I am particularly appreciative of the Historical Society of Pennsylvania and the Library of Congress without which no early American scholarship could get done.

I would like to acknowledge *Pennsylvania History: A Journal of Mid-Atlantic Studies*, in whose pages chapter 6 was originally published, the *Pennsylvania Magazine of History and Biography*, for material that was part of chapter 4, as well as Lehigh University Press, which published an earlier book of mine on the *Rush v. Cobbett* trial that informed chapter 5. A forthcoming book to be published in spring 2024 by the University of Georgia

Press will more extensively address issues related to the law and legal culture of the Whiskey Rebellion.

Finally, it is a pleasure to thank Gautham Rao for his collegiality in taking time off from his own scholarship to make very helpful comments that helped give shape to the complexities of chapter 3, and Christian Fellner, a Bavarian confederate whose kindness in providing offprints rescued me at a difficult and challenging time.

Introduction

From Treason to Runaway Slaves: Legal Culture in New Republic Trials, 1783–1808, studies six trials that together emphasize themes to which early Americans attached special significance, which are central to early republic issues and concepts and demonstrate the criticality of early republic legal culture and legal history from 1783 to 1808 to the development of democracy in the new nation. We thus view trials through three lenses: legal culture, legal history, and democracy.

In terms of legal culture, this study fixes its gaze on law embedded in culture. It contributes to the ongoing reformation of legal thinking by exploring the fault lines of justice, their instability, and privilege. In its examination of conflicts and counterforces, this work accesses the cautionary themes invested in the struggle for power and the condition of powerlessness, in geographical and ideological splits. Its approach to studying legal culture embraces the richness of context that the interdisciplinary study of history, law, and language provides and exploits the potency of conflict analysis, the immediacy of thick description, and the nuance of rhetorical study. It reads legal culture as texts full of ellipses, incoherencies, and transient data to find their shape and how they behave, what their patterns signify. Its interpretations are drawn from the inferences provided by places, language, gestures, and events, from the people who experienced or expressed those events. It draws, as anthropologist Clifford Geertz suggests, "explanatory conclusions" out of the flow of that discourse. If, as he advises, the landscapes of meaning that make up our cultural understanding arise from the microscopic miniature,[1] it is in those gestures and that language we will discover whom the law represented and how those at a distance from power geographically, culturally, by race or ethnicity resisted or accommodated their power or, to the contrary, appropriated and expressed it themselves.

As for legal history, the material out of which the study is crafted, the trials pose questions about threats to the American nation and address questions of American identity, asking whether justice was done and what was learned by putting society on trial and testing its values. The trials raise questions of land ownership, rebellion, libel, urban crime, military and civilian law, state law opposed to federal law, western expansion, popular grievances and governance, republicanism and sedition, internal migration and equal treatment, together with quarrels over legal jurisdiction, constitutional law, and popular justice. Examining newly discovered primary sources and underutilized documents, the study includes two classic trials (the Whiskey Rebellion trials and the Benjamin Rush libel trial) and four that are studied for the first time. It demonstrates chronological changes across the period through these selective moments in time viewed through the intimacy of the courtroom. The trials reveal the transition from a British legal system to an American system that fed on English common law while it developed a body of its own statutory and constitutional law and resolved conflicts between federal and state courts. The study addresses critical conflicts over localism and centralization of the law as it provides a revitalized view of the early history of an American legal system that shaped the country as a novel experiment in self-governance.

The cases can be read like peaks across a landscape narrating democracy. We get from one point (1783) to another (1808) by tracking early democracy at some of its bitterest and most challenging moments. The point the book makes is that viewing events in terms of a continuous, thematic, period history misses something of importance. Yes, events are connected, but the connectedness resides in how these events contribute to an organic culture of varied guises, rejecting homogeneity and universalism. Here, channeling the poet Cavafy,[2] we find the holy grail is the trip itself; having taken this trip, we shall no longer look at democracy or American law in the same way again.

The early republic experienced great change, great instability, tremendous economic growth, and population movement. Like other institutions in the new country, the legal system went through a period of separation anxiety in its move away from English law and its transformation into an American system, navigating by trial and error. On our trip through early republic trials, we discover democracy, like law, is messy. It requires high tolerance for ambiguity and multiplicity, for the many within the one and the oneness of the many, as the Marxist theorist Antonio Gramsci might put it,[3] which leads us to ask: What lies below the surface? What is American society really like? What are the challenges to democracy and how does it change?

While democracy is disorderly, it also produces innovations, flexibility, and adaptation. But to do so, it must cure its essentially undisciplined nature. In this sense, it depends upon the rule of law in its three aspects: its jurisprudence, its jurispractice, and its jurisculture. Democracy requires fairness, equality of treatment, due process, representation, and voice, every bit as much as a court of law does—keeping in mind the frame for this study, that is, that trials represent a stress test for democracy. Democracy, in sum, requires a balance of trust and mutuality with boundaries that can easily be busted. This was the road traveled in the early republic, a road to finding and defining a legal practice fit for a nascent democracy. There is good reason for calling the early republic a critical juncture in the history of democracy.

The American legal experience began during the American Revolution with courts-martial, the first federal courts, which are the subject of chapter 1. Overseen by George Washington, the commander of the Continental Army, military law here is largely that of the British Articles of War, although it both interfaces and conflicts with the rules and procedures of peacetime civil law. Courts-martial expose a series of disputes among officers in a system of military justice rooted in an older, disorderly altercation-style process. In this sense, courts-martials were much like the civil courts but afflicted with a reluctance to acknowledge precedents and an authority structure in which military leadership had control over judgments. State courts, meanwhile, preserved their ability to enforce civil law apart from the military and took from the example of military courts an enhanced desire to reform and strengthen their own legal processes.

In treating military law, this book asks whether law can have legitimacy under conditions of war, as they are contradictory states, the one being based on authority and the other on power. This question invokes the prospect that equal treatment is superseded by the need to mount an effective army, which eclipses all else. How was principled law to operate under such circumstances? What servitude was likely to befall free men called upon to subsist under such conditions? Was the code of military law to be trusted as a counterpart to civil law? This study argues that the articles of war did not command the respect of those it prosecuted nor those who turned to the courts for justice. Indeed, "justice" was a term infrequently used in military law; the term "discipline" had displaced it. At the same time, fairness under the law was less a function of the Articles of War or the proceedings of the court as it was a function of an understood gentlemen's code designed to preserve relations among officers. But those relations had been fractured by feuds and did not protect commanding officers from the jealousy and hostility of their subordinates.

The legal culture of courts-martial was reliant upon the peculiarities of a vague understanding to which, in practice, members of the corps felt allegiance, preferring them to written rules or the precedents of prior cases. Their legal culture was not unlike the habitus of which social theorist Pierre Bourdieu speaks, an understood arrangement rather than a controlling structure, but historically specific to a culture of favoritism and accommodation exemplified in elite relations characteristic of the eighteenth century.[4] Letters to commanding officers to predispose a case in one way or another and directives that indicated a disposition to bend the rules were not only common but carried the appearance of dispositive factors. Judge advocates, some appointed as favors, were insufficiently versed in the law and found themselves tasked with conflicting responsibilities; their multiple roles (prosecuting, assisting the accused, and advising the board) were inescapably compromised. The practice of private prosecution further muddied the proceedings, so that members of the boards were badgered by aggressive plaintiffs, themselves fellow officers, who challenged the authority of the judge advocate. That the army continually moved its camps to follow the flow of battle meant individual courts had to be reconvened several times in different locales and rulings were rarely consistent. In toto, courts-martial proved an amalgam of incompatible elements adaptable to individual cases but incapable of producing predictability or certainty. Since they largely punished deserters while protecting those who profited from their command, they undermined the promise of a rule of laws and not men. They provided order, but little justice and not much law.

Chapter 2 takes us to Pennsylvania's contested western lands, a critical venue for the exercise of law in early America; like the country itself, the frontier was on the margins of an older order and had to create a new order out of chaos. The case examined here considers the dichotomous positioning of Indians as a sovereign nation and an object of Western racism in the legal context of an interracial murder. The myth of the "vanishing Indian" and the deculturation of the Indians took on legal implications not only in the contest over western land but on the question of legal rights in Anglo-American courts. Indian crime and crimes against Indians became an issue for competing legal systems—those of Indigenous people and those of the colonial and American legal cultures. Complicated by the incompatibility of frontier vigilantism, Quaker diplomacy and conciliation, Anglo-American retributive justice, and tribal traditions of reparative justice, Indian trials became a crucible for determining the viability of fair and equal justice in the new nation.

The 1785 trial of Mamachtaga, a Delaware Indian, involved the drunken murder of two white men. The Delawares (Lenni Lenape) had been progressively displaced in Pennsylvania from the Quaker proprietorship's infamous trickery in the 1737 Walking Purchase to massacres of peaceful Indians in the 1760s and 1780s (following the French and Indian War and the American Revolution). The competing needs of a trading relationship and keeping the peace, of settlers pushing the frontier progressively westward into Indian lands and border claims by other states (Connecticut, Virginia, and Maryland), made Indians a useful burden. The French, British, and Americans competed over them as allies in colonial wars and as treaty partners to purchase land. But they were never a protected people, nor were they granted the same rights as other inhabitants of the province, despite William Penn's moral intentions in dealing with the Lenni Lenape.

Traditional tribal courts were agreed upon for the disposition of Indian-on-Indian crimes, but interracial crime was the province of government courts. Justices of the peace and newly established county courts in the western part of the state (1773–1780s) created a flexible local legal system, but they were bypassed by elite interests behind an eastern-based state Supreme Court intent upon asserting its authority over them and preventing local prejudice against the Indians. The efforts of competing courts to produce order and administer justice fell short in the face of local militias and mobs that asserted their own popular justice, reflecting the fact that popular sovereignty had not ended with the revolution. The localism of frontier law and backcountry democracy continued the relative autonomy of colonial law under the British to become a thorn in the side of the centralizing force of national government established by the postwar Constitution. Just as colonial law operated under the surveillance of the British, and the tribal legal system found itself in a coercive relationship with white man's law, so did the states find themselves in conflict with the Federalist approach to the legacy of the revolution, an approach that made national government less of a popular liberating force than a counterrevolutionary one.

The postrevolutionary period is covered in three chapters: the conflict of democratic and antidemocratic forces (addressed in chapter 4, the Whiskey Rebellion); the territorial imperative (in chapter 3 on land disputes); and the treatment of the Indians (chapter 2, Mamachtaga's trial). Chapter 3 looks at the fungibility of land as a form of corruptible currency and at the cult of personality that fed George Washington's aggregation of western land. The case addresses to what extent the elite, who were to lead the country, acted from ambition rather than pure civic virtue, a topic that has divided historians for at least two centuries. Washington used his fame to advance his case over settlers who did not have his kind of influence but also to underscore the deference to which he felt himself entitled. That the Pennsylvania Supreme Court assumed jurisdiction rather than the Washington County Court provides insight into local and state legal practices as well as the competition between eastern and western interests. The lack of record-keeping to document the case exposes a continuing problem for the study of early republic trials. In this case, a rare legal brief, written by Washington, and correspondence between the plaintiff and his lawyer provide exceptional access to the legal strategy of the prosecution, including the importance of political considerations in the formative years of the American legal system.

Just as the Mamachtaga trial questioned whether law could function where backcountry democracy enforced the rule of militia by hue and cry and embraced self-governance of a sort that sidelined courts, Washington's land case raises questions about the ability of a postwar government to repair the confused state of civil courts during the revolution. Local courts preferred settlers over eastern speculators, who appealed to the state Supreme Court to have their land cases heard, while an elite America of inherited English practices opposed nativist innovations that had grown up locally; the state legislature and western inhabitants honored local innovations, while the state Supreme Court and federal law aligned with eastern land interests. Land grabs exploded with the Treaty of Paris that ended the war against Britain and would delay any possibility of court reform. In the case of the federal government, reform would occur with ratification of the Constitution in 1788 and the Judiciary Act of 1789; in the case of the state, it would not occur until the new state constitution of 1790.

The desire for land was the excuse for the wars between the French, British, Indians, and the colonies. It was the means of fulfilling national aspirations on the western front. If it would take massaging the law to get a title, the moneyed class of land companies and land speculators were more than willing to exploit their ties with the government in the East. An ugly struggle privileging holders of vast tracts of land left common soldiers with bounty land grants, homesteaders who improved the land, and Indian land rights in the lurch and undermined the expansion of settlements by homesteaders who would actually live in the West and work the land.

The enhanced constitutional authority of the federal government over national land would pacify Western Pennsylvania by 1795, putting down the anti-tax Whiskey Rebellion and defeating the Indians in the Ohio Valley, a pincer movement of two armies—one led by George Washington against western settlers and one by General Wayne against the Delaware Indians. In this context, chapter 4 takes up the Whiskey Rebellion trials of 1794. The trials take place almost a decade after Washington's land trial, although they follow almost seamlessly from the events of chapter 3. The Whiskey Rebellion deepens our understanding of the conflict between law operating at the margins and that at the center. The struggle over vicinage and the priority given to removing accused rebels from the site of the rebellion to cosmopolitan Philadelphia for trial reflects the distrust that faced the local legal culture of Western Pennsylvania county courts. Legal practices had barely improved over the decade between the trials despite the establishment of federal courts. Disdain for proper procedures in evidence collection as well as biases among Federalist judges and political machinations within the Washington administration lend credence to the view that a responsible federal legal structure was a long way off. With ratification of the Constitution and legislation that established a federal court system, federal courts competed with state courts prepared to engage in a bitter fight to claim their own legitimacy against national law. The spectacle played out in the first treason trials in the newly established United States, a test case that would challenge the judicial bona fides of federal courts and the Constitution.

The central theme of the rebellion was the clash between elite and popular views of the law. Common people felt that backcountry democracy demanded active participation in politics through the exercise of their natural and constitutional rights of assembly, petition, and speech. Western anti-federalist rebels (whose elected representatives had voted against ratification of the federal Constitution) refused to accept the decisions of elected officials in lieu of their understood right to engage directly in making the law, focusing their resistance on the 1791 federal whiskey tax. In their defense, the rebels would tout their allegiance to what they called "constitutional resistance," an oxymoron the government rejected as a contradiction in terms and a mantra, adopted by rebel assemblies, tested in the treason trials that followed. When Pennsylvania lost its fight over vicinage for the trials, anti-federalist fears that federal courts intended to supersede state jurisdiction were confirmed. The rebels were treated no better than the Indians who were removed under state law to Philadelphia for trial.

Nonetheless, the trials demonstrated that a new day had dawned for American law. A Federalist theory of the law privileging central government and asserting civil order, protection of property, and the priority of government authority over popular sovereignty dominated the judicial life of the courts. The trials appeared antidemocratic both in their preference for English common law and their judge-dominated procedures. But the judicial constructions and common law interpretations that obtained in the trials proved inadequate to the government's needs, resulting in only two convictions for treason. Demonstrating the independence of common-man juries and a poorly executed government criminal prosecution, the Whiskey Rebellion verdicts would prove a breaking point for US law. It would turn away from the legacy of English common law, generating rigorous American statutory law and enhancing respect for constitutional law to create a legal system suited to the American terrain.

The last two chapters shift the study to the East to address turn of the century problems in urban America. The trials in these chapters demonstrate that the tide had turned in terms of courtroom management and the development of a stable legal system. As the older style altercation trial (where the accused spoke in his own defense) began to segue into an adversarial mode (where counsel for the defense tested the prosecution case), defendants received full representation by counsel whose high oratory dominated the proceedings. On the one hand, while this change provoked resistance from judges dictating both the facts and the law, performance-minded lawyers appealed to more independent-minded juries susceptible to an influx of cultural sensibility and a movement toward penal reform. On the other hand, lawyers had the contradictory effect of steering courtrooms toward argumentative battles that clouded the truth and of enhancing rules of evidence and legal standards (including exclusionary and procedural rules, reasonable doubt, presumption of innocence, and protection against self-incrimination).

Eastern courts faced a new set of problems informed by continuing hostilities between the French and the English that exacerbated the partisanship of Anglophile and Francophile Americans. Trials conducted under the Alien and Sedition Acts of 1798 pitted newly formed political parties against each other just as elections would lead to the first peaceful transfer of power in the country's history. The courtroom, like the press, had become the tip of the spear for public sphere politics, leading to a rash of libel suits that plagued the late century. The US capital in Philadelphia saw more than its share of personal and press attacks on public figures that threatened not only personal reputations but political authority in a test of how much attacks on public figures would undermine their ability to lead in the new democracy.

In chapter 5, the *Rush v. Cobbett* trial opposed the partisan politics of the British émigré and Federalist journalist William Cobbett to those of a prominent Philadelphian, the Republican physician Benjamin Rush. As in the high-profile Washington land case, the state Supreme Court successfully intervened to claim the trial, having opposed Cobbett's application to have the case tried in a federal court. Rush capitalized on his oversized reputation to lay claim to a heroic cure for yellow fever, a disease that had ravaged the mid-Atlantic states in a series of devastating epidemics, notably one in 1793 that coincided with Cobbett's arrival in Philadelphia. Cobbett, who could abide neither Rush's politics nor his invention, was intent upon destroying the physician's reputation, first in the press and then in the trial where the courtroom turned into a showcase for the rights of a free press. Anticipating the electoral victory the Republican Party would enjoy the following year, partisan prosecution arguments framed Cobbett as the darling of the Federalist press and the scourge of Republican journalists targeted by the Sedition Act. His defense pictured him as the conscience of America warning of a deadly medical treatment during a national health emergency.

The last chapter deals with a looming crisis within cities along the eastern coast and between the North and the South: race and racism. Chapter 6 positions the question of race in terms of urban crime and the internal conflict within the African American community. Black community religious institutions had become involved in a double-edged campaign to defend the morality of its congregants and to take a leadership role in the abolition movement, which meant that support for two Black men charged in an 1808 case with the murder of a white woman would undermine dearly won economic and social advances. The concern was whether Blacks would receive due process and equal treatment in the courtroom at a time when the gradual emancipation of Pennsylvania slaves and a rash of emigrating fugitive slaves had changed the face of the city and a movement to remove Blacks to Africa had sponsored a tense conversation over the position of the community in Philadelphia. The Black population of Philadelphia was economically, legally, and socially vulnerable, an anomalous condition that routinely led to accusations of disorderly conduct, the summary judgment of magistrate courts, and unequal treatment. As a counterforce, Pennsylvania's Gradual Abolition Act of 1780 had declared that all inhabitants of the state had the same rights under criminal law.

With the demographic and economic growth of the North focused on cities, the politics of urban crime played itself out in a very public way in the trial of John Joyce and Peter Matthias. Like the two men, migrants had flocked to the city only to find themselves deprived of sustainable work, while Philadelphia experienced a rising crime rate, much of it tied to crimes committed by Blacks. For many jurors, these trials were their first up-close experience with people who had been enslaved, contributing to imperfect understandings that criminalized Blacks and presumed the worst about the prospects for granting civil rights to free Blacks and those newly emancipated. These perceptions were fed by vernacular legal culture in the form of crime narratives, execution sermons, and confessions. Published to satisfy a growing appetite for popular literature, they created at the same time a perception of "strangerhood" linked to biblical constructs like the mark of Cain and the blackness of sin. By contrast, trials had the effect of endowing accused Blacks with personhood and limited agency. The fact that affirmation of their judicial rights took place while slavery was still allowed in the United States represented a significant advance in justice for a people yet to be fully recognized as citizens.

What the reader will find in this book capitalizes on new historical perspectives. Many new studies have widened the scope of legal culture and its history to include the agency of groups on the geographical or hierarchical periphery whose power, status, and role in creating communities, impacting the Union, or contributing to national expansion have previously been given little importance.[5] Other studies have excavated the transatlantic connections and continuities between European colonialism and new-world settler agency that subjugated Indigenous populations, using violence and appropriating land as it pushed the imperial agenda forward. Settler colonialism replicated colonial legal, economic, and social patterns, as well as legislative authority, while settlers assumed the rights of English citizens.[6]

More importantly, the project reveals the "jurisdictional tensions" of a state in which a plural legal order obtained in the absence of a strong claim by the state of "legal hegemony."[7] To be sure the national government was in the early stages of developing a political system informed by imperial models and practices, and the origins of a federal administrative state and independent local colonial courts were being joined by a federal judicial apparatus under the Judiciary Act of 1789 and the prospect of a more coercive military force with the Militia Act of 1792. But federal institutional growth, though significant, was still in its infancy. With Indigenous, colonial, and emerging confederal polities in contest, negotiations between legal systems and interactions between individuals and groups with the federal and state governments were very much in flux. Legal pluralism was both a necessity and a reality.[8] A variety of unequal systems interfacing and negotiating relationships was the norm in a multicentric legal order that nonetheless "created continuities across diverse regions and politics."[9] At the same time, legal maneuvering, including strategic behaviors and improvisations, promoted fragile justice. Even vulnerable legal actors found opportunities to forum shop, litigate defensively, and appeal within such jurisdictional complexity, seeking forums that showed a greater ability to enforce rulings and capitalize on boundary crossing between multiple legal systems and spheres.[10]

In a final note, readers will find that democracy has been used as a thread to tie together these six trials. The choice reflects recent work that reminds us of democracy's fragility, an attribute rooted in the very nature of democracy, signifying that threats inherited within democracy endure as features that cannot be simply excised. These threats are correlated with political partisanship, conflict over economic resources, the struggle for rights, free elections, and the rule of law, and are glaringly revealed in overweening assertions of executive power, inequality, and racial tension. These are the very questions raised in early republic trials.

Every period experiences one or more of these threats, but it is clear that in the early republic several were present in concert. Certainly conflicts occurred between political parties and over resources; they flared up over racial inequality and the struggle for individual rights.[11] The interface of multiple threats made this historical period more vulnerable than most so that it can legitimately be characterized as a "critical juncture" for democracy, the term applied by Giovanni Capoccia and R. Daniel Keleman.[12] In the space represented by a critical juncture, governments make choices that either reinforce or disable institutions. In fact, each time a crisis appears to be resolved, resolution involves a compromise of some democratic value.[13]

Clashes over leadership, criminalizing political opposition, and conspiratorial and paranoid styles—these are all conditions familiar to the politics of the early republic[14] and clearly familiar to those presently living under such political conditions.[15] National unity depends upon understanding these conditions and generating agreement within the political community over how these transitions are to be negotiated. This is the challenge taken up by the trials presented here and the reason for writing this book. In the spirit of a cautionary tale, then, this book offers its insights on democracy, with the hope that it contributes to rethinking democracy in our own times and to the struggle for democratic values that we wish to see prevail.[16]

NOTES

1. Clifford Geertz, *The Interpretation of Cultures: Selected Essays* (New York: Basic Books, 1973), 7–10, 15–17, 20–21.

2. C. P. Cavafy, "Ithaka," *The Canon: The Original One Hundred and Fifty-Four Poems by C. P. Cavafy*, trans. Stratis Haviaras (Washington, DC: Center for Hellenic Studies, 2007), 90–93.

3. Antonio Gramsci, *Selections from Cultural Writings,* trans. William Boelhower (Cambridge: Harvard University Press, 1985).

4. Pierre Bourdieu, *Outline of a Theory of Practice* (Cambridge: Cambridge University Press, 1977).

5. Jessica Choppin Roney, "1776, Viewed from the West," *Journal of the Early Republic* 37, no. 4 (2017): 656–60; Amy Turner Bushnell and Jack P. Greene, "Peripheries, Centers, and the Construction of Early Modern American Empires," in *Negotiated Empires: Centers and Peripheries in the Americas, 1500–1820*, ed. Christine Daniels and Michael V. Kennedy (London: Taylor and Francis Group, 2002), 6.

6. Jack P. Greene, *The Constitutional Origins of the American Revolution* (Cambridge: Cambridge University Press, 2011), 3–15.

7. Lauren Benton, "Historical Perspectives on Legal Pluralism," *Hague Journal on the Rule of Law* 3, no. 1 (2011): 57.

8. Gautham Rao, "The New Historiography of the Early Federal Government: Institutions, Contexts, and the Imperial State," *The William and Mary Quarterly* 77, no. 1 (2020): 97–128; see Gautham Rao, *National Duties: Custom Houses and the Making of the American State* (Chicago: University of Chicago Press, 2016); Aaron T. Knapp, "From Empire to Law: Customs Collection in the American Founding," *Law & Social Inquiry* 43, no. 2 (2018): 558, 578.

9. Benton, "Legal Pluralism," 57.

10. Benton, "Historical Perspectives," 57–59, 62–65; Lauren Benton, *Law and Colonial Cultures: Legal Regimes in World History, 1400–1900* (Cambridge: Cambridge University Press, 2001), 8.

11. Sonia Mittal and Barry R. Weingast, "Self-Enforcing Constitutions: With an Application to Democratic Stability in America's First Century," *Journal of Law, Economics, and Organization* 29, no. 2 (2013): 278–302; John L. Brooke, "Consent, Civil Society, and the Public Sphere in the Age of Revolution and the Early American Republic," in Jeffrey L. Pasley, Andrew W. Robertson, and David Waldstreicher, eds., *Beyond the Founders: New Approaches to the Political History of the Early American Republic* (Chapel Hill: University of North Carolina Press, 2004), 207–50; Reeve Huston, "Rethinking the Origins of Partisan Democracy in the United States, 1795–1840," in *Practicing Democracy: Popular Politics in the United States from the Constitution to the Civil War*, eds. Daniel Peart and Adam I. P. Smith (Charlottesville: University of Virginia Press, 2015), 46–71; Katlyn Marie Carter, "Denouncing Secrecy and Defining Democracy in the Early American Republic," *Journal of the Early Republic* 40, no. 3 (2020): 409–33.

12. Giovanni Capoccia and R. Daniel Kelemen, "The Study of Critical Junctures: Theory, Narrative, and Counterfactuals in Historical Institutionalism,"

World Politics 59, no. 3 (2007): 341–69; Giovanni Capoccia and Daniel Ziblatt, "The Historical Turn in Democratization Studies: A New Research Agenda for Europe and Beyond," *Comparative Political Studies* 43, nos. 8/9 (2010): 931–68.

13. Suzanne Mettler and Robert C. Lieberman, *Four Threats: The Recurring Crises of American Democracy* (New York: St. Martin's Press, 2020); Steven Levitsky and Daniel Ziblatt, *How Democracies Die* (New York: Crown, 2018).

14. Saunder van der Linden, Costas Panagopoulos, Flavio Azevedo, and John T. Jost, "The Paranoid Style in American Politics Revisited: An Ideological Asymmetry in Conspiratorial Thinking," *Political Psychology* 42, no. 1 (2021): 24–25; Gordon S. Wood, "Conspiracy and the Paranoid Style: Causality and Deceit in the Eighteenth Century," *The William and Mary Quarterly* 39, no. 3 (1982): 401–41; Richard Hofstadter, *The Paranoid Style in American Politics and Other Essays* (New York: Vintage, 1964).

15. Robert C. Lieberman, Suzanne Mettler, Thomas B. Pepinsky, Kenneth M. Roberts, and Richard Valelly, "The Trump Presidency and American Democracy: A Historical and Comparative Analysis," *Perspectives on Politics* 17, no. 2 (2019): 470–79; The Imagination Collectif, "From Whiskey Rebellion to Donald Trump and the Question of Power: An Interview with Isaac Ariail Reed," *Sociaini Studia* 13, no. 4 (2017): 99–104; Michael S. Schmidt and Maggie Haberman, "Trump Weighed Insurrection Act Against Protests," *New York Times*, June 26, 2021; Nicholas Casey, "Making Political Forecasts, and Wincing All the While," *New York Times,* Sunday, November 17, 2019.

16. Francis Fukuyama, "Why is Democracy Performing so Poorly?" in *Democracy in Decline*, eds. Larry Diamond, Marc F. Plattner, and Condoleezza Rice (Baltimore, MD: Johns Hopkins University Press, 2015), 11–24; Larry Diamond, "Facing Up to Democratic Recession," in *Democracy in Decline*, eds. Larry Diamond, Marc F. Plattner, and Condoleezza Rice, 98–118; Steven Levitsky and Lucan Way, "The Myth of Democratic Recession," *Journal of Democracy* 26, no. 1 (2015): 45–58.

Chapter 1

Trying Military Law

The Hazen-Reid Feud and the Case of Judge Advocate General Thomas Edwards, 1780–1783

> How then Sir, am I to act in my present unfortunate Situation?
>
> —Moses Hazen to William Heath, February 8, 1781.

The conduct of courts-martial in the Continental Army is a subject well worth examining for its contribution to understanding the administration of justice under the extreme circumstances and contradictions inherent in war. Operating as a crucible for legal principles, courts-martial and their caretaker the judge advocate were caught in the eye of a whirlwind no better illustrated than in the attempt of a brigadier general and twenty-four officers to try the last of three judge advocates general who served in the Revolutionary War, Thomas Edwards, in 1783. This case, which tested a military justice system during a war that founded a nation, is the subject of this chapter.[1]

William Blackstone, in his *Commentaries on the Laws of England*, warned that the law of war "is built upon no settled principles, but is entirely arbitrary in its decisions, [it] is, as sir Matthew Hale observes, in truth and reality no law, but something indulged, rather than allowed as a law."[2] It was an even greater irony for Blackstone that law bases itself in certainty and predictability, where

> nothing is left to arbitrary discretion. . . . How much therefore is it to be regretted that a set of men, whose bravery has so often preserved the liberties of their country, should be reduced to a state of servitude in the midst of freemen! for sir Edward Coke will inform us, that it is one of the genuine marks of servitude, to have the law, which is our rule of action, either concealed or precarious.[3]

He proclaimed it a miserable slavery where the law is vague or uncertain.

Not all treatise writers agreed with Blackstone, finding military law as much based in rules of evidence as the civil courts and more humane and rational; but they all found it justified by the harsh requirements of war.[4]

Although the Continental Army relied upon the British Articles of War, American military figures were well informed about the theory of war.[5] M. D. Vattel's mid-eighteenth-century treatise, the most cited in the first half century after the revolution,[6] based itself on Hugo Grotius's *De Jure Belli ac Pacis* (On the Law of War and Peace), a seventeenth-century work that proved influential in preconstitutional America.[7] Grotius's third book covered the rights of killing the enemy, spoil and rape committed in war, the right to confiscate property, and the right over captives and the vanquished. His dissertation on "rights of aggression rather than protection" was tempered by sections on moderation in war and discourse on reason and strategy, which proved informative to the framers in forming a declaration of war and informing the standing army debate.

Still, neither Grotius's work nor the Articles of War, a disciplinary manual, was a drill manual or a work on military science.[8] For that, military veterans turned to more practical works from personal libraries to which they had access. Indeed, Washington himself expressed an interest in military studies in proposals, which Congress nonetheless rejected.[9] Such knowledge remained rudimentary, despite a series of colonial wars, because of the association of military education with the idea of a standing army,[10] which was seen as a tool of tyranny. In America, militias took on the burden of self-defense. Their task was to defend liberty at any cost but subordinated to civilian authority.[11] It would take Friedrich Wilhelm von Steuben, in the capacity of inspector general of the Continental Army, to establish a true military force. His 1779 "Blue Book" on order and discipline in the US Army,[12] together with English and French works on organization, fortifications, and supply, provided the bulk of military knowledge on which American officers depended, while in 1780, Henry Knox established a precursor to the later military academy at West Point, which, until it was abandoned in 1783, fostered the notion of systematic military thinking. Washington identified this aspect of the military as one of the four takeaways from the experience of a "long and arduous" war, essential "unless we intend to let the Science become extinct" and mean to rely upon the "friendly aid" of foreigners.[13]

In 1776, the Continental Army adopted almost in toto the British Articles of War, under which American colonials had fought in the French and Indian War. Several authorities were established in the American Articles: the sovereign (the Continental Congress); the judge advocate (who prosecuted on behalf of that sovereign); the court-martial board (which determined the verdict and sentenced the accused); and the commander in chief, or Congress, (who approved or disapproved the verdict). Tellingly, the Articles of War was designed to discipline and punish the troops, for without order soldiers would desert in droves and the army would disintegrate; with severe punishments, on the other hand, mutinies would have a similar effect.[14] The importance of respect for discipline was codified in the culminating "Devil's Article" (Sec. XVIII, Art 5), which infamously gave blanket discretion to military courts for "All crimes not capital, and all disorders and neglects which officers and soldiers may be guilty of, to the prejudice of good order and military discipline."

Congress established court-martial procedures, but as courts-martial predated the federal judiciary it was unclear whether they belonged to the executive or legislative branches. They were nonetheless the first form of federal court authorized in the United States.[15] Soldiers tried in regimental courts-martial were subjected to summary justice and the board of officers served as a combination of judge and jury deciding both fact and law, unlike civil courts. The older form of British military trials (referred to as courts of honor) still obtained in the Continental Army whereby courts-martial relied upon gentlemanly rules and officers' honor.

Although they tried offenses strictly related to the law of military conduct, courts-martial were bound to fundamental principles of law and general rules of evidence and court procedure, which were relied upon unless they conflicted with an express requirement of military law.[16] The Articles of War directed that the court was to adhere to "the custom of war in the like cases," indicating an adherence to written military code and to precedents established by other military courts. Because the articles were largely silent on the role judge advocates were to perform, they frequently resorted to "established usage and practices" (lex non scripta), of army common law. Judge advocates were, however, expected to instruct themselves in civil trial law if they had not practiced law in civilian life.[17] Indicatively, in a case dealing with parties from Connecticut Judge Advocate General John Laurance, an experienced lawyer from the New York bar, felt that "a Court Martial could not properly take Cognizance of the Facts they are charged with, unless the Court acted under a Law of the State."[18]

Courts-martial were thus separate from and yet related to criminal trials under civil law. Reflecting the preadversarial style of civil trial (the altercation-style trial) in which the accused must speak in his own defense and the judge acts as counsel, courts-martial practiced private prosecution where an aggrieved party brings the case forward and must provide proof of the charges.[19] Military trials worked interchangeably in some instances with civil criminal trials (Articles of War, sec. III, article 1; 1, sec. X) and shared some practices, including that civil and military courts both permitted the accused to examine witnesses but neither allowed them to argue their case to the jury;

military and civil law shared as well rules of evidence and procedures. At the same time, courts-martial disfavored introducing legal authority in citations or common law precedents; in practice, despite what the articles allowed, they discouraged military precedents as well. For example, although a soldier could appeal a regimental verdict to a general court-martial, there was no value given in those appeals to precedents from other military cases.[20] And whereas challenges to a member of a general court-martial board (following the example of challenging a juror for cause in a civil court) were sometimes allowed to avoid partiality, judge advocates discouraged such challenges to avoid setting a precedent.[21] This attitude toward precedents of any sort was consistent with the general understanding that each court-martial was unique to itself and its own set of conditions and facts and that decisions depended upon the particulars of a case and not any principle or rule.

JUDGE ADVOCATES

Judge advocates in armies from northern Britain and Bombay to the American colonies used the British Articles of War to train officers in the legality and regularity required in court-martial proceedings. Deputy Judge Advocate Payne Adye in his 1797 treatise on British military law in North America nonetheless noted the incongruity of articles written "to be easily understood by military men" that were nonetheless silent "wherein the assistance of a judge advocate is requisite."[22] Judge Advocate General Vans Kennedy of the Bombay army made the case that with a "penalty undefined and unknown, the law itself may be justly called concealed and precarious." Whereas the penalty attached to the crime was, in his view, the law's "main strength and force," in military law it was most commonly purely discretionary. In this sense, military law did not abide by Blackstone's dictum that the consequence of noncompliance be known; it was in fact vague or unknown law.[23]

Under the British Articles, the judge advocate's functions were to administer an oath to witnesses and members of court-martial boards, to prosecute, as well as to assist, the accused, and to transmit a report of court-martial proceedings as expeditiously as possible to the secretary of war. In the Continental Army, he also submitted the proceedings to the commander in chief or Congress before a sentence could be executed. By custom, judge advocates provided advice to the board, which they were expected to give "with freedom and amplitude," but they were not to vote on the sentence, having "no judicial power."[24] According to Vans Kennedy, the only guide for conducting proceedings was the experience of members of the board and the "knowledge of the Judge-Advocate."[25]

Alexander Macomb, a judge advocate in the US Army, held in his treatise on military justice that the judge advocate must "put the court upon their guard against every deviation, either from any essential or necessary forms in their proceedings, or a violation of justice in their final sentence and judgment." Should an illegal opinion be offered, his duty was to controvert the point (to absolve himself of failing to give counsel), to bring the offense to the commander in chief (to affirm or deny the court's recommendation), or to return the case to be reconsidered.[26] The judge advocate wrote up each day's proceedings as an official report that he read to the court in its final form before it began deliberating.[27] He was to retain the written proceedings and original notes in his possession so that he "may have recourse to them as necessary documents, if he should be called upon to give evidence in relation thereto."[28] The implicit understanding was that once the proceedings were sent to the commander in chief the judge advocate should remain in good stead with his superior. It was also understood that the judge advocate's conduct in a trial could become the subject of an inquiry. Military justice thus incorporated respect for legal forms, but it also depended upon a code of honor and discretionary punishment (guided by either pride in the profession, preconceived opinions, or command influence) and indicated that a degree of self-protection was required on the part of those conducting trials.

The administering of oaths was a matter of some consequence in courts martial. While witnesses swore to give evidence that was wholly truthful, the court swore to "well and truly try and determine" the matter before it according to that evidence so as to "duly administer justice." Due process and proof of a charge were thereby guaranteed. In swearing to act "without partiality, favor, or affection," the court was bound to ensure fairness and equal justice. Similarly, the court's decisions were to be "according to [its] conscience, to the best of [its] understanding," allowing for a degree of the moral certainty or reasonable doubt of civil trials and, importantly, protecting its members from undue command influence.

Primarily, the judge advocate's duty was to prosecute, which involved using his discretion to examine witnesses and evidence he deemed necessary to proving the charges. Collaterally, he was to converse with the accused or his counsel before trial and acquaint himself with the prisoner's defense, but not to exert "his ingenuity to defend the prisoner at all hazards." Rather, his job was to provide exculpatory evidence and include in the written proceedings any matter that would tend to the accused's defense; he was not to influence the court to convict or acquit.[29] Caught in what one treatise considered a "*Proteus-like*" posture, the judge advocate must first prosecute the accused and in the next moment "change sides, and furnish him with means and arguments to overthrow those he has before made use of." Caught in a position "inconsistent with justice and common sense,"[30] he was not to let "his master's cause suffer" (the state being the injured party) nor was he to allow a criminal to go unpunished.[31] As Deputy Judge Advocate of North Britain Alexander Tytler made clear in his treatise, "All that is required is, that, in the same manner as in the Civil courts of criminal jurisdiction, the judges are understood to be of counsel with the person accused."[32] Providing such counsel would ensure "he has law and justice."[33]

In addition, accused officers were allowed private counsel, within strict constraints. The US Army trial of Captain W. Wilson in 1809 is instructive on this point. In one of the earliest full proceedings provided by a judge advocate that has survived, the board complained that the accused's counsel may "suggest Questions or objections to him, to prepare his defence in writing—but he is not to open his mouth in Court." The trial was disapproved by General James Wilkinson, citing strong "grounds of Exception," glaring innovations, and a precedent "if permitted so pernicious in its Tendency." Wilkinson considered the mere fact of admitting defense counsel "to mingle in the deliberations of the Court" offensive in encouraging the temptation "to interrogate, to except, to plead, to teaze, perplex & embarrass by legal subtilties & abstract sophistical Distinctions." Even more, throwing courts-martial open to the bar would lead officers "to direct their attention from the military service & the Art of War, to the study of Law" and to conflate the rules of common law and courts-martial.[34]

Macomb's treatise argued that the animosity toward counsel was in one part the result of military men not being "versed in legal subtilties or abstract and sophistical distinctions" and in another that courts-martial dealt with violations of military discipline rather than questions of law. Counsel who knew little of military practices and procedures, he claimed, tried "to force the axioms and rules" of civil courts on military trials or use their skills to introduce irrelevant procedural matters, particularly where a military offense would not have been criminal under common law.[35] As counsel were not officially recognized, the right to counsel did not greatly concern courts-martial. They were, as a result, required to submit their motions, questions, and communications to the judge advocate in writing, although courts-martial appeared in practice to follow Blackstone's sense of the right to counsel. Thus, the general rule was that the accused might have his own counsel as an adviser in a limited capacity on a point of law, including "what questions to ask, or even to ask questions for him, with respect to matters of fact," but not on general issues. But it was the judge advocate who "shall see that the proceedings against him are legal and strictly regular."[36]

In the American military system, judge advocates general (three were appointed over the course of the war) and deputy judge advocates (of which there were fifteen)[37] tried officers' cases in general courts-martial while regimental and battalion commanders conducted regimental and battalion courts.

The appointment of judge advocate generals was based on the approval of the Continental Congress and the overall commander of the Continental Army, Washington, which meant that they were initially selected from a small pool of elite figures known to the general and his extended circle and were intended to signal the legitimacy of the army's court system. William Tudor was a lawyer of some prominence from Boston who found favor with John Adams, and John Laurance was an eminent jurist who went on to become a federal judge. By contrast, Thomas Edwards, the last of the advocate generals before adoption of the Constitution, was selected in a hasty search after two other candidates avoided accepting the office. Edwards came to the office having served as a deputy judge advocate. Along the same line, deputy judge advocates were an uneven lot, the result of a selection process whereby their commanders raised them up from the line.[38]

The first Continental Army judge advocate general was William Tudor, a Boston lawyer who studied law under John Adams and whom Adams recommended to Washington for his appointment in July 1775.[39] Not only had there been no regular courts-martial "by Reason of their wanting some Person to methodize and conduct the Business," but Tudor realized that "Lords Coke, Holt and Hale are made to give Way to your congressional military Code."[40] He soon learned the workload was enormous and "excessively fatiguing": "One Court is no sooner dissolv'd," he wrote Adams, "than another is ordered to sit."[41] Tudor was to learn, furthermore, that General Washington would not leave important events like courts-martial of his officers completely in someone else's hands. Deeply immersed in the details of the workings of trials under his command, the general took a proprietary interest in the workings of the courts. In fact, Tudor complained of Washington that "he cannot form a competent Opinion of the Court's Judgement, without seeing the whole State of the Evidence, etc."[42] General Washington's decided interest stemmed from his view of the courts as a "fundamental instrument of command and control" in deterring his troops from errant acts as well as disciplining them.[43] Study of the camp at Valley Forge reveals that 60 percent of his daily general orders were in fact about court-martial trials and that Washington personally appointed the officers who would preside over them.[44] Washington was particularly attentive to the crimes of his officers, whom he relied upon to make the army move "like Clock-Work." "[T]here is no Situation upon Earth, less enviable, nor more distressing," he contended, "than that Person's who is [*sic*] at the head of Troops, who are regardless of Order and discipline."[45]

But the military justice system's role served more than a functional need to make the army work. The experience of generating a military capable of defending a union of states was, like the development of an administrative state and the establishment of a federal court system, part of a larger debate about the "power and authority of the central government."[46] The whole effort of the war forced even loyalists to reconsider the role of government and their place in the empire, which was increasingly difficult in the context of extinguishing ties to Britain and the need for self-defense. The military, along with fiscal and administrative continuity and innovations and drawing on traditions of the past and elaborating innovations through artifacts and performative moments,[47] played a role in creating authority for nation-building under a constitution that appreciated the "dual sovereignty" of a strong center accommodating the centrifugal force exerted by the states. State authority over "*internal police*" was necessary, but preservation of a "compact of union" that turned potential enemy states into partners and gave power to national government to patrol international affairs, Indian affairs, interstate affairs, and western lands[48] meant that the power and authority of the military was essential to the common good.

General courts-martial of officers were lengthy and difficult to set up as the war not only kept the troops moving from one place to another but required taking officers from the front line to serve on the board of judges. Ranging from the rank of major to general, thirteen officers were required by the Articles of War for a general court-martial, so that holding one during the war was complicated. The trial of General Lee, second in command to Washington, who prosecuted the case, provides a good illustration of the complexity: thirty-eight witnesses were called; the trial had to be held over twenty-seven sessions; and it covered thirty-eight days and five locations, including houses, taverns, and a church. Washington charged Lee with "misbehavior before the enemy," "disobedience of orders," and "disrespect of the commander in chief." Found guilty on all three charges, Lee was sentenced to suspension of his command for a term of twelve months.[49]

Tudor made it clear that the job of judge advocate general was a revelation to him. Not only had some of the officers he tried "disgrac'd the Country by practicing the meanest Arts of Peculation," but he discovered in them "every Subtlety which Avarice could invent, or Rascality carry on, have been used to cheat the Publick by Men who procur'd Commissions, not to fight for the Liberty of their Country, but to prey upon it's Distresses."[50] He complained to Washington of having to compensate for courts which

> not only expected that I give the proper Orders for procuring the Evidences, & putting all Matters in such a Train, that the Court may have Nothing else to do than to hear the Witnesses & form a Judgement but that I also analyse the Evidence & state the Questions that are involv'd in it for the Opinion of the Court.[51]

His exasperation was only increased by the inadequacy of the 1775 Articles of War under which he labored and which, he complained, "without making

Soldiers, is breeding Highwaymen and Robbers. . . . To inlist an army, without that Severity of Government which will alone make Soldiers, is to collect Numbers only to be slaughtered."[52]

Congress' adoption of a more expansive version of the British articles in 1776 was no panacea, despite increasing punishments by lashes from thirty-nine to one hundred and extending the kinds of crimes for which death was the penalty beyond desertion, mutiny, and misbehaving before the enemy to more explicit crimes like enlisting in more than one regiment to collect a bounty or sleeping on duty. The lack of specificity in sentencing offenders, however, even death penalties, left room for discretion by the court. Penalties were, for example, cast in language like "according to [the court's] discretion," "as it shall see fit," "by its judgment or sentence," "according to the nature of the crime," or "to be taken cognizance of." Indeed, Tudor indicated to Adams that the judge advocate general's workload might be mitigated

> could I prevail on Courts Martial to show that Severity in their Punishments which is essentially necessary for the Good of the Service. There is such a Timidity and Backwardness in Officers to inflict capital Punishments, that it is as difficult to get a Villain hang'd in the Camp, as it used to be in our County of Suffolk.[53]

The number court-martialed at the camp in Valley Forge under the second judge advocate general John Laurance (April 1777–May 1782) suggests, by comparison, that courts-martial were at least to become more numerous. In the three months of 1778, some fifty-one officers, or one-twentieth of those officers serving in the army, were prosecuted.[54] By the middle of that year, the number was as high as ninety-five, with Laurance convicting in 460 of his 605 cases over a twenty-one-month period.[55] Laurance and Washington shared a desire for competent prosecution. Indeed, Washington would only replace Laurance during a twelve-day absence conditioned upon the judge advocate general "being perfectly persuaded" that his replacement "was fully competent" in intricate cases.[56] During his tenure, to be sure, Laurance had expressed an affinity for a more draconian approach to punishment. Desertion, he felt, exemplified the need for attention: "It deserves, undoubtedly, a severe punishment, as it strikes at the Existence of the Army." He did not, however, recommended death as opposed to "Stripes," for the former would deplete army ranks. But the number of allowable lashes was in his view insufficient to deter soldiers from punishable acts. Rather, he would "leave Courts martial at Liberty to sentence offenders to receive as great a Number of Lashes, as they conceive an adequate punishment for the Crime, according to the Nature and Degree of it."[57] The congressional committee to which Washington forwarded Laurance's recommendation considered it excessive and did not act on the request.[58] A second concern for Laurance was the authority to order courts-martial. Laurance advised that waiting for the commander in chief or a state commander was inconvenient and would delay trials: "During this time the Culprits must be kept in confinement, by which means the Continent will lose their personal Services, and the good Effects of a recent Punishment destroyed." Laurance advised delegating the authority to order a court-martial power downward along with the ability to approve or disapprove sentences. An impolitic proposal, it would have had the effect of impinging on Washington's control over courts-martial and did not thereby take effect.[59]

A critical aspect of the military justice system was its jurisdiction over state militias that supplemented the regular army to make up a combined force. When colonial militia joined the British in the French and Indian War, they engaged in fruitless raids and mismanaged expeditions and were responsible for considerable destruction on the frontier. Militia like that of the Paxton Boys acted more like a law unto themselves than as legitimate arms of the community, provoking accusations of terrorism against the Indians and of undermining Pennsylvania's legal and civil institutions. Paxton's followers expressed local grievances related to the government's protection of the Indians as well as unfairness of representation in the state assembly that favored eastern Pennsylvania over the West.[60] Reliance on militia for military operations in the Revolutionary War proved them to be poorly trained and disciplined. Moreover, their civilian ties kept them from being true soldiers. As a home guard they constituted an impregnable and perpetual obstacle for British forces and against the Indians they were fierce fighters; such order on the home front presumed that citizens had committed to look after the common defense. But not only were they an uneasy fit for a European style army like that of the Anglo-American forces,[61] voluntary associations proved unreliable as a source of manpower. By the time of the revolution, the government coerced the citizens to do their share and punished them to maintain discipline.[62]

If we turn to the Pennsylvania militia statute of 1777, the kinds of activities considered actionable by courts-martial and the extent to which militia were held to military law become immediately apparent.[63] First, demands to serve were made of white male "persons" indicating that servants and slaves were either not incorporated or served in menial capacities.[64] Those who refused to "associate" would be fined for each month they were out of military service unless they paid a three pound tax and hired a substitute to serve in their stead; should a party default in paying for a substitute the payment could "be recovered by distress and sale of his goods and chattels, lands and tenements" by justices of the peace in one's home county. Capitalizing on the dishonor of being brought before a court of one's neighbors, the militia statute allowed as well that officers who committed fraud or neglected their duty could be tried before a jury of their county or state.

As for penalties, deserters and those who sold state-owned arms were levied fines; if officers, they could be fined or cashiered. Militiamen who failed to appear with their arms in good order or who were absent from a muster or left before discharged were liable to fines, though not as heavy as officers who failed to attend and exercise their companies; officers' fines were not only more substantial but were differentiated by rank from five shillings to five pounds, indicating the elitist hierarchy that characterized militia. Like the Articles of War, militia penalties were ascribed for those who swore an execrable oath on duty, refused a lawful command, joined in mutiny, struck a superior, behaved in an "infamous manner," or were found drunk under arms or asleep on duty. The fines associated with misconduct were not inconsequential. Indeed, 6,000,000 pounds in militia fines were collected from some fifty thousand delinquent militiamen out of a total of three hundred thousand enrollees.[65]

THE HAZEN-REID COURTS-MARTIAL

The truest test of how the judge advocate and the military justice system functioned came toward the end of the war. It played out over a series of courts-martial and courts of inquiry from 1780–1783 that involved Colonel Moses Hazen (who would become brigadier general before the end of the trials), Major James Randolph Reid, and three judge advocates (Judge Advocate Generals Laurance and Edwards and Deputy Judge Advocate Strong). Only one officer was indicted, censured, or convicted (Reid was punished with a reprimand in one case; in another, his conduct under one charge was so trifling the court declined to censure him). While Hazen represented that the military process essentially punished the innocent and set the guilty free, the court and the commander in chief suggested that Reid was being persecuted. Reid, who accused Hazen of embezzling regimental money and padding the payroll with absentee soldiers and noncommissioned officers, presented himself as a whistleblower representing a regiment that felt Hazen had defrauded them. The twenty-four officers who joined with Hazen, Reid averred, were retaliating for his attack on Hazen. Each side felt the honor of the regiment had been sullied by the other.

Moses Hazen was a rough-and-tumble character with anger issues whose path through life was pockmarked with business misfortunes, litigation, and even debtor's prison. Yet his career was also one of the disappointments of the revolution as he was a man of ability and drive whose temper and circumstances prevented him from being successful.[66] A backwoods warrior, he fought as a captain in Major Rogers's Rangers against Indians who had allied with the French in the French and Indian War of 1754–1763. As a lieutenant in the British Army, he fought in Canada against the French. He worked as a spy for the British only to be captured first by the Americans and then arrested by the British as a double agent. Freed when the Americans captured Montreal, he joined forces with them but continued to be considered both an unconventional fighter and a man who was open to changing sides. Hazen urged the formation of a Canadian force and was made a colonel in the Continental Army with a brief to raise a Canadian regiment against the British that was called "Congress' own," reflecting its special status outside of any state quota and under the auspices of Congress. Hazen raised a small force of 250 men but had to leave Canada with the Americans when they withdrew. He then took part in several campaigns in New York and Pennsylvania but was disappointed that a second invasion of Canada did not materialize.[67]

James R. Reid was a member of a well-to-do family and among the more educated elite who served in the Continental Army, having graduated from Princeton with two degrees; Reid would marry into a family that allied him with a network of important Central Pennsylvania figures. He was commissioned as a lieutenant in Anthony Wayne's newly formed Fourth Pennsylvania Battalion and wound up at Fort Ticonderoga just as Moses Hazen was exonerated by a court-martial initiated by Benedict Arnold on charges of disobeying orders. Reid nonetheless joined up with Hazen as a captain, fought respectably in the battles of Brandywine and Germantown, and was made a major within a year, indicating Hazen's satisfaction with his performance. Their relations devolved when the regiment failed to receive the same level of support as state troops and a feud developed between Hazen and Reid, affecting regiment morale and forcing its officers to take sides.[68]

Coming from such different backgrounds, Hazen and Reid were engaged in one of many feuds between officers that led to courts-martial in the Continental Army. As a subordinate, Reid's humiliation of his superior reflected poorly on the chain of command and undermined troop discipline, risking the kind of conflict that military law was designed to replace—dueling to restore one's honor. Not only did the 1776 Articles of War (section VII) explicitly prohibit challenges to a duel (officers could be cashiered and noncommissioned officers faced corporal punishment), but officers' honor was the glue that maintained both unit order and the integrity of military justice. As a result, the feud between Hazen and Reid and the multiple courts-martial and courts of inquiry it inspired represented an attack on military justice that exposed a system that, for all its efforts at reform, was inconsistent in its verdicts, inadequate to principles of law, and dangerous to the discipline of an army at war.

The narrative of the Hazen-Reid courts-martial broadly tells a story of an army torn by feuds among its officers, afflicted with a dysfunctional, though often well-meaning, legal system, and constituted of elite figures and rough-hewn warriors, of state-based militias and a congressionally overseen general army. Held accountable to a British code of war and informed in its military strategy by European theory and training rooted the army in European practices modified by local pressures of war. The Continental Army struggled under a British-style system of military justice and was beholden to state militia statutes at the same time that it worked to maintain consistency with respect to the rights granted those tried under state civilian courts. The story of the Continental Army military justice system, exemplified in the series of trials to which Hazen and Reid were subject and seen up close in the courtroom, tells us much about the experience of this negotiated law from the perspective of those subject to it. And it introduces us to one of the many legal orders whose jurisdictional jockeying made up the legal pluralism of the founding of the new nation.

Benedict Arnold versus Hazen, 1776; Baron von Steuben versus Hazen, August 1780

Problems inherent in the military justice system were expressed in two earlier prosecutions of Hazen, one by the then-brigadier general Benedict Arnold and a second by Major General Friedrich von Steuben. The Arnold trials tell us much about an officer corps of elite figures trying to dig itself out of a scandalous episode of plundering, cowardice, and embezzlement during the retreat from Canada in which Congress had to direct Washington to inquire about the behavior of all the officers involved. Hazen and Arnold were at the center of the dispute, largely because the army wanted to keep Arnold, a heroic officer, from either being found guilty himself of misconduct in the retreat or of having to apologize for aspersions against Hazen's character. Hazen was unrelenting in pursuing his superior, who had indeed lashed out not only at Hazen but at the court-martial panel as well; Hazen refused to drop the matter, establishing a pattern that persisted through his feud with Reid.

In his July 1776 trial of Hazen, Arnold charged him with disobeying orders and the loss of seized goods. Arnold, rather than Judge Advocate General Tudor, or a deputy, "adduced the Evidence on the Part of the Prosecution." According to Hazen, Arnold "stated the Questions to the Evidences—was allowed to argue on the Propriety of the Proceedings of the Court—and even to file a Protest against them, which was received and read."[69] The court was presided over by an interested figure who had allegedly contributed to the offense for which Hazen was tried, Major John Scott. Arnold had assigned control of the goods to Scott, who claimed Hazen bore responsibility for them. In the court-martial, Scott inexplicably allowed Arnold considerable license, which resulted in a request from Commanding General Horatio Gates that Arnold apologize to the court-martial board. The apology never materialized, and Hazen was acquitted.[70]

On August 23, 1780, in the second court-martial, Major General von Steuben once again charged Hazen with having disobeyed an order, this time regarding the line of march. Hazen had stopped his brigade and thereby created a gap in the line of half a mile, by order, he claimed, of General Stark. Stark testified there was no negligence on the accused's part, but that he had given no such order.[71] Judge Advocate General Laurance prosecuted and allowed von Steuben to express opinions on the evidence, which were included in the proceedings. Hazen was permitted to read a written "Defence," although the judge advocate moved the court to remove the part that reflected on other individuals' character and conduct. Hazen admitted to going "out of common custom" in offering his defense before he brought in evidence but claimed that this was his own defense, and he was taking it on at his own risk. He did so knowing it would count heavily against his conduct as an officer and gentleman should he fail to carry his evidence "fully into proof"; failure to do so, he allowed, "must of Course be taken Cognizance of by the Court." Hazen's alteration of his defense was intended to provide latitude in countering Laurance's questions to witnesses "on a Matter of Opinion." The judge advocate thereupon allowed von Steuben to argue that the defense was improper in a written justification of his own, which the judge entered into the proceedings. As these interventions exceeded von Steuben's function of providing evidence to support his charges, Hazen accused Laurance of neglect of duty, misleading the court, and assuming powers not delegated to him. The court not only decided the case in Hazen's favor but admitted his "Defence" into the proceedings uncorrected.

In reviewing the matter, Washington's general orders warned that disregarding the line of march was not "a matter of question" and that such conduct was "highly improper." He affirmed the court-martial verdict, however,[72] an indication that both levels of review, caught off-guard by Hazen's brazen behavior, hoped this would end the matter. Unfortunately, Hazen was not of the same mind. He countercharged von Steuben with the same conduct unbefitting an officer with which he had been charged, requiring a board of seven officers to meet from September 20–22 to settle the matter to the satisfaction of both parties. One member of the board, Colonel Israel Angell, commented on the feud that provoked the trial: "A troublesome world this. as Soon as one gits out of trouble them Selves, are Calld upon to Settle Disturbances with others."[73]

Reid versus Hazen, November 1780; Hazan versus Reid, December 1780

The charges in these early courts-martial reflect the range of crimes that one finds when indexing Revolutionary War courts-martial involving officers.[74] There, such crimes as leaving one's post without orders, making false accusations, willful disobedience, desertion, drunkenness, selling public equipment, absence from the regiment, embezzling, abusive behavior, conduct unbecoming an officer, and mustering those unfit for service, dominate the charges brought. In addition, the process of the trials demonstrates the looseness of courts-martial proceedings as a work in progress, a function of the need for officers on the line, and a decided uneasiness about undermining officer authority. Negotiations among those responsible for conducting courts-martial are readily apparent as a demonstration of not only the jurisdictional jockeying that affected courts-martial but the influence of the legal pluralism that permitted such bargaining back and forth.

With the experience of these two trials barely behind him, Hazen faced prosecution in November under Major Reid's charges of regimental mismanagement and fraud. The charges included reporting a false muster for a captain's son and claiming gratuities for one hundred soldiers and noncommissioned officers who, if vouchers were produced, were not actually present in the ranks. Reid cited 126 men who had deserted Hazen's command and that four months' pay had been withheld from fifty officers and soldiers; Hazen responded that the payment was prevented by Congress and the state of Connecticut, although he could show no "official authority." Finally, Reid cited Hazen's nephew, his paymaster Captain John White, for covering up Hazen's conduct.[75]

General William Heath felt obliged to order a court-martial. A farmer and a member of the Massachusetts Provincial Congress for thirteen years, Heath had risen in the ranks of the Massachusetts militia and entered the Continental Army as a brigadier general. Promoted to major general, he performed poorly at the Battle of Fort Independence on the Hudson River and thereafter did not serve where there was fighting.

Brigadier General John Stark presided over the trial and Mr. Strong served as deputy judge advocate. Hoping to "have done justice to an injured Regiment," Reid wrote to Washington "to hold up their situation" and justify their expectation of seeing justice done.[76] In a later letter,[77] Hazen complained that Reid had refused to "particularize" the charges or name the evidence in support of them, which he "claimed as a Point of Right in common justice." Hazen felt himself disadvantaged in not being able to prepare properly for trial, not knowing the particulars of his crimes. The court had disagreed and allowed Reid to present the charges as they stood, suggesting a sensitivity to specified charges that were just as likely to provoke dueling behavior as they were to serve the interests of military law. In addition, the court permitted Reid, according to Hazen, to introduce matters immaterial to the charges and to produce new charges well after the prosecution had begun its case. By comparison, one ruling (excluded from the proceedings) prevented Hazen from bringing in cases "foreign to the Charges," while others allowed Reid "the Privilege of Argument in the Court in Point of Form" and to "state the questions to the Evidence," prerogatives of the judge advocate's role. Hazen refused to call a single witness or to ask any questions in cross-examination. Instead, he filed a "bill of exceptions" (written objections with grounds of support) to perceived errors of the court. The bill was quashed and excluded from the proceedings.

Hazen was acquitted again, although not honorably, this time of fraudulent conduct, false musters and returns, and ungentlemanly- and unofficer-like conduct. Reid represented to Washington that the "acquittal is such as leaves no room to doubt that the Court thought [Hazen] guilty of the charges, but the proof was insufficient to convict him." Following Hazen's example, Reid objected to the conduct of the court; he claimed to have been denied the right to challenge the panel of officers selected by Major General Heath, in what Reid called "a profusion of indulgence" to the accused, and he blamed both the board and Deputy Judge Advocate Strong, in his view a man of little ability, for the failure to convict Hazen. As the panel did not include lawyers, he complained, they "were not obliged to understand some points of Law" that came before them; more importantly, they were unwilling to indulge his request to suspend the trial until a judge advocate equal to the task could be appointed.[78] Reid was convinced that Washington, had he seen the proceedings, would find Reid was not motivated by "passion or disappointment," but, rather, that his "Court-Martial abilities" were inferior to those of Hazen. It was a common occurrence in courts-martial that both the accused and those who prosecuted had not the requisite skills, as one judge advocate put it, "to do justice to [their] own cause, or may be deserted by that presence of mind" needed to use whatever skills they had.[79]

Upon hearing the verdict, Hazen immediately arrested and charged Reid with essentially the same offenses that had been directed against him: disobeying orders, unmilitary-like conduct, defrauding the regiment and the United States, embezzling and misapplying public property, and conduct unbecoming an officer. As Reid begged Washington to appoint a board for his trial "as soon as convenient," his court-martial began just a month after Hazen's (on December 21) and lasted until February 8, 1781.[80] The presiding judge in that court-martial was Colonel John Graeton who had served as lieutenant colonel in the Massachusetts militia and succeeded William Heath in command when he joined the Continental Army. As a member of

Washington's army, Graeton fought in the Battles of Trenton and Princeton and in Burgoyne's invasion under Brigadier John Nixon and commanded for a time in the Northern Department of the army. The Graeton trial in 1780 and a subsequent trial under Colonel Putnam in 1782, both prosecutions of Reid by Hazen, became the centerpieces of the series of courts-martial.

In the Graeton trial, Hazen cited Reid's assertion of privilege in the earlier court-martial as precedent and declined to specify his charges or provide evidence to support the charges. The court overruled him. Deputy Judge Advocate Edwards (soon to become judge advocate general) asserted what he "contended for to be his Right" to sum up the evidence. Hazen agreed, provided that the accused abide by the same standards.[81] Reid countered by replicating Hazen's defense in August in the von Steuben prosecution: he began reading a "Manuscript" that constituted his defense. Predictably, Hazen claimed "the Protection of the Court" to the effect that the writing ought not to be read unless corrected as its content was "contrary to the System laid down by that Court." Demanding latitude in his defense, Major Reid pleaded the precedent of Hazen's von Steuben trial. Hazen countered by moving that the reading be considered an instance of conduct unbecoming an officer and gentleman. Instead of declaring the reading immaterial to the proceedings, the judge advocate advised that Reid's "Defence" "could not come under the Cognizance of that Court" as it was not a matter on which Reid had been arrested and charged. The court followed suit and ruled that Reid would be allowed his "own feeling," but if he "impeached any Officer" that "would of Course be a Subject Matter of a new Trial." On February 18, Reid's guilty verdict on two charges—disobeying orders and unofficer-like conduct—was approved and he was sentenced to a reprimand.[82]

It is worth pausing to consider why Reid might not have been found guilty on the embezzlement charge. The problem of supplies was a constant one in the underprovisioned army and occasioned numerous accusations against officers for withholding, failing to seek, selling, or otherwise spoiling or misappropriating goods. Hazen had in fact leveled charges of gross mismanagement and neglect against his own regiment's deputy quartermaster and two deputy commissaries;[83] his officers complained in letters to Washington about desperate shortages while speculators added to the problems. Not only had Hazen himself written a long report in 1779 about the condition of his regiment to Washington, but Reid had joined other officers in a letter to Supreme Executive Council president Joseph Reed of Pennsylvania about the regiment's deficiencies; Hazen advised President Reed he could not support the appeal as it privileged partial provisions for the complaining officers. Major Reid persisted and joined another petition, this time to Washington. For Hazen to later accuse Reid of defrauding the regiment "by embezzling or misapplying public property" was possibly a reflection of his anger at what he considered insubordination by one of his own majors. Moreover, the charge mirrored Reid's charge against Hazen himself in a previous court-martial in which Reid prosecuted his superior and in which Reid "neglected" to specify the charge, suggesting the reciprocal nature of such charges and counter-charges. In any case, the nature of the embezzling and misapplying charge in Reid's court-martial was unclear; the court's request for specification went unaddressed, and, as a result, Reid was exonerated.[84]

Hazen et al. versus Reid, 1782

Having become a brigadier general in June 1781, Hazen treated Reid's defense as an assault on his reputation and that of his regimental officers, twenty-four of whom joined him to press for a public hearing to satisfy their honor. In specifying the charges, Hazen charged Reid with neglecting to prosecute the officers he had impeached in his "Defence," disobeying orders by not joining his regiment as commanded on three instances from November 1781 (by Major General Lincoln) to January 1782 (by General Washington), and failing to apply for a furlough. In addition, he was charged with defrauding his regiment on suspicion of making false musters for which he received money, granting soldiers under confinement certificates of release, withholding money from part of the regiment, ungentlemanlike conduct in his letters to General Hazen, and signing himself major of a battalion that did not exist.[85]

Unlike Reid's first, quickly convened, court, Washington delayed forming a court for six months; it was held in December 1782 under Colonel Putnam,[86] and the prosecuting officers were aided by two counsel, Captain Lloyd and Captain Moses White (Hazen's cousin).[87] The court overruled counsel's objection to the presence of now-Judge Advocate General Edwards for "being interested in the Event." In addition, it permitted Reid to introduce to the military court "Common Law Citations," to which Hazen's team objected as they were unfairly stated and taken out of context. Moreover, the court ruled, Reid was not triable for his "Defence" statement or his conduct in the prior trial on the grounds that there "was nothing improper in it, or the Court would not have received or suffered it."

In protest, counsel cited instances of their evidence being withdrawn, or suppressed. Their request to bring in testimony to specify a charge was denied as was a move to support the "charge in gross as it first stood." In sum, counsel complained of a general lack of rules and system in the proceedings such that Reid's trial had become instead a trial of his twenty-four prosecutors.[88] According to the officers of the regiment, Reid had impeached their honor and reputation in his "Defence" and, by neglecting to prosecute them, had left them without a forum to defend themselves.[89] Reid was acquitted on all charges, with the exception of his erroneous assumption of the title of major of a nonexistent battalion, which the court found "reprehensible" but as "trifling" as "the nature of the whole prosecution against him." It refused to censure Reid on the matter.[90]

What we find throughout these trials is a series of differently authorized and structured systems (Congress, state authority, the army's command structure, and the internal players—the judge advocate and the president of the court) operating through negotiated decisions and appeals. Their mutual concern for the legality of the proceedings and recognition of its imperfections provide a variety of experiences for those subject to military law and different perspectives on both its hierarchical order and its arbitrary character, despite the common articles to which all the parties were beholden. The room for individual initiative and innovation appears to be preserved in the presence of a presumed rules-based process, leaving open the possibility, on the one hand, of continuity and, on the other, of improvisation.

Judge Advocate General Edwards's Court of Inquiry, February 1783

Bottom-up pressure on the courts-martial was as readily exerted as top-down, something we see in operation in the attack on the judge advocate general himself and the call to have him brought up before a court of inquiry. If we had any illusions about victimization of the accused in court-martial proceedings, appeals to courts of inquiry should disabuse us of them and alert us to a democratization of the military system. This is something we shall see more of when the Hazen-Reid related trials come to an end and Washington directs a military board to make a broad inquiry into the system not only to account for the distressing revelations they exposed but as a stress test for the entire system of military justice.

Washington took Hazen and the officers' attack on Edwards's presumed misconduct as an attack on the military system of justice itself, clearly concerned about the damage the case was doing to the system and the perception that it was not addressing complaints about its partiality. Hazen for his part was determined to continue his assault on Reid and to pursue the malpractice to which he felt he had been subjected under military law. He took two courses of action. In a letter to Washington he requested that the Reid verdict be set aside and a new trial convened, and he asked that Judge Advocate General Edwards's conduct be subjected to an inquiry.[91] In the general order of February 9, 1783, the commander in chief responded by ordering a board made up of his general officers; headed by Major General Gates, it was to convene an inquiry within a week "relative to the proceedings of Courts martial, the duties of a judge advocate, and the conduct of Mr. Edwards the present Judge Advocate." He directed the parties to attend and present their "documents and information" and instructed the board to report with dispatch. Washington indicated that he would point out "the particular objects" of the inquiry at a later date.[92]

On February 12, Washington instructed the board to address the following outstanding issues: setting aside Reid's recent trial, inquiring into the conduct of the trial, a "full and fair" retrial of Reid, and the conduct of the judge advocate, which should be investigated first. Washington repeated Hazen's remonstration that the lack of system and established rules in courts-martial led to the innocent being injured and the guilty escaping punishment and that the lack of uniform rules led to similar cases being treated in diametrically opposite ways. He directed that the matter be treated broadly, "In order to prevent a similar complaint against so important a part of our Military System as the Channel appointed for the equal distribution of public justice to every Member of the Army, on account of a defect of some certain rules for the Government of General Courts Martial and their Officer the Judge Advocate."[93]

Washington's desire for a broad review of the military justice system was an extension of his concession that militias would have to play a role in that army, although subordinated to it, and his more general desire for a regular peacetime army. The need to use state militias, accept their general lack of discipline and training, and respect state statutes meant that the military justice system would be stressed to produce fair and equitable treatment of those who broke military rules and put the common defense at risk. A military system of justice was important to a regular army as a guarantee that its power and authority would be properly controlled and appropriately used against geopolitical threats. Without a proper system of justice, military legitimacy would be challenged and support for both the existing army and a future regular peacetime army undermined. More than that, however, Washington saw an opportunity to rethink what kind of an army a young nation would need. Would a standing army be dangerous to the nation's liberties? Only a mercenary army constituted such a threat. Would it no longer command the commitment of citizen soldiers in defense of the homeland? Washington contended that it would be a disgrace to decline such service and that a well-regulated and disciplined force would ensure "the happiness, dignity and Independence" of the country.[94] A dependable military system of justice would confer upon the army an authority citizens could respect and would treat those who served with dignity and humanity while it protected the army's own values in assuring an orderly role as a law keeper. Constrained in that it "exists by the same authority that any other court exists by" and its law is as valid except that it applies to the army, is limited to breaches of military duty, and does not apply to other areas of the body politic,[95] the system's congruence with civilian law would demonstrate continuity with other institutions of importance in an administrative state as well as strengthen a federal government that addressed threats posed by foreign nations and the western hinterland.[96] A broad review of the military justice system was thus, for Washington, only part of a larger critical scheme of which this issue was an essential part, a plan in which, he admitted to von Steuben, he had "hinted at the propriety of a Continental Militia, [but which] glided almost insensibly into . . . A proper Peace establismt [*sic*] for this Country." Washington's 1783 "Sentiments for a Peacetime Establishment" of an army constituted a strategy that outlined this larger scheme.[97] Hamilton took up his plan and saw it through a congressional committee that included James Madison and James Wilson. The plan, delivered in June 1783 would by 1801 become the very Federalist peacetime establishment that Washington had envisioned at war's end.[98]

As regards the broader review related to Hazen's charges against Edwards, Washington directed the board to determine whether they were true and, if so, were they military matters. "The particular items of enquiry" he had promised to point out in the February 9 orders were delineated. They included investigating those matters, which appeared to be the object of Hazen's charges, that is, the judge advocate general's neglect and the court's partiality, under the apprehension that the court was not possessed of all the facts necessary to resolve the case. Washington wanted a report that would allow him to decide what course of action to take. He could either hold a general court-martial, approve the Reid trial proceedings, or refer Hazen and his officers to an inquiry into their conduct where Reid would have to support his charges. Finally, Washington issued instructions that would in effect put the military justice system itself under review. He required a separate general inquiry to report "what in general cases is and ought to be the business of a Judge Advocate, precisely delineating his duties as well with relation to the Court as with respect to the Accuser and accused."[99]

In his January 25 general orders, it appeared that Washington saw the more recent Reid trial in Colonel Putnam's court as the critical case, for he conditioned the release of that court's proceedings upon Hazen's specifying the charges against Edwards. Should the "Memorialists" (the twenty-four officers) wish to prosecute Edwards, it read, "it will be necessary to reduce your Allegations to specific Charges, and transmit them to me without delay, that an investigation may immediately take place."[100] Hazen, however, had in his own "Memorial" to Washington expanded his complaint to include other trials in which he had been involved (and which involved other judge advocates—Deputy Judge Advocate Strong and Judge Advocate General Laurance—and other prosecutors—Baron von Steuben and Benedict Arnold) and other issues related to judges advocate and courts-martial. Thus, Hazen and the twenty-four other officers' January 29 response to Washington's request added cases going back several years and tied the court-martial of Reid under Colonel Greaton in December 1780 to that under Colonel Putnam in December 1782. The procedural and legal issues raised were thus more extensive, more complicated, and of longer duration than merely one problematic trial.[101]

While the trials from 1780–1783 represented a consequential context for considering the Edwards court of inquiry, two documents stood out as a more direct route to the inquiry. Both were forwarded to the commander in chief by Hazen as the organizing force behind the charges: an enclosure from the two counsels appointed by the regiment (included in the joint memorial of January 13, 1783), and the joint communique from Hazen and his twenty-four co-complainants (January 29, 1783), which transmitted and supported the charges against the judge advocate general that Washington's general orders had requested.

The enclosure by counsel expanded on Hazen's acknowledgment that he had "taken up matters on a Larger Scale than I otherwise should have done had it not been to shew the necessity of adopting by authority Some general rules for the government of Courts martial in other cases as well as ours." Lloyd, writing on behalf of himself and White as counsel for the regiment, argued that Edwards was responsible for the Putnam court denying them the opportunity to prosecute Reid's "Defence." They contended that they had exposed Reid's selective common law "extracts" and had wished to enter "many other cases of Common law" to prove there was precedent for bringing the "Defence" into court against Reid. The judge advocate, however, not only suppressed their reasons, refusing to communicate them to the court, but belied his impartiality by speaking "after the manner of an attorney for his client [Reid]." In their role as counsel, Lloyd represented that "we have not had justice done us by the seeming partiality of the Judge Advocate for as the Court had determined they knew no prosecutor but the Judge Advocate and even silenced us when we spoke aloud to him." Moreover, the proceedings, for which Judge Advocate Edwards had responsibility, entered reasons "directly opposite the Opinion of another Court [the Graeton court] on the same matter whereon Mr Edwards also officiated as Judge Advocate." Counsel could have cited, but for some reason did not, an apposite precedent: Hazen's written defense in the von Steuben prosecution, which Hazen, like Reid, had read before the court.[102]

The second document, by Hazen and the twenty-four officers, presented the full case made by counsel against Edwards, reworking the memorial with greater specification on the trials prior to the Graeton and Putnam courts. The "Gentlemen Officers" of Hazen's regiment offered the following global charges against Lieutenant Thomas Edwards, judge advocate: "The Want of Abilities and a regular judicious System in the Office and Duties of a

Judge Advocate," including "The Want of Knowledge in common law and Equity"; "The Want of Candour and Impartiality in conducting Prosecutions as Judge-Advocate in Courts-martial"; and "A Neglect of Duty in the Office of Judge-Advocate."[103] Counsel represented that the charges had "such an immediate Connection the one with the other that the supporting the one will naturally tend to prove the other." Their intent was to demonstrate that the judge advocate's conduct provoked Reid's "infamous libel . . . called his Defence" thereby making him a principal or accessory. The first Reid court-martial's acceptance of the "Defence" had become central to the charges against Edwards as it legitimized the accused's right to say whatever he pleased, however immaterial or prejudicial, and gave the accused free rein to libel his prosecutors. Reid was able in his second court-martial, as a result, to claim that the "Defence" was sanctioned by the original court, which Edwards did not contradict. Reid had, however, admitted to the original court that while the accusations in the "Defence" were not a subject for that court, they were open to determination by another.[104]

The "Defence" contributed to yet other abuses according to Hazen and the officers' counsel. Not only had counsel's own use of common law citations (which they claimed was "admitted by all Authors in Civil Law or Equity to be the best possible Testimony in the World; and not ever before rejected in Military Courts Martial") been rejected, but the court accepted Reid's quoting of common law out of context to "suppress" the record of his public acts, which included the libels read as part of his "Defence." In the Graeton court, Judge Advocate Edwards had determined that Reid should be allowed his "Defence" without holding Reid accountable for material that was "false and criminal"; thereafter as regards the Putnam court, Edwards objected to the "Defence" being admitted (in this instance as a libel by Reid) on the grounds "that it was a new Matter for which [Edwards] had not a precedent," leaving aside that the first trial under Graeton, as the prosecution represented, was "a precedent in Point." In each instance, Edwards's opinion was adopted by the court in Reid's favor. The judge advocate, counsel concluded, neglected his duty to be impartial; his opinions were inconsistent and prejudicial, and he was wanting in legal ability.[105]

Having only been assigned their task eight days earlier, the board under General Gates announced its findings in the February 20, 1783, general orders. The first charge against Edwards ("want of abilities and a regular judicious system" in his office and duties) was "not a Military offence cognizable by a Courtmartial." As for the charges of partiality, lack of candor, and neglect of duty in conducting courts martial, the board had investigated them fully and minutely and was "unanimously of opinion" that they were not supported.[106] The inquiry process thus rejected counsel's argument that because the court had refused to communicate their argument to the court, because it silenced them and refused to recognize any other prosecutor than the judge advocate, the court was partial. Moreover, the court rejected their argument that the accused was granted latitude when it disallowed Reid's "Defence" as a form of conduct under the charges. The commander in chief approved the court's recommendation.

The court of inquiry's position was consonant with that of the Putnam and Graeton courts, a position that would resonate with a later set of reforms recommended by General Henry Knox, who sat on the board. It did not regard the judge advocate as speaking for the accused as a client, and it did not consider him an accomplice of the accused and thereby accountable for Reid's libel. Nor did it find him inconsistent, prejudiced, or partial. Rather, the inquiry board held that the judge advocate's advice was more to be believed and followed than the prosecutors' citations and their claims of precedent. Moreover, the common customs of military courts, with their established usage, practices, and customary constraints were judged sufficient to inform the knowledge and light necessary to deliver decisions in courts-martial, but they still needed reform with respect to the rights of the accused and provisions for general fairness, changes that reflected more than a command perspective. They constituted a recognition that a new governing authority had taken hold of the country, of which the military was an integral part.

GENERAL HENRY KNOX'S REPORT

Within a week and a half of the general orders approving the court of inquiry verdict, General Knox's "Thoughts on Courts Martial and the Duty of Judge Advocate" were submitted to a board of general officers that had been appointed by the commander in chief. At Washington's side as a confidant during the war and at the cusp of replacing Washington as commander in chief in December, Knox wrote his remarks on March 4 at West Point where he had been commander of the garrison since 1782.[107] Washington's general orders of February 9, 1783, had directed the garrison's general officers to serve on Edwards's court of inquiry board and the February 12 general orders directed the board to submit a report on courts-martial "on a General Scale." Knox's remarks thus appear to have either been intended as part of that report or constituted the report itself.[108] His remarks have not been identified as the report requested of the board by Washington in his February 12 communication, likely the result of the burning of the war department and its records in 1800. Nonetheless, the report survives in manuscript in Henry Knox's papers, indicating that it represents Knox's thoughts as a member of the court of inquiry board.[109]

Knox might have been a critic of the court-martial system, but he was an honest broker when it came to fulfilling Washington's request to make recommendations for a uniform code that could work for both a standing army and a militia. The intent of the report was to produce new regulations that expunged unproductive customs and would benefit the common good. These included reforms protecting the innocent in courts-martial as well as delineating the role of the judge advocate in its relation to both the accused and the accuser.[110] Knox began with an acknowledgment of the dilemma that faced military justice:

> A court martial ought to possess the means of obtaining the truth, unrestrained by any forms, but such as common sense and the known maxims of justice dictate. It is therefore difficult to establish rules which shall govern in all cases, as there may be some peculiarly circumstances, which must be decided upon by their own state of things. The following principles, however, may be necessary to be adopted as they appear to be founded upon the unalterable principles of justice.[111]

Here, Knox was reporting the command perspective on courts-martial. He endorsed the rationale that Blackstone, among others, had found concerning: that the law of war could be arbitrary, that it could be particular to one case and based on discretion, and that it was sufficient if it was unclear and uncertain rather than predictable and based on precedent. Yet Knox accepted the need for principled common sense and adherence to known maxims of justice, which was reflected in his recommendations.

In line with this thinking, the question of vague or general charges was a matter of importance to Knox who argued that they should not be admitted and that charges "ought to be distinct and particular," an issue that arose in more than one of the serial Hazen-Reid trials. Moreover, nothing should be admitted on the part of the prosecution or the defense except "what should be pertinent to the charge," a blow to the frequency with which immaterial evidence was introduced at trial and to the constant attacks on the honor of accused officers in courts-martial. The danger, in Knox's view, was that irrelevant expressions were in themselves criminal as they tended to prejudice or influence the court "to such a degree, as to be incapable of performing their duty with propriety." To that end, he recommended bringing attacks on individuals' character before a subsequent court-martial, a process for which Hazen and his officers had aggressively argued.[112]

Knox recommended as well allowing peremptory challenges to members of the court to ensure impartiality, something that Reid had claimed as his right in his prosecution of Hazen. In practice, judge advocates commonly disallowed such challenges as they assaulted the integrity of the presiding officers upon whose honor the proceedings relied. Whereas judge advocates were often "averse to taking away any privilege from a criminal at a court martial, that is enjoyed in any other court," it was also the case that the accused often made such challenges to delay trials and ought to be dissuaded on those grounds.[113] On questions related to witnesses, Knox objected to interrogations that were suggestive, advising that they "ought to be general, bringing the fact into view, without any of its attendant circumstances." This recommendation would have affected reliance on suggestive examinations of witnesses like those that tainted testimony across the Hazen courts-martial, ranging from "pointed evidence" to inducing immaterial testimony and the use of negative proof or prejudicial opinions. Knox, in addition, recognized a need to expand the role of the accused, if only to cross-examine witnesses on the prosecution's evidence, but limited disruptive aspects of the accused's defense like allowing him "to argue upon the proceedings, or to remark on the nature or tendency of the testimony,"[114] a protection that would have obviated the disruptive defense statements that both Hazen and Reid had utilized.

Unwilling to get too far ahead of himself, and consistent with military court practice, Knox rejected introducing legal authorities into a trial "as they would tend to involve the proceedings in endless perplexities and errors." Reid's attempts to confound Hazen's prosecution of him with selective and inapplicable cites and precedents would thereby have been overruled, as would counsels' efforts to introduce common law cases for consideration. Rather, Knox emphasized, it was the judge advocate's duty, under the control of the court, "impartially to bring the whole truth before the court," according to "the principles of equal justice."[115] Nor should the judge advocate in his multiple roles of prosecuting the case for the state, advising the accused, and interpreting the law to the board of officers, curry favor with command authority.

Knox thus fell in line with treatises that embraced the judge advocate's role in counterbalancing prosecution and defense. The judge advocate's role did not end with prosecuting alone, Knox noted, else the institution of the court martial would be "unequal and unjust." Perhaps the remark most applicable to the Hazen-Reid trials, this prohibition argued against merely prosecuting on behalf of the state. In Edwards's inquiry, it illustrated the difficult path a judge advocate must navigate in keeping the accused and the accuser satisfied that they had received a full and fair hearing untainted by inability, partiality, neglect, or unbecoming conduct.[116]

As a comment on the Hazen-Reid courts-martial and the judge advocate general's court of inquiry, Knox's "Thoughts" supported the court's role in determining both the facts and the law and depended on principles of justice understood as a function of common sense and accepted truth, not on civil law legalisms and procedural law. Like the Articles of War, his principles reflected an easily comprehended, yet independent and discretionary application of military law combined with an honor code that served as a foundation of the officer's code of conduct and a bulwark of the military system of justice. Honor underlays the oath taken by members of the board, which guaranteed that they would collectively and in good conscience act as a court of honor to ensure fairness and equal treatment.

In line with that mission, Knox would, in sum, grant the accused the right to challenge board members, to demand precise charges, and to cross-examine the prosecution's evidence, within limits, all innovations informed by civil law. He would not go so far, however, as to allow the accused to cite legal authorities, remark on the nature of the testimony, or argue upon the proceedings. For these functions, the accused must depend upon the judge advocate, a role whose authority Knox elevated to pull the whole together into a more effective operating system. The judge advocate role might have been perceived as a Proteus posture by treatise writers, but Knox understood it as the critical nexus for a three-way balance of prosecution, defense, and the board.

As we see in Knox's report, the military system of justice might have had the authority of the state and the power of force behind it, but it responded to the commonalities inherent in a multicentric world of plural legal orders by adopting more flexible strategies to enhance its legitimacy as a legal order. Within its world, we find improvisations by legal actors based on experience and the application of strategic behaviors to take advantage of the jurisdictional complexity of the outer world as well as opportunities offered within the court-martial system to stretch its limits. It was not insulated against other legal systems but engaged knowingly or otherwise in exchanges among them as part of the larger process of negotiation characteristic of plural legalism.

One cannot argue that the military legal system was hegemonic or self-enclosed; rather, its interactivity logically extended its power and allowed it to incorporate from the international code of war, state militia law, civil, common law, and state law strategies that enhanced its coherence. Its resistance to boundaries, as it turned out, was limited in practice, despite its declared enmity to legal authority, civil common law, and procedural law. Instead, it jockeyed in ways that included pragmatic accommodations and that utilized the flexibility of its vertical command structure to correct imperfections and injustices as well as inconveniences. Like other entities in a plural legal order, its boundaries were permeable sites of contest, sometimes defending traditions and at other times challenging them.[117]

AFTERMATH

Whereas it appeared that the Hazen-Reid feud had played itself out, it had in fact only paused. Reid reacted to the resolution of Judge Advocate General Edward's court of inquiry in a February 22 letter to Washington:

> It is true I unhappily got into a current of ill fortune, and have been twice in arrest and as often embroiled in difficulties which is generally the conduct of a bad man but as your Excellency is fully possessed of the circumstances which occasioned these difficulties, my feelings are perfectly at rest upon that score.[118]

Reid's seemingly apologetic mien had no effect on the continuing saga of his feud with Hazen. The core issue of Reid's accusations against Hazen and the officers of his regiment remained unresolved, as did releasing Reid's second court-martial proceedings. At the beginning of April, Washington ordered a second court of inquiry to examine Reid's attacks, "particularly in his Defence before a General courtmartial" in Graeton's court in 1780. Washington directed the inquiry to meet on May 15, 1783, and proceed without delay "ascertaining the facts fully, with the further admonition that Major Reid and all concerned "will attend accordingly." Washington considered the opinion of this court "the final determination of the matters in question," a statement that expressed his frustration with a case that had escalated exponentially and become unnecessarily complicated and destabilizing.[119]

By May 27, the court concluded its inquiry, which Reid did not attend despite Washington's directive.[120] The court determined it "cannot find Reason to justify the Assertions made" in Reid's prosecution of Hazen in Brigadier General Stark's November 1780 court or in Reid's later "Defence" before the Graeton court. Washington approved the court's findings[121] and on June 1 advised Hazen he had "done every thing in my power to give satisfaction to you . . . and can only lament that the Measures which have been adopted have failed of the wished for effect."[122] On June 23, Washington assembled the general officers of the army (Major Generals Heath, Howe, and von Steuben, and Brigadier Generals Huntington, Hart, and, notably, Greaton) to inquire "Whether all measures which were practicable and proper for giving satisfaction" to Hazen and his twenty-four officers had been pursued, and, if so, whether Reid ought to be brought to trial.[123]

The following day, Major General Heath reported the board was unanimous in declaring that all avenues had been explored and Reid should not be tried as too much time had elapsed ("in the one case nearly Six Years and in the other two Years"); the war was ending, leaving little time to properly try the case to anyone's satisfaction, the army and the public included.[124] Reid had effectively run out the clock. On the same day, Washington anxiously closed the case as commander in chief, satisfied that it arose more "from a spirit of persecution, than a desire to promote Service" and acknowledging it had "given so much trouble to the Army."[125]

Washington's response was somewhat equivocal, as he had previously expressed some empathy for Hazen. In his February 18, 1781, general orders following the Graeton court-martial, Washington had offered that "an inferior officer can never be justifiable in attempts to make his commanding officer suspected and odious to his corps." He found it regretful that officers on trial would indulge in "invective and abuse" inconsistent with decency for others and respect for themselves.[126] He condemned Reid's "Inflammatory expressions" against his commanding officer, which he considered unjustified and exceptionable,[127] noting that an officer should be "as delicate in expressing his resentment as in defending his honor."[128]

Washington revisited the issue in his general orders of February 21, 1783, in relation to the 1782 Putnam court trial where the prosecution strategy had been to use Reid's "Defence" as evidence of conduct unbecoming an officer and gentleman. He blamed Reid's "Defence" for prolonging the feud as Reid used such unwarranted language "impeaching the honor and integrity and reputation of a large majority of the officers of the regiment" that it would render it impossible for them to hold commissions in the army.[129] Washington's concern spoke to five articles in section VII of the Articles of War focused on honor and conflict resolution by means of dueling. The first prohibited provocative speech or gestures as they escalated events and led to challenges. Challenges received the same punishment—being cashiered—as willingly and with knowledge suffering anyone to fight a duel or upbraiding someone for refusing a challenge. By contrast, officers who refused a challenge were "discharged of any disgrace, or opinion of disadvantage," having done their duty and obeyed the will of Congress as well-disciplined soldiers.[130] In Washington's world, containing officers' disputes within the military justice system and addressing them with decorum was paramount. As the Articles directed, members of courts-martial were "to behave with calmness and decency" (article 4, sec. XIV) and refrain from using "menacing words, signs, or gestures" or causing disorder that would disturb the proceedings (article 14, sec. XIV).[131]

Hazen responded to the untenable position in which he found himself in a letter to General Heath, asking, "How then Sir, am I to act in my present unfortunate Situation? Is there any Way by which an [illegible] may reestablish an injured Character?" Either he had to risk his life and challenge Reid to prove himself no coward, "prove to the Regiment and the World that I am not a Felon, a Thief, and a Robber" or he must remain "an infamous Character as a Legacy to my Posterity." Hazen not only expressed his need to avenge his honor and the prevailing view that dueling was the only satisfactory way to do so, but he revealed how close the case had come to being resolved by dueling. How could he and the officers, in Hazan's words, "be admitted to the Society of Gentlemen"? How could such calumny be tolerated "in our Sacred Courts of Justice"?[132] They faced the dilemma of being unable to perform with honor once they had been publicly, and on record, accused of criminal conduct. To avoid breaching the military code, it was crucial that an officer's honor be redeemed by a military court, even if recourse to yet another court-martial seemed fruitless. The alternative of applying to a civil court for redress was inconsistent with one's military character and unappealing to a military man. For Hazen and the officers, it would remain an unresolved dilemma.

CONCLUSION

Just as Judge Advocate General Edwards's court of inquiry had demonstrated, and as General Knox's recommendations reaffirmed, the army recognized it faced a dilemma in trying to reconcile the competing demands of war and law in the military justice system. The Hazen-Reid courts-martial and the two courts of inquiry that emanated from them had exposed that the Articles of War provided poor guidance for the procedures, crimes, and punishments involved in trying officers. Interested parties, for example, routinely participated in courts-martial. Hazen filed a motion to replace Judge Advocate General Edwards for being an interested party in the 1782 court-martial of Reid, while Reid challenged a board he considered partial to the accused in his 1780 prosecution of Hazen. Major Scott, who had played a role in Hazen's offense, presided over Benedict Arnold's prosecution of Hazen; Colonel Greaton appeared on the board of Reid's court of inquiry, which investigated the very court-martial over which he had presided; and Baron von Steuben—who had himself prosecuted Hazen—served on the same board.

The usurpation of the judge advocate's prerogatives by those who filed charges was another destabilizing feature of courts-martial. Arnold, von Steuben, and Reid were all accused by Hazen of overriding the judge advocate, while Hazen himself admitted he had impinged on the judge advocate's authority when accused by von Steuben. Prosecutors legitimately assumed certain powers, including to charge the accused, but could demand unwarranted influence by refusing to specify the charges or provide evidence to support the charges, or by introducing new charges well into the trial. The interference of counsel and prosecutors in making motions, arguing on procedure, and filing protests, or by reading written justifications into the proceedings, questioning the evidence, and interjecting opinions on witness testimony contributed to disruptive courts-martial. Judge advocates permitted some innovations in trying to deal with obstreperous prosecutors and defendants, including negotiation of an agreement to hold both parties to a common set of rules. But they were firm in resisting pressure to assert military and common law precedents that countered their advice to the court. In practice, they endeavored to sideline private counsel and restrict legal authority to the Articles of War, established military usage, and military-specific laws passed by Congress, in an effort to keep military trials separate from civil law. Knox's recommendations and the findings of Judge Advocate Edward's court of inquiry positioned the judge advocate at the critical center of courts-martial, effectively putting his conduct beyond the reach of investigations by general officers and making charges against him a nonmilitary matter outside of their judgment.

In sum, the courts-martial and courts of inquiry that constituted the corpus of the Hazen-Reid feud provided a rich body of material to trace the fault lines of the military system of justice, but they also left room for innovations and borrowings. Still, courts-martial left decisional autonomy in the hands of an inexperienced board of officers without legal training who reposed their confidence in the judge advocate; the judge advocate, for his part, had to accommodate prosecutors with a vested interest in the proceedings as well as the accused who had no realistic means of defending themselves. The goal Washington had set of maintaining military discipline and keeping military officers in the field posed an almost insurmountable obstacle to a fair and just outcome. If Blackstone wanted to point out the incongruity of law and war, he needed to look no further than the Continental Army and its military justice system. As a court of law in a time of war, and despite its acknowledgment of the need for reform, it was barely adequate.

As for the issues in the Hazan-Reid courts-martial, they appear in one way to be no more than a feud writ large. The court, in this reading, served as a venue for a slander suit that capitalized on military referees to avoid the damning prospect of undermining military discipline and justice by dueling. Feuds addressed by courts-martial might have had some effect on the unravelling of respect for the officer corps, but the result was little more than the appearance of justice being done.

America, still in its infancy as a nation, was characterized not so much by stability or cohesiveness as it was held together by an older order of honor culture, reputation, and character. We shall see something of this in chapter 3 as General Washington relies upon his reputation on the frontier to secure private land holdings and in chapter 5 when the physician Benjamin Rush defends his medical reputation against the libelous attacks of British-born journalist William Cobbett. The honor code that served as a glue for officers in the Continental Army functioned in the civil world as a means of avoiding going to court or, in the alternative, of regaining one's honor by gaining a favorable trial verdict. Banking on one's reputation to protect one's interests required a surface of gentility backed by a threat of violence. The value of one's honor depended upon the credibility of the threat of dueling or of winning at court, with reputation acting as a form of fungible currency expended toward that end.[133] But whereas dueling represented a means of operationalizing the reputation upon which honor relied and through which one's character was displayed, the Articles of War prohibited it. The court-martial was intended to fill this role. Through its verdict it resolved disputes and certified order at a time when predictability and reliability were very much at issue; one's name, one's character depended upon it.

Looking at courts-martial through the prism of feuds[134] suggests that their prevalence in the military justice system had the potential to destabilize the war effort and allow for status differentials and backroom deals that affected the neutrality and fairness necessary to equal treatment under the law, proportional punishments, and certainty of application. The mere threat of a feud could have a deterrence value, but it did not prevent the back-and-forth prosecutions of Hazen and Reid or the routinized counterattacks we shall take up in the Rush and Cobbett feud. Nor was there much precision in the Hazen-Reid courts-martial as neither party chose to specify his charges, as required by court-martial procedures, possibly because it might provoke a duel by violating an understood code of honor. But if justice was not the ultimate objective of the court-martial, for which discipline and order were the overriding considerations, the system was at least concerned with innocence, with peremptory challenges, with vague charges, with evidentiary proof, with representation for the accused, protections reinforced by the military system's interactivity with civil courts and state law, the result of a negotiated interface with other legal systems.

Importantly, at the macro level the military system was part of a larger fabric. We don't want to miss the institutional development exerted by reconceiving the military through such inventions as the experiment of an academy at West Point, the recommendations and analyses of courts of inquiry boards, and Washington's submission to Congress of his thoughts for a reconceived army, his Sentiments on a Peacetime Establishment. These efforts were in the process of reinventing the administrative fabric of the military consistent with parallel judicial efforts in establishing a federal court system and civil efforts like national administrative changes in customs collection, banking, insurance companies, and the US Post Office, which sparked a revolution in communications. Looking forward, new governing authorities were already creating a federal political culture of a "modern state capable of collecting revenue, exerting regulatory authority, and utilizing military force," a culture with the energy of a fiscal-military state.[135]

NOTES

1. Bibliographical note: Chris Bray, *Court Martial: How Military Justice Has Shaped America from the Revolution to 9/11 and Beyond* (New York: W. W. Norton & Co., 2016); William F. Fratcher, "History of the Judge Advocate General's Corps, United States Army," *Military Law Review* 4 (1959): 89–122; James C. Neagles, *Summer Soldiers: A Survey and Index of Revolutionary War Courts-Martial* (Salt Lake City, UT: Ancestry Incorporated, 1986); Bradley J. Nicholson, "Courts in the Legion Army: American Military Law in the Early Republic: 1792–1796," *Military Law Review* 144 (1994): 77–109; David A. Schlueter, "The Court-Martial: A Historical Survey," *Military Law Review* 87 (1980); George James Stansfield, "A History of the Judge Advocate General's Department United States Army," *Military Affairs* 9, no. 3 (1945): 219–37; G. A. Steppler, "British Military Law, Discipline, and the Conduct of Regimental Courts Martial in the Later Eighteenth Century," *The English Historical Review* 102, no. 405 (1987): 859–86; Jonathan Turley, "Tribunals and Tribulations: The Antithetical Elements of Military Governance in a Madisonian Democracy," *George Washington Law Review* 70, no. 4 (2002): 649–734. Cases: Charles Lee, *Proceedings of a General Court Martial Held at Brunswick, in the State of New-Jersey, by Order of His Excellency General Washington, General and Commander-in-Chief of the Army of the United States of America, for the Trial of Major-General Lee, July 4th, 1778* (New York: Privately Printed, 1864); *Proceedings of a General Court Martial of the Line, Held at Raritan, in the State of New-Jersey, by Order of His Excellency General Washington, General and Commander-in-Chief of the Army of the United States of America, for the Trial of Major-General Arnold, June 1, 1779, Major General Howe, President* (Philadelphia: Francis Bailey, 1780); *Proceedings of a General Court Martial, Convened at Fish-Kill, on the 25th Day of October, 1780, by Order of His Excellency General Washington, Commander in Chief of the Army of the United States of America, on the Trial of Colonel Elisha Sheldon* (Hartford, CT: Hudson and Goodwin, 1780).

2. William Blackstone, *Commentaries on the Laws of England*, 15th ed. (London: A. Strahan, 1809), I, 412.

3. Blackstone, *Commentaries*, 415–16.

4. Alexander Fraser Tytler, *An Essay on Military Law, and the Practice of Courts Martial* (Edinburgh: Murray & Cochrane, 1800); Payne Adye, *A Treatise on Courts Martial. Also an Essay on Military Punishments and Rewards*, 4th ed. (London: J. Murray and S. Highley, 1797). Ala Alryyes makes the point that historically eighteenth-century military justice and courts-martial have not received much scholarly assessment until recently; Ala Alryyes, "War at a Distance: Court-Martial Narratives in the Eighteenth Century," *Eighteenth-Century Studies* 41, no. 4 (2008): 539n3.

5. Jonathan Lurie, *Military Justice in America: The U.S. Court of Appeals for the Armed Forces, 1775–1980* (Lawrence: University Press of Kansas, 2001), 1.

6. Emmerich De Vattel, *The Law of Nations; or Principles of the Law of Nature, Applied to the Conduct and Affairs of Nations and Sovereigns*, Joseph Chitty, ed., 1834. (Cambridge: Cambridge University Press, 2011).

7. Hugo Grotius, *The Most Excellent Hugo Grotius, His Three Books Treating of the Rights of War and Peace*, William Evats, trans. (London: M. W. for Thomas Basset and Ralph Smith, 1682).

8. Patrick O. Gudridge, "Ely, Black, Grotius & Vattel," *University of Miami Law Review* 50, no. 1 (1995): 89–90, 93–94.

9. Ian C. Hope, *A Scientific Way of War: Antebellum Military Science, West Point, and the Origins of American Military Thought* (Lincoln: University of Nebraska Press, 2015), 23–28.

10. Hope, *A Scientific Way of War*, 19–20; Robert D. Duke and Howard S. Vogel, "The Constitution and the Standing Army: Another Problem of Court-Martial Jurisdiction," *Vanderbilt Law Review* 13, no. 2 (1960): 435–60.

11. Lurie, *Military Justice in America*, 9–10; James Kirby Martin and Mark Edward Lender, *"A Respectable Army": The Military Origins of the Republic, 1763–1789* (Hoboken, NJ: Wiley Blackwell, 2015), 8.

12. Friedrich Wilhelm Ludolf Gerard Augustus, Baron von Steuben, *Regulations for the Order and Discipline of the Troops of the United States* (Philadelphia: Styner and Cist, 1779).

13. "Washington's Sentiments on a Peace Establishment, May 1, 1783," Founders Online, accessed 9/4/2023, https://founders.archives.gov/documents.

14. Arthur N. Gilbert, "Military and Civilian Justice in Eighteenth-Century England: An Assessment," *Journal of British Studies* 17, no. 2 (1978): 42–43; Francis H. Heller, "Military Law in the Continental Army," *University of Kansas Law Review* 25, no. 3 (1977): 353–55.

15. Lurie, *Military Justice in America*, 1–5.

16. Alexander Macomb, *A Treatise on Martial Law, and Courts-Martial; as Practised in the United States of America* (Charleston, SC: J. Hoff, 1809), 166–67.

17. Tytler, *An Essay on Military Law*, 359–60; Harry M. Ward, *George Washington's Enforcers: Policing the Continental Army* (Carbondale: Southern Illinois University Press, 2006), 39.

18. John Laurance to George Washington, May 17, 1781, Founders Online, https://founders.archives.gov/documents.

19. John H. Langbein, *The Origins of Adversary Criminal Trial* (Oxford: Oxford University Press, 2003); Barbara Shapiro, *"Beyond Reasonable Doubt" and "Probable Cause": Historical Perspectives on the Anglo-American Law of Evidence* (Berkeley: University of California Press, 1991); Allen Steinberg, *The Transformation of Criminal Justice, 1800–1880* (Chapel Hill: The University of North Carolina Press, 1989).

20. Maurer Maurer, "Military Justice Under General Washington," *Military Affairs* 28, no. 1 (1964): 14.

21. Adye, *A Treatise on Courts* Martial, 117n, 117–18, 120. After the Constitution, conflict arose not only between the judge advocate and the board (which was not obliged to take his advice), but between the power of the legislative and the executive branches of government (the objective of ensuring proper command and discipline fell within the prerogatives not of the judicial or legislative but the executive function). Statutes governing civil courts have no effect on military courts, which are not

courts in a traditional sense, and their findings cannot be reviewed by the judiciary. William Winthrop, *Military Law and Precedents* (Washington, DC: Government Printing Office, [1896] 1920), ch. V, 49–65.

22. Adye, *A Treatise on Courts Martial*, 110–11.

23. Major Vans Kennedy, *Practical Remarks on the Proceedings of General Courts Martial* (London: A Strahan, 1825), iv, vi–vii.

24. In practice, members of the board who had not voted with the majority on a verdict did not vote on the sentence. Macomb, *A Treatise on Martial Law*, 167–68; Tytler, *An Essay on Military Law*, 361.

25. Vans Kennedy, *Practical Remarks*, vii, x–xi.

26. Macomb, *A Treatise on Martial Law*, 168–69.

27. Tytler, *An Essay on Military Law*, 369.

28. Tytler, *An Essay on Military Law*, 371.

29. Macomb, *A Treatise on Martial Law*, 170–71; Tytler, *An Essay on Military Law*, 364, 367–368.

30. Adye, *A Treatise on Courts Martial*, 113; Tytler, *An Essay on Military Law*, 363–64.

31. Adye, *A Treatise on Courts Martial*, 115; Macomb, *A Treatise on Martial Law*, 165.

32. Tytler, *An Essay on Military Law*, 364.

33. Adye, *A Treatise on Courts Martial*, 111–12.

34. Full proceedings of courts-martial date from 1808; earlier trials were preserved in part in order books; Proceedings of Courts-Martial, War office, Mss. National Archives Record Group 153, Entry 14, 2, at 142–43; Frederick Bernays Wiener, "Courts-Martial and the Bill of Rights: The Original Practice I," *Harvard Law Review* 72, no. 1 (1958): 27–28; *The Army Lawyer: A History of the Judge Advocate Generals Corps, 1775–1795* (Washington, DC: US Government Printing Office, 1975), 29.

35. Macomb, *A Treatise on Martial Law*, 93–96; Wiener, "Courts-Martial and the Bill of Rights," 10–12, 20.

36. Blackstone, *Commentaries*, 349–50; Wiener, "Courts-Martial and the Bill of Rights," 22–23, 44–45, 49; Wiener on the 1824 trial of Captain Charles Stewart, 34; on the 1810 trial of Captain Thomas Howe, 40.

37. Major Norman Thompson, "Before we had Wings," *The Reporter* 26 (1999): 56, 58.

38. George James Stansfield, "A History of the Judge Advocate General's Department United States Army," *Military Affairs* 9, no. 3 (1945): 222.

39. George Washington to John Hancock, July 21, 1775, Founders Online, https://founders.archives.gov/documents.

40. William Tudor to John Adams, July 19, 1775, Founders Online, https://founders.archives.gov/documents.

41. William Tudor to John Adams, July 31, 1775, Founders Online, https://founders.archives.gov/documents.

42. William Tudor to John Adams, [no date] August 1775, Founders Online, https://founders.archives.gov/documents.

43. Keith Marshall Jones III, "John Laurance and the Role of Military Justice at Valley Forge," *Pennsylvania Magazine of History and Biography* 141, no. 1 (2017): 9.
44. Jones, "John Laurance and the Role of Military Justice," 11.
45. George Washington to President of Congress [John Hancock], September 24, 1776, in *The Writings of George Washington from the Original Manuscript Sources, 1745–1799*, ed. John C. Fitzpatrick (Washington, DC: U. S. Printing Office, 1932), vol. 6, 106–16.
46. Tal Tovy, "Militia or Regular Army? The Debate on the Character of the American Army during the Revolution," *European Journal of American Studies* (2010), https://journals.openedition.org/ejas/7814.
47. Benjamin H. Irvin, *Clothed in Robes of Sovereignty: The Continental Congress and the People out of Doors* (New York: Oxford University Press, 2011), 5–6, 11–13.
48. Max M. Edling, *Perfecting the Union: National and State Authority in the U.S. Constitution* (New York: Oxford University Press, 2021), 11, 135–36.
49. Christian M. McBurney, *George Washington's Nemesis: The Outrageous Treason and Unfair Court-Martial of Major General Charles Lee During the Revolutionary War* (El Dorado Hills, CA: Savas Beatie, 2020), 168–69, 188–90.
50. William Tudor to John Adams, October 28, 1775, Founders Online, https://founders.archives.gov/documents.
51. William Tudor to George Washington, August 23, 1775, Founders Online, https://founders.archives.gov/documents.
52. William Tudor to John Adams, September 6, 1776, Founders Online, https://founders.archives.gov/documents.
53. William Tudor to John Adams, October 3, 1776, Founders Online, https://founders.archives.gov/documents.
54. Laurance read for the law under the New York Lieutenant Governor Cadwallader Colden, was admitted to the New York bar, and had tried more than 220 cases by the time of Valley Forge in 1778. He was appointed judge advocate general in April 1777 and oversaw half a dozen military lawyers in the middle, southern, and middle departments of the army; Jones, "John Laurance and the Role of Military Justice," 13–14.
55. Jones, "John Laurance and the Role of Military Justice," 26.
56. James McHenry wrote to Laurance on George Washington's behalf, May 16, 1779, Founders Online, https://founders.archives.gov/documents.
57. John Laurance to George Washington, February 5, 1778, Founders Online, https://founders.archives.gov/documents.
58. Jones, "John Laurance and the Role of Military Justice," 24.
59. Laurance to Washington, February 5, 1778.
60. Nathan R. Kozuskanich, "Pennsylvania, the Militia, and the Second Amendment," *The Pennsylvania Magazine of History and Biography* 133, no. 2 (2009): 130.
61. Gregory J. W. Urwin, "'The Army of the Constitution': The Military, American Values, and the Early Republic," *Foreign Policy Research Institute Footnotes*, March 9, 2012, 3, https://www.fpri.org/article/2012/03/the-army-of-the-constitution-the-military-american-values-and-the-early-republic/; Steven Eames,

Rustic Warriors: Warfare and the Provincial Soldier on the New England Border, 1689–1748 (New York: New York University Press, 2011), 4–5, 7–8.

62. Kozuskanich, "Pennsylvania, the Militia, and the Second Amendment," 133.

63. The Statutes at Large of Pennsylvania, 22–30; passed March 17, 1777. See the Acts of Assembly passed June 19, 1777, chapter 760; December 30, 1777, chapter 781; April 5, 1779, chapter 843; (repealed by the Act of Assembly passed) March 20,1180, chapter 902.

64. Isaac Rhys, *The Transformation of Virginia, 1740–1790* (Durham: University of North Carolina Press, 1999), 105; Kozuskanich, "Pennsylvania, the Militia, and the Second Amendment," 141.

65. Francis S. Fox, "Pennsylvania's Revolutionary Militia Law: The Statute that Transformed the State," *Pennsylvania History: A Journal of Trans-Atlantic Studies* 80, no. 2 (2013): 204–14.

66. Allan S. Everest, *Moses Hazen and the Canadian Refugees in the American Revolution* (Syracuse, NY: Syracuse University Press, 1976), 174.

67. Harry Schenawolf, "General Moses Hazen of the Infernals: Ruthless and Fierce, He Was Just the Man Washington Needed," *Revolutionary War Journal* (July 16, 2019): 1–59, www.revolutionarywarjournal.com/; Everest, *Moses Hazen*.

68. "Maj. James Randolph Reid," The State Society of the Cincinnati of Pennsylvania, https://pasocietyofthecincinnati.org/gallery_post/maj-james-randolph-reid/.

69. Moses Hazen to George Washington, January 13, 1783, enclosure, Founders Online, https://founders.archives.gov/documents.

70. Schenawolf, "General Moses Hazen of the Infernals," 22; Everest, *Moses Hazen and the Canadian Refugees*, 42–45.

71. Everest, *Moses Hazen and the Canadian Refugees*, 80.

72. Fitzpatrick, General Orders, September 17, 1780, vol. 20, 65–66; Hazen to Washington, January 13, 1783; Moses Hazen to William Heath, February 8, 1781, George Washington Papers, ser. 4, general correspondence, LOC.

73. Throughout this study, all quotes retain the spelling and grammar of the original source. Israel Angell, *Diary of Colonel Israel Angell, Commanding the Second Rhode Island Continental Regiment during the American Revolution, 1778–1781*, ed. Edward Field (Providence, RI: Preston and Rounds Company, 1899), 120; Everest, *Moses Hazen and the Canadian Refugees*, 80–81; Schenawolf, "General Moses Hazen of the Infernals," 38; Hazen to Washington, January 13, 1783, enclosure.

74. See James C. Neagles's survey of 136 orderly books in *Summer Soldiers: A Survey and Index of Revolutionary Courts-Martial* (Salt Lake City, UT: Ancestry Incorporated, 1986).

75. James Reid to George Washington, December 7, 1780, Founders Online, https://founders.archives.gov/documents ; Everest, *Moses Hazen and the Canadian Refugees*, 145.

76. Reid to Washington, December 7, 1780.

77. Hazen to Washington, January 13, 1783, Founders Online, https://founders.archives.gov/.

78. Reid to Washington, December 7, 1780.

79. Macomb, *A Treatise on Martial Law*, 93–96.

80. Reid to Washington, December 7, 1780; Everest, *Moses Hazen and the Canadian Refugees*, 87.

81. Hazen to Heath, February 8, 1781; Hazen to Washington, January 13, 1783, enclosure.

82. General Orders, February 18, 1781, Fitzpatrick, vol. 21, 239–40; Reid to Washington, December 7, 1780; Hazen to Heath, February 8, 1781; Hazen to Washington, January 13, 1783, enclosure.

83. Everest, *Moses Hazen and the Canadian Refugees*, 75.

84. Everest, *Moses Hazen and the Canadian Refugees*, 75, 86–87; Moses Hazen to George Washington, January 13, 1783, Founders Online, https://founders.archives.gov/; "Maj. James Randolph Reid."

85. General Orders, February 21, 1783, Fitzpatrick, vol. 26, 149–51; George Washington Papers, Subseries 3G, Varick Transcripts, Letterbook 7, February 21, 1783, General Orders.

86. Everest, *Moses Hazen and the Canadian Refugees*, 103–4.

87. Everest, *Moses Hazen and the Canadian Refugees*, 104, 145.

88. Hazen to Washington, January 13, 1783, enclosure.

89. General Orders, February 21, 1783, Fitzpatrick, vol. 26, 149–50; George Washington Papers, Subseries 3G, Varick Transcripts, Letterbook 7, February 21, 1783, General Orders. The officers had refused to serve with Reid, given his remarks about them in the previous trial; Everest, *Moses Hazen and the Canadian Refugees*, 103.

90. General Orders, February 21, 1783, Fitzpatrick, vol. 26, 152; George Washington Papers, Subseries 3G, Varick Transcripts, Letterbook 7, February 21, 1783, General Orders.

91. Hazen to Washington, January 13, 1783.

92. George Washington Papers, Subseries 3G, Varick Transcripts, Letterbook 7, February 9, 1783, General Orders.

93. George Washington Papers, Series 4, General Correspondence: George Washington to Horatio Gates and the Board of General Officers, February 12, 1783, LOC.

94. "Washington's Sentiments on a Peace Establishment."

95. S. V. Benet, *A Treatise on Military Law and the Practice of Courts-Martial* (New York: D. Van Nostrand, 1862), 8.

96. See Michael Shurkin, *The Evolution of U. S. Military Policy From the Constitution to the Present, Volume I: The Old Regime: The Army, Militia, and Volunteers From Colonial Times to the Spanish-American War* (Santa Monica, CA: Rand Corporation, 2020); Tovy, "Militia or Regular Army?"

97. Tovy, "Militia or Regular Army?," 13; Max M. Edling, *Perfecting the Union: National and State Authority in the US Constitution* (New York: Oxford University Press, 2021), 1; Richard H. Kohn, *Eagle and Sword: The Federalists and the Creation of the Military Establishment in America, 1783–1802* (New York: The Free Press, 1975), 8–9, 44–48. Washington submitted his plan to thirteen state governors to relay to their legislatures; he copied his advisors in the army who had provided him with end of the war analyses that the need for "some regular establishment was imperative because the militia was unquestionably unsound militarily"; Kohn, *Eagle and Sword*, 44. See "Washington's Sentiments on a Peace Establishment"; "Continental

Congress Report on a Military Peace Establishment," [June 18, 1783], https://founders.archives.gov/documents; George Washington to Steuben, March 15, 1784, https://founders.archives.gov/documents; Alexander Hamilton to George Washington, [April 8, 1783], https://founders.archives.gov/documents; Friedrich Wilhelm von Steuben, *A Letter on the Subject of an Established Militia and Military Arrangements: Addressed to the Inhabitants of the United States* (New York: J. McLean and Co., 1784).

98. Kohn, *Eagle and Sword*, 48.

99. George Washington Papers, Subseries 3G, Varick Transcripts, Letterbook 7, February 9, 1783, General Orders.

100. Captain Richard Lloyd to Washington, January 10, 1783, enclosure; Hazen to Washington, January13, 1783, enclosure; Moses Hazen to George Washington, January 29, 1783, https://founders.archives.gov/documents; General Orders, January 25, 1783, Fitzpatrick, vol. 26, 65–67.

101. Hazen to Heath, 8 February 1781; Hazen to Washington, January 13, 1783, enclosure; Hazen to Washington, January 29, 1783; George Washington Papers, Subseries 3G, Varick Transcripts, Letterbook 7, General Orders, February 21, 1783; General Orders, February 21. 1783, Fitzpatrick, vol. 26, 149–52; General Orders, January 25, 1783, Fitzpatrick, vol. 26, 65–67.

102. Lloyd to Washington, January 10, 1783, enclosure; Hazen to Washington, January 13, 1783.

103. Hazen to Washington, January 29, 1783.

104. Hazen to Washington, January 29, 1783.

105. Lloyd to Washington, January 10, 1783, enclosure; Hazen to Washington, January 13, 1783.

106. George Washington Papers, Subseries 3G, Varick Transcripts, Letterbook 7, General Orders, February 20, 1783; General Orders, February 20, 1783, Fitzpatrick, vol. 26, 148–49.

107. Knox experienced his fair share of presiding over courts-martial given his rank; he served on one of the most infamous trials, that of Major John Andre, Brigadier General Benedict Arnold's British contact.

108. Washington's general orders of February 9, 1783, had directed "A Board consisting of all the General officers in this Cantonment and at the Garrison at Westpoint"; George Washington Papers, Series 4, General Correspondence: George Washington to Horatio Gates, February 12, 1783, LOC; Henry Knox, Westpoint, March 4, 1783, "Thoughts on Courts Martial and the Duty of Judge Advocate," in the hand of Samuel Shaw; "submitted to a board of Genrl officers, appointed by the Commander in chief," April 83, LOC. Henry Knox Papers, microfilm edition (Boston: Massachusetts Historical Society, 1960), 3: 12–13; Gilder Lehrman Collection, #GLC02437.01979.

109. Ward, *George Washington's Enforcers*, 42–43. Court-martial proceedings were housed with the war department, whose records reveal the following: "On Saturday evening, November 8, 1800, the War Department building, with the records and files, was consumed by fire"; *Business Methods in the War Department: Report of the Board Appointed in Compliance with the Request of the Senate Select Committee*

to Investigate the Methods of Business in the Executive Departments (Washington, DC: Government Printing Office, 1889), 184.

110. Ward, *George Washington's Enforcers*, 42–43.

111. Knox, "Thoughts," Henry Knox Papers.

112. Knox, "Thoughts," Henry Knox Papers.

113. Adye, *A Treatise on Courts Martial*, 116–21. Courts of inquiry allowed some challenges for cause; Verne D. J. Philips, "The American Military Court of Inquiry," *The Military History of Texas and the Southwest* 14 no. 1 (1978): 48.

114. Knox, "Thoughts," Henry Knox Papers.

115. Knox, "Thoughts," Henry Knox Papers.

116. Knox held that witnesses ought to be allowed to put their testimony in writing, so long as they were cross-examined. He did not extend that privilege to testimony taken out of court. In 1789, Secretary of War Knox argued that ratification of the Constitution required that the Articles of War be revised. This would not occur until seventeen years later, in 1806; Wiener, "Courts-Martial and the Bill of Rights, 8.

117. See Lauren Benton, "Historical Perspectives on Legal Pluralism," *Hague Journal on the Rule of Law* 3, no. 1 (2011): 57–69; Lauren Benton, *Law and Colonial Culture: Legal Regimes in World History, 1400–1900* (Cambridge: Cambridge University Press, 2001).

118. James Reid to George Washington, February 22, 1783, Founders Online, https://founders.archives.gov/documents.

119. General Orders, April 3, 1783, Fitzpatrick, vol. 26, 283; George Washington to Jedediah Huntington, May 17, 1783, Founders Online, https://founders.archives.gov/documents.

120. Lewis Nicola to George Washington, May 27, 1783, Founders Online, https://founders.archives.gov/documents.

121. Nicola to Washington, May 27, 178; General Orders, April 3, 1783, Fitzpatrick, vol. 26, 283; General Orders, May 29, 1783, Fitzgerald, vol. 26, 458–59; Everest, 105.

122. George Washington to Moses Hazen, June 1, 1783, Fitzpatrick, vol. 26, 460–61.

123. "To the General Officers of the Army," June 23, 1783, Fitzpatrick, vol. 27, 29.

124. William Heath to George Washington, June 24, 1783, Founders Online, https://founders.archives.gov/documents.

125. "To Brigadier General Moses Hazen," June 24, 1783, Fitzpatrick, vol. 27, 30–31.

126. Everest, 88; General Orders, February 18, 1781, Fitzpatrick, vol. 21, 239.

127. General Orders, February 18, 1781, Fitzpatrick, vol. 21, 240.

128. General Orders, February 18, 1781, Fitzpatrick, vol. 21, 241.

129. George Washington Papers, Subseries 3G, Varick Transcripts, Letterbook 7, General Orders, February 21, 1783.

130. Linda Myrsiades, *Medical Culture in Revolutionary America: Feuds, Duels, and a Court-Martial* (Madison, NJ: Fairleigh Dickinson University Press, 2009), 118–73, for a 1780 court-martial based on a feud involving three prestigious early

American figures serving in the Continental Army: Benjamin Rush, John Morgan, and William Shippen.

131. Moses Hazen to William Heath, February 8, 1781, George Washington Papers, ser. 4, General Correspondence, February 8, 1781, LOC.

132. Moses Hazen to William Heath, February 8, 1781, George Washington Papers, ser. 4, General Correspondence, February 8, 1781, LOC.

133. Warren F. Schwartz, Keith Baxter, and David Ryan, “The Duel: Can these Gentlemen be Acting Efficiently,” *Journal of Legal Studies* 13 (1884): 321–55; David Harley, “Honour and Property: The Structure of Professional Disputes in Eighteenth-Century English Medicine,” in *The Medical Enlightenment of the Eighteenth Century*, eds. Andrew Cunningham and Roger French, (Cambridge: Cambridge University Press, 1990), 138–64.

134. Dov Cohen and Joe Vandello, “Social Norms, Social Meaning, and the Economic Analysis of Law: Meanings of Violence,” *Journal of Legal Studies* 27, no. 2 (1988): 567–84; Robert C. Ellickson, *Order Without Law: How Neighbors Settle Disputes* (Cambridge, MA: Harvard University Press, 1991).

135. Gautham Rao, “The New Historiography of the Early Federal Government: Institutions, Contexts, and the Imperial State,” *The William and Mary Quarterly* 77, no. 1 (2020): 106–9. See Max M. Edling, *A Revolution in Favor of Government: Origins of the U. S. Constitution and the Making of the American State* (New York: Oxford University Press, 2003); Max M. Edling, *A Hercules in the Cradle: War, Money, and the American State, 1783–1867* (Chicago: University of Chicago Press, 2014).

Chapter 2

"The Crooks of the Law"

The Trial of Mamachtaga, the Delaware Indian, 1785

And these brown tribes, who snuff the desert air,/ Are aunts and cousins to the skunk and bear

—After Hugh Henry Brackenridge, in *The Echo*[1]

There was not a thing that had ever seen a squaw, or a half king, or a chief, or had heard the guttural sound of a Kickapoo, or a Delaware, but would have it that he understood fifty Indian languages, and could interpret, and could draw all the tribes after him just as a boy would whistle pigeons. Hence, treaty and not war.

—Hugh Henry Brackenridge, "Farther and Concluding Thoughts on the Indian War," *National Gazette*, February 6, 1792

The trial of the Delaware Indian Mamachtaga in Hanna's Town, Westmoreland County, Pennsylvania, took place in the context of a frontier history characterized by settlers squatting on Indian land, government treaties with the Indians for large land purchases, land bounties the army gifted to soldiers for their service in the French and Indian War and the American Revolution, and multiple states making overlapping land claims. Militia parties raided Indian settlements just as Indians raided white settlements and engaged in intertribal wars, while foreign powers vied for alliances with the Indians to support their own territorial claims.

Indian self-governance might have been the plan under the Penn family's government, but that concept soon turned into white control over Indians.[2] The history of the Delaware Indians (the name given them by

American colonists, as opposed to their exonym, Lenni Lenape) included a Pennsylvania treaty in 1736 whereby the Quaker government of Pennsylvania recognized the Iroquois Five Nations as supreme over other Indian tribes in the region, an arrangement that allowed the Iroquois to make treaties in the name of the Delaware.[3] The Walking Purchase of 1737 that tricked the tribe of its land in the Delaware Valley forced them to move west and form the Four Nations of the Susquehanna, a coalition designed to offset the Iroquois alliance.[4] Thinking they had a commitment from Penn to settle in the Susquehanna Valley, the Delaware found the Iroquois had claimed similar rights. The Delaware were pushed further west; a twice-displaced people, their new home was on the Alleghany River.[5]

The underlying theory was that Indians lost their rights over the land the moment they were "discovered."[6] Indeed, English common law that treated Indian tribes as subordinated, presumably racially inferior people, privileged white settlers and frontiersmen driven by racial animus who intended to dislodge Indians from the land and retaliate for Indian outrages.[7] A rash of murders contested Indian land throughout the 1760s and resurged in the 1780s with the end of the revolution. Frontier people had begun to see Indians in the aggregate rather than as individual native groups, which exacerbated racism in Pennsylvania, challenged the government, and transformed colonial-Indian relations. Increasingly, the myth of the "vanishing Indian" took hold and the idea that Indian culture would survive civilization was displaced by one whereby the tribes would either assimilate entirely or disappear.[8]

Having sided with the French in the French and Indian War and with the anti-English Indian alliance in Pontiac's War, the Delaware split over supporting the American Revolution. American grievances about the Indians incorporated in the Declaration of Independence were not encouraging as they allowed that the English King "excited domestic Innovations amongst us, and has endeavoured to bring on the Inhabitants of our Frontiers, the merciless Indian Savages, whose known Rule of Warfare, is an undistinguished Destruction of all Ages, Sexes and Conditions." Nonetheless, the Treaty of Fort Pitt, which the Delaware signed in 1778, recognized them as a sovereign nation and essentially kept them at peace during the revolution.

The western country, meanwhile, had begun to assert its political importance. The East had become a transatlantic frontier threatened by the British, so that the potential for Indian disruptions in the West placed frontier people in the optimal political position of ensuring a second front would not open. The criticality of the frontier enabled westerners to gain power in the legislature and inform the government in the East.[9] This gave rise to settlers' movements that took control of land and Indian issues away from provincial officials and enabled western inhabitants to dictate local solutions. Once Cornwallis surrendered to Washington in 1783, any consensus on the frontier would henceforth have to accommodate western settlers and militias, for whom the war was anything but over.[10] Westerners still faced the presence of British forts, the enmity of British-allied Indians, and pent-up resistance to being constrained under a revolutionary government intent on avoiding a full-scale Indian war while the war against Britain was still on-going. As frontier inhabitants took Indian relations into their own hands, the Delaware faced the brunt of the anti-Indian animus that animated local militias.

The 1784 Treaty of Fort Stanwix promised respite for settlers as it effectively resolved the question of Pennsylvania's borders as a state, if not its status as a frontier. The expectation was that the US government would assume responsibility for order on the frontier, as it did three years later by means of the Constitution (Article IX), which assigned the United States the "sole and exclusive right and power" to manage Indian affairs and regulate trade. This was the situation in Western Pennsylvania at the time of the trial of the Delaware Indian Mamachtaga in 1785.

INDIANS AND THE LAW

The law, as it related to Indians, changed relative to several variables including, prominently, different colonial and state governments and wars that involved Europeans, the Indians, and the colonies. Even more importantly, it depended upon the desire for land. What was clear amid this complexity was that the government considered Indians neither citizens nor a protected group. They had only those legal rights colonial governments chose to grant them or that their treaties permitted, discretionary rights that were essentially disregarded by frontier settlers.[11]

In Pennsylvania, William Penn's letter to the "Kings of the Indians in Pennsylvania" in 1681 was the earliest notice we have of the law to which Indians would be subject under colonial rule. Presumably addressing himself to Chief Tamanend of the Lenni Lenape, Penn made a promise of fair and equal treatment, allowing that "if in any thing any shall offend you or your people, you shall have a full and Speedy satisfaction for the same by an equal number of honest men on both sides that by no means you may have just occasion of being offended against them."[12] In a second letter two years later to the Committee of the Free Society of Traders, Penn recognized that natives had their own legal system, referring to their system as restorative atonement:

> The Justice they have is Pecuniary: In case of any Wrong or evil Fact, be it Murther it self, they Attone by Feasts and Presents of their *Wampon*, which is proportioned to the quality of the Offence or Person injured, or of the Sex they are of: for in case they kill a Woman, they pay double, and the Reason they

> render, is, That she breedeth Children, which Men cannot do. 'Tis rare they fall out, if Sober; and if Drunk, they forgive it, saying, It was the Drink, and not the Man, that abused them.[13]

In the same year, the proprietorship passed a statute that applied to trials of Indians, which demonstrated a principled and diplomatic approach to Indian relations.[14] First, it respected tribal hierarchy in requiring that "notice shall be given to the king of the Indians hee relates to that the offender be brought to his tryall."[15] Thereafter, it makes clear that "the king to whom Such Indians doth belong, shall have Notice thereof, That So hee may be present and See Justice done on both Sides." It is worth noting that the term "king" is kept in the lower case (presumably not to offend Penn's own "King" in England) even as the author shows the ruler the respect he ought to be accorded. The "sachem"—the word for "chief" in Algonquin (the language the Lenape spoke)—was thereby represented in the Anglo-American court, where he sometimes interpreted for and advised the accused; he also informed the court on Indian legal practices. The law proceeded to stipulate that the accused "shall be tryed by six of the free-man of the same County where the Abuse was Committed, and Six of the Indians that are Nearest to that place." As the Indians had no experience with juries, this provision most likely originated in a British practice with which Penn would have been familiar from cases involving foreign merchants. Called a jury "de medietate linguae" ("of half tongue"), it referred to members of the same community whose shared customs enabled them to understand the situation and the parties involved; it did not necessarily mean the parties spoke the same language or, in the case of the Indians, were members of the same tribe.[16] Penn had previously negotiated with the Lenni Lenape to the effect that "We have agreed, that in all Differences between us, Six of each side shall end the matter."[17] The statute confirmed that understanding, specifying a mixed jury in matters where "any person in this Province or territories therof shall at any time hereafter Committ or do any dammage or Injury to any Indian." Indians in Anglo-American courts thereby had the right of a mixed jury for crimes committed against them by whites or for crimes they committed against whites, that is, white courts were assigned interracial crimes.

Finally, the law clarified that should any Indian refuse to be tried, such courts were authorized to "impose such fine or punishment on the offender as they shall think fit." This ex parte alternative was less beneficent than the rest of the law as it excluded a hearing, a defense, and representation for the accused. A warning in 1715 by the Provincial Council to the Conestoga Indians to bring their cases to government courts suggested further that the government jealously protected its jurisdiction in interracial cases and that

Indian authority only covered cases between Indians of the same tribe.[18] Thus, the council directed that the Conestoga Indians should

> be very careful on their parts that no difference should arise between any of their and our people, or if there should that they would acquaint us with it immediately, that we might duly inquire into it, and Justice should be done them if they were in any way wronged.[19]

The proprietorship had not imposed its legal system because the Algonquins were unfamiliar with concepts of law, for they had operated under a set of Indian principles and practices long before colonists imposed their courts. Katharine Hermes in her study, for example, cites tribal customs as well as Indigenous legal rules in asserting that the Algonquins' legal approach constituted a mentality about the law expressed through practices.[20] The central feature entailed convening a community of the accused, the victim, relatives, and witnesses to reach an accommodation. It was a loose and rambling procedure; everyone got a say without regard to rules of evidence, hierarchy among the parties, or the amount of time the process took. Ada Pecos Melton refers to the convening as "a circle of justice" that focused on harmony for the community and reparation, with the victim's well-being the focal point. Conducted in the language of the tribal community, the circle considered all relevant aspects of the situation, broadly understood, to resolve underlying issues. Its central feature, however, was its treatment of individual conduct in relation to the wider kinship group, all of whom shared the blame and responsibility for rectifying relationships. In this clan system model, the expression of remorse and rituals that cleansed the spirit were essential to lead to binding agreements.[21]

The two legal systems were not completely separate. Notably, the Algonquins and the colonists shared the legal concept of reciprocity, so that Indian practices and rules infiltrated Anglo-American courts when Indian issues were brought there. Because each community was bound to support the other's law, colonists had to protect Indians by punishing whites who "offended" them, while Indians had to turn over those who were accused of crimes against whites and to allow white courts to punish them.[22] Imperfect as it was, the limited reciprocity of the coexisting systems demonstrated the need to stretch definitions as well as to negotiate jurisdiction, especially when Indian populations were in decline and tribes were unwilling to have their people face justice at the hands of the whites.[23]

The origin of unequal treatment in this judicial arrangement was apparent. Indian crimes against colonists had to be resolved in colonial courts, whereas the crimes of colonists did not come under Indian jurisdiction. Penn's conviction that fair treatment would cover this difference ("Don't abuse them, but let them have Justice, and you win them," he wrote)[24] left the Indians at a disadvantage in that they had no authority to call white witnesses to their own courts, while in white courts their customs and practices were either misunderstood or disregarded. Unavoidably, questions arose whether Indians in white courts received equal treatment and whether whites received more favorable verdicts there. Moreover, trying white crimes against Indians in white courts belied the pretense that Indian courts were meaningful or capable of delivering justice. Because tribes could not police Indians who were not of their tribe, referring Indians to tribal law for punishment was compromised as well; nor could one tribe be held accountable for the actions of other tribes. On the one hand, legal protections guaranteed by treaty (provisions that Indian offenses would be treated under the law just as those committed by any subject of Great Britain and that juries for Indians would be mixed juries) eroded over time and promises made in conferences (aimed at preventing the sale of liquor to the tribes and protecting the sanctity of Indian lands) went unfulfilled. On the other hand, whites complained that treaty agreements superseded the authority of their courts and that Indians received lenient treatment in tribal courts.

In truth, more whites appeared before Anglo courts for violating the law than Indians,[25] which contributed to local juries refusing to convict whites who murdered Indians. Yet, civil authorities needed to punish murders of Indians to maintain treaties, placate the tribes, and avoid further violence. One unavailing effort required the removal of Indians who committed interracial crimes to Philadelphia for trial under the Act of 1744.[26] Incensed, settlers demanded that sentences be dealt out by local justices of the peace in their own settlements, rather than in distant courts unlikely to reflect local sentiments about Indians. In line with such attitudes, settlers objected to Indians and whites receiving the same legal protections in the courts, arguing that white crimes against Indians should be treated as acts of war.[27]

Significantly, few settlers supported the idea of sovereign Indian nations living within the bounds of an independent commonwealth, with all the implications that brought for the legal rights and systems of law of both whites and Indians. The complications added by mob law and Indian wars, and the competing demands from both Indians and colonials for government protection, made the prospect of sensible jurisdiction and adjudication improbable. In reality, the presence of militias and armies on the frontier ensured that they were increasingly likely to handle Indian problems spontaneously through vigilantism and expeditions against the Indians rather than in the courts, a likelihood reflected in law reports covering newly formed county courts in Westmoreland, Washington, Fayette, and Alleghany[28] and those seconded to the state Supreme Court on circuit or in Philadelphia; they included only a handful of cases related to Indians.[29]

Overall, despite an assertive Indian presence in Anglo-American courts (either representing themselves or bringing their own complaints against colonists), failed prosecutions for the murder of Indians, more lax procedures, and a general breakdown of trust gradually undermined confidence that interracial justice would be delivered in the western counties. Indians began to refuse to appear for trial, while courts less and less frequently charged whites for crimes against Indians or dismissed their cases. The 1780s represented a period of decline for a reciprocal accommodation between the two presumably sovereign groups.[30]

THE INDIAN PERSPECTIVE

Contemporary commentary by westerners provides a unique perspective on the Indian response to the law. For our purposes, James Adair, a trader who lived in Indian country for forty years, provides useful counsel.[31] Adair held, for example, that Indians' poor opinion of white law emanated from their experience in Anglo courts with interpreters—Indians, mixed race, or Euro-Americans who learned Indian languages through trade, captivity, or as missionaries; only rarely were they professional translators. As interpreters needed some knowledge of Indian customs and protocol to capture the content and tone of the speaker, and as they often advised as well as translated, they ran into a variety of problems, among them that they were often mistrusted.[32] Of some interest, Indians who served on mixed juries in capital cases often consulted, advised, and interpreted to keep trials flowing smoothly. They took their task to be that of protecting Indian interests and were considered by Indians among the wisest and most even-tempered of their tribe. As Yasuhide Kawashima contends, however, mostly white men served as jurors and Indians merely supplemented rather than substituted for them when they were seated as jurors.[33]

Indians also objected to lawyers. One description depicted lawyers as snakes with "cunning heads and strong mouths" who hid the truth from the searching eye and fed on the harmless. Others felt that lawyers were too much tempted by "rich people's yellow stone" or that they bought justice, which the "honest poor" were unable to do, leaving Indians the great losers in the "litigious, expensive, and tedious suits" encouraged by lawyers and legislators.[34] Indians complained that whites did not give their judgments freely and without delay and that court punishments were not proportionate to the damage done, unlike the Indian system. On the other hand, bad causes were not met with severe judgments "to check vice, and promote virtue in social life."[35] Adair even refers to one Indian speaker who protested that the white man's law ought not to be "so weak as not to condemn those to death; who took away the lives of low innocent people."[36]

Adair expresses some common ideas associated with what has been called Indigenous, primitive, or Indian law. Its justice, for example, included few principles: the truth was clear, "its native dress is always simple, and it never resides in troubled waters, but under the striking beams of the sun." In this system, "there are only two contraries; that simple nature enables every person to be a proper judge of promoting good and preventing evil, either by determinations, rewards, or punishments," another way of saying that Indian law was embedded in communal relations. Although Indian law appeared to be indelibly tailored to immediate cases, it maintained a clear, foundational principle: a victim and his relatives ought to "revenge their blood . . . in order to quench innocent blood, and teach unwary people to avoid and detest the execrated criminals." If, on the other hand, Indian law failed to condemn to death those who took the lives of the innocent, it was at least able "to incite the surviving relations of the murdered persons, to revenge their blood on the murderers by beating them with long knobbed poles" that they might teach the unwary what to "avoid and detest."[37] The concept, as Adair relates, was highly regarded among the Indians for its "wisdom and justice."[38]

Although Indians often extended to whites their own traditions of sparing someone's life or forgiving crimes as sufficient means of addressing offenses,[39] they found white law largely unresponsive and perplexing, particularly its voluminous written laws. Adair explained to Indians he dealt with that the white man's laws were fixed and recorded in books to preserve trading contracts in the white man's empire and to accommodate "different abilities of the parties." Even whites, he admitted to a group of natives, could not easily understand these books or the lawyer's language, so they recorded "decisions of right and wrong" to guide them "in future similar disputes." Another problematic aspect of white man's law was the presumption that Indians were cognizant of Anglo-American law. They protested "that people cannot in justice be accused of violating any laws, when it is out of their power to have a proper knowledge of them."[40] Moreover, according to Adair, Indians felt that white "chieftains" supported "their own bad actions by bad laws" and that such laws ought not to be honored if the Indians were to live in peace as free men.[41] From the Indian's point of view, the merits of Indian law—like offering gifts to officials as payments for crimes—were much to be preferred.

Hugh Henry Brackenridge, whose firsthand experience of Indian justice was as a western lawyer (he represented Mamachtaga as counsel, for example), regarded the Indian view with less nuance. In fact, he published observations he made just three years before the Mamachtaga trial alongside collected narratives of captivity and torture. Brackenridge questioned whether Indians ought not to be regarded as whole nations of murderers, based on their treatment of captives, which, he claimed, departed from the laws of nature. Such conduct, he argued, was of "a sufficient order to exterminate the whole brood. As the Seceder (a member of the Scottish Presbyterian sect that refused communion) said of Satan, what will you make of them, my beloved, but ill, vile, evil devils?"[42] Far from respecting Indian traditions, Brackenridge ridiculed "the mystery of agent-craft and the mummery of Indian speechifying" as a parlor trick more profitable "than a tame bear or a lion presented for a show."[43] He claimed to possess a clear-eyed view of Indians, unlike those he accused of being unacquainted with the Indian character, discounting, for example, the validity of Indian claims to the land. Who, Brackenridge argued, plants themselves upon the earth to "prevent all others from having any?" God Himself did not permit aliens from Jupiter, nor Noah after the flood, to lay claim to "a greater proportion of the soil than others and, without sharing equally."[44] Brackenridge considered, as well, that years of Indian wars had required recruits and replacement labor at home that were particularly burdensome to the western counties.[45] Thus, he disavowed treaties with the Indians and supported the right to settle on Indian land.

While Brackenridge treated issues of land rights, Indian character, and revenge as typical Indian problems, criminal complaints against Indians largely centered on the sale and use of alcohol. The economic appeal of alcohol trafficking, together with liquor's ability to undermine the viability of tribal communities, defeated the best efforts of both whites and Indians to address the problem. Indeed, in the 1770s, the Delaware Indians warned colonial authorities that the tribe had appointed people to break open any kegs brought onto their lands; other tribes threatened to stop the fur trade to end liquor trading. Still, Indian communities exonerated those who committed crimes that involved the use of alcohol so long as the victims were not badly harmed. As Penn allowed in holding alcohol responsible for their drunken acts, Indians were not normally quarrelsome when sober.[46] Nonetheless, in serious crimes involving alcohol, Indians called for the perpetrator's death.[47] The dangers of disorderly behavior, drunken brawls, and inter-racial violence, together with the negative effect on cultural identity, had made alcohol a major player in Western Pennsylvania's troubles with its Native population. It would certainly play havoc with Mamachtaga, who would suffer the ultimate consequence of its use.

THE MAMACHTAGA CASE

The trial of the Delaware Indian Mamachtaga began on November 4, 1785, with Chief Justice Thomas McKean and Justice George Bryan of the

Pennsylvania Supreme Court presiding. It was convened six months after Mamachtaga murdered two white men and wounded two more on May 11.[48] In the interim, the Indian was held in a "black hole" that served as a brig at Fort Pitt, the only secure place to jail him; the garrison held a mere skeleton force of six soldiers. He was tried in Hanna's Town, the capital seat of Westmoreland County, in Robert Hanna's house that served as the only courthouse in the area; it was thirty miles from the fort.[49] The court was founded along with the county seat in 1773 as the first Anglo court west of the Alleghanies. The town itself had been burned to the ground by Seneca Indians and their British supporters in 1782, the same year that a local militia attacked and killed Moravian village Delaware Indians in the Gnadenhutten massacre.[50]

In March 1783, a party of whites from Chartiers (south of the Monongahela River) had attacked a friendly Delaware Indian settlement on Killbuck Island that was protected by the garrison at Fort Pitt, killing most of the Indians. Among them were some who had served the whites on expeditions against Indian villages and as scouts to prevent attacks on the settlements.[51] It was on this island, on the west side of the Alleghany River, that the crime was committed in an Indian camp; the camp had been established there by Delaware Indians who, like Mamachtaga, had fought against the settlements. Friendly Delaware who supported the Americans had moved with their chief, Killbuck, to be near Fort Pitt, although some remained behind on the island with other Delaware who "had come in, it being just after the war."[52]

The first official notice of Mamachtaga's murders came on May 13 from Michael Huffnagle, a justice of the peace, to General J. Armstrong, secretary to the Supreme Council of Pennsylvania.[53] The notice advised that whereas an inquest had found the deaths "Wilfull Murder" and authorities had secured the Indian in the Pittsburgh garrison, the court should arrange some mode of trial as quickly as possible. Huffnagle was anxious that a chief of the nation be notified to be present at the trial. He was less concerned that justice be done or an Indian reprisal be prevented than that there were only a few soldiers at the fort and action should be swift "for fear of an escape or force." Huffnagle's fear was well-justified; vigilantes planned to seize and summarily execute the accused.[54]

Brackenridge blamed notice of his acting for the defense ("that I was to appear for the Indian, and having acquired some reputation in the defence of criminals") for a rumor that the Indian would get off "by *the crooks of the law.*" Public talk of raising a party to "hang the interpreter, and exact an oath from me not to appear in behalf of the Indian," he reported, led a party to raid the garrison so they might hang the Indian.[55] Indeed, as Robert Galbraith wrote to John Dickinson, president of Pennsylvania, the militia of Washington County attacked twice "to break the Dungeon where [Mamachtaga] is confined, and

Tommihawk him." Galbraith reported that fifty men with rifles and guns at 11:00 at night and thirty at daybreak made the attempt, which garrison commander Captain Luckett headed off: he "ordered the gate closed, they cocked their rifles at his chest; a JOP [Justice of the Peace] read them the Riot act, whereupon they presented their guns at him; inhabitants disarmed them and no lives were lost."[56] Captured, the assailants somehow escaped from the hands of the undersheriff, suggesting official complicity with the jailbreak.

Reflecting the urgency of the situation, Huffnagle wrote a second letter, on May 27, to Major-General James Irvine of the Pennsylvania militia.[57] This time he made a specific request for a special commission to conduct a local trial and for a blank death warrant, presuming a guilty verdict. His request was peculiar, given that under Pennsylvania law a county criminal court or the Pennsylvania Supreme Court would have tried the case, a matter that would soon prove to be in dispute. Further, Huffnagle advised Irvine of two pressing concerns. First, that "the Indians lately committed several Murders and Robberies down the Ohio River," indicating the fort faced the dire prospect of an Indian uprising. Second, that Brackenridge had brought "an order of ejectment from the garrison" against the commander on another matter, related to the fort's deed; Luckett refused to be relieved of his command until officially ordered to do so. The matter was of grave concern since, as Galbraith had warned in his letter, the garrison was so undermanned that local residents had to stand guard until reinforcements were sent by Colonel Josiah Hamar of the US Army, then serving in the Ohio Valley.[58]

A narrative by Brackenridge was the sole account of the murders. The facts were simple. The incident occurred in a cabin in the island camp where white traders and Indians frequently met and drank. Mamachtaga, liquored up, rushed into the cabin, according to both Indians and whites who were present. He stabbed four white men, including William Freeman, referred to as a dwarf. According to Brackenridge, a man named John Smith and another, William Evans, died of their wounds.[59] When he sobered up the next morning, Mamachtaga made no attempt to escape. Rather, he turned himself over to a guard and claimed to have no knowledge of the events of the preceding night.[60] His drunken state and how he got the liquor would become issues in the trial.

Brackenridge learned of the case because one of the victims, Smith, had worked for him shingling his house in Pittsburgh. Smith borrowed a blanket from Brackenridge and then crossed the river to visit the camp. Brackenridge followed the next morning to find two men dead and two wounded. Mamachtaga, Brackenridge related, was confined in "something resembling that kind of hole which is depressed in the floor . . . in which [the southern people] keep their succulent roots, from the frost in the winter season . . . [and] in which delinquent or refractory soldiery had been confined occasionally for punishment."[61] The pit was eight feet deep, though it could hold two or three men; when Brackenridge interviewed his client, he did so peering down from the floor above the pit.

Brackenridge approached an interpreter in the area, Joseph Nicholas, to inquire whether Mamachtaga was able to pay a lawyer to defend him, that is, whether he had "any fur or peltry, or has any interest in his nation that he could collect some." Nicholas was well informed about native people, "having been some years amongst the Indians in early life a prisoner, and since a good deal employed in the Indian trade." The whole exchange was treated with the solemnity of a formal contract. It involved Nicholas consulting with the Indian and a trader, William Amberson, who held some of Mamachtaga's pelts in town, as well as Mamachtaga's brother, who set off to Indian settlements to procure additional pelts from the tribe. Nicholas brought back "an order for the beaver in the hand of the trader," which had Mamachtaga's mark on it, in the form of a turkey's foot. Brackenridge commented, "These people have no idea of an hieroglyphic merely abstract, as a strait line or a curve, but it must bear some resemblance to a thing in nature." Mamachtaga's name, for example, meant "hurricane" (indicating trees blown as if by a tempest), suggesting both a force of nature and the great ferocity of his appearance. It was apparently "given him from the ungovernable nature of his passion,"[62] for, as Galbraith told President Dickinson, his name defined him as "the most violent and Bloody Catiff of the Delaware Tribe."[63]

For his part in the affair, Nicholas charged a broker's fee of half the pelts, which he and Brackenridge settled on in negotiations. Brackenridge then set off to consult with his client by way of determining whether he could arrange a defense "on which a probable face could be put." To this end, he and the interpreter were admitted to the garrison and the interpreter put Brackenridge's questions to the Indian. Brackenridge explained the process: he was there to help him and to learn the truth, thereby to prepare a defense. The disconnect between the expectations of the Anglo-American legal system and that of the Indian became immediately apparent. Mamachtaga refused to offer a defense and presented the beaver pelts "as a commutation for his life." In a similar way, Indians understood pretrial confinement as satisfaction for the crime. Brackenridge was not about to negotiate any further. Recognizing there was nothing he could do for the Indian, he decided it was improper to accept a fee at all. The interpreter, by contrast, decided to keep his share, which Brackenridge paid from his own pocket. Brackenridge proceeded to turn the signed order for pelts over to a trader in town, presumably Amberson, to use in procuring occasional necessities—a blanket and food—for the Indian.[64]

To this point, Brackenridge merely intended to provide competent legal counsel to Mamachtaga, as he would for any other defendant. He had not counted on the vigilantes, who were not about to allow Mamachtaga to be tried. Considering the interpreter an abettor for having assisted the Indian in employing counsel, they chased him into Indian country whereupon he relinquished entirely his share of the pelts to disassociate himself from the case. Brackenridge, on the other hand, was determined to see the case through to trial, largely to preserve his professional character and his reputation for being independent: "It did not appear to me adviseable to relinquish the defence of the Indian, fee or no fee, least it be supposed that I yielded to the popular impression." In fact, the "fury" of the people spent itself and subsided.[65]

The Law

By June, it was clear that local pressures favored trying the Indian within the vicinage, which sponsored a legal debate. A letter from Justice of the Peace John Whitehill (delegate to the Supreme Executive Council 1784–1787) to Justice Bryan inquired "how, where, & by what authority the Homicide should be inquired of and adjudged."[66] Despite his acknowledged difficulty in dealing with so few specifics, Bryan (who, with McKean, would hear the case on circuit) provided an opinion on the matter. Supposing the crime was committed in Westmoreland, Bryan considered whether it was "*remote from inhabitants*" to determine whether it fell under the 1744 Act for trials of Indians in remote areas.[67] If so, it should be tried in Philadelphia; if not, by common law the trial should be held in the vicinage.[68] In the end, he regarded Hanna's Town the proper site for the trial, as "The Act for setting off the county of Westmoreland directs that all courts for said county be holden in the house of Robert Hanna." Bryan made clear, "This should be the place of judgment, if it be not altered by some later law." As a sidenote, Bryan had been appointed to the Supreme Court "in part to ease tension between the Council and the court,"[69] which might have influenced his inclination to value local justice. In any case, he indicated that "Perhaps the County Courts of Common Pleas & Sessions of Westmoreland are more expressly fixed at Hanna's house, than the Supreme & Oyer & Terminer [criminal court] for capital matters."

A second question (whether there should be a special commission to try the case) depended on the authority of the Supreme Executive Council to appoint a commission of "persons who are not judges of the Supreme Court to hear & determine concerning this or other similar cases."[70] Bryan acknowledged their authority to do so, which he qualified by citing the Act of 1744 to the effect that Supreme Court judges were not "the only justices of oyer, terminer & goal delivery competent to try capital offenses."[71] Bryan offered that "the practice was not unknown" before the revolution and that since the revolution such a commission had appeared in Bedford to inflict capital punishment.

Bryan had addressed a similar question in an earlier opinion in 1783. There, President Dickinson and the Executive Council asked whether appointed commissions of oyer and terminer, which had commonly been issued since the revolution and as "lately issued for Westmoreland & Washington Counties," were consistent with the Constitution and laws of the state.[72] Working his way through the possibilities, Bryan cited the Act of 1722 establishing the Pennsylvania Supreme Court (where its justices were commissioned to preside over oyer and terminer), the Act of 1718 for the advancement of justice, and "long contrary usage & acting,"[73] but concluded its justices were not the only ones allowed for capital cases, that "long contrary usage" decided the point, and that nothing since the revolution altered it. Furthermore, Bryan warned, the council's authority to appoint commissions risked being abused, as it had the ability to select judges with the idea of preventing "a fair & equal hearing."[74] The commissions for Westmoreland and Washington Counties presented examples of such abuse and were void in that they contained blanks for the names of the accused. A companion opinion by Chief Justice McKean, although facially more open to the history of commissions, holding that they were not restrained by statute or the Constitution and had the sanction of long and constant usage prior to the revolution, was equally cautious: "But we humbly conceive, they should be granted with great caution, and only upon very urgent occasions, when the offences are of a very heinous nature and require immediate punishment." McKean's concern was for the authority of the Supreme Court, holding that in all cases the proceedings for such commissions should be returned to that body.[75]

Bryan addressed yet another question raised in the Whitehill letter—Robert Galbraith's request to send a death warrant before the Indian trial. The idea, as Galbraith posed it, was to "ease the minds of the people. There can be no doubt of his conviction."[76] Bryan found the idea "extravagant." By common law, the court that tried the case ought to "pronounce judgment & award Execution thereof also."[77] Involving the council might have been an old practice related to clemency and suitable when the province was made up of small counties, Bryan commented, but the judges ought to disregard it. McKean recalled the precedent of the commissions issued in Washington and Westmoreland Counties, remarking that "the names of the persons to be tried were not inserted by the Council, but by another hand after it had passed the seal, etc., and after it arrived in those counties, [which] is in our opinion bad." McKean considered such warrants void,[78] as did Bryan who concluded they gave no authority to any commissioners who might use them.[79] The commission for the Indian, by contrast, ought to be "special to the very case, & to limit the power to the trial of the Indian now in custody, by name, & the homicides already committed."[80]

There were other protections that favored the Indian, in Bryan's opinion, including that an Indian, should he demand it, had a right to a jury of "half foreigners." Bryan knew Penn had established such a practice and that a precedent from Chester County called upon six Indians for a rape trial;[81] he concluded the law supported a mixed jury but did not necessarily require members of the accused's nation.[82] The chief justice, less impressed by such precedents,[83] overruled him and Mamachtaga was tried without the benefit of a mixed panel of jurors. The Indian would, in the end, be tried by a local jury in the western county where the crime occurred, but with judges from the state Supreme Court on circuit presiding to offset local prejudice.

Case law, which did not appear in law reports until the 1790s,[84] throws additional light on Mamachtaga's trial.[85] Despite the paucity and selectivity of law reports related to Indians, a review of Pennsylvania cases reveals a case in 1794 that is instructive for Indian drunkenness and one in 1799 where Indians served as plaintiffs. A third case involved the murder of a drunken Indian by a white man (1794) and a fourth the theft of Indian goods by whites (1799). Five additional cases, reviewed for comparison, involved a drunken murder of a white victim by a white man (1793–1799). The only other cases that were reported in which Indians were involved (seven cases) dealt with the disposition of land titles (1799–1805).

In the murder case, *Pennsylvania v. Andrew Robertson*, 1794,[86] a white man named Robertson killed a Munfey Indian (probably a Munsee Indian, a sub-tribe of the Delaware) who had approached him as he was cooking meat in his home. The Indian, reported to be strong and over six feet tall and a member of a tribe some of whose members white men considered hostile, was "supposed to be dangerous" and had a knife, although the knife was not a factor in the crime. In charging the jury, presiding judge Alexander Addison asked whether the crime constituted manslaughter, as it was lawful for the defendant to exert force to remove the Indian from the house and the force used was not excessive. Moreover, the Indian was not only drunk but had made the first move by kicking the defendant. According to Addison, the defendant Robertson, alarmed and fearing for his safety, was induced "to prevent the danger of the *Indian's* attack, and save his own life."[87] The jury found the defendant not guilty on the grounds of homicide in self-defense, having discounted the prospect that the defendant could have escaped.

To determine whether the murder of an Indian received the same verdict as the murder of a white man, we can compare five cases where a white man killed a white and drunkenness was involved. In three cases where the crime was murder in the first degree and the judge sentenced the defendant to death, the US Supreme Court reversed one of the convictions[88] while the governor pardoned the defendant in the second.[89] In the third case, the party, unprovoked, threatened to kill the victim and committed the crime while drunk and in the heat of passion. Whereas his drunkenness could have served as a mitigating factor, the court sentenced the defendant to death.[90] In the remaining two cases, the sentence was not death. In one of those, the jury convicted the defendants of murder "in the lowest degree" for having been "troublesome and fought with guests" at a wedding. They had attended without an invitation, and an old man subsequently died of his injuries.[91] Of some interest, the prosecutor compared the crime to how Indians behaved: "We have no custom in this country of killing old men at weddings. The *Indians* have a custom, of killing one another when drunk; and if we indulge such practices, as have appeared in this case, we shall soon be as barbarous, as the savages of the wilderness."[92] He went on to argue for protecting the aged and the infant, for whom society has a particular responsibility, with the implication that such concern was a sign of civilization. The court sentenced the accused to five years imprisonment. In the other case, a malicious crime, a drunken defendant threw his wife twice on a fire, held her there, and subsequently refused to call a physician.[93] Her death three weeks later led to a conviction for manslaughter and a sentence of five years hard labor. Women, the aged, and Indians shared something in common in terms of being devalued by juries.

Despite the hostility with which whites frequently greeted Indians, courts usually treated them with a modicum of care, partly for fear of Indian uprisings or reprisals. In a 1799 case where Indians appeared as plaintiffs, *Pennsylvania v. Henry Becomb, John Reading, James Eckles, and Samuel Dickson*, the court felt a special obligation to express the benevolence of the white community. A group of peaceful, trading Indians had, by signs, complained of their loss of skins from their camp:

> The *Indians* were present at the trial: they appeared to be poor, and from a sense of the loss which they had sustained, and of the danger which resentment for such loss might bring on the frontier inhabitants, and a desire to shew the *Indians* the benefit of appealing to our tribunals for redress; some gentlemen contributed about 40 dollars, which were laid out in cloathing, and other useful articles for the two *Indians*; with which, and assurances of restitution for their property lost, they departed well pleased.[94]

This show of concern was offset by Brackenridge, who argued for the defense. He held that "the taking" was not a felony and that the Indians themselves had trespassed: "The property was abandoned, and not in the possession of anyone. The *Indians* had no property in the things taken. They had no right to come upon our lands to hunt. They were trespassers on the lands of the state, or of some private person." The judge disagreed, charging the jury there was no law preventing Indians from hunting on the land of others: "Whether the *Indians* were trespassers or not, the authorities cited prove that they were not thieves." To the contrary, "Their labor in killing the wild animals gave them a property right in the skins and meat." The jury found two defendants guilty, and the court sentenced them to be confined "in the goal and penitentiary house in Philadelphia," one for eighteen months and the other for twenty-four months; a third defendant broke out of jail.[95]

The fact that law reports were remiss in reporting Indian cases by itself speaks volumes about the possibility for equal treatment by courts, given the hysteria in the western counties over Indian crimes and the brutal renderings in captivity narratives. The mixed treatment courts dealt out to Indians, depended, of course, on the crimes charged, but the most egregious crimes were not likely to have reached the courtroom as local gangs and militia assumed the role of a public police to protect communities and revenge outrages. From the meager evidence available, in sum, Indians appeared in two guises: those who were peaceful or in the charge of missionaries as opposed to those who were still very much in "the woods," living in the wild or on the margins of white settlements but unassimilated. Just as their conditions differed, so did their crimes and so did their treatment in the courtroom. It was their treatment outside the courtroom that, unfortunately, spoke most persuasively about the nature of western prejudice and popular justice.

The Trial

In general, there was a disconnect between Indian and white legal systems, which was evident in the court's effort to elicit a plea from Mamachtaga at his trial. A new interpreter, Handlyn, translated into the Delaware language what the indictment meant, and that the Indian could deny the charge by pleading not guilty. Mamachtaga did not comprehend this matter of legal form and was "unwilling to deny the truth." He said he had been drunk and that he did not know what he had or had not done. He could not, as a result, say he killed the men and for that reason would not confess to the crimes. In the alternative, he "supposed he should know when he was under the ground."[96] After the court entered a plea for him, the interpreter explained to him that the jury was under oath and what that meant, so that he might appreciate "the solemnity and fairness of the trial." The interpreter then advised Mamachtaga he could challenge jurors, which he proceeded to do "according to the sourness, or chearfulness of the countenance, and what he thought indications of a mild temper." As for the jurors, their prejudices as well as their familiarity with the language of the court, and even with the English language, were themselves questionable. In Mamachtaga's trial, for example, one German, asked to "look upon the prisoner at the bar" and to consider whether he was related to the prisoner, responded in anger that "he thought it a uncivil way to treat Dutch peoples as if he could be the brothers, or cousins, of an Indian."

A fellow German explained the process to him, upon which he was sworn onto the jury.[97]

Nonetheless, as Brackenridge represents, so far as the fairness of the trial proceedings was concerned, "the usual forms were preserved" by the justices presiding, and witness testimony "put the homicide beyond a doubt." The Act of 1718 for the advancement of justice, previously cited by Justice Bryan,[98] ensured that all manner of crimes were "to be inquired of, heard, tried and determined by virtue of this or any other act or law of this province . . . [and] heard, tried and determined by judges, justices, inquests and witnesses" qualified by taking an oath.[99] In addition, it provided that in all trials of capital crimes "lawful challenges shall be allowed, and learned counsel assigned to the prisoners, and shall have process to compel witnesses to appear for them upon any of the said trials" upon oath or affirmation.[100]

Several issues of consequence suggest nonetheless that the trial was compromised. For one, the trial did not address questions of motive, intent, or malice, aspects of the common law that would have informed the verdict at the very least as mitigating factors. For another, Brackenridge was denied the only plausible line of defense once the facts of the homicide were presented—"to prove that [the defendant] was in liquor, and that this had been given to him by the white people; the traders in town." The Indian's drunkenness could have cleared the Indian had the liquor been provided by the dead men, "which was alleged to be the case." The surviving victim, William Freeman, undermined this potential defense by denying the claim, although, in the best of circumstances, he would have made a poor witness. As Brackenridge put it, "His testimony it was thought would not be much regarded as he could not be said to be *man grown*, and had been convicted at the quarter sessions of stealing a keg of whiskey some time before." The court, in any case, closed the door on this defense, overruling any testimony related to drunkenness as "the being drunk could not by our law excuse the murder."[101] One analysis attributes the ruling against considering drunkenness to Chief Justice McKean, who had also ruled against a half jury of aliens.[102]

Not only Freeman's reputation but the Indian's character, a crucial element in a criminal trial, spoke against him. His own nation thought him to be a bad man. He had been a great warrior, but "mischievous in his liquor, having killed two of his own people." His people, as a result, would not be sad to hear of his death and only his brother would give anything to free him. Indeed, the Indian custom of a clan turning in one of their own to recompense a crime reinforced the likelihood that the tribe would not interfere on his behalf. That lack of support might easily have affected the court's judgment.[103]

Brackenridge was right about the importance of offering testimony that the Indian's alcohol had been supplied by his white victims, certainly from a historical perspective. The custom of sealing trade and treaty negotiations with rum provided by the colonists meant that alcohol had become habitual in peaceful economic interactions, a practice that went well beyond profits made from the sale of alcohol and extended to treaties and compacts that cheated the Indians of their land and instigated violence. Initially, those who sold more than an allowed amount of alcohol to Indians were fined with an eye to morality; rampant intoxication soon led to an outright ban by the middle of the eighteenth century. Complaints from Indian leaders of many tribes from 1750–1775, including the Delaware, were joined by those of colonists as both groups believed that Indian drunkenness threatened peaceful relations.[104] Legal and religious proscriptions that were somewhat effective with the colonists had little effect on the Indians. Cultural appeals by Delaware leaders to the tribe to abstain, to return to traditional customs and desert white ways, also went unheeded. Traders evaded the law and continued to cheat Indians of their skins and wampum while they were drunk, which further impoverished Indians and led them to neglect hunting and agriculture. Drunkenness interfered as well with Christian conversions and public safety, while enforcement of prohibition was ineffective with Indian groups living independent of colonial settlements in the woods where it was common to exonerate those who committed crimes that involved the use of alcohol.[105] It was a situation that Samuel Danforth directly addressed in his 1709 execution sermon on the evils of drink at the hanging of two Indians. Danforth was particularly incensed at those who, like the white traders in Mamachtaga's case, "for the sake of a little Gain" supplied the liquor that did Satan's work. They were, he preached, "judicially given up . . . to Errors, Ignorance and Profaneness." Danforth held traders equally liable to punishment and was not surprised they "should be suffered by God to be carried into Captivity, among the wild Salvages of *America*: or that those wild *Indians*, should be Commissioned to destroy them & their *Estates*."[106]

The jury declared Mamachtaga guilty on November 25, three weeks after the trial began; Brackenridge made sure to note that it rendered its decision "without leaving the bar," which was, in any case, a common practice. On the same day the court sentenced Mamachtaga, it also sentenced another defendant charged with homicide, John Bradly; the jury found Bradly "guilty of *manslaughter* only."[107] Hung on December 20, Mamachtaga was the first Native American west of the Alleghany Mountains convicted of murder in a civil trial, not as a war crime, and executed by the state of Pennsylvania.[108]

AFTERWORD

Looking at the trial from the perspective of the white western community, it served its purpose. Neither malicious prosecution nor ill-informed judges affected Mamachtaga's trial—the presence of Bryan and McKean on the bench was ample evidence of that. Brackenridge was already enjoying a career as an eminent western litigator that would earn him a seat on the Pennsylvania Supreme Court in 1799. Western society had every motive to hold a fair trial and the government certainly wanted one; the alternative was to allow vigilantism to quench its thirst for vengeance. The West would benefit from proving that a court could conduct a trial that justified trying such cases and using a local jury in its vicinage.

From the Indian perspective, however, the trial revealed Mamachtaga's almost total lack of understanding of what was happening, his unfamiliarity with court procedures, language, and forms, and his reactive reliance upon the Indian customs he presumed were the norm for resolving crimes. All these factors contributed to his inability to mount a proper defense, despite having a more than competent lawyer. Asked, for example, what he had to say to the sentence of death, Mamachtaga answered "that he would rather *run awhile*." He was referring to the custom among the Indians of giving the murderer time to visit the victims' families and arrive at some form of compensation. As Brackenridge explained,

> If he could satisfy the relations of the deceased, by a commutation for his life, a gun, a horse, fur and the like, it is in their power to dispense with the punishment, but if this cannot be done, having not enough to give, or the relations not consenting to take a commutation, he must come at the end of the time appointed to the spot assigned, and there, by a warrior of the nation, or some relative, son, brother, etc. of the deceased, be put to death, in which case the tomahawk is the usual instrument.

Despite his largely pessimistic view of Indians, Brackenridge was convinced that, should it have been allowed, the condemned man would doubtless have returned within the time set as a point of honor. Mamachtaga was not, however, permitted to follow Indian custom, and he was not prepared for the sentence he received: "Being a simple man, he made a hedious outcry, and gave a most woeful look to the court and country and begged for mercy."[109]

On receiving his sentence, Mamachtaga did not understand that he was not about to be hanged at that moment, or that the charge might be converted to manslaughter should the condemned ask for benefit of clergy. If he were able to recite a "neck verse" (a passage from the Bible), he could be spared execution. To initiate the process, "the sheriff came in with a rope to bind up his hand to a beam of the low and wooden court-house," which would have allowed for a "sentence of *burning in the hand*"; the burning ensured that the condemned could not receive a "neck reprieve" for a subsequent crime. From the Indian's point of view, these were alien judicial forms. Mistaking the rope for the hangman's noose, the Indian cried out and begged for mercy and was only calmed when the process was explained to him.[110] This was not the only misapprehension Mamachtaga was under. Asked as he was taken from the courtroom who the judge was

> and who [the judges] were on the bench in scarlet robes, which was the official custom of that time, and being of the Delaware nation, amongst whom Moravian missionaries had been a great deal . . . he answered that the one, meaning the chief justice, was God, and the other Jesus Christ.

Under this illusion, he stopped "to acknowledge, that his trial had been fair, and to express a wish, that his nation would not revenge his death, or come to war on his account."[111]

As an Indian tried in a white man's court, Mamachtaga was at the mercy of a system that made little sense to him, but with which he had incentives to cooperate. Not only would his tribe have surrendered him to the white man's court to be tried, given the interracial and capital nature of the crime, but the presumed reciprocity of principles of justice between the Indian and white nations seemed to guarantee Indian customs would be respected. The sovereignty of native justice in Indian affairs and the protections of American law for all its inhabitants appeared to guarantee fairness and equal treatment, which might have made the court's justice easier to bear. Complications arose where whites had so encroached on Indian land that they now lived cheek by jowl. There, Indian crimes increased, and whites took advantage to avenge themselves on Indians, peaceful or not, with the result that vigilantism and militia justice usurped the state's efforts to contain the application of justice to the courtroom. In some ways, the courtroom appeared a refuge for Indians some of whom took cases to white courts, despite local juries reluctant to convict whites who committed crimes against them and local officials who cooperated with escapes and "rescues" of white offenders.

In one way, the court was a site of contest over cultural identity. Deracinated, deculturated, and separated from the land that gave them personhood as natural stewards, Indians in the white man's land struggled to assert themselves nowhere more than in the court. On that site, the struggle was overtly over liberty and over life and death, but, just as consequentially, over how one was to be disposed of as a person. Defined by the collective good of his nation, an Indian held to individual responsibility was reduced in the most consequential social sense. He was deprived of the entire set of obligations and benefits distributed across the people to which he belonged. He stood uniquely alone, stripped of his clan and devoid of honor. His vision of collective life and custom was neither understood nor appreciated by those who would judge him. In some ways, the court, which to the Indian was nominally superfluous, became the most important forum in which he operated. It expressed hierarchy, power, and punishment, not the consensus and restorative justice familiar to Indian councils. What was important here was who was wrong, not reconciling affected parties. Victims were not present to participate in a search for solutions; truth was contested, not mutually accepted as a baseline for returning people to good relations within a community. There was more than daylight between the Indian and the white legal systems; there was an unbreachable divide.

Mamachtaga had conceded to the white man's legal system by making no attempt to escape and giving himself up. But at least in this regard he understood that the Indian way would have had the same result, an acceptance of the right of retaliation to redress a violation. That he was denied a mixed jury of whites and Indians was a violation of hospitality as much as a broken legal promise, an obligation the Indian felt keenly. How was his vision to be respected if no one on the jury understood the Indian way or his relationship to its customs? If Indian interpreters, who were largely women, were displaced in favor of whites who had lived among the Indians, in what way could they be said to speak for him? If Anglos were not tried before the councils of his people, how was it just that an Indian should be tried in the white man's court? In the absence of extenuating factors like intent, duress, or malice in their own justice system, Indians had difficulty understanding rulings that did not deliver a decisive result or that left malefactors free. Eclipsing the truth, which to them was plain to see and simple, by means of obfuscating terms and technicalities preserved in voluminous written texts was the opposite of seeing justice done. It was, rather, a way of hiding justice from the people.

Even Mamachtaga's name and his mark reflected that his trial was a travesty on his way of life. The evocation of a hurricane and sign of a turkey's foot spoke to signs of nature and a resemblance to the natural world. While offering his beaver pelts in commutation for his life was, in his experience, a fair bargain, he experienced nothing fair or natural in the trial process—the plea of not guilty, understanding the indictment, his inability to confess, the countenance of the jury, the meaning of an oath, benefit of clergy, and the scarlet robes. In the end, although Mamachtaga hoped he would be able to "run awhile," he was only allowed his freedom to find roots from the forest to cure his jailer's daughter. As Brackenridge indicated, "This was during the Indian War, and this place on the verge of the settlement" so that, had he chosen to run, Mamachtaga might easily have escaped.[112] That he did not was a function of "the way of thinking amongst the Indians," not that he lacked the physical force to do so.

Mamachtaga's resolution was tested in two other incidents before his end. Kept in a cell with a white man set to be hung for a "crime against nature," the Indian declined the man's offer of whiskey in exchange for killing him to save him from the "disgrace of being hanged"; Mamachtaga claimed "he had killed white men enough already." On the gallows, the rope broke as he fell, upon which "he rose with a smile, and went up again."[113] Asked how he felt about the disgrace of a hanging, he was hesitant but responded that he might rather choose to "be shot or be tomahawked." He figured that the good man above would excuse him.[114]

The Mamachtaga trial is not a typical case for several reasons.[115] Mamachtaga represented a subset of those who lived near white settlements, accustomed to white ways but not assimilating. Such Indians were partway between those who remained independent in the wild and those who associated themselves with missionary settlements. At the same time, the case represents an instance of negotiating intersecting Indian and white law which was characteristic of the legal pluralism that typified the western country.

On the one hand, the white man's court became the venue because the trial was not a crime committed by an Indian on an Indian; on the other hand, Mamachtaga expected that court to honor Indian ways. The Indian did not have the opportunity to forum shop; the crime was a capital one and the county court was the most obvious venue. Of the available options, it was the most likely to enforce its verdict, a critical factor for the settler community and its vigilante element if they were to accept the court's findings.[116] The vigilantes who tried to lynch Mamachtaga were a common feature of western law as they constituted the home front militias called upon by settler colonists to defend against Indian raids and to attack Indian villages, acting not only as their arm in pushing the Indians out of western lands but as an essential feature of self-governance and extra-legal force that gave settlers a great deal of autonomy.[117] For Mamachtaga, they represented a hostile and intimidating force trying to capture and hang him, his interpreter, and his lawyer as well.

Mamachtaga's greatest legal obstacle, by comparison, was his inability to represent himself. His communication problem involved a variety of interpreters and intermediaries, the first of which, Nicholas, was readily available in the community, had lived among the Indians, and had traded with them; Nicholas engaged a trader to deal with Mamachtaga's tribe. Once he was scared off by the vigilantes, a second interpreter, Handlyn, presumably provided by the court, translated the charges, their meaning, and the Indian's rights in Delaware to Mamachtaga. Separately, the court wished to have the chief of the tribe present at the trial, a common practice that allowed another opportunity to translate for and represent the Indian. In addition, an Indian woman who attended Mamachtaga out of sympathy at the place where he was detained spoke Delaware but refused to assist the lawyer in posing any questions. Finally, Mamachtaga was represented by legal counsel. These multiple intermediaries acted as a variety of go-betweens between the white and Indian systems of justice, offering, on the one hand, the possibility of representation and, on the other, the prospect of a confusing array of voices and perspectives that apparently confounded the Indian, who had his own view of the way justice for Indians should operate.[118] Except for Brackenridge, they were not "fully subjects of the law" and had an ambiguous status as intermediaries who not only cast doubt on the legitimacy of Indigenous law but did little to enhance respect for state courts.[119]

Whether other tribes shared Mamachtaga's experiences or took a more activist interventionist role with the settler justice system leads us to the question of agency. The answer depends upon whether an Indigenous group actively sought the legitimacy of an alternative forum or equal terms with colonizing settlers. Certainly, missionary Indians constituted such a group as did trading Indians; continuity across boundaries was necessary to preserve orderly accommodations, advocate within the white man's system, or preserve access to more than one legal system. Indians in the woods were less likely to submit to white man's law except by treaty, although Indigenous authorities worked in different ways to defend and reinvent traditional authority. Not only did they cheat and resist the state, but they challenged state representations, enhanced cultural inclusiveness, and even broadened colonizing jurisdiction to claim special status. In fact, the native experience demonstrated the limitations of state authority when it tried to enforce its Indian policies and dominate western land. If nothing else, that experience proved that Native American polities were highly varied and harder to contain, some increasing in strength as others lost their autonomy.[120]

As for Mamachtaga, he was a creature of the history of his people—their experience with Penn and with the missionaries, the white settlers' assault on their stewardship of the land and their tribal traditions. His trial might have denied him his life, but it did something of possibly greater importance to him—it took away his connection to his land, his people, and his identity. Insofar as his crime was tied to the pressure of expansion that characterized America from its founding, it was connected to the thirst for land that is exemplified in the next chapter in which George Washington takes up the thread of the story of the white man's burden, bringing civilization to the frontier and profiting himself in the meantime. This next step in playing out the democratic experiment explores the conflicts in American land law and the growing importance of lawyers.

NOTES

1. Claude Milton Newlin, *The Life and Writings of Hugh Henry Brackenridge* (Princeton, NJ: Princeton University Press, 1932), 128n10.

2. The Lenni Lenape made a peace treaty with Penn's government in 1682. They inhabited land in the Brandywine River valley in Chester County only to be ejected between 1720–1760s; G. S. Rowe and Jack D. Marietta, *Troubled Experiment: Crime and Justice in Pennsylvania, 1682–1800* (Philadelphia: University of Pennsylvania Press, 2006), 67–68.

3. The Lenni Lenape (the native name) spoke the Algonquin language and became the leading voice in the Four Nations of Indians upon the Susquehanna—Delaware, Shawnee, Conoy (Piscataway), and Conestoga (Susquehannock/Mingo) Indians—formed to offset the Iroquois organization of the Five Nations (the Covenant Chain)—Mohawk, Oneida, Onondaga, Cayuga, and Seneca—that colluded with the colonists to dominate the other tribes. This study refers to them as "Delaware" Indians in deference to common usage.

4. The "Walking Purchase" was a fraud perpetrated against the Delaware Indians by arranging a cleared path and choosing the fastest runners to "walk" out the boundary of a land purchase.

5. Paul Douglas Newman, "The 'Four Nations of Indians Upon the Susquehanna': Mid-Atlantic Murder, Diplomacy, and Political Identity, 1717–1723," *Pennsylvania History: A Journal of Mid-Atlantic Studies* 88, no. 3 (2021): 290, 294, 313; Steven C. Harper, "Delawares and Pennsylvanians After the Walking Purchase," in *Friends and Enemies in Penn's Woods: Indians, Colonists, and the Racial Construction of Pennsylvania*, eds. William A. Pencak and Daniel K. Richter (University Park: Pennsylvania State University Press, 2004), 167–79; Patrick Spero, *Frontier Country: The Politics of War in Early Pennsylvania* (Philadelphia: University of Pennsylvania Press, 2016), 2, 6–13, 94–95.

6. Grant Christensen and Melissa L. Tatum, "Core Concepts," in *Reading American Indian Law: Foundational Principles*, Grant Christensen and Melissa L. Tatum, eds. (Cambridge: Cambridge University Press, 2020), 19–21.

7. G. S. Rowe and Jack D. Marietta, *Troubled Experiment: Crime and Justice in Pennsylvania, 1682–1800* (Philadelphia: University of Pennsylvania Press, 2006), 168–77; see Morris N. Shenk, "Crimes and Punishments in Provincial Cumberland County," *Cumberland County History* 18, no.1 (2001): 10–14.

8. Harper, "Delawares and Pennsylvanians," 179; Patrick Griffin, *American Leviathan: Empire, Nation, and Revolutionary Frontier* (New York: Hill and Wang, 2007), 167–80; Peter Silver, *Our Savage Neighbors: How Indian War Transformed Early America* ((New York: W. W. Norton & Company, 2008), 154–59, 177–90, 265–85; Spero, *Frontier Country*, 142–52, 159–64, 177–91, 233–46; Gleb Aleksandrov, "Power, History, and Native-Colonial Conflicts in the Early Native American Literary Tradition (OAH 2020)," *Law and History Review* (March 2020); Francis Bailey, *Narratives of a Late Expedition against the Indians; with an Account of the Barbarous Execution of Col. Crawford; and the Wonderful Escape of Dr. Knight and John Slover from Captivity, in 1782* (Philadelphia: Francis Bailey, 1783), 4–15.

9. Spero, *Frontier Country*, 13, 230, 240.

10. Spero, *Frontier Country*, 244–47, 255; Silver, *Our Savage Neighbors*, 285, 291–92; Griffin, *American Leviathan*, 184–85.

11. Yashuhide Kawashima, *Puritan Justice and the Indian: White Man's Law in Massachusetts, 1630–1763* (Middletown, CT: Wesleyan University Press, 1986), 148, 150; Yashuhide Kawashima, "Forced Conformity: Puritan Criminal Justice and Indians," *Kansas Law* Review 25, no .3 (1977): 361–74.

12. William Penn, first letter to the Kings of the Indians in Pennsylvania, October 18, 1681, Historical Society of Pennsylvania (HSP). Lenni Lenape Chief Tamanend presumably signed the Treaty of Shackamaxon with Penn in late 1682, but no evidence of the treaty has survived. It was possibly destroyed by Penn's son in order to be free from complying with the treaty's commitments.

13. William Penn, "A letter from William Penn, Proprietary and Governor of Pennsylvania in America, to the Committee of the Free Society of Traders, 1683," in *Narrative of Early Pennsylvania, West New Jersey, and Delaware, 1630–1701*, ed. Albert Cook Myers (New York: Charles Scribner's Sons, 1912), 236.

14. Whereas William Penn has been referred to as the Proprietor and the Quaker government has been referred to as the Proprietary government of Pennsylvania, the Quaker government has also been referred to as a colonial government. The terms indicate, on the one hand, a beneficent government and, on the other, colonialism. See essays in William A. Pencak and Daniel K. Richter, eds., *Friends and Enemies in Penn's Woods: Indians, Colonists, and the Racial Construction of Pennsylvania* (University Park: Pennsylvania State University Press, 2004).

15. Robert L. Cable, ed., "Law About Trial of Indians (1793)," *The Statutes at Large of Pennsylvania*, vol. 1, 1682–1700 (Harrisburg, PA: Legislative Reference Bureau, 2001), chapter 73, 64–65; John Smolenski, *Friends and Strangers: The Making of a Creole Culture in Colonial Pennsylvania* (Philadelphia: University of Pennsylvania Press, 2010), 99.

16. Allowing aliens on a mixed jury became explicit in the fourteenth century in relation to merchant cases, but without specifying which aliens, so that aliens initially did not have to be alien merchants, aliens from the same country, or even speak the same language, a practice that continued on the Pennsylvania frontier where Indians of any language group might sit on a mixed jury. Marianne Constable, *The Law of the Other: The Mixed Jury and Changing Conceptions of Citizenship, Law, and Knowledge* (Chicago: The University of Chicago Press, 1994), 98, 112–13, 124–27.

17. Penn, in Myers, *Narrative of Early Pennsylvania*, 236; Katherine Hermes, "'Justice Will Be Done Us': Algonquin Demands for Reciprocity in the Courts of European Settlers," in *The Many Legalities of Early America*, eds. Christopher Tomlins and Bruce H. Mann (Chapel Hill: University of North Carolina Press, 2001), 131–34.

18. Using a 1772 Connecticut case, *Mohegan Indians v. Connecticut*, Mark D. Walters contends that where there were treaties and Indigenous people were "not subject to local municipal law" in British North America their own customary law was in force. Thus, the authority of courts in the North American colonies coexisted with native sovereignty over its own legal traditions independent of the colonies' legal systems. Mark D. Walters, "*Mohegan Indians v. Connecticut* (1705–1773) and the Legal Status of Aboriginal Customary Laws and Government in British North America," *Osgood Hall Law Journal* 33, no. 4 (1995): 786–88, 827–29; Mark D. Walters, "The

Judicial Rcognition of Indigenous Legal Traditions: *Connolly v. Woolrich at 150*," *Review of Constitutional Studies* 22, no. 3 (2017): 347–77.

19. Pennsylvania Colony Provincial Council, *Minutes of the Provincial Council of Pennsylvania*, vol. 2 (London: Forgotten Books, 2018), 608; John Smolenski, "The Death of Sawantaeny and the Problem of Justice on the Frontier," in *Friends and Enemies in Penn's* Woods, eds. Pencak and Richter, 117.

20. Hermes, "'Justice Will Be Done Us,'" 126–27, 130.

21. Ada Pecos Melton, "Indigenous Justice Systems and Tribal Society," *Judicature* 79, no. 3 (1995): 126–28, 132.

22. Hermes, "'Justice Will Be Done Us,'" 126–27; Smolenski, "Sawantaeny," 122–24.

23. Louis M. Waddell, "Justice, Retribution, and the Case of John Toby," in *Friends and Enemies in Penn's Woods*, eds. Pencak and Richter, 130.

24. Penn, in *Narrative of Early Pennsylvania*, ed. Myers, 236.

25. Smolenski, "Sawantaeny," 107–8, 113, 116.

26. *The Statutes at Large of Pennsylvania, 1744,* vol. 5, session 1744, An Act for the Speedy Trial of Capital Offenses Committed by any Indian or Indians in the Remote Parts of the Province, no. 362, 5–6.

27. Rowe and Marietta, *Troubled Experiment*, 206–8.

28. County courts were founded in the western counties as follows: Westmoreland (1773), Washington (1781), Fayette (1784), and Alleghany (1788).

29. Alexander Addison, *Reports of Cases in the County Courts of the Fifth Circuit, and in the High Court of Errors and Appeals of the State of Pennsylvania* (Philadelphia: John Colerick, 1800): Allegheny County, 1794, *Pennsylvania v. Andrew Robertson*, 246–48 (a case which an Indian was murdered by a white man; the defendant was found not guilty "on the grounds of homicide in self-defense"); Westmoreland County, 1799, *Pennsylvania v. Henry Becomb, John Reading, James Eckles, and Samuel Dickson*, 386–89 (a case in which the state prosecuted three white men for robbing Indians; the defendants were found guilty); Washington County, *Pennsylvania v. Samuel Lewis, Ch. Hobbes, Isaac Hobbes, Nathan Lewis, and Isaac Braden*, 1796, 279–83, the prosecution ("Young for the state") made a relevant reference to Indians, 281. Alexander J. Dallas, *Reports of Cases Ruled and Adjudged in the Several Courts of the United States and of Pennsylvania, Before and Since the Revolution Held at the Seat of the Federal Government,* 4 vols. (Philadelphia: T. Bradford, 1790–1807): seven Indian cases involving land titles: *Sims Lessee versus Irvine* (1799), III, 425–66; *Commonwealth v. Tench Coxe, Esq.* (1800), IV, 170–205; *Morris' Lessee versus Neighman* (1800), IV, 209–10; *Attorney-General versus the Grantees under the Act of April 1792* (1802), IV, 237–45; *Balfour's Lessee versus Meade* (1803), IV, 363–70; *Penn's Lessee versus Klyne* (1805), IV, 403–10; *Huidekoper's Lessee versus Douglas* (1805), 392–401. G. S. Rowe, "Crime and its Resolution in 18th Century Cumberland County," *Cumberland County History* 3, no. 1 (1986): 22–26; A. B. Reid, "Early Courts, Judges, and Lawyers of Alleghany County," *Western Pennsylvania Historical Magazine* 5, no. 3 (1922): 185–202; J. W. F. White, "The Judiciary of Allegheny County," *Pennsylvania Magazine of History and Biography* 7, no. 2 (1883): 143–193; Shenk, "Crimes and Punishments."

30. Hermes, "'Justice Will Be Done Us,'" 139, 143–45, 148.

31. James Adair, "Extracts," *The History of the American Indians*, in *A Selection of Some of the Most Interesting Narratives, or Outrages, Committed by the Indians in Their War with the White People*, ed. Archibald Loudon (Carlisle: A. Loudon, 1808), vol. II.

32. Nancy L Hagedorn, "'A Friend to Go Between Them': The Interpreter as Cultural Broker During Anglo-Iroquois Councils, 1740–70," *Ethnohistory* 35, no. 1 (1988): 62, 69; Yasuhide Kawashima, "Forest Diplomats: The Role of Interpreters in Indian-White Relations on the Early American Frontier," *American Indian Quarterly* 13 no. 1 (1989): 3–4, 6–7, 12.

33. Kawashima, "Forest Diplomats," 2.

34. Adair, "Extracts," 349–50.

35. Adair, "Extracts," 352

36. Adair, "Extracts," 354.

37. Adair, "Extracts," 351–54.

38. Adair, "Extracts," 353–54.

39. Smolenski, "Sawantaeny," 120–22; Waddell, "Justice, Retribution, and the Case of John Toby," 136–141.

40. Adair, "Extracts," 349–350.

41. Adair, "Extracts," 349–350.

42. Hugh Henry Brackenridge, "Observations," in Bailey, 36–37; Brackenridge edited the account of Crawford's capture and execution featured by Bailey.

43. Hugh Henry Brackenridge, "Thoughts on the Present Indian War," in Daniel Marder, ed., *Incidents of the Insurrection* (New Haven: College & University Press, 1972), 44.

44. Brackenridge, "Observations," 32–33; Hugh Henry Brackenridge, "Indian Right of Soil" *Gazette Publications* (Carlisle: Alexander and Phillips, 1806), 103.

45. Indian troubles had cost the national economy five sixths of its budget from 1790–1796. Thomas P. Slaughter, *The Whiskey Rebellion: Frontier Epilogue to the American Revolution* (New York: Oxford University Press, 1986), 93–94.

46. Penn, in *Narratives of Early Pennsylvania*, ed. Myers, 236.

47. Waddell, "Justice, Retribution, and the Case of John Toby," 136–38.

48. William S. Lofquist, "Justice on the Western Frontier: The Death Penalty in Pre-Industrial Pittsburgh, 1754–1840," *Pennsylvania History: A Journal of Mid-Atlantic Studies* 85, no. 4 (2018): 574–75; *Pennsylvania Packet*, November 24, 1785; Bill Lofquist "State Killings in the Steel City: The History of the Death Penalty in Pittsburgh," https://state-killings-in-the-steel-city.org/2018/01/09/mamachtaga/; Hugh Henry Brackenridge, "The Trial of Mamachtaga, an Indian, at a Court of Oyer and Terminer for the County of Westmoreland, in the Year 1784–5," Brackenridge, in *A Selection*, ed. Loudon, I, 49–50.

49. Brackenridge, in *A Selection*, ed. Loudon, I, 50; Hugh Henry Brackenridge, "The Trial of Mamachtaga," in *Incidents*, ed. Daniel Marder, 25–35; Hugh Henry Brackenridge, "The Trial of Mamachtaga," *Litigation* 14, no. 4 (1988): 47–50; Judge Hugh Henry Brackenridge, "The Trial of Mamachtaga, a Delaware Indian, the First Person Convicted of Murder West of the Alleghany Mountains, and Hanged for His

Crime," *Western Pennsylvania Historical Magazine* 1, no. 1 (1918): 27–36. The Loudon text, the source from which quotes are taken in the present chapter, was the first published version of Brackenridge's "Trial"; Daniel Marder, *Hugh Henry Brackenridge* (New York: Twayne Publishers, Inc., 1967), 105.

50. Brady J. Crytzer, "Frontier Justice: The Trial and Execution of Mamachtaga," *Westmoreland History* 20, no. 2 (2015): 4–5; Lofquist, "Justice," 573.

51. Brackenridge, in *A Selection*, ed. Loudon, I, 54–55.

52. Brackenridge, in *A Selection*, ed. Loudon, I, 49. See Margaret Pearson Bothwell, "Killbuck and Killbuck Island," *Western Pennsylvania History* 44, no. 4 (1961): 343–60; The Historical Dilettante (blog): "Pittsburgh's Lost Islands," posted by Sue Morris, May 11, 206. historicaldilettante.blogspot.com/2016/05/things-that-arent-there-any-more.html.

53. See "Opinion of Hon. Geo. Bryan," George Bryan to John Whitehill, June 10, 1785, *Pennsylvania Archives*, ser. 1, vol. 10 (Philadelphia: Joseph Severans & Co.), 473–75; Box 2, Case 63, Bryan Papers, Historical Society of Pennsylvania (HSP); Michael Huffnagle to Gen. John Armstrong, May 13, 1785, *Pennsylvania Archives*, ser. I, vol. 10, 464–65; Michael Huffnagle to James Irvine, May 27, 1785, *Pennsylvania Archives*, ser. 1, vol. 10, 467–68; Robert Galbraith to John Dickinson, May 25, 1785, *Pennsylvania Archives*, ser. 1, vol. 10, 466–67; George Morgan to Council, October 23, 1785, *Pennsylvania Archives*, ser. 1, vol. 10, 526.

54. Crytzer, "Frontier Justice," 7.

55. Brackenridge, in *A Selection*, ed. Loudon, I, 53–54.

56. Galbraith to Dickinson, May 25, 1785, *Pennsylvania Archives*, ser. 1, vol. 10, 466–67.

57. Huffnagle to Irvine, May 27, 1785, *Pennsylvania Archives*, ser. I, vol. 10, 467–68.

58. On a deed made in 1784 for the land occupied by Fort Pitt, Major Isaac Craig and Colonel Stephen Bayard filed through Brackenridge for Captain Luckett's ejectment as he had refused to allow them to occupy some of the buildings. Huffnagle asked Congress to order him to relinquish possession. Charles W. Dahlinger, "The Last Days of Fort Pitt," *Western Pennsylvania Historical Magazine* 5, no. 2 (1922): 99–107.

59. Lofquist disagrees with Brackenridge, naming Benjamin Jones as the second man killed and not Evans. Brackenridge claims that his account was related to him by the two wounded men and that he had himself "found the Indians" at the scene the morning after the murders. Brackenridge, in *A Selection*, ed. Loudon, I, 49–50; Lofquist, "Justice," 574.

60. Brackenridge, in *A Selection*, ed. Loudon, I, 49–50.

61. Brackenridge, in *A Selection*, ed. Loudon, I, 49, 51.

62. Brackenridge, in *A Selection*, ed. Loudon, I, 50–51, 54–56.

63. Galbraith to Dickinson, May 25, 1785, *Pennsylvania Archives*, ser. 1, vol. 10, 467.

64. Brackenridge, in *A Selection*, ed. Loudon, I, 52, 54.

65. Brackenridge, in *A Selection*, ed. Loudon, I, 56.

66. “Opinion of Hon. Geo. Bryan,” June 10, 1785, *Pennsylvania Archives*, ser. 1, vol. 10, 473–75. Burton A. Konkle, *George Bryan and the Constitution* (Philadelphia, 1932), 288–93.

67. 1744 Act for the Speedy Trial of Capital Offenses Committed by any Indian or Indians in the Remote Parts of the Province, 5 Stat. 5 chpt. 362.

68. “Opinion of Hon. Geo. Bryan,” June 10, 1785, *Pennsylvania Archives*, ser. 1, vol. 10, 473–75.

69. G. S. Rowe, *Embattled Bench: The Pennsylvania Supreme Court and the Forging of a Democratic Society, 1684–1809* (Newark: University of Delaware Press, 1994), 158; Bryan was appointed in 1780 as a fourth justice to expand the original three-person bench.

70. “Opinion of Hon. Geo. Bryan,” June 10, 1785, *Pennsylvania Archives*, ser. 1, vol. 10, 474.

71. “Opinion of Hon. Geo. Bryan,” June 10, 1785, *Pennsylvania Archives*, ser. 1, vol. 10, 474; Act of 1744, 4–5.

72. George Bryan to His Excellency John Dickinson, Esq. and the Council, March 24, 1783, *Pennsylvania Archives*, ser. I, vol. 10, 16–19.

73. *The Statutes at Large of Pennsylvania,* vol. 3, sessions 1713–1724, An Act for Establishing Courts of Judicature in the Province, 1722, no. 255, 298–309; *The Statutes at Large of Pennsylvania,* vol. 3, sessions 1713–1724, An Act for the Advancement of Justice and More Certain Administration Thereof, 1718, no. 236, 199–221.

74. Bryan to Dickinson and the Council, March 24, 1783, *Pennsylvania Archives*, ser. I, vol. 10, 17.

75. “Answers of C. J. McKean,” March 27, 1783, *Pennsylvania Archives*, ser. I, vol. 10, 20; Rowe, *Embattled Bench,* 188–89.

76. Robert Galbraith to President Dickinson, May 25, 1785, *Pennsylvania Archives*, ser. I, vol. 10, 467.

77. “Opinion of Hon. Geo. Bryan,” June 10, 1785, *Pennsylvania Archives*, ser. 1, vol. 10, 474.

78. “Answers of C. J. McKean,” March 27, 1783, *Pennsylvania Archives*, ser. I, vol. 10, 20.

79. Bryan to Dickinson and the Council, March 24, 1783, *Pennsylvania Archives*, ser. I, vol. 10, 17.

80. “Opinion of Hon. Geo. Bryan,” June 10, 1785, *Pennsylvania Archives*, ser. 1, vol. 10, 474–75.

81. “Opinion of Hon. Geo. Bryan,” June 10, 1785, *Pennsylvania Archives*, ser. 1, vol. 10, 474. In 1764, the Pennsylvania Supreme Court granted “a moiety of foreigners” on the jury of a German immigrant, while as recently as 1783 the court had awarded a mixed jury to Italian sailors; *Respublica v. Mesca*, 1783, Dallas, *Reports of Cases Ruled*, I, 73–75. Apparently, Pennsylvania had wrestled unsuccessfully for years “with the need to offer special courts involving Indians”; Rowe, *Embattled Bench,* 168–69, 189.

82. “Opinion of Hon. Geo. Bryan,” June 10, 1785, *Pennsylvania Archives*, ser. 1, vol. 10, 474.

83. Rowe, *Embattled Bench*, 189.

84. Alexander Addison covered the Pennsylvania courts of the western counties; his law reports were not published until 1800 and went back to 1791; Alexander Dallas covered Pennsylvania Supreme Court cases; his reports went back to 1754.

85. The reform law of 1794 changed the law on murder, eliminating numerous crimes for which the death penalty applied and distinguishing murder by degrees to make murder in the first degree the only crime punishable by death. Lawrence M. Friedman, *A History of American Law* 1973 (New York: Simon and Schuster, 2005), 207–8.

86. *Pennsylvania v. Robertson*, Addison, *Reports of Cases*, 246–48.

87. *Pennsylvania v. Robertson,* Addison, *Reports of Cases*, 248.

88. Allegheny County, *Pennsylvania v. James Honeyman* (1793), Addison, *Reports of Cases*, 147–50.

89. Washington County, *Pennsylvania v. John Bell* (1793), Addison, *Reports of Cases*, 156–80.

90. Fayette County, *Pennsylvania v. John M'Fall* (1794), Addison, *Reports of Cases*, 255–57.

91. *Pennsylvania v. Lewis, et al.*, Addison, *Reports of Cases*, 279–83.

92. *Pennsylvania v. Lewis, et al.*, Addison, *Reports of Cases*, 281.

93. Allegheny County, *Pennsylvania v. James Stoops* (1799), Addison, *Reports of Cases*, 381–384.

94. *Pennsylvania v. Becomb, et al.*, Addison, *Reports of Cases*, 389.

95. *Pennsylvania v. Becomb, et al.*, Addison, *Reports of Cases*, 388–89.

96. Brackenridge, in *A Selection*, ed. Loudon, I, 56–57.

97. Brackenridge, in *A Selection*, ed. Loudon, I, 57.

98. *The Statutes at Large of Pennsylvania,* 1717–18, An Act for the Advancement of Justice, 1718, 199–214.

99. Act of 1718, Section III, 200.

100. Act of 1718, Section III, 201.

101. Brackenridge, in *A Selection*, ed. Loudon, I, 58.

102. Rowe, *Embattled Bench,* 189.

103. Brackenridge, in *A Selection*, ed. Loudon, I, 55–56.

104. Peter C. Mancall, *Deadly Medicine: Indians and Alcohol in Early America* (Ithaca, NY: Cornell University Press, 1995), 101, 106–7, 121, 123–24, 127.

105. Mancall, *Deadly Medicine*, 109–10, 114, 116, 119–20.

106. Samuel Danforth, *The Woeful Effects of Drunkenness,a Sermon preached at Bristol, Octob. 12. 1709. When Two Indians, Josias and Joseph, Were Executed for Murther, Occasioned by the Drunkenness both of the Murthering & Murthered Parties* (Boston: B. Green, 1710), 34, 37. Indian execution sermons became a genre of their own. Mamachtaga was not himself, however, memorialized in such a way. Katherine Grandjean, "'Our Fellow-Creatures & our Fellow-Christians': Race and Religion in Eighteenth-Century Narratives of Indian Culture," *American Quarterly* 62, no. 4 (2010): 925–50; Ava Chamberlain, "The Execution of Moses Paul: A Story of Crime and Contact in Eighteenth-Century Connecticut," *The New England Quarterly* 77, no. 3 (2004): 414–50.

107. Brackenridge, in *A Selection*, ed. Loudon, I, 58.

108. Rowe, *Embattled Bench*, 189; Lofquist, "Justice," 563, 575; Lofquist, "State Killings." Lofquist argues that Mamachtaga's case "could well have been treated as an act of war and tried by military authorities." Trying it as a civil case thus demonstrated a separation of military and civilian systems and the legitimacy of the civilian system.

109. Brackenridge, in *A Selection*, ed. Loudon, I, 58–59.

110. Brackenridge, in *A Selection*, ed. Loudon, I, 59–60.

111. Brackenridge, in *A Selection*, ed. Loudon, I, 60–61.

112. Brackenridge, in *A Selection*, ed. Loudon, I, 63.

113. Brackenridge, in *A Selection*, ed. Loudon, I, 61–82.

114. Brackenridge, in *A Selection*, ed. Loudon, I, 53, 57–60.

115. See for the distinction between trouble-less, or typical, cases and trouble-cases, Karl N. Llewellyn and E. A. Hoebel, *The Cheyenne Way: Conflict and Case Law in Primitive Jurisprudence* (Norman: University of Oklahoma Press, 1941); J. F. Holleman, "Trouble-Cases and Trouble-Less Cases in the Study of Customary Law and Legal Reform," *Law and Society Review* 7, no. 4 (1973): 585–610; William Twining, "Two Works of Karl Llewellyn-II," *The Modern Law Review* 31 (1968): 165–82; Simon Verdun-Jones, "The Jurisprudence of Karl Llewellyn," *Dalhousie Law Journal* 1, no. 3 (1973–1974): 453, 460–65.

116. Lauren Benton, "Historical Perspectives on Legal Pluralism," *Hague Journal on the Rule of Law* 3 (2011): 57.

117. Spero, *Frontier Country*, 141.

118. See Hagedorn, "'A Friend to Go Between Them'"; Kawashima, "Forest Diplomats."

119. Lauren Benton, *Law and Colonial Cultures: Legal Regimes in World History, 1400–1900* (Cambridge: Cambridge University Press, 2001), 17–18.

120. Benton, *Law*, 8, 10. Gautham Rao, "The New Historiography of the Early Federal Government: Institutions, Context, and the Imperial State," *The William and Mary Quarterly* 77, no. 1 (2020), 117, 125; Amy Turner Bushnell, "Indigenous America and the Limits of the Atlantic World, 1493–1825," in *Atlantic History: A Critical Appraisal*, eds. Jack P. Greene and Philip D. Morgan (New York: Oxford University Press, 2008), 194.

Chapter 3

"A fine peace of Land"

Settlers' Rights and Land Titles in George Washington v. James Scott, et al., 1786

A fine peace of Land

—Letter from James Crawford to George Washington, September 29, 1767

Land in what is now Western Pennsylvania was central to the definition of the colonies in America and to the United States as a nation from the 1750s through the 1790s. A major player in the western lands, George Washington had his hand in almost every aspect of its disposition—from his role representing the First Virginia Regiment in claiming the military bounty promised by the British for service in the French and Indian War to his substantial land speculation from 1767 until he became the new democracy's first president in 1789. His involvement was expressed as well through his support of Virginia's cessation of western lands in 1780 in favor of national authority and his vision of a waterway to connect the country from the Potomac to Lake Erie.[1] Indeed, Alan Taylor constructs a story of how American freedom depended upon whether settlers' pursuit of land "in the West would undermine the construction of a viable national government." Among his concerns are the critical moment when Americans breached the Alleghany mountains and the government's fear that settlers were too free of public authority to allow integration of the frontier into the nation.[2]

Irrespective of a 1763 Proclamation Line established by the British and the Virginia Executive Council to close Indian territory, land speculators in Virginia sought grants to open it for settlement. By 1774, Colonial Secretary

Lord Dartmouth and the British Privy Council directed Virginia's Governor Dunmore to abolish all land grants, including military bounties like those granted to Washington's regiment. The Quebec Act in the same year established a barrier to access land west of the Ohio, encouraging speculators to seek an excuse to incite a war with the Indians. Numbers of influential Virginians like Richard Henry Lee, Patrick Henry, Thomas Jefferson, and Washington felt threatened by the freeze on land acquisition, a major contributor to the gentry's willingness to separate from the British Empire.[3]

This fascinating period in American history is encapsulated in microcosm in a legal case that was a scandal in its own time but has been lost to history: Washington's suit against squatters on his Millers Run tract in Washington County, Pennsylvania. That case was tried at the cusp of the Constitutional Convention where Washington was elected its president and just three years before he would become the first president of the new nation.[4] By the time he instituted his ejectment suit in 1784, Washington held as much as forty thousand acres of western land to make him one of the largest individual landholders in the nation.[5] However desirable the Millers Run land, it was a small part of Washington's holdings that entailed evicting thirteen poor families who claimed homesteads averaging thirty-one improved acres per settler (403 acres of Washington's tract), from the smallest at three acres to the largest at ninety-one.[6]

Washington's attachment to the West was the fruit of three and a half decades of service there in several capacities. He made four trips from 1748 as a surveyor and served as a colonel in the French and Indian War (1755–1758); he returned in 1770 to locate bounty land for his regiment and in 1784 to check on his western property and explore an east-west transportation waterway.[7] Washington had a decided advantage in the Millers Run land dispute, for the very county to which the tract would be assigned when a boundary was run between Virginia and Pennsylvania was named after him in 1781 to honor his role as commander in chief of the Continental Army. His reputation was such that he was often deferred to in Virginia by the Masters of William and Mary College (whose royal charter gave them the authority to nominate surveyors for the counties) and the Land Office (whose regulations controlled the granting of land titles). Parties who claimed land on tracts about which Washington expressed an interest routinely avoided conflicts with him by giving up their claims.

Washington was intensely interested in the property, leading him to write probably the only legal brief of his career;[8] like the legal strategy for the case, it has never really been studied. Though the brief was transcribed and has been noted in several works, the manuscript itself has disappeared;[9] nor was there a law report, newspaper account, or published transcript of the trial.[10] Washington enclosed his brief in a letter to his lawyer Thomas

Smith.[11] He subsequently sought legal advice from John Harvie and Edmund Randolph on Virginia law.[12] Smith exchanged letters with Washington to develop a strategy for the trial, while Washington shared his analysis with Charles Simms and Thomas Lewis as sounding boards.[13] Together, these materials construct the legal strategy developed for the Millers Run trial.

Whereas he was not a lawyer, Washington's brief reflects a determination to capitalize on his experience with the law. At the Virginia House of Burgesses (1758–1775) and as a delegate to the Continental Congress (1774–1775), he would have consulted the colony charter, Virginia's code of laws, English common law, and law books. Having served six years as a justice of the peace (c. 1768–1774) and four as a judge on Virginia's Fairfax County Court (1770–1774), Washington was a "gentleman justice," a role usually filled by a property owner of some influence.[14] He served as an arbitrator, admitted lawyers to the bar, and gained experience in civil, probate, criminal, and chancery cases. He would have dealt with grand jury and petit jury pleadings, practices, and procedures and was exposed to as much law as those who apprenticed or read for the bar. County courts, importantly, served as the main judicial bodies for local disputes, both civil and criminal.[15]

Washington's larger than life persona as the recently retired commander in chief of the Continental Army proved one the most daunting factors in trying the case. In the public sphere, he was compared to the Roman general Cincinnatus who left public life to retire to his farm, the mythical figure Atlas who bore the weight of the world on his shoulders, an apotheosized divinity, the biblical Joshua, and even Moses the lawgiver.[16] This is not to say that those without the fame of a founder were without support.

On the one hand, settlers conceived of themselves as founders of communities and sponsors of the growth of towns; they had support in the countryside, backing in the legislature, and friends on juries chosen from the locale. They cultivated and lived on the land, pushed back the frontier, and captured territory for the new nation. Unlike land companies and individual speculators, they were not interested in profiteering, and they were not absentee owners, making this nearly forgotten trial a test case for the struggle in Western Pennsylvania between western homesteaders and largescale eastern speculators.

There is a story somewhere in all of this, however, about the establishment of local militia, the automatic nature of community call-ups, and the harshness of vigilantism in western communities as a means of fostering an imperial western-style colonialism. It begins with what military historian Richard H. Kohn calls the inconceivable idea that colonials would give up their local settler-based militias, because they were so ingrained in colonial culture as community "defense against invading savages."[17] The idea is picked up by Washington as he retired from command of the Continental Army. In his

"Sentiments on a Peaceful Establishment," his most strategic and realistic postwar thinking on a regular military, Washington recognized both the need to subordinate militias and their connection to settlers on the frontier "forming a barrier against the Indians," which would give great security to settlements.[18] This is a long way from endorsing the terroristic stratagems used by settler colonists in pursuing and eradicating Indian tribes and settling on their land. But it does explain a western perspective that was favorable to settlers as insiders whose lived experience on the frontier attracted support from the East among those with visions of a western empire and from the West among those with little power or wealth and only their hunger for land and desperation to guide them. The western experience, one recognizes, expressly characterized itself in terms of "popular racial ideology and the construction of a White male nation" in which settler colonists saw themselves pitting "White patriarchy against a racialized Native American enemy."[19] One need only look for the historical roots of such a construction in the legacy bequeathed to the West by the violence perpetrated by the Paxton Boys, a 1763 massacre of peaceful Conestoga Indians by a collection of some fifty frontiersmen to whom Benjamin Franklin referred as "CHRISTIAN WHITE SAVAGES."[20]

Continuing grievances of the settler colonists over the next thirty years contributed to the Whiskey Rebellion, the first rebellion against the federal government, its new president, Washington, and the Union itself. As for the Seceders whom Washington met at Millers Run, they became involved in the rebellion that shook the nation,[21] along with their counsel Brackenridge, who would play a leading role, and Washington, who would end it by invading the very country he had liberated from the British, using a federal army made up of militia from several states to quell the rebels of Western Pennsylvania.

FACTS OF THE CASE

Washington and Crawford

Washington's involvement with the Millers Run property began with Virginia governor Dinwiddie's proclamation of February 19, 1754, in which bounties were offered to entice the service of officers and soldiers in the French and Indian War. When the war was over, grants were reaffirmed in greater detail by the Royal Proclamation of October 7, 1763, as part of a project to prevent uncontrolled settlement in the West until Indian boundaries were established. Settlers inhabiting Indian lands before the 1768 Treaty of Fort Stanwix (covering land west of the Alleghany Mountains and south of the Ohio River) had to remove themselves.[22] The question was whether the land was open to survey by those who held military warrants. Shockingly, Pennsylvania began selling off protected land, to which Virginia objected as it had fought in the war to claim the same land.[23] Virginians feared that land grants from the king would similarly be seized or at the very least that they would be at the mercy of Pennsylvania law.

A lack of good faith on both sides exacerbated grievances as Virginia, too, granted hundreds of land certificates. The conflict between the two states went unresolved until they agreed on a boundary between them in 1779, resolving to respect each other's titles based on which had the earliest date.[24] In the same year, the Penn family divested its proprietorship of Pennsylvania land, granting it to the commonwealth in what many considered a wartime seizure.[25] In three of the Pennsylvania counties affected (Westmoreland, Fayette, and Washington), the rigorous system left behind by the Penns was challenged by permissive Virginia land laws, which meant that by 1785 some five hundred ejectments were initiated.[26] Still, some 659 settlers from November 1779 to June 1780 had their titles approved by commissioners appointed under the Virginia-Pennsylvania Agreement, and, based on the records of Washington, Alleghany, and Fayette Counties, Pennsylvania courts honored the agreement in all the claims brought before it.

Indian troubles, meanwhile, continued even in lands the Indians had ceded, and in 1782, with the defeat of troops under William Crawford's command in Sandusky, Ohio, attacks became even more frequent than when the British had allied with the Indians at the height of the revolution.[27] Nonetheless, with the establishment of a Land Office in 1781, Pennsylvania opened the 1768 land purchase and later the1784 "last purchase" from the Indians that essentially extended to the present western border of Pennsylvania.[28] The land rush to settle land west of the Alleghanies was on.[29]

This was the background of the collaboration between Washington and William Crawford, a friend and member of his regiment who became his land agent. Anxious to accrue lands for themselves, Washington and Crawford colluded as early as September 1767 to violate the proscriptions against entering Indian territory to claim land. In one illustrative instance, Washington proposed to secure "some of the most valuable Lands in the Kings part . . . notwithstanding the Proclamation that restrains it at present & prohibits the Settling of them at all."[30] Washington suggested to Crawford that since Pennsylvania would not allow the amount of land he wanted, he might evade its proscription by making several smaller entries if the cost was not too great, "but this I only drop as a hint leaving the whole to your discretion & good management." He asked Crawford to keep his secret and confide only in those he trusted to help him. Washington was concerned that he might meet with disapproval if discovered and that the scheme he was proposing might be overturned, "all which may be avoided by a Silent management & the [scheme] snugly carried on by you under the pretence of hunting other

Game."[31] Crawford confirmed Washington's plan: "I had the same Sceem in my head but was at a loss how to accomplish it, wanting a Person in home I cold confide"; "you may Depend upon my Keeping the hole as a profond secreet and Trust the Seaching out the Land to my own Care." Six years later,when Crawford had trouble getting a warrant of his own, he offered to locate a spot, Little Kanhawa, "for [Washington's] own benefit & mine" such that Washington might depend upon his making "any Equil Devesion you shall propose." Washington's claim to the bounty land would be used to cover the whole amount, which Crawford would then divide with Washington however he wished.[32]

Washington had previously allied with Crawford when he tried to activate a land grant of two hundred thousand acres made to the 1st Virginia Regiment. He petitioned the then governor Botetourt and the Council of Colonial Virginia in 1769 to permit the regiment to appoint a surveyor and pursue its own surveys, by which he meant Crawford, with the excuse that should the work be done by a county surveyor, it would "be greatly retarded."[33] He later elaborated: there were "few men at that early day, hardy enough to undertake a work, in a wilderness where none but Savages & wild beasts inhabited."[34]

On October 18, 1770, following an August meeting of the regiment, Washington and Crawford traveled to the western lands to explore possible sites on the Ohio River; Washington was to give the orders and Crawford was to report to him.[35] Even before Crawford was directed to begin surveying (on November 3, 1771) under a "special commission,"[36] he and Washington were "at home all day Plotting & Measuring [Crawford's] Surveys."[37] Complaints surfaced from regimental grant holders that prime lands went to Washington while their own plots were void of rich flatland.[38] Among others, one veteran, George Muse, objected to the Virginia Council on being shortchanged in his allotment and was given his full share; Washington defended his process at length, complaining that it was an impossible task and "the source of much discontent at a division."[39]

In 1774, convinced Crawford's reputation was suspect, Augusta County surveyor Thomas Lewis refused to record surveys Crawford "returned," intimating that his commission was only gotten through Washington's efforts. Officials of Fincastle County complained as well, accusing him of encroaching on other claims in his surveys.[40] The Masters of William and Mary College, however, deferred to Crawford and brought no charges against him.[41] But one incident raised serious questions for Washington, who heard that patents authorized under the Proclamation of 1754 had been nullified. He appealed on April 3, 1775, to Virginia governor Dunmore, pained to hear that regimental land surveys were invalid after the great expense members had undergone and "after we had proceeded in all respects agreeably to the orders of Government." Dunmore stood firm. He responded that the information referred to a report that the surveyor of those lands, Crawford, was not qualified under the Act of Assembly of 1748. "[I]f this is the Case," he advised, "the Patents will of Consequence be declared Null and Void."[42]

While the catastrophe Dunmore predicted was avoided,[43] this was the second time Washington's patents were threatened. On September 24, 1773, Governor Dunmore had advised Washington that he did "not mean to grant any patents on the Western Waters." Washington countered that the king had removed any constraints on doing so; a council directive followed to the same effect.[44] Washington went further. He sent a letter on February 17, 1774, to county surveyor Thomas Lewis of Augusta County, Virginia, the jurisdiction in which Millers Run was then located. Washington argued that the survey he enclosed was made for him "in that country" by Crawford (that is to say, "actually" made on the ground, as required). He intended either to use the survey for a patent under the Proclamation of 1763 or to use his bounty grant for a "New Colony" on the Ohio being pursued by disaffected settlers.[45] Having heard provincial officers like himself might not be covered by the royal grant, Washington proposed that Lewis provide him with a certificate of survey for a patent on Millers Run; he would pay Lewis "the same fees, as if actually surveyed by yourself, or Deputy."[46] Indeed, neither the grant in Governor Dinwiddie's 1754 Proclamation (to "all who shall voluntarily enter into" the King's service) nor the affirmation in the Royal 1763 Proclamation (to "the Officers and Soldiers of our Armies") specifically incorporated provincials. Washington attributed the omission to a "malignant disposition towards us poor Americans,"[47] an "injustice" to provincial officers whose service was "as worthy of regard" as that of regular officers.[48]

Washington's complaint had an unintended effect. Andrew Lewis, the brother of the Augusta County surveyor and a surveyor himself, advised Washington in March that any patent on "two Surveys You Send the Work of" would be illegal and void and the surveyor (Crawford) could lose his bond.[49] Lewis promised to conceal that Washington's two surveys were not part of the two hundred thousand acres granted to the regiment, but he felt it was unsafe to certify Crawford's work: "Obtaining a Patent in a way similar to what You desire" had in another case "made so great a Noise that it is in every bodys Mouth, & in Particular the Lawyers who say that it may be set a side at any time."[50] County surveyor Thomas Lewis appears to have advised Washington to have his tracts resurveyed by a surveyor commissioned by the county; Washington pursued a commission for Crawford, uncertain whether Lewis would accept him as a deputy. He then recruited Peter Hog[51] to assist Crawford in his immediate and "highly necessary" qualification, which would require Hog to act as a surety for Crawford's bond; Washington promised to indemnify him. Aware the county court was not going to meet, Washington asked Hog "through your Means" to get Crawford sworn, "as a few of the Magistrates, & Clerk, may be convened to do this business."[52]

Despite Andrew Lewis's warnings, Washington persisted in working with Crawford to gain patents for lands Crawford discovered for him. He was especially interested in an attractive tract of 2,813 acres called Millers Run (sometimes referred to as Chartiers Creek or Sh[e]rtees Creek),[53] which Crawford first identified in September 1767 (Crawford did not specify its location until April 20, 1771, or claim to have drafted a survey until August 2 of the same year).[54] A month before the 1786 trial, however, Washington backdated the survey, claiming it was first done "in the fall of 1770 or early in the following year" (presumably when Crawford and he located regimental bounty land).[55] In any event, Crawford did not send a "draft" of the "Shertees Land don Agreeable to Mr Lewis Derection" until May 8, 1774, which Washington forwarded to Thomas Lewis.[56] On July 5, 1774, Washington's patent for Millers Run was awarded. This did not, unfortunately, mean that Washington had unimpeded title to the land. Seceder settlers (a breakaway sect from the Presbyterian Church of Scotland)[57] had occupied the property continuously from 1773 until 1784 when Washington traveled to view the land and "receive the final determination of those who live upon it." They refused his offer of tenancy. Two days later, Washington met with and engaged Thomas Smith to file an ejectment suit.[58]

The problems related to Crawford's status as a surveyor and the legitimacy of his survey (upon which the patent's validity and Washington's legal title depended) thus resurfaced after a hiatus of ten years, by which time Crawford had been killed at the 1782 battle of Sandusky.[59] Washington had already reached out to Thomas Lewis on February 1, 1784, reminding him of Crawford's 1774 survey and revealing he could not account for it. Suggesting the survey had been "arrested" in the land office "by some very ungenerous, & unjustifiable attempts of different people, at different times, to disturb me in my right to it," he reminded Lewis that Crawford acted as a deputy surveyor under Lewis's direction. Washington was beginning to inoculate his case against accusations that could be made against Crawford, although he was reluctant to speak ill of his dead friend.[60]

Washington's Brief

Once he decided to file the ejectment suit on the Millers Run property, Washington prepared a brief of his arguments. The provenance of Washington's brief on the ejectment case is as follows. It was enclosed with a July 14, 1785, letter of instruction to his lawyer. Washington referred to the brief in the following terms: "I have a paper enclosed, put down the foundations and evidence in support of my title. . . . As also the pleas which

I *suppose* will be urged in behalf of my opponents, in opposition thereto," much like notes of a trial argument. Smith assured Washington he kept the papers in Bedford "locked up in a Private drawer of mine," trusting no one else to handle them.[61] He planned to return the papers to his client after the trial but apparently never did so;[62] they were rediscovered in the basement of an old building in Carlisle, where Smith had his office.[63] Burton Alva Konkle, who recovered and transcribed the manuscript brief, describes the document as

> eight foolscap pages, each page arranged in two columns, the first showing the "Ground" and the second the "Evidence" [the plaintiff's case]. These are followed by five pages, arranged in similar manner . . . showing the "Pleas" in one column and the "Answers" in the other [the defendants' case].[64]

In Konkle's transcription of the papers, a list of witnesses is included on which the title "George Washington's Brief" appears as well as notes, which Konkle affirms are in Smith's hand, of an interview with Washington titled "Brief of General Washington's Land on Miller's Run."

Washington's Grounds

Under "Grounds," Washington listed thirteen premises upon which to build his case for title to Millers Run: the military claim (1), Crawford's survey (2), his bond, warrant, and patent (3), previous occupancy (4, 5, 6, 7), Washington's improvements (8), the patent (9), disputed claims (10, 11), Land Office regulations (12), and respect for state titles (13). First, he argued that William Crawford and he each had the right to a military claim and joined forces, Crawford to find land and Washington to secure warrants. As evidence, he cited letters between them. Second, Washington claimed that, at his request, the Masters of William and Mary College granted Crawford a surveyor's commission; based on that commission, Crawford made an "actual survey" covered by the 1754 proclamation's offer of military land bounties. Washington claimed the survey was created prior to occupation of the land by the defendants and Crawford returned a certificate of the survey to Washington. Washington did not claim to have "entered" the survey with the county surveyor or the county court at that time and admitted he was unable to find evidence of it, "tho' he well recollects to have been possessed of it."[65]

Washington then vindicated his position under the proclamation of 1763. Only those entitled to grants for military service were permitted "before, at, and after this period" to occupy the western lands, locate lands, or take patents, so that the defendants were in violation of "then existing Government." Even supposing he had no prior claim to the land, his survey was made long before the settlers arrived "consequent of a Military claim which I had purchased from Capt, Posey." Here, Washington's brief claims that John Posey's bond for the land was dated October 14, 1770; that "the Land was covered [for survey] as soon as a Warrant could be obtained"; and that the warrant "as he presumes it will appear by the Patent . . . is not dated until the 25thof Nov.r." He admits he cannot explain the lapse of time between "purchase of the Right, and the obtainment of the Warrant" but acknowledges it advantages the defendants who "pretend they came to the Land in Octobr. 1773," a month before the warrant. Thus, the settlers "will say Washington can derive no benefit" from the warrant, which "should be guarded against." According to Washington, on the one hand the settlers had no "legal, or equitable claim" because of the bond and the presumed warrant (assuming it was confirmed by the patent); on the other hand, should they discover the lapse of time "it is supposed they will lay much stress on it."[66]

Washington thereafter presented the grounds of occupancy. Two prior parties attempted to occupy the land. The first was bought off by Crawford and the second discovered "marked trees" (regarded as a "tomahawk" claim) and "upon tracing them, finding a regular Survey" made by Crawford for the benefit of Washington, they quit the land. A letter from Crawford and the testimony of Colonel Cannon were evidence of this. As for notice, Washington argued the settlers had been informed repeatedly of his claim and "ordered to leave the Land." The settlers "expressed that they had seen the advertisements" and might "deny it all or be silent at the trial," but letters (from Crawford and his brother Valentine, both deceased) and witnesses (he names nine of them) evidenced this. Moreover, that the land was "generally believed" to be Washington's from before the settlers occupied his tract was, for Washington, sufficient evidence to overcome any "plea of ignorance" as justification for their possession of the land. They had either to become tenants or suffer the consequences, as he "was determined to prosecute his Right." Washington thereafter represented that he had expended money and made improvements on the land prior to their arrival, while they blocked the entrance to the one cabin that "remains there to this day unless it has been removed, or destroyed," to which several of the same witnesses could attest.[67]

With the history of the property dispatched, Washington asserted Crawford's appointment by the College of William and Mary in the spring of 1774 as deputy to the county surveyor Thomas Lewis in Augusta County, "in which County the Land *then* lay."[68] Crawford thereafter returned a "certificate" (of the survey) to the secretary of the Land Office, upon which a patent was awarded with the colony's seal and the governor's signature. As no records survived to support Crawford's commission or the return of the certificate, Washington provided a certification from the Virginia register of the Land Office "that the Survey with many other papers" were destroyed by the enemy during the war so that records antecedent to the patent could not be produced. Washington claimed that June or July of the year of the patent (1774) "was as early as any legal survey were made, or could be made, in that country." Critically central to his brief, he presented his most lawyerly argument: that the survey "with the proceedings antecedent thereto which were of record, being lost, nothing but presumptive proof can be drawn from thence—this however must be as strong as any presumptive proof whatever can be." He argued that since public offices must act according to the rules, regulations, "Law and Constitution of the Country in which they are instituted," to doubt his patent—"the last act for transferring the right of the crown"—was no less than to charge the executive of the state with "mal-administration."[69]

Reviewing the law, Washington cited the Virginia Act of 1779 for settling claims to the effect that all surveys before January 1, 1778, were "good & valid" so long as they were made "by the Surveyor of the County" and against which no caveat had been entered (sec. I). He added, moreover, that "*Military* locations by *actual* Surveys made under *special* commission, should *become* valid upon taking out Warrants and resurveying according to Law." Washington called special attention to a letter from John Harvie, register of the Land Office, which provided "much useful information" and the rules of the land office. While he conceded that the steps outlined in the 1779 act should have been taken, he argued they were "altogether unnecessary" for he had complied with all the legal forms four years before the Act, presumably referring to his patent.[70]

Finally, Washington's "grounds" undermined the claims of the defendants to title. First, they never offered a caveat to issuance of his patent during the nine months from their occupation of the land to Washington's patent. Nor had they made any attempt to secure the land legally for themselves in Virginia or Pennsylvania, leaving them entirely reliant upon their "violent intrusion" onto the land. Washington offered a declaration by the Virginia register of the Land Office to the effect that there were no caveats or applications for title on that office's records, that is, there was no location made "in this State" by the occupants, or on their behalf, and the defendants did not appear "from the records" to have applied to commissioners established under the 1779 Virginia Act "to hear & determine disputed titles."[71] Contrarily, the agreement between Pennsylvania and Virginia respected the rights of those who held titles under "either Country" prior to running the boundary. Washington enclosed authenticated copies of both documents.[72]

Settlers' Pleas

Having laid out the case for legal title, Washington constructed the presumed defense of the settlers in terms of nine sets of "Pleas" and

"Answers": Crawford's reputation (1), the survey (2), the settlers' occupancy (3), Washington's improvements (4), conflicting claims (5, 6, 7), and previous occupancy (8, 9). They would rely upon an attack on Crawford's involvement as a "land jobber" whose survey, "a private one," was unauthorized and thereby invalid. They would argue that Crawford used "the names of people of influence" to "cover his claims" so that those who wanted land would have to purchase it from him. Washington answered he had no hand in Crawford's enterprises and "no credit could be given" to the charge that Crawford's land belonged to Washington. Nor had he "a foot of Land in the Western Country," other than by military right and two tracts he had purchased, so that "to attempt to deprive me of the little I have is, considering the circumstances under which I have been, and the inability of attending to my own affairs, not only unjust, but pitifully mean."[73]

The settlers would claim to have searched the land office and found no record of a patent or survey certifying Washington's title. Had they taken "proper pains" to obtain the evidence, he answered in response, they would have known "this land was reputed" to be his. They would claim their occupancy preceded legal action on Washington's part, referring to Crawford's deputation and legal return of the survey, so that preference should be given to their possession of the land, which was "prior to the *date* of the Warr. and to Capt.n Posey." The burden was on the defendants to prove that fact, Washington answered, alleging he had taken measures under the Act of 1779 that "must obviate every plea of this kind." The defendants were bound to claim the land was abandoned when they arrived; Washington would argue the settlers themselves had obstructed the entrance to the house built there and Crawford had placed an agent, who was away, "to keep possession," to which witnesses and a letter from Crawford would attest.[74]

Further, they would argue even a good patent might be forfeited for lack of improvement on the land, "which was required by Law, and which is conditional of the Grant." Washington's answer was that he was the victim, having had his land "violently detained" from him; that his people working from the Great Kanhawa lands toward the tract could have "saved this tract" but for the Indians who "forced them to abandon the work . . . and the unjustifiable conduct of themselves." Moreover, the settlers could not claim they had no "*legal* notice" to quit his land. "What *really* is, or *may* be construed, legal notice in such a case, is not for me to decide," he answered, claiming he had in effect provided "legal" notice through Crawford or otherwise. Finally, he argued, the settlers would contend they had improved the land "at great expence" under the conviction that it was unclaimed, so that they "ought not in Law or equity to be deprived of it." Washington answered that they "certainly must be in their own wrong, and not to the loss of my property—for was the case otherwise, no one could be secure in Lands at a distance—as possession & occupancy would set aside the best title, and put legal right at defiance."[75]

Strategic Considerations

Viewing Washington's brief in the context of his correspondence helps to assess his argument. Before Washington crafted his brief, Smith had written to lay out his progress since his hire.[76] He addressed procedural matters, advising his client that while he was at the Washington County court he prepared and delivered ejectments against the defendants and that the sheriff served them "with a degree of regularity not very usual in that County," an indication of Smith's political skills. His most immediate problem was lack of information. He asked for authentication of Posey's bond and the entry of the warrant by the county surveyor. On Virginia law, he asked Washington to point out any that might apply: "Does the occupier forfeit his right of Pre-emption if he does not apply for an office-right, in a given Time?"; "If so, when?"; "by what Law? or is it by the regulations established in the Land office?"

Smith had filed the case in the county court on Washington's instructions and planned to move the case to the highest Pennsylvania court with speed. He had already delivered writs to that purpose so that prothonotary Thomas Scott (brother of one of the defendants) might certify and transmit them.[77] If "safe conveyance" could not be had, Smith would forward them himself to "enter" the case with the Supreme Court before the next term "that they might be ready for Trial as soon as it may be thought proper." Smith described his procedural tactics:

> I had good information that James Scott Junr had the most plausible claim, & that he was the ringleader or director of the rest; I therefore resolved to take the Bull by the horns, & removed the Ejectments into the Supreme Court in such order, as to have it in my power to try the Ejectment against him before the rest, reserving the Rule; so that had any unforeseen point turned up against me, I could try the rest or not as I pleased.[78]

Anticipating the trial, Smith and Washington discussed possible co-counsel. Smith considered the case "a matter of too much importance" for him to proceed unassisted: "especially as I would have the strong & fomented prejudices of Party to contend with, and I have some reason to believe that a good deal of art & management were used, before the People were prevailed with to stand the Ejectments." He suggested Lancaster County lawyer Jasper Yeates[79] in the event Washington's choice, James Wilson,[80] were unavailable, with an eye to his experience in Western Pennsylvania. Washington acknowledged that he felt an obligation to Wilson, implying legal expertise was not his first consideration. He was later to confirm the case was "so clear & self-evident, that I think nothing more is necessary but to state facts."[81] Although Wilson would have lent a name of some consequence to the proceedings, Washington left the matter to Smith who chose in the end neophyte Washington County lawyer James Ross,[82] with whom Washington was perfectly satisfied.[83] Smith appears to have used Ross as little more than an assistant.

On a more substantive matter, Washington expressed to Smith his preference for prosecuting based on Virginia law, an acknowledgment that Pennsylvania's customs and usage would benefit settlers' preemption rights. The pattern of migration to Western Pennsylvania is telling on the question of the choice of law for Washington's suit. One stream of settlers came from the northeast; these more ethnically diverse settlers had a mid-Atlantic sensibility and were loyal to Pennsylvania. A second stream came from Maryland and Virginia and had a more homogeneous English character and were loyal to Virginia. The boundary dispute between Virginia and Pennsylvania was related to the conflicting loyalties of these two streams. But it was also a question of the different land systems and grants associated with each state. Virginia's system was much looser and the validity of its grants to individuals was tenuous, while Pennsylvania had an established system of applications and patents, a difference that burdened the court system.[84] The irony was that settlers used the courts (or avoided them) of either or both states, paid taxes, and voted (or did not) in either or both without a preference for one jurisdiction or another, so that by 1785 they had a more inclusive sense of citizenship and one less identified with individual states, a process begun when states embraced common cause and minimized their differences in the war.[85]

For Virginia's stability, it was vital that its "territorial integrity as a fundamental attribute of independent statehood" be respected; only with its rights as a state and its sovereignty protected (as a condition of its cession of western land to the Union—allowing Congress to sell public land and establish new states—and its resolution of conflicting land claims with Pennsylvania) could Virginia define state boundaries with its neighbors and accept Congress' power to oversee commerce and taxation.[86] Pennsylvanians were frustrated that Virginia's land rights would supersede those of Pennsylvania, and that Congress was intent on authority over western land; proposals for a new state represented an enticing prospect for Western Pennsylvania's territorial integrity.[87] Pennsylvania was slow to pick up on what settlers wanted. Even when the agreement with Virginia should have made for clean transfers and peaceful jurisdiction, confusion still reigned based on popular unrest, confusion about the arrangements, and a sense that it was not permanent, together with growing separatist support in the West and antiwestern sentiment in the East.[88] In the midst of such jurisdictional fluidity, people's rights were in flux, a problem the state failed to recognize or address and which would contribute to the rebellion that would follow in 1794.[89] Settlers had begun to think of themselves as national citizens, and statehood was devalued as citizens felt they had been denied the benefits of citizenship promised by the revolution. Pennsylvanians would insist on having a say about how they were governed.

In his pursuit of a legal strategy, and at Smith's request, Washington had solicited from John Harvie of the Virginia Land Office advice on applicable Virginia land law.[90] Washington framed his request in terms of the "manner in which titles to Lands were acquired by improvement or occupancy, by the Laws & customs of Virginia."[91] Harvie responded with a fulsome review of the law and regulations "by which I Conceive your Title must be determin'd."[92] They included the 1763 proclamation, the 1779 Virginia and Pennsylvania Agreement, the 1779 act for resolving claimants' disputes, and the 1748 act on surveyors' duties. Harvie saw no general principle in the laws or ordinances of Virginia regarding Washington's title to Millers Run. He did, however, note that according to the 1779 act for settling claims[93] Washington's surveys on all military rights were "good and valid" with the exception that where "locations" on military warrants conflicted with the rights of settlers, settlers were to be preferred. This did not apply, however, where "Warrants [were] Carry'd into Effect by actual Survey, and much less so to Patents which have been Regularly Obtain'd under our former Government." Washington's survey had not, of course, carried a warrant into effect, nor was his patent obtained regularly (as the survey was not entered), although his title was tied to a military bounty, which entailed a more permissive process. Harvie concluded the law favored Washington's title. He made the case that from the 1763 proclamation until the opening of the Virginia commonwealth Land Office in 1779, only patents upon surveys for lands given as bounty for military service were permitted; titles by occupancy were not recognized by Virginia law until 1775. Moreover, no county surveyor could "enter" (record) lands on any other than a military right, and in 1778 a resolution prohibited any farther settlement of the western lands until a Land Office had opened. Settlers, Harvie reported, "were by repeated proclimations Order'd off from those Lands."

Contrary to Harvie's reading, the settlers' occupancy in 1773 fell outside the 1778 prohibition, although they could not enter a survey; yet should Washington's survey be invalid so might his patent, which relied upon it. Putting Washington's patent and survey aside (and discounting Pennsylvania case law), Harvie described the only way the occupants could conceivably prevail based on the 1779 act. They could establish "a Right of Settlement founded upon a Residence of twelve months or raiseing a Crop of Corn in the Country" (sec. V) upon which the commissioners were to grant the entitled party a "Certificate of such Right," which authorized the county surveyor to survey the lands. Once the survey was returned to the Land Office and six months had passed for any "caveat" to be offered against the land, "an ex officio grant would issue." Should the occupants proceed on this course, however, Harvie presumed Washington's prior attempts at settlement and improvement preceded theirs. Harvie also held Washington's patent was "Conclusive to the Title" since the settlers failed to enter a caveat against it and could not show a commissioner's certificate giving them preference.[94] On these grounds, Washington's title was "Unimpeachable." Finally, Harvie claimed, the Virginia-Pennsylvania boundary agreement of 1779 gave "permanency" to Washington's title. Like other military grantees who feared their land would be confiscated if the boundary agreement was not honored, Washington considered Pennsylvania legally bound by its 1779 compact to respect land claims Virginia had certified; the two states had a duty of honor to which they could be held accountable. As he was to affirm throughout his life as a private and public man, a state no less than an individual retained a reputation for honor that bespoke its character.

Applying Virginia law in a Pennsylvania court, however, posed a problem for Washington's case: Why would a Pennsylvania court use Virginia law to settle a question on Pennsylvania land when Pennsylvania law tended to support settlers and Virginia law preferred land titles? As counsel Hugh Henry Brackenridge for the Millers Run occupants admonished, it was settlers who had "defended and cultivated during the Indian depredations upon that quarter, at the expence [*sic*] of life in many instances." Westerners especially objected to the prospect of ejecting settlers and ceding the rights of Pennsylvanians to Virginians. Such moves smacked of a taking by eminent domain that could not be justified without compensation, which neither Washington nor the state of Pennsylvania was prepared to do.[95] Still, Smith appreciated the Pennsylvania Supreme Court's affinity for legal title and its willingness to reverse the legislature's preference for settlers. Nor was the high court impressed by rulings of county courts, which protected settlers' improvement claims measured by marks made on trees. Washington and his lawyer had, in fact, decided to pursue a jury trial (nisi prius) before the higher court on circuit from Philadelphia.[96] It was much more likely to prove deferential to a figure who had just secured the nation's independence and was prepared to invest in creating new wealth for the country.

Washington was not yet on solid ground. His alternative argument depended upon a settlement right of his own based on improvements, which meant he had to address the law on abandonment and its requirement that he ought to have lived on the land. The 1779 act required a "crop of corn in that country" or at least one year of residence, which would disqualify Washington. There was also a question of "what has always been the law and usage of this State" (identified in the 1786 act on a limited right of preemption), which would also have disqualified him. Such usage required "an actual personal resident settlement, with a manifest intention of making it a place of abode, and the means of supporting a family, and continued from time to time."[97] Even the terms of his patent required cultivating and improving within three years three acres of every fifteen,[98] giving Washington until June or July 1777 to comply. As Pennsylvania Supreme Court Chief Justice McKean held in a dispute dating from 1784–1785, "It could not be seriously pretended that [a] four log improvement, never prosecuted for twenty-eight years, could be deemed the shadow of a right. To give an improvement any equity whatsoever, it must not have the smallest cast of an abandonment."[99]

No matter how he argued the case, Washington faced a procedural block that was an explicit criterion in weighing legal title against actual settlement: the standard for reasonable time. The Millers Run settlers had resided on Washington's land for eleven years before he filed for ejectment. The Pennsylvania Supreme Court in *Patrick Campbell, Lessee v. Benjamin Kidd* (1774) considered such a time frame encouragement to settlers to improve the land, an assent to usage that "amounts to an implied contract" between the parties, limiting legal title and supporting the settler's right to preemption. The time frame extended well beyond the seven years that settlers had to wait to gain possession under a 1705 act "still in force" and under a 1785 act.[100] Even the survey was untimely. On this issue, Brackenridge had asked "will a settler be bound to read a survey in appearance years old, as one which had been recently made?" Here, a 1783 act[101] required that a distinction be made between a survey years old and a recent one; as Brackenridge noted, "The surveyor general had no power to take such surveys off the file and attach them to a warrant,"[102] a subterfuge that applied to Washington's management of his claim.

Washington's wait for over a decade to file for ejection added to his inability to validate his title. Having represented in his brief that he had been "violently detained" from the land by the settlers and his people had been prevented from reaching the tract by the Indians, he could have invoked a provision of the March 26, 1785, act (sec. V) that permitted a person driven away "except by the judicial authority of the state"[103] to recover his lands. He did explain in a letter to John Harvie[104] that his absence from home for nine years and efforts to keep his papers "out of the enemy's reach" accounted for his failure to provide proof of title, a foundation upon which Smith would build to engender favorable treatment from Chief Justice McKean. In any case, the time was ripe for Washington to file his case. Property prosecutions tended to increase sharply when a war ended,[105] congressional jurisdiction had resolved conflicting land claims by Virginia, New York, Maryland, and Connecticut,[106] and Pennsylvania's newly opened Land Office became fully operational by 1784, leading squatters to petition the Pennsylvania Assembly repeatedly for preference on lands they had improved.[107] For Washington, it was now or never to address the situation at Millers Run.

WASHINGTON'S ARGUMENT

With the suit moving forward, Washington had to face immediate problems related to his evidence. Smith's notes in response to Washington's brief[108] were, for example, preoccupied with Washington's mistaken dates, missing or unauthenticated documents, and erroneous timelines, which were confused further as Smith tried to clarify them. Washington himself attributed an "unaccountable," "unlucky," "incomprehensible" "mistake" for his inability to provide proof of the bond and warrant verifying his right to Millers Run.[109] John Posey's bond transferred his military bounty of three thousand acres in exchange for relief of a debt he owed Washington.[110] The date of Posey's warrant was critical as authorization to survey the property. Having claimed in his legal brief that the date of Posey's bond was October 14, 1770 (preceding the October 1773 occupation of Millers Run), Washington was "exceedingly surprised" to find "Posey's Warrant was not dated till the 25th day of Novr 1773," postdating the occupancy by a month.[111] Furthermore, Posey had offered his right to the land to Washington in a letter of May 25, 1771, well after the presumed date of the bond.[112] Washington assumed the patent he ultimately received for Millers Run on July 5, 1774, would include the date for the warrant,[113] but it stated only that the grant was made by means of an assignment by Captain John Posey to Washington of his right by proclamation to a military land bounty of three thousand acres.[114] In fact, it included no date whatever for a bond, warrant, or survey.

Washington tried as well to resolve that part of his argument upon which the validity of his patent most depended: the persistent questions of Crawford's commission and the missing survey and warrant. In summary, Washington had argued in a 1769 petition that the regiment did not want a county surveyor; it received permission for a special commission for the regiment's military bounty acreage, the right to appoint its own surveyor, and to pursue its own survey, resulting in Crawford's appointment and survey. Five years later, Andrew Lewis revealed that Washington's land was not covered by the special commission as his tracts were not part of the regimental acreage. Washington continued to rely on Crawford's special commission, arguing a military warrant covered the survey he could not produce and ignoring the requirement that a county surveyor ought to have conducted the survey. Washington promised the missing survey would show the date of the warrant and the patent would show the date of the warrant (which it did not).

To have it both ways, Washington noted "at the time this survey was *returned* to the Office—Mr Crawford was Deputy surveyor to Mr [Thomas] Lewis," recalling in a letter to Harvie that Crawford qualified as a deputy to the county surveyor of Augusta in 1774.[115] Washington thus presumed that "no person could more legally" have acted than Crawford, although Crawford's deputation occurred after the "regimental" survey and after occupancy, but before the "return" and the patent. In addition, Washington consistently referred to a single survey, which raises the question of Washington's offer to pay Thomas Lewis for Crawford's 1774 survey on the pretext it was made by the county surveyor. In support of his single-survey argument, Washington also declared in the Harvie letter "that no survey was ever made of this Land, but the first one by Crawford," effectively discounting a second one in 1774. Washington thus appeared to have arrived at the position he posited in his brief: that a legally appointed person had conducted his survey; that it was covered by military warrant, validated by the county surveyor, and patents were issued on them.[116]

Just before the trial,[117] Washington tried to coordinate the commissions, warrants, surveys, and returns further. He now claimed two surveys, such that "the legal return of the first differing in dates, were both made by Captn (afterwards Col.) Crawford." This version had the land "explored & surveyed for me the first time, in the fall of 1770, or early in the following year," so that Crawford's "first" survey was now dated significantly earlier than the August 2, 1771, date when Crawford produced a draft. Washington held that the "first" survey was made under the military commission. The "second" survey (which appears to have been a resurvey and which Washington, for some reason, refers to both as the "second" survey and the "return") was made after Crawford's deputation by Lewis, which Washington believed "did not happen, 'till Feby 1774." In truth, the "second" survey could not have been returned until after Crawford provided Washington in May of that year a "second" survey draft "don agreeable" to Lewis's direction.[118]

The development of Washington's argument tells us several things. For one, it supports Governor Dunmore's (1775) and Andrew Lewis's (1774) cautions about the illegality of the survey(s). Washington's arguments about "one" or "two" survey(s) were evidence of deception; his offer to pay Thomas Lewis a fee "as if" the county office had surveyed the property was evidence of misrepresentation; his pretense that his land fell within the penumbra of regimental acreage, his denial that the survey was the work of a friend or a private agent, and his representation that Crawford's first survey was proper, were potentially evidence of fraud.[119] Similarly, Washington fudged his argument to conflate the 1771 and the 1774 surveys, so that the "return" would represent a second step to the first survey rather than a resurvey. The link from the first to the second survey was unsustainable, as was the connection between Crawford's 1771 special commission and his 1774 county deputation. Washington could not conflate them however mightily he tried; they were separate qualifications under separate agencies with separate justifications.

If Washington's patent depended upon the survey, it also depended upon how Crawford qualified as a surveyor. Regulations in the 1748 act covering the duties of surveyors required his oath and that the bond be certified by a justice of the county court (sec. I); otherwise, "every survey, and other matter of thing, so by him done under colour of office, shall be illegal and void" (sec. I). Further, a surveyor must "enter for lands" before a justice, and not an assistant of the county or some other official like the county surveyor. Should he fail to do so, the entry was "illegal and void," such that another person could survey and apply for a patent on the same land (sec. III). As no county court was held in March 1774, no justice was available the month Crawford intended to be sworn, making it likely a clerk or other county official administered his oath. Moreover, there was no record Crawford had entered the survey. Failing on either count, Crawford's "Work" (Andrew Lewis's term) was illegal and void.[120] If any more proof were needed, Crawford's authorization to begin surveying for the regiment came a month after Washington and Crawford had already divided up and assigned the regimental bounty land; and Washington did not have the required warrant to authorize the survey until two years after the survey. Importantly, the challenge to Crawford's surveyor's license was only fully resolved by the Masters of the College of William and Mary through his deputation under County Surveyor Lewis after the occupancy. These were the elements out of which Washington crafted his legal brief.

TRYING THE SETTLERS

There was really only one option for which state would try the Millers Run case after Virginia and Pennsylvania resolved their boundary conflict in 1780; Pennsylvania now had clear jurisdiction over the Millers Run land. In the Pennsylvania system, the Washington County Court of Common Pleas would, as a matter of course, try the case as a civil case, with the right of appeal before the Pennsylvania Supreme Court acting in its role as appellate court. But the plaintiff successfully applied to the state's high court to take on the case in original jurisdiction, that is to act as trier of fact as a trial court, or nisi prius, and thereby to remove the case from the county court. The case was transferred to the Supreme Court with two of its justices set to preside and a local jury to render the verdict. In this role, the Supreme Court was not acting as an appeals court, which meant that any appeal would require a second appearance before the high court in its role as an appellate court, which would then review its own work as a trial court. In another turn of the screw, Washington's lawyer chose to try two other land cases in the Westmoreland County Court that he hoped would act as precedent for the Supreme Court in trying the Millers Run defendants. In fact, successful verdicts in those cases did aid him in the trial.

The appearance docket for the December 1784 term of the Washington County Court of Common Pleas shows a Washington ejectment suit set with a trial date for the twenty-eighth. The case was listed as *Lessee of George Washington, Esq. vs. Timothy Turnout, with notice to thirteen settlers.* The filing indirectly invoked Washington as the party who "demised" the tract to John Goodright. Represented by Thomas Smith, Goodright had taken possession of "3000" acres on July 7 for twenty years, a term, according to the docket, not yet expired. The docket accused the defendant, Timothy Turnout (a common placeholder name used on such suits) of ejecting Goodright from his seventeen "messuages" (a dwelling house, including any outbuildings), seventeen barns, and three thousand acres by "force and arms" on July 7. The "casual ejector" assigned to the case directed the defendant to appear, having been informed that Turnout had a claim to the title or was in possession of one for the premises. Should Turnout fail "to be made Defendant," judgment would be entered by default against the ejector and Turnout would "be turned out of possession." Konkle refers to this as "the preliminary entry to the case."[121] If Konkle is right (the case refers to 3,000 acres; Millers Run was 2,813 acres), the day after Washington received his patent he must have assigned the tract to Goodright who was ejected the next day by the thirteen settlers.

Who were these western settlers and what kind of social power did they have? Pennsylvania faced the incursion of large numbers of settlers, their preference for no government at all, and the separatism of those who wished to form a new state. Supported by the ideology of Indian removal, a system of trading posts, and a land office, the appetite of settlers for land overwhelmed forces for coexistence; treaties, proclamations, boundary lines, and laws could not hold back the settlers' westward expansion.[122] Clearly, they were locally based and integrated into their communities. On the one hand, competition for land meant they were engaged in considerable claim jumping, overlapping claims, and ejectments, as well as raids against Indian households and settlements to force Natives from the land. The power of county and state courts was not in their favor as land companies from the East amassed large tracts of land and Congress had turned its attention to creating new states in the western territory.[123] But settlers were well placed locally, including as justices of the peace, militia officers, and leaders of churches. The brother of the named defendant in Washington's Millers Run suit, for example, was Washington County clerk of courts and prothonotary. Settlers petitioned the state assembly for fairer representation and for preference over land titles, and they elected officials like Sheriff James Marshel friendly to their cause. In fact, Marshel's election prompted Washington's lawyer to delay proceedings until a more favorable judge could be seated.

Twenty years before the Seceder group at Millers Run settled there, Seceders, or Associate Presbyterians, broke from the Church of Scotland. They split from the Scottish church over taking communion and had the reputation of the sternest of Calvinists.[124] Their principled stubbornness was expressed in their intransigence regarding Washington's proposal that they buy the land rather than face a suit; in addressing Washington, each Seceder stood separately to refuse the offer. Similarly, in the Whiskey Rebellion, the subject of the next chapter, Seceder settlers refused to submit to the federal government and support the excise tax; they would pay their share of the federal revenue through their support of the state of Pennsylvania.[125]

In preparing for prosecuting the settlers in the Supreme Court, Washington produced the outline of a plan he hoped Smith and his cocounsel James Ross would follow.[126] Whether Smith in fact relied upon the plan is open to question, although he told Washington after the trial "it gave us [Ross and Smith] satisfaction that we had agreed to conduct the trial upon the Plan pointed out in that Letter, & that I had transcribed & brought up the cases from the Books [law reports and legal commentary], which were not to be had at Washington [County], to support the points on which you directed us to rely."[127] Washington's plan relied on two Virginia documents—orders of the Virginia Council and the Proclamation of 1763—which proved to his satisfaction that his military right and "warrants of survey" preceded the defendants' occupancy. He argued that their settlement contravened Virginia's express proclamation and was thereby illegal, that it invaded a private right (having been informed it was land "surveyed for me"), and that their conduct expressed "contempt for publick Authority." Washington neglected to mention that the same proclamation (like the 1779 act, usage codified in the 1786 act, the terms of his patent, and Pennsylvania case law on improvements) required of military claimants "the necessary and expedient . . . improvement and settlement [of the land]," conditions that interfered with Washington's intention to lease or sell his land.[128]

What followed in Washington's pretrial letter was an iteration of the core of his argument: the patent resolved all other issues as the "last solemn act of the Government"; he had been prevented from taking legal steps until the 1763 proclamation's restriction on military rights to the land had been lifted (evidenced by the issuance of the patent); in the alternative, he was still entitled to the land because his improvements proved preoccupancy; and he had the right of any citizen to own land and ought not to be deprived because he had absented himself to serve his country.

Washington's alternate theory depended upon witnesses, many of whom (including the most critical—William Crawford and his brother Valentine) were dead, others unwilling, and still others with only hearsay or presumptive knowledge.[129] Smith was cool to the alternate theory and even Washington raised questions about "indubitable facts" (his preoccupancy of the land, the evidence of his own improvements, the recognition of his claim by a previous occupant, and the repeated notices and warnings given the settlers), admitting "where the evidences are, or by what means they can be drawn forward to prove them" were questions he was unable to solve.[130] He recognized his witnesses would have no legal effect unless Crawford's letters were admitted and the witnesses he named appeared.[131]As one court opinion indicated, his fears were well founded; it held the use of witnesses "would make the titles of lands, which should be permanent and fixed . . . depend on parole evidence, and open a wide door to perjury."[132]

Beyond his instructions to Smith, Washington was open to using his personal appeal to sway the case. He repeatedly asked Smith when he thought the case would be scheduled and promised to attend if "nothing of greater importance should happen to prevent it" and he was in Western Pennsylvania at the time. Ultimately, however, he claimed the trial was "inconvenient" and that he did not see what he might add if he was present at the trial.[133] Smith remained unperturbed as he had not depended on Washington being present, relying more heavily on his knowledge of the courts, Pennsylvania precedents, and his political instincts. The choice of private prosecution, for example, allowed the plaintiff more leeway in presenting the crime, framing the law, and challenging the defendant's case. A creative form of localism linked to self-governance, it fit well with current ideas in rural areas and became so popular and accessible that the state tried to discourage it in 1804.[134] Western areas in Pennsylvania, Indiana, and Kentucky adopted it, while Virginia relied more heavily on the state to prosecute.[135] As law reports from 1791 to 1798 in the western counties of Alleghany, Washington, and Westmoreland demonstrated, land cases dealing with forcible entry, trespass, ejectments, and titles were prosecuted more frequently by private parties than the state at a rate of more than three to one (seventeen to five cases).[136] Largely used in property crimes, private prosecution's cost was sustained by the victim, tending to advantage the well-to-do.[137]

Smith's conduct of the case, as Washington related to Randolph, was also affected by "significant local interest in the issues of this case." Washington had been told that those "whose rights are disputed on similar grounds" were interested in the case as was the "lately chosen" high sheriff of the county who was dependent upon "the suffrages of these people in his election."[138] Washington expressed confidence that his title was so clear his opponents had little to argue "that can have the least weight with an impartial

Court & Jury";[139] still, he was attuned to the prospect that "as I apprehend there will be some management in obtaining the latter." The high local interest in the case and a western prejudice for settlers' improvements over legal titles led to concern for the independence of the jury, which concerned Washington: he believed summoning the jury so long before the case began would be "very much against me; for there can be no doubt but that every indirect (if not direct) means which the Defendts & their friends can adopt will be used to impress the members who constitute it."[140]

Aware of the political aspects of the case and the need to treat the jury with special care, Smith's attentiveness in following the Pennsylvania Supreme Court's circuit throughout the western courts and his familiarity with the justices had already proved profitable in getting the case scheduled before that court. His legal practice in multiple western counties enabled him to facilitate cooperation with filings and the certification and delivery of writs. To that purpose, according to Smith, prothonotary Scott proved helpful in speeding up the transition from the County Common Pleas Court to the state Supreme Court "that they might be ready for Trial, as soon as it may be thought proper."[141] Smith was a political animal focused on exploiting his connections and capitalizing on his knowledge of western courts. He explained to Washington he had been busy in Carlisle at the Cumberland County court, where from 1785 to 1790 he litigated an average of fifty cases a year, more than one-third of the court's yearly docket.[142] From Carlisle, he followed the Pennsylvania Supreme Court on its western circuit to Westmoreland where he met Chief Justice McKean, with whom he had a familiar relationship. McKean agreed to postpone the county court at Smith's request and told him he could share with Washington that the Supreme Court might hold a court of nisi prius in Washington County at the end of May or early June of the next year. Smith was not shy about telling McKean that as "several points of law would arise in [Washington's] Ejectments" he wanted to try the case in the higher court. Mc Kean responded that when the judges made their arrangements for the spring circuit "if Mr [Jacob] Rush will cross the mountains, he will come with him—(the difficulty is occasioned by some coolness, about rank, which subsists between the two other Judges)."[143] McKean would tell him as soon as the judges had fixed who would be going westward, and Smith promised to alert Washington should he "discover anything new." Washington's case, it became clear, received uncommon attention as comparable land disputes were often delayed as long as ten to twenty years.[144] Not only was this case pulled from the county court almost as soon as it appeared on the docket, but it was tried within two years as a civil case before Pennsylvania's highest court.[145] As an added bonus, when the high court tried a case in original jurisdiction, appeals were largely redundant, leaving the losing party without meaningful recourse.

Smith's apparent ease in navigating the venue was extended to his application for a struck jury to address Washington's concerns. Under Pennsylvania law, jurors could be drawn from a pool specific to one trial. Assuming local sentiment preferred the settlers, Smith ordered the appointing of the jury "in such a manner, as to be as free from objections of influence as possible." In fact, he advised Washington, a new law had jurors drawn by lot from a pool four times larger than the jury itself: "Neither party can certainly know one of the Men who may try his cause." Smith proposed to uncover the inclinations of the sheriff who would return the jurors, adding that if he had "the least reason to suspect that he will not be impartial" he would have the court name a special jury, which he would strike "with the assistance of your friends." When a local judge likely to be more favorable to the settlers, James Marshel, was elected in October 1785, Smith began considering a special jury.[146] He filed his request in the summer of 1786 after a potentially more friendly judge had been seated. Smith and Ross used most of their eighteen challenges to select a jury whose "social background" was wealthier than most juries, according to David Porter, and included the politically influential (two), elected militia officers (six), local office holders (seven justices of the peace), and leaders in their church (five). Compared to the Seceder settlers who occupied Millers Run, this jury was made up, importantly, of seven jurors who had held office when the area was under Virginia jurisdiction.[147] Short of actual jury-rigging, Smith chose jurors who had more in common with Washington than the settlers.

Smith's knowledge of western legal precedents and Pennsylvania law was equally significant as it offset the weakness attributable to witnesses. The witnesses that Smith interviewed had proved unreliable and "could not tell [him] with precision what they could testify." Nonetheless he considered that on the issue of land improvements the Supreme Court was "so materially variant from those of the County Courts of late" that he did not believe Washington's title would depend upon his witnesses, even if he suspected their testimony might prove useful. Several local precedents were in Smith's favor. He noted, for example, that "some ejectments have been Tried in Westmoreland; in which the Title of the Defendants was their improvement, made before the Plaintiffs had obtained their office right, notwithstanding which, the Plaintiffs recovered." In one trial where the jury was too decidedly in favor of improvements, the judge declared that an appeal for a new trial would be granted as the verdict "was contrary to Law." Smith drew the lesson that the jury was "so pointedly" opposed to "office rights" that under Pennsylvania jurisdiction the case must work as a precedent in Washington's favor.[148]

Before the trial, Smith tried an ejectment case that created a precedent for the Millers Run case, having brought improvements "fully before the Court" with an eye to Washington's ejectments. The plaintiff produced a survey;

Smith objected to settlers' improvements "being given in evidence" to challenge legal title; the defendant failed to give evidence; and Justice McKean gave the verdict to Smith's client. Smith expressed confidence that "this decision will produce very important effects on the Property of that County and will, I think shake the confidence of your opponents in the goodness of their Title"; he admitted to being "more sanguine" than previously about Washington's legal title. "I believe," he told Washington, "their decision [the Westmoreland cases] must very materially operate in your favour."[149]

On another matter of strategic importance, Washington had instructed Smith to bring actions of trespass against each of the Millers Run settlers on grounds of "mesne profit" (profits taken by a tenant in wrongful possession). Smith advised Washington this might convince the settlers he was determined to seek "every satisfaction which the Law can give you," but it might, equally, "produce a bad effect, in the minds of the jury": jurors might well find the defendants unfortunate rather than blameworthy, "as these double actions will well nigh ruin most of them."[150] Smith excused himself for taking the liberty of offering contrary advice and cited a trial that was very much on point in Westmoreland, "*a recovery* in ejectment." In that case jurors thought the defendants' improvements were more valuable than the plaintiff's "expences & loss." They found for the defendants, whereupon counsel on both sides agreed to send the jury out to reconsider. It returned with the same verdict, upon which the defense counsel agreed to damages to avoid the cost of a writ of error. According to Smith, had the action been taken "*before* the recovery in Ejectment," as Washington preferred, and should the defendant have gone to trial on the title again, the plaintiff might well have been obliged to pay the costs. Attentiveness to Pennsylvania law reports and attending other court cases clearly marked the difference between Smith's conduct of the case and Washington's argument.

James Scott's trial began after dinner on October 24, ran through the next day, and until eleven o'clock the morning of the twenty-sixth. With the verdict against Scott, Smith expected the defendants "would have confessed Judgments" rather than risk weaker cases with the same jury. He was, he admitted, mistaken; each insisted on a separate trial. But Smith, anticipating "that we had very strong prejudices, artfully fomented, to encounter" and that many of the jurors preferred to award the verdict to the settlers, had consolidated the cases so that reaching a verdict did not take long. He explained to Washington he "had applied to the Court to name the jury at a Time when the Bench was filled with such of the Justices as I believed would make out the most impartial list." When the defendants refused to strike the jury, he gave "them notice to attend [him] a certain Day at the Prothonotary's office in Philadelphia to strike." They not only struck the jury on the spot, but Smith rushed the jury list to Philadelphia, discovered what witnesses would be necessary, and "even *served* the Subpoenas on as many as attended the preceding County Court."[151] Like the rest of his preparation, Smith's management of the jury accounted for his client's wishes, western practices, legal precedents, and procedural niceties.

On a final note, there remains the question of payment for the lawyers. It appeared that Washington was interested in being compensated by the Seceders for his legal costs, which must have been substantial given Carlisle lawyer Smith's prodigious efforts in prosecuting on Washington's behalf and the fact that each defendant asked for a separate jury trial.[152] Smith's letters to Washington following the trial indicate his persistence in settling his fee. As for Brackenridge, he was no innocent bystander or pro bono altruist. Law reports show that previously Brackenridge had taken on cases on both sides of the ejectment question and that he had written to a Philadelphia speculator, Bernard Gratz, that he had given up representing settlers against whom Gratz had brought ejectments, as well as many whom Colonel Croghan (a land-grabber with whom Washington contested for western land) had ejected, intimating (presumably tongue-in-cheek) that Gratz should "soon begin to think it time the executors give me a handsome retaining fee to indemnify me."[153]

In the case of the Seceders, how and whether they paid Brackenridge's fees—particularly as he lost their case and their small farms suggested meager incomes—is unclear.[154] The Seceder church is a possible candidate. The Seceders had a congregation (Chartiers Associate Presbyterian) from the late 1770s and a minister, Reverend Matthew Henderson. The Seceders might have found payment in kind useful, given the scarcity of cash. Nonetheless when Washington suggested it to them as a means of settling their dispute, they turned it down.[155] Of some interest, once the Seceders lost the case, they offered Washington 80 percent of his original asking price for the land (which he summarily refused), an indication that they were not without funds to pursue their defense of the land.

Brackenridge might well have worked against his own best interest in getting paid, as in September, less than a month before the trial took place, he announced his candidacy for the state legislature, pursuing the office through anonymous letters to the *Pittsburgh Gazette*. Whereas the notoriety of the Millers Run trial probably generated votes, Brackenridge's campaigning was not likely to endear him to the dour Seceders; compensated or not for his trial defense, he was elected to the state assembly.[156]

CONCLUSION

Washington's legal brief formed a critical starting point for the strategy used in the Millers Run trial. His experience serving as a justice of the peace and on the county court was put to good use in considering the applicability and validity of statutes, documentary evidence, and witness testimony, as well as the value of appeals to emotion and political horse trading. Washington's brief and his subsequent arguments show him doggedly exploiting political connections, solving problems, trading favors, soliciting advice, and pursuing leads; he stated and reimagined his case in iterations that developed and shifted over time. If Washington was not a trained lawyer, he was also not above serving his own interests and benefiting from the law. Using collaborative techniques like those he applied working with members of his cabinet in his presidential years,[157] Washington was able to capitalize on Smith's talents in managing the case, the venue, and the jury, and exploiting contacts in legal circles. Smith complemented Washington's skills in accounting for legal technicalities and precedents and the nuances of courtroom practice from jury selection to judicial authority and the venue for the trial. Never a mere instrument of Washington's instructions, he shifted the emphasis of the case from Virginia to Pennsylvania law and pushed back where an alternate line of attack expressed weakness, unnecessarily complicated the case, or might prejudice the jury. In sum, the case took advantage of Washington's reputational capital and Virginia contacts and combined them with Smith's political instincts and ingenious application of western land law. The legal system in America was in a formative state. State assemblies debated laws with passion and rigor only to find custom and usage often had equal or greater sway. Statutes subjected to judicial interpretation yielded results that differed from those intended in assembly while the politics of choosing jurors and delivering jury verdicts had its own local effect on courts. Navigating the courtroom in the early years of the American republic required equal measures of procedural smarts, political acumen, and knowledge of courts and legal precedents.

On another front, Washington's local ambitions as a landholder and speculator had tested his ability to rise above collusion and corruption even if they did not define him in the same way they did James Wilson—who was ruined by them. Larger national needs would call him from entanglements over his properties, while his personal ownership of western land would tarnish his reputation for service and duty to the country. We cannot, as a result, fairly conclude the Millers Run case without addressing what Joseph J. Ellis calls the "patriarchal Problem." Washington's dealings with the thirteen settler families constituted, after all, a portrait of a not-altogether admirable character advancing his ambitions in a time of chaos and ambiguity with a sharp eye to navigating within the margins of legal constraints. Washington was, in this regard, a man like other men, even if he possessed considerably more natural and political resources to work with.[158] Washington's land policy when he was president, while it began with a gentlemanly pursuit of territory, somewhat like William Penn's diplomatic proprietorship, was in the end caught up in the great western land grab.[159]

Washington's engagement with the poor settlers who had to face off against the most powerful figure of the recent war presaged a career in government in which he guarded a hard-won reputation for service and yet benefited from that reputation legally and politically. In the Millers Run case, he initially took offense at what he considered a sinfully willful invasion of what he had hoped would be an impregnable source of his fortune. Later, his complicated relationship with the West informed his conviction that efforts to prevent people from breaching the land beyond the Alleghanies were a fool's errand as the region represented the future and the fortune of the new country, to which he was entitled a generous share.[160]

According to one critic, Washington was in a class of men despised in the western country as a "rapacious speculator" and a man whose public decisions were influenced by his private interests.[161] The Millers Run case is revealing, as a result, for the light it sheds on the question of Washington's character and for the importance of character to the stability of communities. As someone at the top of the plantation culture and a military officer, Washington was used to being greeted with deference by his lower-class neighbors, by Indians, merchants, slaves, and by his troops and fellow officers.[162] Whereas his lack of control over events in the Indian wars and against the French assaulted his pride, he accepted the experience as an opportunity to learn his craft as a warrior. His preoccupation with troop discipline and courts-martial, as we saw in the preceding chapter, suggests his sense of ownership of the role he had taken on and his protectiveness toward his men, while his involvement with the western rebellion that we shall take up in the next chapter speaks as much to his ability to navigate among competing egos as to his proprietary feelings about the West where he spent so much of his early career.

If we have learned anything from the Millers Run trial, it is that character is at the heart of understanding how Washington operated, for good or for ill. As a military man and a politician, he scrutinized how he was seen and what the public thought of him. Fulfilling his ambitions and tailoring his standing accounted for much of his posturing, his policies, and his politics, while the scales of republican virtue balanced his realistic goals against his grand schemes, enabling him to avoid the appearance of a democratic monarch and protect his credentials as a public servant.[163] As Gary Wills intimates, the secular pantheon that Washington shared with Jefferson and Franklin was as much a trap as it was a display case.[164]

Although he took pride in being "authorized" by the men he led and the people he liberated and he considered the source of his authority to derive from "genuine Principles of Liberty" and the "uncorrupted Choice of a brave and free People,"[165] Washington accepted the title "His Excellency" when it was proffered during the revolution, endowing him, as Ellis puts it, with "semi-royal status."[166] He did so, however, at a price in the eyes of men whose recognition he prized just as much, Jefferson and Madison, when in the midst of a rebellion during his service as president—a rebellion of common men on the western frontier that Washington so loved—Jefferson was reminded of Madison's observation

> that the satellites and sycophants which surrounded [Washington] had wound up the ceremonials of the government to a pitch of stateliness which nothing but his personal character could have supported. . . . Naked he could have been sanctimoniously reverenced. But inveloped in the rags of royalty, they can hardly be torn off without laceration.[167]

This chapter has thrown light on the contention that in the critical interim between the war and the presidency, that is, during the years culminating in the trial of the thirteen squatters and a mere four years before he assumed the office of president, Washington's reputation hung in doubt. With his return to the West after the revolution, the common focus for the political cooperation between the states had dissolved and the West beckoned as a means of binding them together once state conflicts over land were resolved in favor of congressional oversight. In ascending to the presidency in 1790, Washington was about to redefine how western land would be divided, sold, and governed, how the Indians would be squeezed out, and how new states and territories would be formed. Having won the country's independence, he was positioned to claim the "great prize," western land, for both himself, and the new nation.[168]

As for the legacy of the Millers Run case, another force was at play. Washington, Westmoreland, and Fayette County settlers petitioned the Pennsylvania Assembly from April through November 1786, supported by defense counsel Brackenridge when he took his seat in the Assembly.[169] On December 30, an act was passed giving a right of preemption to qualified settlers, too late to help the Seceder settlers and only offering relief until 1788.[170] Nor did it quell grievances over land rights by occupancy leading into the Whiskey Rebellion of 1794. "Among other causes of discontent," the US Commission to the President reported, the rebels "complained of the decisions of the State Courts, which discountenanced improvement titles, and gave the preference to paper titles."[171] Brackenridge was the rebel delegate who constructed and read the list of rebel grievances to the Commission. That rebellion and how Washington's presidency proceeded in relation to it are the subjects of the next chapter.

NOTES

1. Thomas Perkins Abernathy, *Western Lands and the American Revolution* (Richmond: University of Virginia Institute of Research in the Social Sciences, 1937), 243–46; W. W. Abbot, "George Washington and the Union," *Indiana Magazine of History* 84, no. 1 (1988): 8, 10–14; Merrill Jensen, "The Creation of the National Domain, 1781–1784," *The Mississippi Valley Historical Review* 26, no. 3 (1939): 323–42; George Washington to Edmund Randolph, August 13, 1785, https://foundersarchives.gov/documents; George Washington to Benjamin Harrison, October 10, 1784, https://foundersarchives.gov/documents; Archer Butler Hulbert, *Washington and the West, being George Washington's Diary of September, 1784, Kept During his Journey into the Ohio Basin in the Interest of a Commercial Union Between the Great Lakes and the Potomac River* (New York: Century Co., 1905), 175–86.

2. Alan Taylor, "Land and Liberty on the Post-Revolutionary Frontier," in *Devising Liberty: Preserving and Creating Freedom in the New American Republic*, ed. David Thomas Konig (Stanford, CA: Stanford University Press, 1995), 81–83; Gordon S. Wood, *Empire of Liberty: A History of the Early Republic, 1789–1815* (New York: Oxford University Press, 2009).

3. Woody Holton, *Forced Founders: Indians, Debtors, Slaves, and the Making of the American Revolution in Virginia* (Chapel Hill: University of North Carolina Press, 1999), 11–13, 28–38.

4. The Constitutional Convention ran from May 25, 1787, to September 17, 1787.

5. George Washington to John Witherspoon, March 10, 1784, https://foundersarchives.gov/documents; Roy Bird Cook, *Washington's Western Lands* (Strasburg, VA: Shenandoah Publishing Inc., 1930), 121–22, 139. Washington's holdings at the time of his death in 1799 was reportedly 60,200 acres.

6. Adding uncleared land, their claim came to most of the 2,813 acres. Note 1 to George Washington Diary entry, September 20, 1784, https://foundersarchives.gov/documents; Hulbert, *Washington and the West*, 50–53.

7. Cook, *Washington's Western Lands*, 148–63; Abbot, "George Washington and the Union," 3–4; Hulbert, *Washington and the West*, 175–86.

8. Burton Alva Konkle, *The Life and Times of Thomas Smith, 1745–1809* (Philadelphia: Campion & Company, 1904), 176n1, 185.

9. In conjunction with Ron McColl, faculty research librarian at West Chester University, an extensive search for the manuscript was conducted in state and federal archives, private collections, historical societies, college and university libraries, bar associations, and history centers, with special attention to the Library of Congress.

10. Washington's brief appears in full transcription in the following sources: Boyd Crumrine, in an editorial note to a letter from Thomas Smith to George Washington, February 9, 1785, https://foundersarchives.gov/documents; see n21, n22; Burton Alva Konkle Papers deposited at the University of Georgia; a partial transcription, William

Henry Egle, ed., *Notes and Queries: Historical, Biographical and Genealogical: Relating Chiefly to Interior Pennsylvania* (Harrisburg, PA: Harrisburg Publishing Company, 1893), 38–41. This study relies on Konkle, who affirms his transcription is "a complete, accurate and even exact copy of the original papers" (1904, 173–89); Joel Achenbach, *The Grand Idea: George Washington's Potomac and the Race to the West* (New York: Simon and Schuster, 2004), 111–13, 119–20, 144–50; Boyd Crumrine and Franklin Ellis, *History of Washington County, Pennsylvania, with Biographical Sketches of Many of its Pioneers and Prominent Men* (Philadelphia: H. L. Everts & Co., 1882), 856–60; Hulbert, *Washington and the West*, 143–59; G. S. Rowe, *Embattled Bench: The Pennsylvania Supreme Court and the Forging of Democratic Society, 1684–1809* (Newark: University of Delaware Press, 1994), 189–91; G. S. Rowe, *Thomas McKean: The Shaping of an American Republicanism* (Boulder: Colorado University Press, 1978), 193–94.

11. George Washington to Thomas Smith, July 14, 1785, https://founders.archives.gov/documents. Known for his expertise in land cases, Thomas Smith practiced in Carlisle and Bedford, "largely before the Judges of the Supreme Court"; he was appointed to the Pennsylvania Supreme Court in 1794; Konkle, *The Life and Times of Thomas Smith*, 187–88.

12. John Harvie was Virginia land office register, 1780–1791, mayor of Richmond 1785–1786, and secretary of the Commonwealth of Virginia 1788–1789. Edmund Randolph was a member of the Continental Congress 1779–1782, Virginia governor in 1786, and US attorney general 1789–1794.

13. Charles Simms was a Virginia lawyer and a member of the House of Delegates in 1786 when Washington approached him. Thomas Lewis was county surveyor for Augusta County, 1745–1777 and a Virginia commissioner who negotiated the 1799 land agreement between Virginia and Pennsylvania; John E. Potter, "The Pennsylvania and Virginia Boundary Dispute," *The Pennsylvania Magazine of History and Biography* 38, no .4 (1914): 416, 418.

14. R. Walton Moore, "George Washington as a Judge and His Attitude Towards Courts and Lawyers," *American Bar Association Journal* 18, no. 3 (1932): 151–55; George Washington Nordham, *George Washington and the Law* (Chicago: Adams Press, 1982), 10–13. While county court order books record Washington for four years (1770–1774), Washington's diary, April 18, 1768, suggests he served from 1768–1774.

15. G. Edward White, *Law in American History: From the Colonial Years Through the Civil War* (New York: Oxford University Press, 2012), 48–49.

16. Garry Wills, *Cincinnatus: George Washington and the Enlightenment* (Garden City, NY: Doubleday, 1984), 3–13, 151–72, 182–85; Jason S. Lantzer, "Washington as Cincinnatus: A Model of Leadership," in *George Washington, Foundation of Presidential Leadership and Character*, eds. Ethan Fishman, William D. Peterson, and Mark J. Rozell (Westport, CT: Praeger, 2001), 33–51; Kathleen Bartoloni-Tuazon, *For Fear of an Elective King: George Washington and the Presidential Title Controversy* (Ithaca, NY: Cornell University Press, 2014).

17. Richard H. Kohn, *Eagle and Sword: The Beginnings of Military Establishment in America* (New York: The Free Press, 1975), 8.

18. "Washington's Sentiments on a Peace Establishment, 1 May 1783," Founders Online, accessed 9/4/2023, May 1, 1783, https://founders.archives.gov/documents/Washington/99-01-02-11202; Tal Tovy, "Militia or Regular Army? The Debate on the Character of the American Army during the Revolution," *European Journal of American Studies* 13 (2010), https://journals.openedition.org/ejas/7814.

19. Gregory T. Knouff, "Whiteness and Warfare on a Revolutionary Frontier" in *Friends and Enemies in Penn's Woods*, eds. William A. Pencak and Daniel K. Richter (University Park: The Pennsylvania State University Press, 2004), 238–39; Krista Camenzind, "Violence, Race, and the Paxton Boys," in *Friends and Enemies in Penn's Woods: Indians, Colonists, and the Racial Construction of Pennsylvania*, eds. William A. Pencak and Daniel K. Richter (University Park: Pennsylvania State University Press, 2004), 219.

20. Benjamin Franklin, "A Narrative of the Late Massacres in Lancaster County, of a Number of Indians," in *The Papers of Benjamin Franklin*, vol. II, ed. Leonard W. Labaree, (New Haven, CT: Yale University Press, 1967), 53.

21. David Porter, "Washington v. Anarchy: A Prelude to the Whiskey Rebellion," *Topic* 45 (1994): 11–17.

22. C. H. Laub, "Revolutionary Virginia and the Crown Lands (1775–1783)," *The William and Mary Quarterly* 2 no. 4 (1931): 306.

23. R. Eugene Harper, *The Transformation of Western Pennsylvania, 1770–1800* (Pittsburgh: University of Pittsburgh Press, 1991), 8; Patrick Spero, *Frontier Country: The Politics of War in Early Pennsylvania* (Philadelphia: University of Pennsylvania Press, 2016), 12; Peter Silver, *Our Savage Neighbors: How Indian War Transformed Early America* (New York: Norton, 2009); Patrick Griffin, *American Leviathan: Empire, Nation, and Revolutionary Frontier* (New York: Hill and Wang, 2007).

24. Spero, *Frontier Country*, 197, 199, 201, 206–11. Pennsylvania and Virginia agreed to a boundary on August 31, 1779, confirmed it September 23, 1780, and ran the boundary line 1784–1785. Charles Huston, *An Essay on the History and Nature of Original Titles to Land in the Province and State of Pennsylvania* (Philadelphia: T. & J. W. Johnson, 1849), 10–12; Boyd Crumrine, ed., "The Boundary Controversy between Pennsylvania and Virginia, 1748–1785: Minute Book of the Virginia Court Held at Fort Dunmore (Pittsburgh) for the District of West Augusta, 1775–1776," one of four papers from The Annals of the Carnegie Museum, 1903; Harper, *The Transformation of Western Pennsylvania*, 9; Laub, "Revolutionary Virginia and the Crown Lands," 313; Potter, "The Pennsylvania and Virginia Boundary Dispute," 411, 416–19; Norman Wilkinson, *Land Policy and Speculation in Pennsylvania, 1779–1800: A Test of the New Democracy* (New York: Arno Press, 1979), 4–6.

25. November 27, 1779, An Act for Vesting the Estate of the Late Proprietaries in this Commonwealth [Pennsylvania], Huston, *An Essay*, 362–67.

26. Potter, "The Pennsylvania and Virginia Boundary Dispute," 417, 420, 422; Harper, *The Transformation of Western Pennsylvania*, 9–10.

27. Harper, *The Transformation of Western Pennsylvania*, 11.

28. April 9, 1781, Act for Establishing a Land Office, and for the Purpose Therein Mentioned, 1 Smith's Laws, 521; Huston, *An Essay*, 369–74; March 12, 1783, Act for

the Sale of Certain Lands Mentioned, for the Purpose of Redeeming and Paying off the Certificates of Depreciation given to the Officers and Soldiers of the Pennsylvania Line, 2 Smith's Laws, 62; Huston, *An Essay*, 379–82.

29. David M. Friedenberg, *Life, Liberty and the Pursuit of Land: The Plunder of Early America* (New York: Prometheus, 1992), 184, 187, 190; Harper, *The Transformation of Western Pennsylvania*, 9–10; Wilkinson, *Land Policy and Speculation in Pennsylvania*, 41.

30. George Washington to William Crawford, September 17, 1767, https://foundersarchives.gov/documents.

31. William Crawford to George Washington, September 29, 1767, https://foundersarchives.gov/documents; C. W. Butterfield, ed., *The Washington-Crawford Letters, Being the Correspondence between George Washington and William Crawford, from 1767 to 1781, Concerning Western Lands* (Cincinnati, OH: Robert Clarke & Co., 1877).

32. William Crawford to George Washington, November 12, 1773, https://foundersarchives.gov/documents; George Washington to Thomas Lewis, February 1, 1784, https://foundersarchives.gov/documents.

33. George Washington Petition, December 15, 1769, https://foundersarchives.gov/documents. The council referred Washington to the Masters of the College of William and Mary, which appointed surveyors; Washington enlisted the support of Andrew Lewis (a captain in his 1754 regiment). Benjamin J. Hillman, *Executive Journals of the Council of Colonial Virginia (June 20, 1754–May 3, 1775)* (Richmond: Virginia State Library, 1966), VI, 337–38. Andrew Lewis to George Washington, March 1, 1770, https://foundersarchives.gov/documents.

34. George Washington to John Murray Dunmore, April 3, 1775, https://foundersarchives.gov/documents.

35. Minutes of March 5, 1771, regimental meeting, https://foundersarchives.gov/documents.

36. Washington's legal brief, July 14, 1785; Washington's brief, Konkle Papers, G2, G9, E9.

37. George Washington's diary, items, October 10, 11, 1771, https://foundersarchives.gov/documents; Cook, *Washington's Western Lands*, 37.

38. William Hogeland, *Autumn of the Black Snake: George Washington, Mad Anthony Wayne, and the Invasion that Opened the West* (New York: Farrar, Straus and Giroux, 2017), 69–70; Joseph J. Ellis, *His Excellency, George Washington* (New York: Vintage Books, 2004), 56–57.

39. George Washington to George Muse, January 29, 1774, https://foundersarchives.gov/documents; George Washington to George Mercer, November 7, 1771, https://foundersarchives.gov/documents.

40. Thomas Lewis to Col. Preston, May 15, 1774; in Cook, *Washington's Western Lands*, 38.

41. John Camm to Col. Preston, March 22, 1775; Col. Preston to John Camm, April 18, 1775; in Cook, *Washington's Western Lands*, 38.

42. John Murray Dunmore to George Washington, April 18, 1775, https://foundersarchives.gov/documents; October 22, 1748, An Act Directing the Duty of

Surveyors of Land; William Waller Hening, *The Statutes at Large; Being a Collection of all the Laws of Virginia, from the First Session of the Legislature, in the Year 1619* (Richmond, VA: George Cochran, 1822), VI, 33–38.

43. The Ohio Land Company commissioned Crawford in 1773 to survey two hundred thousand acres. In 1775, the Loyal Company challenged the legality of Crawford's appointment, implicating most of Washington's land under the proclamation; Crawford was replaced by Willis Lee, an uncommissioned surveyor. Abernathy, *Western Lands and the American Revolution*, 133–34.

44. George Washington to John Murray Dunmore, November 2, 1773, https://foundersarchives.gov/documents; Hillman, VI, November 3, 1773; Abernathy, *Western Lands and the American Revolution*, 84–89.

45. Dissatisfaction with Virginia's 1782 reformed land taxes and its administration of vacant lands led to an attempt to create a new government in the Ohio valley; Laub, "Revolutionary Virginia and the Crown Lands," 312–13.

46. George Washington to Thomas Lewis, February 17, 1774, https://foundersarchives.gov/documents.

47. George Washington to James Wood, February 20, 1774, https://foundersarchives.gov/documents.

48. Washington to Thomas Lewis, February 17, 1774, https://foundersarchives.gov/documents.

49. Andrew Lewis to George Washington, March 9, 1774, https://foundersarchives.gov/documents.

50. Andrew Lewis to George Washington, March 9, 1774, https://foundersarchives.gov/documents.

51. Peter Hog served as a captain in Washington's 1754 regiment.

52. George Washington to Peter Hog, March 21, 1774, https://foundersarchives.gov/documents; George Washington to Thomas Lewis, May 5, 1774, https://foundersarchives.gov/documents.

53. Crawford identified the land to Washington as "Shirtees Creek," which included Millers Run in the southwestern part of the "new purchase" of 1768 in Augusta County, Virginia (which in 1781 would become Washington County, Pennsylvania); Crawford to Washington, September 29, 1767, https://foundersarchives.gov/documents.

54. Washington's legal brief says Millers Run was surveyed on March 23, 1771. George Washington to George McCarmick, July 12, 1784, https://foundersarchives.gov/documents. Crawford did not claim to have drafted a survey until August 2, 1771; William Crawford to George Washington, April 20, 1771, August 2, 1771, https://foundersarchives.gov/documents.

55. George Washington to Charles Simms, September 22, 1786, https://foundersarchives.gov/documents.

56. William Crawford to George Washington, May 8, 1774, https://foundersarchives.gov/documents.

57. Porter, "Washington v. Anarchy," 1, 17n3.

58. George Washington Diary, September 20, 1784, September 22, 1784, in Hulbert, *Washington and the West*, 49–50, 56. Donald Jackson and Dorothy Twohig, eds.,

The Diaries of George Washington, Volume IV, 1784–June 1786 (Charlottesville: University Press of Virginia, 1978), 20–38; Konkle, 187–88; Rowe, *Embattled*, 255.

59. Crawford was tortured and killed by the Indians June 11, 1782; James H. Anderson, "Colonel William Crawford," *Ohio History Journal* 6, no. 1 (1898): 1–34.

60. Washington to Thomas Lewis, February 1, 1784, https://foundersarchives.gov/documents.

61. Thomas Smith to George Washington, November 17–26, 1785, https://foundersarchives.gov/documents.

62. Thomas Smith to George Washington, November 17–26, 1785, November 7, 1786, https://foundersarchives.gov/documents. Smith wrote that Bedford was "where I leave all the Papers respecting my business in the Western Courts, which are not necessary to be brought to this Place"; "I will take your Papers to Carlisle & will send them from thence to such place, either in Philadelphia, or Baltimore, as you will please to point out."

63. Konkle, *The Life and Times of Thomas Smith*, 175 n1. Konkle gives the address as "18 High Street, Carlisle, Pa."; the papers were "in the possession of C[hristian]. P[hilip]. Humrich, Esq., of that place." Konkle photographed the first page of the original manuscript brief, which reads "Original from Library of Congress" and "Digitized by Internet Archive."

64. Konkle, *The Life and Times of Thomas Smith*, 176.

65. George Washington's brief, Burton Alva Konkle Papers, University of Georgia, G2, E2; cites from Washingtons briefs are entered as "G" for Grounds, "E" for Evidence, "P" for Pleas, and "A" for Answers, followed by the number given the item in the brief.

66. Washington's brief, Konkle Papers, G3, E3.

67. Washington's brief, Konkle Papers, G5, G6, G7, E6, E8.

68. Italics within quotes are consistent with the original text, as is the spelling.

69. Washington's brief, Konkle Papers, G9, E9.

70. Washington's brief, Konkle Papers, G10, G12.

71. Land records for the West Augusta District were transferred from Virginia to Washington County, Pennsylvania, when it was founded in March 1781; Potter, "The Pennsylvania and Virginia Boundary Dispute," 413.

72. Washington's brief, Konkle Papers, G11, G13, E11.

73. Washington's brief, Konkle Papers, P1, P2, A1.

74. Washington's brief, Konkle Papers, P8, A7, A8, A9.

75. Washinton's brief, Konkle Papers, P4, P6, P9, A4, A6, A9.

76. Thomas Smith to George Washington, February 9, 1785, https://foundersarchives.gov/documents.

77. Thomas Scott, the brother of James Scott, the lead defendant in the Millers Run case, was prothonotary of Washington County from 1781–1789 and served two terms in Congress, 1789–1791 and 1793–1795; like Washington, he was a Federalist. Thomas was apparently influential in getting the Seceders to stand up to Washington. The April before the trial, Thomas Scott read a petition to the state assembly supporting Washington County residents on the issue of giving preference to continued

settlement and time to gain a legal title; Porter, "The Pennsylvania and Virginia Boundary Dispute," 7–8.

78. Smith to Washington, November 7, 1786, https://foundersarchives.gov/documents.

79. Jasper Yeates was a successful lawyer in Lancaster County and was appointed to the Pennsylvania Supreme Court in 1791. He served with James Ross on Washington's Whiskey Rebellion Commission.

80. A Framer of the Constitution, second only to James Madison, James Wilson was appointed by Washington to the US Supreme Court in 1789 and was law professor at the College of Philadelphia (now the University of Pennsylvania) from 1790–1798. Impoverished by his land speculation, he was imprisoned briefly and died in penury in 1798 while still on the highest bench.

81. Washington to Smith, July 14, 1785, https://foundersarchives.gov/documents.

82. James Ross, born in 1762, was admitted to the Washington County bar in 1784. He became a US senator in 1794 and served on Washington's Whiskey Rebellion Commission; James L. Brownson, *The Life and Times of Senator James Ross* (Washington, PA: The Observer Job Rooms, 1910), 1, 15.

83. George Washington to Thomas Smith, September 22, 1786, https://foundersarchives.gov/documents.

84. Harper, *The Transformation of Western Pennsylvania*, 5, 8, 10.

85. Peter S. Onuf, *The Origins of the Federal Republic: Jurisdictional Controversies in the United States, 1775–1787* (Philadelphia: University of Pennsylvania Press, 1983), 64–65.

86. Onuf, *The Origins of the Federal Republic*, 76, 82, 94–100.

87. Onuf, *The Origins of the Federal Republic*, 69.

88. Onuf, *The Origins of the Federal Republic*, 61.

89. Onuf, *The Origins of the Federal Republic*, 62–63.

90. George Washington to John Harvie, March 19, 1785, https://foundersarchives.gov/documents.

91. To aid Harvie in his research, Washington provided a summary of "a state of the whole matter" from the point of view of the present occupiers of the land.

92. John Harvie to George Washington, April 22, 1785, https://foundersarchives.gov/documents.

93. Hening, *The Statutes at Large*, X, 35–50.

94. The commissioners' certificate was not something for which the settlers could have applied; it was awarded upon resolution of a dispute by the commissioners; 1779 Act for Adjusting Claims, sec. VIII.

95. Hugh Henry Brackenridge, *Law Miscellanies: Containing an Introduction to the Study of the Law, Notes on Blackstone's Commentaries, Shewing the Law of Pennsylvania from the Law of England and What Acts of Assembly Might Require to be Repealed or Modified* (Philadelphia: P. Sterne, 1814), 258.

96. Two cases were filed: *Lessee of George Washington v. James Scott* and *Lessee of George Washington v. Samuel McBride et al.*; *Appearance Dockets, Records of the Eastern Docket, Records of the Pennsylvania Supreme Court* (Pennsylvania State

Archives, Harrisburg, RG-33), microfilm roll 4, p. 132 (496); Porter, "Washington v. Anarchy," 17n2, 19n38; Rowe, *Embattled*, 189–91; Rowe, *McKean*, 193–94.

97. December 30, 1786, An Act for Giving, during a Limited Time, a Right of Pre-emption to the Actual Settlers within that Part of this State, which is within the Territory Purchased [by the King of Great Britain] of or from the Indians, at Fort Stanwix, in the Year of our Lord One Thousand Seven Hundred and Sixty-Eight (sec. III); 2 Smith's Laws; Huston, *An Essay*, 128–33; 397–99.

98. Washington's brief, Konkle Papers, P4; Virginia State Land Office Patents No. 42, 1773-1774, pp. 516–18 (Reel 41).

99. *Lessee of Thomas Smith, Esq. v. Bezel Brown* (1795) 1 Yeates, 513; Huston, *An Essay*, 132–33.

100. Brackenridge, *Law Miscellanies*, 171–72; March 26, 1785, Act, Huston, *An Essay*, 132.

101. March 12, 1783, An Act for the Sale of Certain Lands; 2 Smith's Laws, 62; Huston, *An Essay*, 379–82.

102. Brackenridge, *Law Miscellanies*, 276–77. In *Lessee of Bernard Gratz v. Patrick Campbell* (1800), an excessive period of time (from 1761 settlement to the 1784 warrant) voided the preference for a military permit; 2 Smith's Laws, 129. *Plumstead's Lessee v. Rudebagh* (1795), a 1761 settlement with a military permit that did not come into a warrant until 1784 (which could not have "pretended to be in due and convenient time") or a patent until 1787, reached the same conclusion in spite of "uninterrupted possession" and considerable improvements; 2 Smith's Laws, 127.

103. March 26, 1785, An Act for the Limitation of Actions to be Brought for the Inheritance or Possession of Real Property, or upon Penal Acts of Assembly, *Laws of the Commonwealth of Pennsylvania, May 24, 1781–September 3, 1790* (Philadelphia: John Bioren, 1810), II, 299–307.

104. George Washington to John Harvie, February 10, 1784, https://foundersarchives.gov/documents.

105. J. M. Beattie, *Crime and the Courts in England: 1660–1800* (Oxford: Clarendon Press, 1986), 215, 220, 233.

106. Abernathy, *Western Lands and the American Revolution*, 242–47, 254.

107. Taylor, "Land and Liberty on the Post-Revolutionary Frontier," 87–88, 322n15; Porter, "Washington v. Anarchy," 8–9.

108. Smith's "brief" notes are included in Konkle's papers at the University of Georgia.

109. Washington to Simms, September 22, 1786, https://foundersarchives.gov/documents.

110. John Posey had served in Washington's regiment. He was also a neighbor of Washington's and owed him money, which accounts for his transferring his land bounty to Washington.

111. Washington allowed that he had bought the right from Posey for the "express purpose [of buying Millers Run] two or three years before." George Washington to Thomas Smith, July 28, 1786, https://foundersarchives.gov/documents.

112. John Posey to George Washington, May 25, 1771, https://foundersarchives.gov/documents; Washington to Smith, July 14, 1785, July 28, 1786.

113. Washington's brief, Konkle's Papers, A2, A5, G9. Virginia State Land Office Patents No. 42, 1773-1774, pp. 516–18 (Reel 41). Virginia Colonial Land Office, Library of Virginia Archives. Patentee George Washington, July 5, 1774.

114. Washington also received rights from Charles Mynn Thruston, John Rootes, William Athel, John Bishop, John Paty, Thomas Jones, Jesse Scott, Robert Scott, John Poe, Marshall Pratt, and Goodrich Crump; Boyd Crumrine and Franklin Ellis, *History of Washington County, Pennsylvania, with Biographical Sketches of Many of its Pioneers and Prominent Men* (Philadelphia: H. L. Everts & Co., 1882), 856; Cook, *Washington's Western Lands*, 93.

115. Washington to Harvie, March 19, 1785, https://foundersarchives.gov/documents.

116. Washington's brief, Konkle Papers, P2.

117. Washington to Simms, September 22, 1786, https://foundersarchives.gov/documents.

118. Crawford to Washington, May 8, 1774, https://foundersarchives.gov/documents.

119. Huston, *An Essay*, 117, 418–19; Sec. 1 1779 Act for Adjusting Claims.

120. Andrew Lewis to George Washington, March 9, 1774, https://foundersarchives.gov/documents.

121. Konkle, *The Life and Times of Thomas Smith*, 175. Appearance Docket, December 1784, term of the Washington County Court of Common Pleas, June 1782–June 1792, cause no. 110, p. 195; on deposit, Dartmouth College.

122. Gautham Rao, "The New Historiography of the Early Federal Government: Institutions, Contexts, and the Imperial State," *The William and Mary Quarterly* 77, no. 1 (2020): 103, 113, 117–18.

123. Onuf, *The Origins of the Federal Republic*, 60.

124. Porter, "Washington v. Anarchy," 17n3.

125. Porter, "Washington v. Anarchy," 13.

126. Washington to Smith, September 22, 1786; Smith to Washington, November 7, 1786, https://foundersarchives.gov/documents.

127. Smith to Washington, November 7, 1786, https://foundersarchives.gov/documents.

128. "Actual" settlement was a continuous theme from the proprietorship of William Penn to the end of the century. The ruling in *Blaine's Lessee v. Cawford* (1793) reflected what the Proclamation of 1763 required in laying out that "a military permit to settle and improve lands, is not to be regarded, unless followed by a settlement and improvement"; 2 Smith's Laws, 128–29.

129. Washington to Simms, September 22, 1786, https://foundersarchives.gov/documents.

130. Washington to Smith, September 22, 1786, https://foundersarchives.gov/documents.

131. Smith to Washington, November 17–26, 1785, https://foundersarchives.gov/documents.

132. *Plumstead's Lessee v. Rudebagh* (1795), 2 Smith's Laws, 127.

133. Washington to Smith, July 14, 1785; July 28, 1786; September 22, 1786, https://foundersarchives.gov/documents.

134. Allen Steinberg, *The Transformation of Criminal Justice: Philadelphia, 1800–1880* (Chapel Hill: The University of North Carolina Press, 1989), 5–7; Allen Steinberg, "'The Spirit of Litigation': Private Prosecution and Criminal Justice in Nineteenth Century Philadelphia," *Journal of Social History* 20, no. 2 (1986): 231–32; Kermit L. Hall, Peter Hoffer, David Bodenhamer, and Allen Steinberg, "Allen Steinberg's The Transformation of Criminal Justice in Philadelphia: 1800–1880: A Symposium," *Pennsylvania History* 59, no. 2 (1992): 145–69.

135. Hall, et al., "Allen Steinberg's The Transformation," 151–59, 163–66.

136. Alexander Addison, *Reports of Cases in the County Courts of the Fifth Circuit, and in the High Court of Errors and Appeals, of the State of Pennsylvania* (Philadelphia: John Colerick, 1800).

137. Beattie, *Crime and the Courts in England*, 8–10. John D. Bessler refers to private prosecution as a participatory process whereby an ordinary citizen, usually the victim or his family, took another to court without official intervention as a form of private justice; in Philadelphia it was the basis of law enforcement from colonial times until the mid-nineteenth century. John D. Bessler, *Private Prosecution in America: Its Origins, History, and Unconstitutionality in the Twenty-First Century* (Durham, NC: Carolina Academic Press, 2022), 107–26; John D. Bessler, "The Public Interest and the Unconstitutionality of Private Prosecutors," *Arkansas Law Review* 47, no. 3 (1994): 511–602; Josephine Gittler, "Expanding the Role of the Victim in a Criminal Action: An Overview of Issues and Problems," *Pepperdine Law Review*, 11, no. 117 (1984): 125–26, 130–33.

138. Washington to Randolph, August 13, 1785, https://foundersarchives.gov/documents.

139. Washington to Smith, September 10, 1785, https://foundersarchives.gov/documents.

140. Washington to Smith, September 22, 1786, https://foundersarchives.gov/documents.

141. Smith to Washington, February 9, 1785, https://foundersarchives.gov/documents.

142. Smith to Washington, November 17–26, 1785, https://foundersarchives.gov/documents; Konkle, *The Life and Times of Thomas Smith*, 187–88.

143. George Bryan wanted the position of third justice to go to him following Justice John Evans's death rather than to Evan's replacement, Jacob Rush. G. S. Rowe, "Judicial Tyrant and Vox Populi: Pennsylvanians View Their State Supreme Court, 1777–1799," *Pennsylvania Magazine of History and Biography* 118, no. 1 (1994), 40–41. Brackenridge (1799–1816) and Smith (1794–1809) became Pennsylvania Supreme Court justices.

144. *Lessee of Samuel Howard v. Pollack*, 1 Yeates, 509 (1780 to 1795); *Lessee of Thomas Smith, Esq. v. Bazel Brown,* 1 Yeates, 513 (1784–1785 to 1795); *Lessee of Samuel Simpson v. John Williams & James Green*, 3 Yeates, 402 (1784 to 1802); *Lessee of Abraham M'Kinney v. Jacob Houser*, 2 Smith's Laws, 190 (1783–1787 to 1800); *Miles's Lessee v. Potter*, 2 Binney, 65 (1783–1788 to 1809); *Lessee of Duncan*

v. Curry et al., 3 Binney, 14 (1775, 1797 to 1810); *Lessee of Henry Drinker v. William Holliday, Jr.*, 2 Yeates, 87 (1765, 1774 to 1796).

145. Konkle, *The Life and Times of Thomas Smith*, 173, 175.

146. Several other likely judges were Virginian partisans during the dispute with Pennsylvania over jurisdiction; Porter, "Washington v. Anarchy," 7.

147. Porter, "Washington v. Anarchy," 8.

148. Porter, "Washington v. Anarchy," 7, 19n35; note 5, Smith to Washington, November 17–26, 1785, https://foundersarchives.gov/documents. *Richard Smith, lessee of James Campbell v. Joseph Budd and Josiah Budd,* and *John Goodright, lessee of Robert Thompson v. Jacob Whitsell and Thomas McBride. Appearance and Continuance Dockets, Records of the Eastern District, Supreme Court,* roll 4 (750), (September Term 1783–January Term 1787) Pennsylvania State Archives, Harrisburg, p. 271 (607).

149. Smith to Washington, November 17–26, 1785, https://foundersarchives.gov/documents.

150. Smith to Washington, November 17–26, 1785, https://foundersarchives.gov/documents.

151. Smith to Washington, November 7, 1786, https://foundersarchives.gov/documents.

152. Porter, "Washington v. Anarchy," 10.

153. Margaret Pearson Bothwell, "The Astonishing Croghans," *The Western Pennsylvania Historical Magazine* 48, no. 2 (1965): 138–45; Gratz Manuscript Collection, Historical Society of Pennsylvania; see Claude Milton Newlin, *The Life and Writings of Hugh Henry Brackenridge* (Princeton, NJ: Princeton University Press, 1932), 62.

154. Neither of Brackenridge's biographers (Daniel Marder and Claude Milton Newlin) mention how he got paid or where the funds might have come from; nor has David Porter who has worked in detail on the Millers Run settlers.

155. Porter, "Washington v. Anarchy," 4–5; See Joel Achenbach, *The Grand Idea: George Washington's Potomac and the Race to the West* (New York: Simon and Schuster, 2004), 83–102.

156. Daniel Marder, *Hugh Henry Brackenridge* (New York: Twayne Publishers, Inc., 1967), 38–39.

157. Lindsay M. Chervinsky, *The Cabinet: George Washington and the Creation of an American Institution* (Cambridge, MA: Belnap Press, 2020).

158. Ellis, *His Excellency*, xi–xiv; Joseph J. Ellis, *American Dialogue: The Founders and Us* (New York: Vintage, 2018), 174–75.

159. Wood, *Empire of Liberty*, 114–15, 126–27; Ellis, *American Dialogue*, 176–81, 186, 190–91.

160. Ellis, *His Excellency*, 55–58, 156–57.

161. Thomas Slaughter, *The Whiskey Rebellion: Frontier Epilogue to the American Revolution* (New York: Oxford University Press, 1986), 85, 88–89; Taylor, "Land and Liberty on the Post-Revolutionary Frontier," 102–05; Abernathy, *Western Lands and the American Revolution*, 359, 361; Friedenberg, *Life, Liberty and the Pursuit of Land*, 336, 345, 347, 353–54.

162. Holton, *Forced Founders*, xvi–xvii.

163. Bartoloni-Tuazon, *For Fear of an Elective King*; Wills, *Cincinnatus*, 102–05; Ellis, *His Excellency*, 77–78, 147–49. Colleen J. Shogan, "George Washington: Can Aristotle Recapture What his Countrymen Have Forgotten?" in *George Washington, Foundation of Presidential Leadership and Character*, eds. Ethan Fishman, William D. Peterson, and Mark J. Rozell (Westport, CT: Praeger, 2001), 53–69; David Hein, "George Washington and the Patience of Power," *Modern Age* 57, no .4 (2015): 35–43.

164. Wills, *Cincinnatus*, 129. Barry Schwartz, "Social Change and Collective Memory: The Democratization of George Washington," *American Sociological Review* 56, no. 2 (1991): 222, 224–25; Forrest McDonald, "Presidential Character: The Example of George Washington," *Perspectives on Political Science* 26, no. 3 (1997): 134–39; Todd C. Harris, "George Washington: A Revolutionary Approach to Leadership," *Leadership & Organization Development Journal* 39, no. 8 (2018): 1003–04; Gordon S. Wood, "The Greatness of George Washington," *Virginia Quarterly Review* 68 (1992): 189–207.

165. George Washington to Thomas Gage, February 25, 1775, August 19, 1775, https://foundersarchives.gov/documents; Thomas Gage to George Washington, August 13, 1775, https://foundersarchives.gov/documents.

166. Ellis, *His Excellency*, 78.

167. Thomas Jefferson to James Madison, June 9, 1793, https://foundersarchives.gov/documents.

168. Ellis, *American Dialogue*, 175, 177, 179–184.

169. Porter, "Washington v. Anarchy," 8; Rowe, *Embattled,* 191; Huston, *An Essay*, 119.

170. "Act for Giving a Limited Time, a Right of Preemption to the Actual Settlers within the Area Purchased from the Indians at Ft. Stanwix in 1768," *Statutes at Large of Pennsylvania, from 1682–1801* (Harrisburg, PA: State Printer, 1896–1909), IX, 350–51.

171. James Ross, Jasper Yeates, William Bradford, "From the Commissioners Sent to Western Pennsylvania," September 24, 1794, https://foundersarchives.gov/documents.

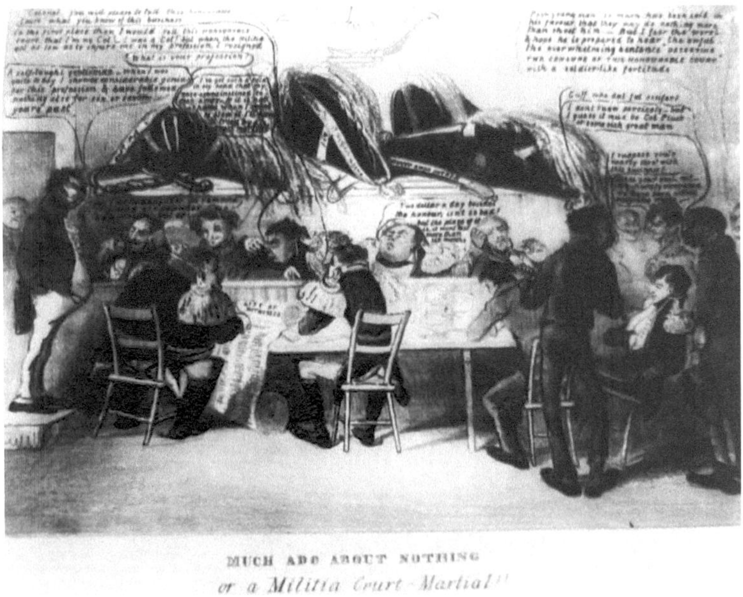

Figure 1. Much Ado About Nothing or a Militia Court Martial, 1832. David Claypoole.
Courtesy of the Library of Congress.

Figure 2. A Scene on the Frontier as Practiced by the Humane British and their Worthy Allies, 1812. William Charles.
Courtesy of the Library of Congress.

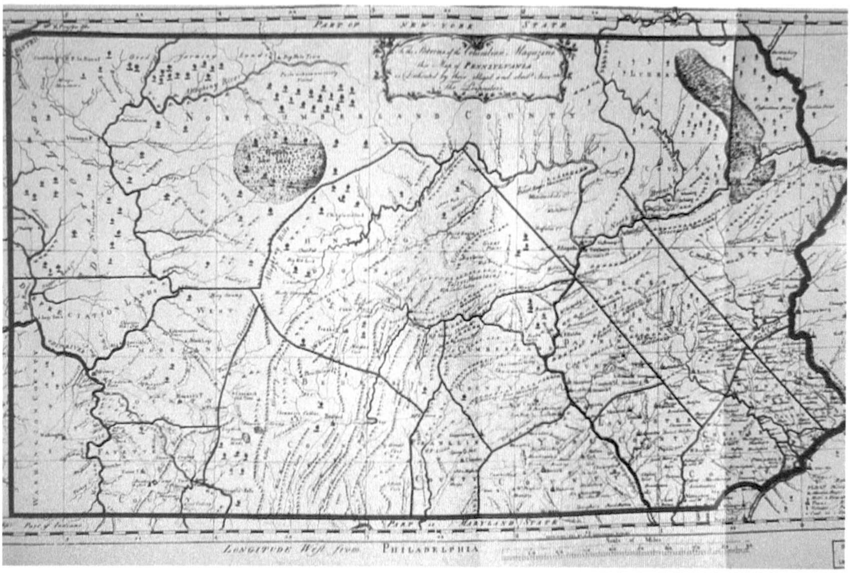

Figure 3. **Map of Western Pennsylvania. *Columbia Magazine*, vol. 2, 1788.**

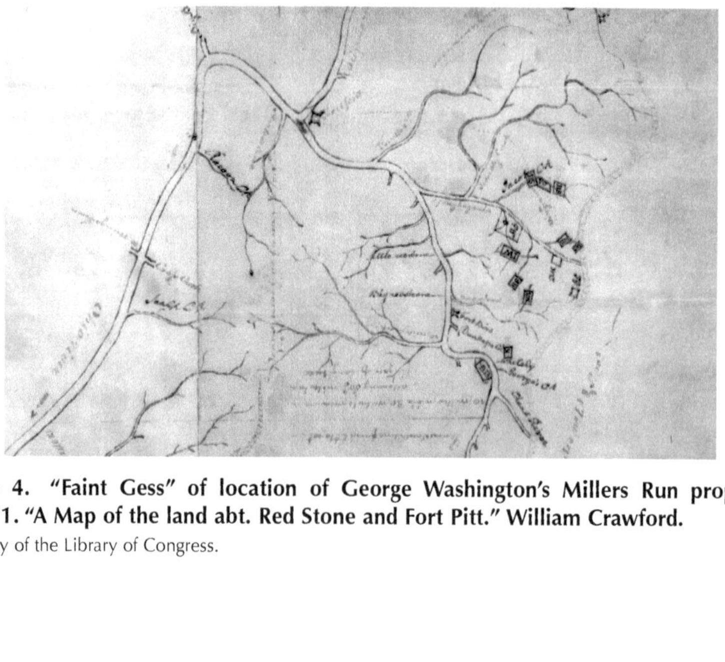

Figure 4. "Faint Gess" of location of George Washington's Millers Run property, c. 1771. "A Map of the land abt. Red Stone and Fort Pitt." William Crawford.

Courtesy of the Library of Congress.

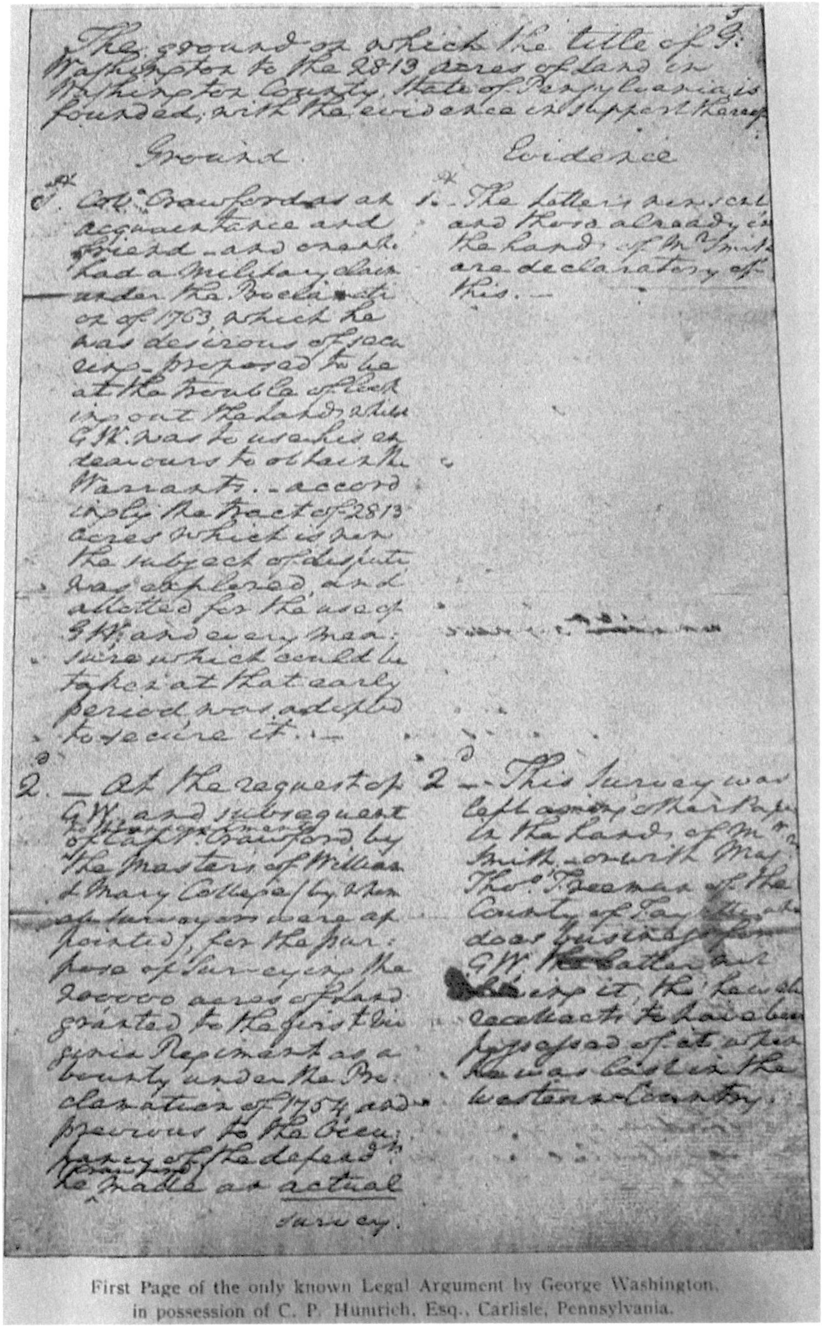

The ground on which the title of G: Washington to the 2813 acres of Land in Washington County, State of Pennsylvania is founded, with the evidence in support thereof:

Ground	Evidence
1. Colo. Crawford was an acquaintance and friend—and one who had a Military claim under the Proclamation of 1763, which he was desirous of securing—proposed to be at the trouble of looking out the Lands, while G.W. was to use his endeavours to obtain the Warrants.—accordingly the tract of 2813 acres which is now the subject of dispute was explored, and allotted for the use of G.W. and every measure which could be taken at that early period, was adopted to secure it.—	1.—The letters now sent and those already in the hands of Mr. Smith are declaratory of this.—
2.—At the request of G.W. and subsequent to the appointment of Capt. Wm. Crawford, by the Masters of William & Mary College (by whom the surveyors were appointed), for the purpose of Surveying the 200,000 acres of Land granted to the first Virginia Regiment as a bounty under the Proclamation of 1754 and previous to the occupancy of the defendants he [Crawford] made an actual survey.	2.—This Survey was left among other Papers in the hands of Mr. [illegible] Smith—or with Maj. Thos. Freeman of the County of Fayette, who does business for G.W. the latter not having it, the former [illegible] recollects to have been possessed of it when he was last in the western Country.

First Page of the only known Legal Argument by George Washington, in possession of C. P. Humrich, Esq., Carlisle, Pennsylvania.

Figure 5. Legal Argument: Brief. George Washington. Burton Alva Konkle, The Life and Times of Thomas Smith, 1745–1809.

Figure 6. A Peep into the Antifederalist Club, 1793.
Courtesy of the Library Company of Philadelphia.

Figure 7. The Times; a Political Portrait, 1793–1797. ***New York Historical Society Quarterly Bulletin*****, 15, no. 4 (January 1732).**

Figure 8. US Circuit Court for Eastern District of PA, in US Supreme Court, Independence Hall, Philadelphia, 1790–1791.

Courtesy of Kostas Myrsiades.

Figure 9. A Case of Infectious Fever (from "81 South Street 4 doors from Callowhill Street" Philadelphia).

Courtesy of the University of Pennsylvania Archives.

Figure 10. Pennsylvania Supreme Court in Independence Hall, Philadelphia, 1740s.
Courtesy of Kostas Myrsiades.

Figure 11. Lawyers in Term, 1786.
Courtesy of the Library of Congress.

Figure 12. G. Washington in his last illness attended by Doc.rs Craik and Brown, 1800.
Courtesy of the New York Historical Society.

Figure 13. Black Horse Alley. Courtesy of Kostas Myrsiades.

Figure 14. "Nigger Jack, The Slave." Walter L. Grayson.
Courtesy of Swarthmore College Library.

Chapter 4

"Whiskey Boys" and the "Pole Gentry"

Treason and the Whiskey Rebellion Trials, 1795

> [U]pwards of 120 of the pole gentry were confined in that town, and more hourly collected—information had been received at Hagerstown of the erecting of a pole.
>
> —"Extract of a letter from a gentleman in Hagerstown," *Carlisle Gazette*, September 24, 1794

> [The]President of the United States . . . preaches against insurrections and rebellions, and this drew upon him the resentment of the "*Whiskey boys*."
>
> —"No. VI," *The Medley or Newbedford Marine Journal*, June 5, 1795

An important aspect of the Whiskey Rebellion—and something that resonates with contemporary angst—is what it tells us about mob psychology and participatory democracy.[1] With ratification of the 1787 Constitution, common people felt their voluntarily given allegiance meant they held the reins of power. As a question of representative democracy, they understood democracy to mean engaging directly in making the law. In tandem with such popular traditions as liberty pole raisings and the "rough justice" of ritual forms of humiliation like tarring and feathering officials and hangings in effigy, people organized in the out-of-door politics of meetings and assemblies, mounted extralegal courts, and spread their message through agitation-propaganda posted on trees or advertised in handbills and newspapers to express their might be divided, but it could not be shared without ensuring the death of the states. Western anti-Federalists warned that the whiskey tax was a conspiracy to undermine states and create a powerful central government, which would "abrogate and repeal" state laws, a battle the central government would win with the use of a national army, indeed with the use of one state's militia to enforce taxes in another state.[14]

The Washington administration saw the protest as problematic, unlike evading a direct tax or customs duties, because it threatened a balanced tax policy and the need to access more than the substantial proceeds of customs duties, which accounted for over 90 percent of federal revenue and which fell on a small defined group, sparing the population at large.[15] Federal assumption of state debts had left the states better off (so that their direct taxes were reduced substantially) and gave the nation the chance to develop sound public credit, but that demanded government revenue. Hamilton felt that customs duties (impost) would not be enough, and that the Shays' Rebellion had proved taxation could threaten public order.[16]

Hamilton had expected more gratitude from the states over assuming their war debt and saving them from a devastating economic dilemma.[17] Beyond that, the spectacle of the Treasury secretary's tax collectors being intimidated fed Hamilton's paranoia about what he saw as partisan Republican motives intended to subvert the government.[18] This fear was exacerbated by Pennsylvania's Republican government and its intransigence in enforcing the tax law through its courts and its resistance to calling up its militia.[19] Nonetheless, it did not appear that Hamilton was intentionally goading westerners to provoke a rebellion that would justify calling in military force; the federal government could not stem the rebellion by itself—it had no army and federal courts were just being established. Still, the rebellion occurred on the closest frontier to the US capital in Philadelphia in an area transitioning from a frontier to a settled space; Western Pennsylvania would pose a dangerous precedent to the rest of the country if it was not pacified.[20]

In the end, the whiskey tax was important because levying a direct peacetime federal tax for the first time as an extension of federal authority, and in the backcountry reformed the relationship of the federal government and its citizens; it demonstrated the federal presence in peacetime in a distinct way in local communities—something that had been avoided with custom duties. The move was interpreted just as anti-Federalists had warned: establishing big government through heavy taxes, not in response to a crisis, which expanded the sphere of federal government through direct taxation of its citizenry as a general matter, not limited to a discrete entity or passed on by merchants. Moreover, it would, as they had anticipated, be enforced by the military and by the presence of myriad tax collectors entering their houses.[21]

More than the conflict between local control and national power and more than the legitimacy of federal government, differing visions of the union and federalism represented the larger stakes for the nation. What is important here is that the debate was not merely about the "local" and the "national" but about flouting Federalists, on the one hand, and punishing anti-Federalists, on the other. The real complication, early American historian Max Edling argues, was that the union was one of dual sovereignty, that of a cohering national framework and disparate sovereign states. Practically speaking, the union produced by the Constitution was essentially a compact of the states to provide for common concerns. The national government was granted the "authority and capacity" to legislate directly for citizens and inhabitants of the United States, to implement legislation through national administration and courts, and to wield powers to tax and regulate commerce, while the states reserved for themselves internal improvements, property, and civic rights.[22]

But this is not to say that there was a clear line separating state and federal authority as there were interactive interests that operated through managing the country's debts together with its defense (a fiscal-military model), opening and organizing western territory, creating a common market, and activating foreign policies using the collective instrument of the federal government; moreover, there were implications for the general government arising from the range of state regulation of internal improvements and economies. It was at the interface of these interactions that the Federalist and anti-Federalist visions of union came to a head.

THE REBELLION

It was unclear which of two paths the rebellion would take in the summer of 1794: issue-oriented gatherings like those held from 1791 to 1793 or acts of outright rebellion like the violent militia-led attack in 1794 at Bower Hill, the home of tax inspector John Neville. With the movement in drift, the radical David Bradford called for a "common cause" in support of the mob, a decision deferred by an assembly at Mingo Creek (July 21) until an assembly at Parkinson's Ferry (August 14).[23] In the interim, Bradford instigated a robbery of the US Mail[24] and called militia groups to assemble at Braddock's Field (August 1). Whereas that assembly sponsored a march on Pittsburgh that resolved into a peaceful, if drunken, riot, the pivotal Parkinson's Ferry assembly that followed reset the trajectory of the rebellion, offsetting Bradford's plan to prepare for war and establish a new state. Washington sent a presidential commission to deliver an ultimatum (August 20–22), which had the effect of reinforcing momentum by a more moderate rebel faction. With the rebellion realigned, an assembly at Brownsville (August 28) presented the government's offer of amnesty in exchange for submission.

Over time, the parameters of the conflict codified as a clash of narratives. The rebel narrative read as a popular struggle for political subjecthood through speech, petition, and assembly. The government narrative reduced rights-bearing people to a senseless mob at the margins of civilized life. Reinforcing the opposed values of the narratives, the passage of both the Bill of Rights and the whiskey tax in 1791 had placed the federal government's right to tax its citizens and the guarantee of individual rights on an unavoidable collision course.

The government accused those who refused to pay the whiskey tax of acting as outlaws, "banditti," and called popular meetings criminal, unlawful combinations promoting insurrection, making the rebellion the first contest over the Constitution's guarantee of individual rights. Prominent western politician William Findley argued that the accepted right to petition against a law bespoke the people's right to assemble, to "publish their sentiments and correspond" throughout the territory affected by that law "without the imputation of combining against the government."[25] From as early as a contentious June 1791 meeting in Pittsburgh, he added, Hamilton's attacks on the rebels had got it wrong: "I never knew that a meeting to petition government respectfully, was esteemed criminal in any country that had the least pretensions to freedom."[26] According to Findley, Hamilton knew Attorney General Randolph did not find the meetings "actionable" and that the government had proved unresponsive to western petitions.[27] The people, Findley argued, were entitled to remonstrate against officials even in a representative democracy and even if officials they elected had legitimately enforced the law.[28] Not having "the remotest intention" to overthrow the government, they had a "moral obligation" to preserve their own rights.[29]

The role played by local militias undermined Findley's argument and complicated the ability to peacefully assembly. Some of the 1794 assemblies—Mingo Creek, Couch's Fort, Braddock's Field—in fact, originated in militia musters. Under the mantle of popular sovereignty, the right to bear arms implied a natural right of revolution against an unjust government, as William Pitt Smith and St. George Tucker represented,[30] and was essential to control Indian incursions, provide security for settlers, and muster members of the community for self-defense.[31] Confirming the value of militia in the context of the constitutional ratification debate, the Federalist Tench Coxe[32] allowed that "the powers of the sword" were in the hands of the militia, who were none other than "ourselves"; as arms were "the birth right of an American,"[33] even Federalists like Coxe who supported national power believed Congress was powerless to disarm the militia.

As a necessary alternative to a standing army, militias had armed themselves with impunity and were duty-bound to do so;[34] that is, unlike the rights of speech, petition, and assembly, serving in the militia could be compelled of a citizen by the state.[35] The sticking point was over a natural right to revolution and whether a voluntarily undertaken compact, the Constitution, superseded that right.[36] Radical, localist rebels were willing to test the proposition in a rebellion,[37] while Federalists refused to condone armed mobs that did not constitute the well-regulated militia the second amendment required.[38] In the backcountry of Pennsylvania, the formation of militia units was, to be sure, beyond state control. But because Whiskey Rebellion militias were far from assuring the Second Amendment's "security of a free state,"[39] the possibility that bearing arms would secure a democratic result was a weak one, which led the government to charge rebels who armed themselves with treason. Treating the local militia as a minority unwilling to submit to the will of the majority had the added value of allowing the government to argue for a standing army.[40]

The militia was the only popularly-based form of organization other than meetings that westerners knew and the most natural vehicle for rebel resistance. Admittedly, without the force of arms the development of a wide body of support for the antitax effort was unlikely. Yet once the rebellion grew ideologically and organizationally, that right became less of a weapon and more of a liability, which moderates capitalized on by exploiting the right of assembly and the collateral rights of petition, speech, and press to reach a peaceful resolution. It soon became apparent that the right to peaceful assembly conflicted with the popular understanding of militia and the realities of how militias operated.

Assemblies nonetheless came with their own problems. The appearance of a representative body suggested an alternative to Congress and clearly agitated the Washington administration. The upside was the assembly's ability to undermine disruptive factions and to speak for the body of the people. Once moderates attended in progressively larger numbers, they defused tendencies to mobocracy by organizing debate and controlling dissent; forms of democratic process emerged that tamped down the criminal aspect of mob rule and military arms. Under the influence of an increasingly moderate rebel leadership, assemblies thus came to represent a crossover between western popular sovereignty and eastern constitutional democracy. The government might have considered the result—"constitutional resistance"—an oxymoron, as Hamilton made sure to argue, but it was a construction that fit well with the rights on which the assemblies relied for their viability.

Which takes to a third consideration: the conflict of participatory democracy and constitutional government. The Whiskey Rebellion directly confronted the very existence of national government and its laws, making it the first significant threat to national authority and the innovative form of a representative federal government. Importantly, the period of the 1790s represented the first years of implementing the Constitution and a time when social forces at odds with each other interrupted national unity and cohesion within the political community, a critical feature of the new democracy.

What settlers wanted was an exchange of obedience to the law, peaceful relations, and "allegiance for protection and other benefits of government."[41] They wanted civil and property rights like those rights and privileges citizens in the East enjoyed, a "full extension of political rights" and benefits[42] such as participation and representation in elections with results that secured settlers' land titles and did not discriminate by burdening them with taxes affecting their economic situation. Settlers expected the state to respect their regional grievances as legitimate participants in a democracy and to adopt policies friendly to the western condition. These included a military that did not enforce the law against them but protected them by controlling the Indians. They wanted settlers to keep their land and authorities to favor them over speculators; they wanted Indian lands and the Mississippi River opened to expand development.[43] The revolution had not ended in the West. Settlers preferred the more fulsome rights of the 1776 state constitution and demanded the fulfillment of the promise of equality and liberty made by the revolution.

Ideological conflict and autocratic tendencies featured the Whiskey Rebellion's split between elites and backcountry democrats and the attendant erosion of democratic norms. The main conflict was between the power of government and the rights of its subjects, particularly how political stakes incited extraconstitutional actions and under what circumstances. The problem was that popular democracy demanded citizens defend against transgressions of government, whereas the government demanded their support. The mob action that resulted exposed democracy's Achilles' heel.[44] But with no incentive for the people to cooperate in a crisis, and with the state unable to contain emerging threats, the national government was incapable of preventing extraconstitutional conduct.[45] The Whiskey Rebellion thus illustrated the competing visions of direct local community control and national power exerted by a distant representative government. Similarly, idiosyncratic violence by militia-based rebels seemed to be at odds with political organization in assemblies that mimicked legitimate representative institutions and imbued popular grievances with authority.[46] Both drew down the ire of the government.

The antifederalism that infused popular sovereignty on the frontier and which opposed the new Constitution contributed to this double bind.[47] Its opposition to strong central government institutionalized in a constitution provoked a deep split between local politics and national authority that would last through the first half of the 1790s. Western politicians had not participated in the convention that wrote the Constitution and from 1785–1795 they were in the minority in the state assembly. Anti-Federalists, however, made up the majority of the western delegation to the state ratification convention where westerners voted 7–2 against ratifying the Constitution.

The western part of the state felt itself undermined by the diminution of state power under the federal Constitution and by the replacement of the 1776 state constitution in 1790 with a less democratic version. These losses informed the eruption of backcountry democracy in 1794, which fed anti-Federalist feelings of powerlessness within the state.[48] In fact, five of the seven westerners who voted against the Constitution (William Findley, Albert Gallatin, John Smilie, James Edgar, and James Marshall) became leaders of the rebellion and architects of the popular assemblies organized by the communities of the four insurgent Pennsylvania counties (Washington, Westmoreland, Fayette, and Alleghany).

In sum, the Whiskey Rebellion and its popular assemblies were unlike the bourgeoise democratic societies (Republican clubs that arose in 1793 to contest federalism) against which Washington railed and which he called the first fruit of the rebellion. Rather, the insurgency was a more volatile combination of social classes that mixed a local political elite with common laborers to constitute popularly-based, western-style, backcountry democracy.[49] At the same time, the insurgency through its assemblies was, according to James Roger Sharp, "the first major challenge to the authority of the national government and a catalyst for reopening the debate concerning the nature of representation."[50] Wanting in western anti-Federalist thinking, the Constitution especially provoked westerners by authorizing a national government to federalize a militia and enforce a federal tax; it seemed to incentivize the government to delegitimize large-scale meetings and petitions and to assault the competency of state courts to administer the law. The Whiskey Rebellion thus resonated with the constitutional ratification fight on the cornerstone issues of anti-Federalist participatory democracy: the radical politics of localism and egalitarianism.[51]

THE EVIDENCE

The rebellion ended with the dispatch of Washington's Watermelon Army[52] (so-called for a large New Jersey contingent where watermelons grew) to quell a rebellion that had spread to twenty frontier counties, eight in Pennsylvania alone.[53] President Washington marched with the troops as far as Carlisle, Pennsylvania, and Treasury Secretary Hamilton tagged along. With the army launched, the president returned home, and Hamilton continued on in the company of US district judge Richard Peters and US district attorney for Pennsylvania William Rawle. The army roused rebels from their homes in the dead of night on November 13, whereupon 150 of them were driven before horses at a seven-mile trot through the mud to Pittsburgh, many in bare feet.[54] There, Hamilton later admitted, interrogations revealed that the tempering influence of moderates in the rebellion had been larger than his spies had represented.[55]

The evidence upon which Hamilton had been relying had been gathered by a network of informants over the three years of antitax protests. Aggravated by the insults they had endured at the hands of distillers who challenged their authority, Hamilton's officers documented the smallest acts of "disrespect to themselves or the law."[56] They proved themselves, as Findley reported, "very attentive to record incidents of little importance, and arrange them in the most criminal dress suited to [their] design." The information, which proved inaccurate and full of misrepresentations, was "usual with the information of spies of all countries," Findley noted, and turned out to be largely useless in punishing breaches of the peace.[57]

In accord with the requirements of the Militia Act of 1792, Supreme Court justice James Wilson had provided the certification necessary to send a federal militia, relying on "evidence, which has been laid before me."[58] Findley referred to the evidence as the "general notoriety of the acts and some private communications as sufficient vouchers."[59] Attorney General William Bradford begrudgingly claimed it was difficult to say that Wilson's certification was more than "sufficient in point of law"[60] and advised Washington to render his own judgment on the facts. Having become secretary of state in 1794, Randolph recommended Washington delay sending the militia as the certification "specifies no particular law that has been opposed"[61] and the certificate itself might sufficiently terrify the insurgents. Like Randolph and Bradford, Pennsylvania governor Thomas Mifflin counselled care, implying the supporting facts were not evidence and the information provided was short on proof "on which an act of Government was to be founded."[62] Where civil law would be suspended and military order replace judiciary instruments on matters of treason or felony, greater caution was required. Speaking through Randolph, the president declared that federal law would control in this case, "leaving it to the understanding and conscience of [Wilson], upon his responsibility to pronounce what kind and degree [of evidence] should suffice."[63]

The cabinet members' hesitancy about the evidence was only reinforced by the performance of the judicial arm of the federal militia. Although General Henry Lee's orders[64] established that Judge Peters was not to be "controlled in his functions,"[65] Hamilton ensured that interested parties were allowed to give evidence, turncoat rebels were enticed with offers of amnesty, and tax inspector Neville was permitted to serve as witness, investigator, and prosecutor without regard to the compromising effect of his involvement.[66] Hamilton dismissed out of hand the expertise of officials familiar with the local legal scene, including judges. He blamed unsafe conditions and his inability to "foresee what cases in the view of the Governor" would be brought for the delay in collecting formal evidence. Willing witnesses were prevented from volunteering and their testimony was considered "liable to specious controversy about their true import and nature." Hamilton thereby begged off providing proof on the specious grounds that events appeared "in forms so plausibly disguised and with so much duplicity of aspect, as not to be capable of being rendered palpable by precise specification and proof."[67]

With the number of accused significantly reduced by the interrogations, several dozen rebels were marched over the Alleghany mountains and across the state to Philadelphia. Their trials were held before the US Circuit Court of the Eastern District of Pennsylvania in the chambers of the US Supreme Court. Charles Nisbet, corresponding with Judge Alexander Addison of the western courts, predicted the prisoners would "have a sham Trial"[68] and "soon return home in Triumph";[69] Hugh Henry Brackenridge intimated that the trials in Philadelphia would "differ little from a revolutionary tribunal of Paris."[70] In the end, two relatively unimportant rebels were convicted of treason, sentenced to death, and ultimately pardoned, making them the first Americans to receive a presidential pardon.[71] More important rebels had escaped custody, so that only ten of the twenty-four indicted for treason were tried. Twenty-six speech-related misdemeanors were indicted, none of which ended in conviction.[72]

Beyond procedural questions of vicinage, lack of pretrial hearings, habeas corpus petitions, witness lists, and copies of indictments, the defense focused on the venire to select jurors from the communities in which the crimes occurred. The prosecution reflected an aversion to independent-minded jurors and conditions in the West in navigating the question of jury composition, acknowledging that its preparations were unpersuasive in the circuit court. Citizens were unwilling to speak against fellow citizens; juries were reluctant "to convict the smaller engine on the testimony of their ringleaders," and found capital convictions repugnant, which "occasioned some unexpected acquittals; and in some instances, bills were returned ignoramus, equally contrary to what appears a grounded expectation."[73]

On the other hand, Gallatin, a rebel witness, called the grand jury "respectable" and not "suspected of partiality."[74] Western trial jurors "summoned from Fayette," he reported, "are good, those from Washington only middling." Those from Alleghany were such that Porter's defense counsel "challenged all of them but one and chose rather to trust his life to the decision of jurors from the counties in the neighborhood of Philadelphia."[75] The defense's strategy proved prescient as the judge directed a verdict of not guilty in *Porter*, which the jury delivered within minutes.[76] Gallatin cited defense counsel William Lewis' choice in *Barnet* of "a jury of a different complexion," which was out a mere fifteen minutes and delivered a not guilty verdict.[77] In truth, efforts to exclude jurors from Philadelphia and neighboring counties in favor of western jurors seemed to be largely unavailing, according to Gallatin, as those from the West "had been picked up with such care" that they were of little use to the defense.[78]

A longer look at trial documents, however, suggests that western jurors were often favorable to the accused.[79] None of the Alleghany County residents, for example, ever voted guilty. Lewis selected in *Barnet* the same Alleghany juror who had voted innocent in the trial of Marmaduke Curtis; Barnet was acquitted. A juror from Alleghany County served on [Thomas] Miller's jury as well; Miller was also acquitted.[80] Unfortunately, all those from Alleghany were excluded from Mitchell's jury, which included no one from the West; Mitchell was convicted. Defense counsel Thomas had "left the case to twelve Quakers (many of them probably old Tories)," under the presumption that Quakers would not condemn the prisoner.[81]

The verdict on this issue appears to be mixed. The venire, or panel, from which jurors were selected might have been more important than the choice of counsel, as Gallatin seemed to feel,[82] but the political inclination of the jury and its independence were also important, as when no western jurors were available for four trials in the October term of the circuit court and jurors from York acquitted in all the cases.[83] Equally, the voir dire, or examination, of jurors mattered in seating eastern jurors who were not aligned with the government or the prosecution's views. Predicting a verdict through the make-up of the jury appears, in sum, to have been as much a calculated gamble as geography or legal savvy.

THE TREASON TRIALS

In many ways the most important treason trial was that of John Mitchell, one of the two trials in which the defendant was convicted of treason. Not only is *U.S. V. Mitchell* the most studied rebellion trial, but it was the most detailed of those in Dallas's law reports.[84] The trial was framed by Justice Paterson in an aside to the defense where he asked counsel to address two considerations, both related to the assembly at Couch's Fort: "Whether the conspiracy to levy war at *Couche's Fort*, was not, in legal contemplation, an actual levying of war"; and "Whether the *proceedings* at General Neville's house were not a continuation of the act, which originated at *Couche's Fort.*"[85] This unusually direct assignment exposed a preoccupation of the trials as a whole. How might the rights of assembly and militia contribute to a charge of levying war as a proper constitutional standard for treason?[86]

Many of the failed indictments and numerous misdemeanor charges implicated attendance at meetings. They referred to such charges as seditious speech and symbolic speech, which were most often associated with one's presence at a meeting. For example, John Corbly was specifically charged for his "expressions" at meetings and Herman Husband for reading an incendiary pamphlet.[87] Paterson's bench notes in other trials prominently remarked on the presence of several figures (John Barnet, Thomas Miller, Robert Philson, and Husband) at specific meetings (Couch's Fort, Braddock's Field, Parkinson's Ferry), which reinforced the judge's preoccupation with how the assemblies fit into the conspiracy and into overt act charges against the rebels.[88]

In charging the *Mitchell* jury, Justice Paterson connected the violence at Bower Hill and conspiracy at assemblies to reach the two-witness standard necessary to proof of treason and to link rebel conduct to a treasonous scheme. His jury charge provided a full sense of the government's preoccupation with assemblies, but not merely as a form of organization or as a vehicle for crafting and expressing oppositional speech to undermine confidence in the government. Rather, his goal, like the government's, was twofold: to create a crime out of the right to assemble and petition for redress of grievances and to allege a conspiracy between rebels who did not commit violent "outrages" and those who supported a common cause with those who did.

The prosecution's approach to the assemblies was apparent as early as the indictment, which relied on the presence of the defendant at Couch's Fort where a group congregated following an initial foray by an armed company at Inspector Neville's Bower Hill house.[89] From Couch's, a second party of rebels marched on Bower Hill and was met by a contingent of soldiers led by Major James Kirkpatrick who confronted and killed the rebel commander, James McFarland, as he tried to negotiate under a white flag. With Kirkpatrick taken prisoner, the rebels returned once more to Couch's Fort.[90] The prosecution thereafter examined Couch's Fort as the site of a conspiracy to commit a treasonous act with the intent of levying war, without claiming war was actually levied against the United States. As applied to the assemblies, the prosecution held that "whenever a lawless meeting is convened, whether it shall be treated as riot, or treason, will depend on the *quo animo*" (intent).[91] What took place at Couch's Fort was a conspiracy whose object was "to suppress the offices of excise in the Fourth Survey." Subsequently, some persons from Couch's Fort engaged in "lawless and outrageous proceedings" at Bower Hill. Having "originally combined with the conspirators" (Mitchell was seen at Couch's Fort) and presuming that those persons who engaged in lawlessness had "a treasonable purpose," Rawle held that it was not necessary that

Mitchell (whom other witnesses also placed at Bower Hill) himself act on the purpose to charge him with treason.[92]

As Rawle applied his argument to the assembly at Braddock's Field (the gathering of militia from four counties that followed the events at Bower Hill), he held it was "not necessary to consider [that] meeting an independent treason." The conduct of the prisoner—"concurring in every violent proposition that was made" and refusing to sign a "declaration of submission to the laws"—was sufficient to establish his state of mind, "that *mala mens*, that dark and dreary turbulence of soul, which is regardless of every social, moral, and religious obligation." Thus, Rawle considered Mitchell's state of mind at a subsequent assembly evidence of his combining with conspirators at a previous assembly, which, combined with an act of a fellow conspirator, was sufficient to prove an act of treason.[93]

Defense counsel Edward Tilghman and William Thomas retorted that events at Couch's Fort and Neville's house cannot "be so combined and interwoven as to form one action." At Braddock's Field, there was no act of treason nor was a plan for levying war devised or executed.[94] Likewise, the prisoner made "some vaunting declarations of a traitorous intention," but such an "intention there, is no proof of his having levied war against the government at another time, and in another place." Counsel argued that the assembly at Couch's Fort did not convene to force a repeal of the excise law nor to suppress the excise offices. Rather, those assembled at the meeting intended to consider their best course of action; they composed a committee and sent Neville a flag, making the prisoner's conduct at the fort "immaterial" to a charge of treason.[95]

William Bradford's take on assemblies in his closing argument for the prosecution reprised Rawle's panoptic of the rebellion with a few variations. He offered that "in every stage of their proceedings, at Couch's Fort, at the General's house, and at Braddock's field, [the insurgents] were actuated by one single, traitorous, motive," to oppose execution of the excise law. He continued, "If his intention was traitorous, his offense was treason." In this construction, Bradford discounted his own premise that a man must both have been present and have acted along with the insurgents to render him a criminal. And he discounted the Constitution's requirement of an overt act. It was enough for Bradford that "war may be levied, though not actually made," assigning himself the task of proving a negative and raising the question "what constitutes the act itself."[96] Bradford was satisfied that assembling, arming, and arraying at Couch's Fort made manifest a treasonous purpose, which itself was "an act of levying war" whether "every witness should have seen him at the same spot, at the same moment, and in the same act."[97] The "design" of the Braddock's meeting had included decisions to prevent execution of the excise law, to overawe the government, and to attack the fort at

Pittsburgh. Whether enacted or not, Bradford held, those decisions were sufficient to prove a "substantive act of Treason."

In his charge to the trial jury, Justice Paterson followed suit. He conveyed that the prisoner was seen at Couch's Fort and at Neville's home. Attending armed at Braddock's Field would in Paterson's view have amounted to treason "if [Mitchell's] design was treasonable." Similarly, Paterson considered "the very act of marching . . . as carrying the traiterous intention into effect." He went on to endorse the prosecution plan for connecting the events, so that, if the jury connected the conspiracy at Couch's Fort and the acts at Neville's house, the prisoner was guilty of treason; in the alternative, if the jury deemed the conspiracy at Couch's treason, the prisoner was also guilty. In either construction, the prisoner was guilty. The prisoner's presence at the two assemblies—rather than an overt act at the actual site where the violence occurred—was the critical element of the prosecutor's case and the judge's charge. Being present at assemblies had implicated Mitchell in a conspiracy and rendered him an accomplice to an act of treason committed by another party.[98]

If the prosecution argument for treason implicated deliberative assemblies, it also implicated the operational arm of the rebellion, the local militia. Paterson and Rawle had applied a convenient stratagem: attacking the militia undermined the right to assemble; attacking the assemblies neutered the right to an armed militia. What could not be successfully attacked was the right to bear arms, although Paterson's bench notes for *Porter* indicated that if Federalist judges could have done so, they would have. There were several complicating factors. One was that militia musters were a customary practice tied to local democracy. Another was that several of the assemblies were actual extensions of militia musters—Mingo Creek, Couch's Fort, and Braddock's Field—and the militia remained linked to assemblies throughout the rebellion. John Hamilton's Mingo Creek militia was, notably, responsible for the destruction at Bower Hill.[99] Yet another troublesome connection was the link between the Mingo Creek militia (responsible for the violence at Bower Hill) and the Mingo Creek Democratic Society (formed by militia members, many of whom participated in the assemblies).

When the prosecution made the case for treason in *Mitchell* based on a posture of war or the people being armed, it not only went against common usage but it transgressed a right that was beyond dispute.[100] Indeed, the Militia Act of 1792 that established standards for organizing the militia made it a duty of "each dragoon to furnish himself" with weapons and ammunition in support of a militia.[101] Nevertheless, Rawle cited common law precedents in *Mitchell* ("raising a body of men," "an assembly armed and arrayed," "they affected the military forms")[102] as did Justice Paterson in *Porter* ("stand to their arms," "generally armed," "appeared to have command") that questioned the militia's commonly accepted right to bear arms.[103] The very language, rituals, gestures, and forms of militia—majors commanding battalions and captains their companies, organization integral to self-defense on the frontier—created the appearance of war that the prosecution felt demanded a charge of treason. This was the horns of a dilemma on which the prosecution was stuck.

There was confusion in the defense camp as well. As defense witness testimony in *Porter* demonstrated, militia members were torn over attending assemblies. Should they obey a call to join their unit or risk being delinquent; should they wear their "military accoutrements" or not? Officers were conflicted over whether to issue "regular militia orders" or to refuse, like Porter, to take command of their troops. As a result, charging treason for levying war was bound to be a hard sell to a common man jury. It raised too many conflicting feelings, making an attack on arms and militia less a weapon than a liability, as the directed verdict dismissing the *Porter* case demonstrated. Irrespective, Rawle insisted English common law bound American courts and that it "uniformly and clearly" defined levying war, with "no room for excuse or extenuation."[104] His position ignored that common law on treason was contradictory, indeterminate, and expansive and that Article III of the Constitution constituted the controlling language on treason.

Bradford, by comparison, converted threats against officers and interference with serving writs into obstructing the legitimate operations of the government in the execution of its laws and the administration of public affairs.[105] The first to propose to the president a constructivist strategy on treason (the foundation on which the prosecution argument in *Mitchell* was based),[106] Bradford avowed that the insurgents' acts, "settled by uniform judicial construction," rose up to "alter the lawful missions of government" and change established law. He included in that definition the redress of grievances, real or pretended, or to achieve "innovations of a general concern." Because "such violence [had] a direct tendency to dissolve all the bonds of society and to destroy all property and all government too by numbers and armed force," these acts were "cognizable in the Courts of the United States" as high treason. Under this description, Bradford presumed to jump the hurdle of the Constitution's restricted view of treason. He focused on dissolving bonds, innovations, withstanding authority, and altering the mission of government, while minimizing overt acts, intent, and overthrow of the government. Bradford's choice of terms was critical ("lawful missions," "the established law") in that it conduced to the standard of a general matter (i.e., public rather than private, general rather than specific) demanded in common law. Similarly, his argument extended to the dissolution of social order and the authority of government generally, discounting that the case dealt with the execution of one law. Bradford had privately communicated to Congressman Elias Boudinot that the success of a presumed insurgent plan to undermine the general government was so formidable that it undermined the authority "of the president who is the Atlas that supports it";[107] "the authority of the civil government is so frustrated," he complained, it was too weak to afford protection to citizens who applied for its care.

Defense counsel Tilghman and Thomas rejected Bradford's constructions as "the dread and scourge of any nation that allows them."[108] They argued that such a construction of treason was "calculated to annul all distinctions heretofore wisely established in the grades and punishments of crimes" so that magically, a mob became a conspiracy and a riot became treason,[109] which was not what Congress intended. Suppressing one officer—a mere misdemeanor, not a "traiterous offence"—was not to suppress all officers. A bare conspiracy to levy war did not amount to a treasonous act.[110] Nor should a crime against a government agent be counted as "a crime of the same denomination" as compelling Congress by violence to repeal a law, since a single officer was not the government. Indeed, if a risk to all law was claimed where one law, the excise law, was resisted (abrogating the common law generality principle regarding "all laws"), "one must equally [do] so, in relation to every other law."[111] The government's proclivity in compounding descriptions of treason "incautiously, into a system,"[112] they claimed, would in fact lead to the "too easy admission of future cases" that was guarded against by Article III.

Justice Paterson's jury charge mirrored the prosecution's expansionism and promoted the idea that a single law signified all law and a usurpation of government authority "of a general nature."[113] His reading also dismissed the Constitution's restricted definition of treason. Paterson implied that treason could be construed as mere political willfulness and that the people's refusal to obey a single law rendered the nation just as ineffectual as if they had overthrown its established laws by violent, direct attack; whether, or not, the intent was to subvert the government, the effect would arguably be the same. Paterson followed the prosecution as well in representing to the jury that, taken together, individual acts that prevented the execution of a law constituted a general usurpation of government authority.[114] This reading was what English common law authorities had warned against as a doubtful construction of a treasonable act.[115]

In a final distortion of constitutional constraints—the two-witness rule of proof for an overt act of treason—the prosecution argued that four witnesses proved Mitchell was where the conspirators assembled and it did not matter that two witnesses to a single overt act could not place him where the violence occurred, that is, at Bower Hill.[116] Since Mitchell originally conspired "in a treasonable purpose," the purpose need not have been enacted. Nor did he need to be present at "the consummation of their plot"; reconnoitering was sufficient. The defense responded that the requisite two witnesses were not present where a treasonous act occurred and that where two witnesses were present no treason had occurred. Moreover, an act like reconnoitering that did "not amount to an overt act of treason by levying war" was not treason, no matter "if it were proved by fifty witnesses."[117]

Paterson's charge to the jury resolved the disparity to his satisfaction. He held that forming an intention at a meeting at one time and place, marching to carry "the traitorous intention into effect" at another, and committing a violent act at yet another could be regarded as a composite transaction. Witnesses to separate parts of that "act" could thus be aggregated to meet the standard of proof for two witnesses to a single overt act of treason.[118] Paterson's construction of Mitchell's "personal motives and conduct" (aggregating each scene in which "he makes a conspicuous appearance") confounded the generality principle and finessed the two-witness rule.[119]As a general matter, the defense had warned that weaving "various descriptions of treason" into a system would allow the government to contort resistance to the execution of a law into an act of compelling Congress to repeal a law "by violence or intimidation."[120] Paterson saw no harm in applying just such chain logic. If the "general object . . . was to suppress the excise offices, and to prevent the execution of an act of Congress, by force and intimidation," it was indeed "an usurpation of the authority of the government; it is High Treason by levying of war." Similarly, Paterson aligned with Bradford's construal of guilt by association, whereby "a base conspiracy is not treason to levy war," yet to be part of a conspiracy where others "execute the plot" makes all guilty.[121]

Paterson's unpublished bench notes for three treason trials (*Porter*, *Barnet*, *Miller*) and one trial for a misdemeanor (*Philson and Husband*)—none of which were reported in Dallas's law reports—illuminate his thinking behind Mitchell's conviction. The three treason cases charged defendants for the attack on Inspector Neville's house (*Miller*, *Barnet*, and *Porter*); they supplement the *Mitchell* law report, the only other treason trial related to that critically important event.[122] Introduced here for the first time, they substantially expand the number of cases open to examination and enable us to gauge Paterson's approach to the trials.

As the defense anticipated, it faced a number of difficulties with witnesses in these trials. It was difficult to procure defense witnesses at a distance, for one thing, and the appropriation of turncoat rebels who bought themselves relief by testifying for the prosecution (two in *Porter*, four in *Miller*, and one in *Barnet*) compromised much of the testimony. The fear of being associated with the rebellion also reduced the number of witnesses willing to testify for the defense. As a result, prosecution witnesses significantly outnumbered defense witnesses. In *Miller*, for example, we find two defense witnesses as against fourteen prosecution witnesses and in *Barnet* four defense witnesses and eight prosecution witnesses; prosecution witnesses exhausted seven times as many pages of witness testimony in *Miller* and eight times as many in *Barnet*.[123] The jury nonetheless acquitted Miller and Barnet. In *Porter*, only prosecution witnesses appeared; no defense was offered as the prosecution failed to prove its case. Porter's case was dismissed.

Paterson's notes summarized testimony witness by witness, marking the text in ways that indicate he reread his summaries more than once to emphasize significant testimony. Paterson's transcription of witness testimony focused on establishing the facts, for which he used marginal notes, marks, sidelining, and underlining to provide an unmediated view of his in-the-moment reactions to the trials. He related not to principles but to the facts of the case and the patterns they formed, along the lines of common law fact patterns. His working process created a narrative of events out of the evidence, identifying categories and patterns, like common agreement among the rebels, forceful interference with official acts, or the formation of bodies of armed men. Paterson's process was one of stitching together a narrative of events and conduct out of summaries that initially read like a historical chronicle. His objective was not to educate a jury or persuade a fellow jurist or counsel—it was to test the prosecution case on the facts and to assist himself as a judge.

Sidelining created an economy of text that privileged testimony of greater interest, while underlining isolated details that deserved attention. Thus, we find Paterson progressively narrowing his view through his markings. Underlining isolated, for example, items with potential legal significance (intent, planning, conspiracy) or critical speech-related acts (proposals, and petitions, public readings of papers). To fully engage with how assemblies operated, Paterson monitored the logistics of calling and organizing meetings and identified incriminating notifications and letters. To determine the use of force, he tracked the buying and selling of weapons and the mobilizing of armed men. Underlining preserved evidence of provocation, coercion, individual rights, and belief, as well as evidence that mitigated or incriminated the accused's conduct, and commitments that indicated one's level of involvement.

A limited number of items were clarified with a marginal note, marked with an "X," or double-marked (e.g., an underlined margin note), emphatic forms of reference likely intended for Paterson's charge to the jury. Thus, the judge referenced the prisoner being present at the edge of a site where violence occurred. He identified members of the mob as terrified rather than terrifying (indicating they were coerced). He referred to the agitator Tom the Tinker as not many men but one man (limiting general culpability). He allowed that buying and selling arms was much spoken of, but that such talk was common practice (mitigating the threat of being armed) and noted that persons and property were not meant to be hurt (speaking to intent). On accomplices, Paterson noted that whatever capacity one served still made one part of a whole (for the purpose of conspiracy or treason) and that defendants had committed themselves to be present as part of the whole (speaking to intent and making common cause).

In sum, having access to Paterson's notes allows us a rare peek into how a judge works on a case in preparation for writing a jury charge. Observing him work through the testimony provides a picture of a judge who is anything but a legal purist or a Federalist stooge, but it also leaves open the question of how to reconcile his jury charge with his bench notes. We might have been able to predict his attention to rebel drunkenness, demands for the resignation of officials, and treasonous intent, but the notes were also noteworthy for balancing such testimony with that which supported peace and constitutional remedies, spoke of protection of captives and property, and cited provocations against the rebels. Here, Paterson reveals what appears to have been consistent eighteenth-century courtroom practice, a judge who refused to stick to the law and to leave the facts to a jury. Rather, Paterson's transcription of trial testimony was faithfully aligned with the facts and his markings were carefully attuned to a common law treatment of those facts rather than legal technicalities, abstract principles, precedents, or constitutional reasoning. Here, Paterson demonstrated he was a pragmatic, rather than a partisan, judge and that he was more independent than his critics or the law reports portrayed him.

What followed in his jury charge was another matter entirely. There, Paterson took on the mantle of a justice of the court navigating his responsibilities to the government (represented by the prosecution) and the people (represented by the jury) by way of the law as he understood it. A conservative jurist, Paterson was beholden to a judicial philosophy that did not desert him in the Whiskey Rebellion trials. He might have been a legal reformer as a governor of New Jersey, but on the court his affinity for stability, order, and national government were decisive influences. Despite his refusal to identify with a political party or faction and his insistence on neutrality in foreign affairs, Paterson held firm for submission to the law.[124]

BRACKENRIDGE'S NOTES ON TREASON

Hugh Henry Brackenridge's notes on treason, a little noticed addendum to the trials, fill in much of the defense perspective that is missing from Dallas's law reports.[125] Brackenridge was a rebel himself and although charges were not brought against him (and despite having been requested to represent one or more of the rebels in the trials) he understood his presence on the defense team would have been a mistake. Brackenridge attended the trials and made notes that he published as a "dissertation on treason," indicating that they were "the notes of the arguments, I had projected in my mind, had I appeared in defence of the prisoners." Brackenridge had expected that a law report would be published "with advantage from the argument of that very able lawyer, and distinguished philanthropist [William Lewis]." Unfortunately, Lewis, "a careless man, negligent of his papers," kept no records of his trial notes.[126] In fact, of all the legal figures who participated in the trials, only Brackenridge left behind an account of the legal arguments.

Brackenridge's notes addressed three aspects of the trials: allegiance, common law, and judicial constructions. His most consequential question was whether the rebels owed allegiance to the US government. In fact, neither the Constitutional Convention, the Constitution, nor the statute of Edward III (upon which the Constitution based its definition of treason) considered a duty of allegiance in relation to treason. The Pennsylvania Supreme Court in *Respublica v. Chapman* (1781) addressed the question during the war and held that where a functioning government existed allegiance encompassed all within that territory, whereas the absence of such government destroyed the reciprocity of protection and allegiance, as in a civil war or the American Revolution, and there a party might choose his own side.[127] The first session of Congress, convened in 1789, passed the Act of 1790, which explicitly required allegiance.[128]

Thomas Jefferson had warned in relation to *Henfield* in 1793 (a case of an American's allegiance to France in its war with England) that if one citizen can claim a right to go to war, then all may do so. And if all may do so, then the nation ("by the authority of its individual citizens") is free to do so; but the US Constitution gave that power to Congress, not to the people. In concluding that "no citizen has a right to go to war of his own authority," Jefferson warned that treason could not be rendered "innocent by giving it the force of a dissolution of the obligations of the criminal to his Country."[129]

Concerning the Whiskey Rebellion, Brackenridge disagreed. He considered it lawful to remove from a chaotic situation by expatriating and asked whether it was not more lawful to protect oneself against a parent society that has wronged one and thereby to protect oneself against trespass of person or property. As one's allegiance was a natural right, it would be "contrary to the laws of nature" to make such an act treasonable once a child reached his majority and could assume the rights to which he was entitled.[130] In taking this position, Brackenridge rejected William Blackstone's feudal dictum *ne excere patriam* (one cannot escape subjugation by the parent society) in which allegiance was fundamental to "the first and most obvious division of the people,"[131] the relation between the ruler and the ruled. In common law, that division represented, as Matthew Hale said, mutual trust between master and servant and mutual duties to protect and to serve.[132] Blackstone bound the subject not by power or ownership but by an "implied, original, and virtual allegiance, owing . . . antecedently to any express promise."[133] It was "a principle of universal law" unalterable by any act of one's own, "written by the finger of the law in their hearts."[134]

Brackenridge reasoned that such law treated "a subject as the *king's* or the *nation's* property"[135] and authorized a universal and "perpetual allegiance"[136] that superseded free will. Feudal in it nature,[137] it constituted "a slavish principle," not a social compact.[138] Unable to dislodge from such allegiance, a human was not a free-born agent and society's entitlement to his service was anathema.[139] Allegiance was thus at the heart of treason law.[140] Man was more than vegetation that "must belong to a bed of loam," just as he happened to find himself; at the age of reason he could contract for himself.[141] This "*prohibition to expatriate*" and this allegiance that "cannot be forfeited" were, for Brackenridge, "contrary to the laws of nature"; they could not bind the whiskey rebels.[142] Yet Brackenridge had his limits. An individual might secede, but he rejected the prospect of state secession, civil war, or dissolution of the Union. The land remained entrusted to the nation.

The second part of Brackenridge's argument, the authority of English common law, addressed a contradictory tradition going back centuries. On the one hand, common law proliferated options for interpreting what was treason while on the other it embraced stare decisis, that is, the necessity to follow earlier judicial opinions on the same point of law. Brackenridge aligned with James Wilson (the architect of the Constitution's language on treason) in rejecting the arbitrary nature of common law, warning that such indeterminateness can "degenerate into arbitrary power."[143] Indeterminateness was the very doubt against which the corrective English statute 25 Edw. III stood—the doubt that constructive treasons left in the minds of men as to their conduct and fate.[144]

For Brackenridge, prosecutors Rawle and Bradford had embraced a contradictory, indeterminate, and expansive common law by labelling the execution of the law and administrative operations of the government treason. But, he objected, an act that did not directly attack the government with the purpose of subversion or overthrow was mere riot;[145] without intent, there was no treason but only trespass, a breach of the peace, or riot.[146] Absent an intention to overthrow the government or conspiring to do so, American law held from its founding that neither domestic disturbance nor political opposition was treason. Was it then necessary to the preservation of the government to hold that the attack at Bower Hill was treason? No rebel present at Neville's house, Brackenridge argued, would have accepted such a presumption of intent; they had no intent "to shake the foundation of the government" to which they had sworn allegiance.[147] Brackenridge's North Star was clear: treason required one to engage knowingly in an attack meant to overthrow the government.

In terms of treason as a form of levying war, riot and treason must be distinguished.[148] Where risings involved maintaining a private right[149]—even to breaking persons out of prison—these were not treason by levying war.[150] Resistance (like that of the rebellion) to an officer or to serving a process of a US court was no more than "an aggravated trespass" and thereby no more than a maximum twelve-month sentence and $300 fine.[151] Moreover, resistance of a particular and not a general design was not a levying of war for it did not attempt to subvert or overthrow government by obstructing some necessary part of its operation and stopping the whole machine.[152] Brackenridge's view of the matter dismissed altogether any definition of treason that did not confine the law to a singular reading: "The accused had meditated death to the government, and the law in this case, and in this case only, will meditate death to him."[153]

By way of correcting judicial constructions, Brackenridge once more held that the law needed to "procure uniformity . . . produce certainty,"[154] the very role the Constitution played: "hitherto," Brackenridge argued, "the law will go, and no further."[155] In that the common law on treason amounted to an aggregation of instances, a fact pattern or a set of circumstantial inferences, Brackenridge was certain that unlearned judges "ignorant of the law"—men whom he compared to "muddy waters [that] produce ignoble fish"—were incapable of administering a standard that required proof of an overt act with the intent to subvert government.[156]

The looming question of judicial constructions constituted the last piece of Brackenridge's argument on treason. Blackstone had labeled constructivist judges "creatures of tyrannical princes"; they had the latitude to decide what was treason; they had the opportunity to raise "forced and arbitrary constructions . . . which never were expected to be such."[157] For Brackenridge, constructive treason had been "rendered sanguinary" by judges for whom even trespass constituted subversion of the government;[158] he was apprehensive that "a liberal construction given, concludes against a more rigorous one in future cases" and should make jurists wary "for we know not where we will end."[159] If legislation affirmed such constructions, Brackenridge proposed that American judges should disable precedents and construe the law "on principle of reason,"[160] for they were not beholden to discretionary law created by English judges and case law was not "law itself."[161]

Brackenridge found Whiskey Rebellion cases were no exception to constructivist tendencies.[162] Indeed, Western Pennsylvania's Judge Addison[163] construed defiance of one law and discrete acts of disobedience as defiance of all law, such that the citizenry, the government, and the nation "must cease to exist."[164] Federal District Judge Peters argued that the duty to defend the government disallowed any dissent against a legitimate government should it act illegitimately. Power, by Peters's description, superseded liberty and circumscribed participation by the people in democratic processes.[165] Justice Paterson, too, adopted an expansive English version of treason where he construed obedience to government ("mistaken for slavery") as a function of "order . . . Heaven's first law,"[166] having constructed treason to mean resisting the execution of the law or the administration of justice and having aggregated nontreasonous acts to reach treason.[167] Brackenridge responded that only "the decision of the English judges" could make the attack on Inspector Neville's house and the rebel march to assemble at Braddock's Field treason;[168] any in the jury who would "fix [a treasonous] design" were not in line with the Constitution's "meliorating spirit," for "only a fixed, formed, deliberate intention of subverting the government" and a defined offense "will construe high treason."[169]

JOHN MARSHALL AND *U. S. V. BURR*

With the resolution of the Whiskey Rebellion trials, it became clear that the spectacle of a president calling upon a national militia to quell a state rebellion and a federal circuit court presiding over a treason trial posed risks not only for federal-state relations but for civil war, the nation's treasury, and the country's public reputation. A second rebellion against federal taxation, the Fries Rebellion in eastern Pennsylvania, did not help the situation; it was tried in 1799 in the same circuit court—with three figures from the Whiskey Rebellion trials: defense counsel William Lewis, prosecutor William Rawle, and Judge Richard Peters—and confirmed the legal analysis of the earlier trials.[170] This was not, however, the end of the story for treason law in the early republic.

In 1806, Aaron Burr (Jefferson's vice president in his first administration) conspired to conduct a military expedition against Spanish territory in Louisiana in violation of the 1794 Neutrality Act. Jefferson felt that Paterson's opinions in the Whiskey Rebellion trials had opened the way to a broad indictment against Burr,[171] which led him to file charges for treason on which Burr was tried in 1807 before the US Supreme Court.[172] This left Chief Justice John Marshall with the task of clarifying the differences between the circumstances of 1795 and 1799 and Burr's involvement in the events of 1806. Pitting a founder and president of the republic against a recent vice president, the case was a public scandal. But it was also a personal embarrassment for Jefferson because he had privately represented that the 1787 Shays' Rebellion (a debt crisis that turned into a rebellion against a Massachusetts state tax) was an evil "productive of good" under a government in which "the will of everyone has a just influence," "A little rebellion now and then," he had impoliticly offered, "is a good thing."[173] The Burr case was a challenge to that observation.

Chief Justice John Marshall's opinion in *U. S. v. Burr*[174] supposed that Justice William Paterson was "inclined" in *Mitchell* to think that a conspiracy at Couch's Fort to force tax inspector Neville to resign paired with a march to his house constituted an act of war. Marshall put it that Paterson did not "precisely state the employment of force as necessary to constitute a levying war," but that in other cases where force was employed Paterson had considered the crime "dependent on the intention" or an instance of "actual force with a treasonable design," which led Paterson to determine "the crime is high treason." Marshall drew the conclusion that Whiskey Rebellion judges (Paterson and Peters) and Fries Rebellion judges (Peters, James Iredell, and Samuel Chase) "seem to have required the actual exercise of force, the actual employment of some degree of violence," which "may be, and probably is" based on the grounds that "such an assemblage as would be sufficient for the purpose would require the actual employment of force to render the object unequivocal." Marshall argued that Paterson and Iredell implied "an actual assembling of men, though they rather designed to remark on the purpose to which the force was to be applied than on the nature of the force itself." Finally, he concluded with what he believed was "the particular point the court meant to establish": that an assemblage was necessary and "the idea of force was never separated from this assemblage."[175]

Apart from Marshall's tortuous parsing of Paterson's argument, the critical obstacle was Paterson's construction of the overt act that constituted treason. As Marshall framed it, "The overt act laid in the indictment was consummated by the assemblage at Couch's and the marching from thence," where Mitchell was seen by two witnesses. But Paterson proceeded "without deciding this to be the law" and considered "the meeting at Couch's, the immediate marching to Neville's house, and the attack and burning of the house, as one transaction." Finding more than two witnesses to "that transaction," according to Marshall, Paterson "declared it to be unnecessary that all should have seen him at the same time and place."[176] Paterson's approach raised a number of questions for Marshall: What if no one had seen Mitchell at the fort or house or on the march? What if Mitchell had been "notoriously absent in a different state"? Could anyone who knew how cautious Paterson was, Marshal asked, have believed he would say Mitchell was "constructively present, and might, on that straining of a legal fiction" find him guilty of treason? Had Paterson, he noted, "given this opinion, it would have required all the correctness of his life to strike his name from that bloody list in which the name of Jeffreys is enrolled."[177]

Marshall went on to qualify his recently departed colleague's analysis, indicating that Paterson did not "precisely state" what Marshall claimed, that

Paterson "was inclined to think," and that Marshall "estimated Paterson's opinion." Assisted by such equivocations, Marshall presumed Paterson was referring to an unequivocal intent on the part of an assemblage to use force to resist through an overt act the execution of a law, substantially short of overturning the government.[178] In addition, the *Burr* opinion clarified that the law on conspiracy did not make it "treason in all" when one conspirator committed a treasonous act based on a conspiracy; that part of treason law, Marshall noted, applied only to counterfeiting and had not been "stated . . . as a general proposition."[179] Those tried for conspiracy rather than an overt act or considered part of a treason because they had conspired but not acted, were not thereby guilty of treason.

Justice Paterson's loose constructions on constitutional concerns such as the proof for treason, intent, and an actual act were thus largely disavowed by *Burr* where the law on treason was brought back in line with thinking in the constitutional convention. "I consider the principles laid down in [the *Burr*] trial," Brackenridge wrote, "as gaining much to the citizen of the United States." Referring to the debate over the legacy of English common law and English statutes in American legal practice, Brackenridge considered *Burr* "a barrier against the application of British rules in the construction of treason," adding that Marshall's opinion "contains some excellent landmarks, that may serve to guide in aftertimes, when [political] parties may prevail, and [Federalist] *judges may have the same leaning with the prosecutors for the state*."[180] Indeed, *Burr* became settled law on the questions of an overt act and levying war, reorienting the interpretation of treason law in much the way the whiskey rebel defense had indicated.[181]

CONCLUSION

In a final irony of history, one of the most important events of the rebellion turned out to have occurred on the site of the most significant event of Washington's early military career in the western lands. Washington had fought in 1755 alongside then-Captain Thomas Gage of the British Army in a battle referred to as the Monongahela massacre. Whereas General Edward Braddock commanded the colonial forces, it would be Washington who walked away with the honors by taking over from the mortally wounded Braddock and overseeing an orderly retreat from the disaster. The retreat would haunt him for at least the four decades between this painful lesson in frontier warfare and his decision to mount a militia against his own citizens in 1794.[182] Braddock's Field, it would turn out, was the site of the largest rebel assembly in the Whiskey Rebellion.

Benefitting from what John L. Brooke calls the "expectations of democracy" created by the revolution, the Whiskey Rebellion reinforced public square dissent that turned the tables on dominant entities. With the insurgency operating to put pressure from the margins, and the democratic societies exercising influence within the public sphere of discourse, the early republic "saw a real democratization of polity" earlier than the Jacksonian era, the period that is often given credit for the breakout of popular democracy.[183] Reeve Huston attributes this change to the 1790s' emergence of "a new class of political leaders," the people's "friends" (Republicans), who challenged the "genteel" friends of government (Federalists). This rise of "popular egalitarianism," partisan newspapers (the subject of the next chapter), and political mobilization instigated enhanced political participation and polarization.[184]

The new growth of political awareness and opposition did not express a singularity of purpose as it split the elite at national and state levels, popular leaders locally, and regional activists in states as diverse as Virginia, Pennsylvania, New York, and Massachusetts. This split meant that genteel patron-client relations would survive side-by-side with changing ideas and political practices until 1840 to produce different definitions of democracy.[185] In the western parts of states, popular movements (regulators, whiskey rebels, agrarian rebellion) that were not party based disappeared after 1800 when they merged with Republican opposition to Federalists. What we thus find are breaks from an emerging party system in the 1790s that produced a "proliferation of competing blueprints for democracy" that has lasted until today.[186]

What one does not want to miss here, however, is that beyond the 1790s the rivalry between local and national politics led to a reinvented republicanism that departed from its earlier classical thought and balanced government to one that recognized public culture emanating from capitalist development and responsive to populism. With the introduction of a direct tax and expansion of the army, Republicans could generate political support by playing on popular aversions to standing armies and oppressive taxation, aversions that dated back to political action against Britain, the constitutional ratification debate, and now the Whiskey Rebellion. Through democratic-republican societies, they were already organizing, electioneering, and creating political alliances in building a political party.[187] With the assistance of a partisan press, Republicans could extend their influence and generate more antipathy to the general government.[188] This transformed Republican brand would become dominant into the Jacksonian era and beyond as a controlling form of national politics that favored popular participation and republican self-government.[189]

Looking toward the next step in the progress of democracy across the early republic takes us from the frontier to the center, from the West to the East and the issues faced there in making democracy. It leaves behind a culture of law dealing with war, land grabs, and debt-crisis rebellion. It removes us from the interdisciplinary prisms of war and peace, reputation and the legal system, and popular sovereignty and treason. With George Washington featured in the three trials already studied, we have passed through the thrall of a cult of personality in which the founding figures were invested. Following Washington through his roles of Continental Army commander in chief to private citizen and then to first president of the United States played out all the permutations of Washington's career, leaving us with a clearer view of an ambitious plantation owner, military leader, and land speculator growing into the role of a head of state.

The law of the East speaks more of solidifying the gains of the revolution in reforming the courts and laws while addressing an explosion of litigation and facing the dark side of human crime, slave labor, and prejudice. It takes us to the nation's transatlantic relations and partisan politics, individual rights and institutional freedoms, urban crime, and the strain between the North and South over slavery. In doing so, eastern trials explore a legal culture made up of high rhetoric and flamboyant lawyering challenging judge-dominated courtrooms. They introduce a shift toward laws of evidence and enhanced due process in an adversarial style of trial. And they provide the influence of African American churches in the struggle for justice, the emergence of abolitionism, and the excesses of a popular press.

NOTES

1. Steven Wilf, "The First Republican Revival: Virtue, Judging, and Rhetoric in the Early Republic," *Connecticut Law Review* 32, no. 5 (2000): 1676–77.

2. Steven Wilf, *Law's Imagined Republic: Popular Politics and Criminal Justice in Revolutionary America* (Cambridge: Cambridge University Press, 2010), 1–13, 64–65, 193–96.

3. William Pencak, "Introduction: A Historical Perspective," in *Riot and Revelry in Early America*, eds. William Pencak, Matthew Dennis, and Simon P. Newman (University Park: Penn State University Press, 2002), 7, 16; William Pencak, "White Indians in Penn's City: The Loyal Sons of St. Tammany," in *Riot and Revelry in Early America*, eds. William Pencak, Matthew Dennis, and Simon P. Newman (University Park: Penn State University Press, 2002), 179–205.

4. Rachel N. Klein, "Ordering the Backcountry: The South Carolina Regulation," *William and Mary Quarterly* 38, no. 4 (1981): 662, 668–69, 675; Dorothy Elaine Fennell, *From Rebelliousness to Insurrection: A Social History of the Whiskey Rebellion, 1765–1802* (PhD diss., University of Pittsburgh,1981), 147–48, 151, 176, DA8213093. On early American crowds, Edward Countryman, "The Problem of the Early American Crowds," *Journal of American Studies* 7, no. 1 (1973): 77–90; Paul A. Gilje, *The Road to Mobocracy: Popular Disorder in New York City, 1763–1834*

(Durham: University of North Carolina Press, 1987); Pauline Maier, "Popular Uprisings and Civil Authority in Eighteenth-Century America," *William and Mary Quarterly* 27 (1970): 3–35; Pauline Maier, *From Resistance to Revolution: Colonial Radicals and the Development of American Opposition to Britain, 1765–1776* (New York: W. W. Norton and Company, 1992); Gordon S. Wood, "A Note on Mobs in the American Revolution," *William and Mary Quarterly* 23, no. 4 (1966): 635–42; Gordon S. Wood, *The Radicalism of the American Revolution* (New York: Vintage Books, 1993).

5. E. P. Thompson, "The Moral Economy of the English Crowd in the Eighteenth Century," *Past and Present* 50 (1991): 78–79.

6. Roger D. Abrahams, "Introduction: A Folklore Perspective," in *Riot and Revelry in Early America*, eds. William Pencak, Matthew Dennis, and Simon P. Newman (University Park: Penn State University Press, 2002), 30, 34.

7. Klein, "Ordering the Backcountry," 661n1, 662, 678–79.

8. James Roger Sharp, *American Politics in the Early Republic: The New Nation in Crisis* (New Haven, CT: Yale University Press, 1993), 108–11.

9. Terry Bouton, *Taming Democracy: "The People," the Founders, and the Troubled Ending of the American Revolution* (Oxford: Oxford University Press, 2007), 217–19; Paul Douglas Newman, *Fries Rebellion: The Enduring Struggle for the American Revolution* (Philadelphia: University of Pennsylvania Press, 2004), 146–64; G. E. Connor, "The Politics of Insurrection: A Comparative Analysis of the Shays,' Whiskey, and Fries' Rebellions," *Social Science Journal* 29, no. 3 (1992): 259–81. Bouton favors the term "regulation," which links the Whiskey Rebellion to earlier and later agitation in North Carolina, Massachusetts, and Maine, but the term "Whiskey Rebellion" tends to be more widely used.

10. Thomas P. Slaughter, *The Whiskey Rebellion: Frontier Epilogue to the American Revolution* (New York: Oxford University Press, 1986), 32–33, 39–40, 53.

11. Slaughter, *The Whiskey Rebellion*, 84–89, 118, 121, 177; R. Eugene Harper, *The Transformation of Western Pennsylvania, 1770–1800* (Pittsburgh: University of Pittsburgh Press, 1991); Thomas Perkins Abernathy, *Western Lands and the American Revolution* (Richmond: University of Virginia Institute of Research in the Social Sciences, 1937); David M. Friedenberg, *Life, Liberty and the Pursuit of Land: The Plunder of Early America* (New York: Prometheus, 1992); Andrew Shankman, *Crucible of American Democracy: The Struggle to Fuse Egalitarianism and Capitalism in Jeffersonian Pennsylvania* (Lawrence: University Press of Kansas, 2004); Alan Taylor, "Land and Liberty on the Post-Revolutionary Frontier," in *Devising Liberty: Preserving and Creating Freedom in the New American Republic*, ed. David Thomas Konig (Stanford: Stanford University Press, 1995), 81–108; Norman Wilkinson, *Land Policy and Speculation in Pennsylvania, 1779–1800: A Test of the New Democracy* (New York: Arno Press, 1979); William Hogeland, *The Whiskey Rebellion: George Washington, Alexander Hamilton, and the Frontier Rebels who Challenged America's Newfound Sovereignty* (New York: Simon and Schuster, 2006); Patrick Spero, *Frontier Country: The Politics of War in Early Pennsylvania* (Philadelphia: University of Pennsylvania Press, 2016); Patrick Griffin, *American Leviathan: Empire, Nation, and*

Revolutionary Frontier (New York: Hill and Wang, 2007); Peter Silver, *Our Savage Neighbors: How Indian War Transformed Early America* (New York: Norton, 2009).

12. Max M. Edling, *A Revolution in Favor of Government: Origins of the U.S. Constitution and the Making of the American State* (New York: Oxford University Press, 2003), 212–13.

13. Stanley Elkins and Eric McKitrick, *The Age of Federalism: The Early American Republic, 1788–1800* (New York: Oxford University Press, 1993), 467–69.

14. Thomas P. Slaughter, "The Tax Man Cometh: Ideological Opposition to Internal Taxes, 1760–1790," *William and Mary Quarterly* 41, no. 4 (1984):585–90.

15. Edling, *A Revolution in Favor of Government*, 209–10.

16. Edling, *A Revolution in Favor of Government*, 207–12; Gautham Rao, *National Duties: Custom Houses and the Making of the American State* (Chicago: University of Chicago Press, 2016).

17. See Richard H. Kohn, "The Washington Administration's Decision to Crush the Whiskey Rebellion," *Journal of American History* 59, no. 3 (1972): 567–84; William D. Barber, "'Among the Most Techy Articles of Civil Police': Federal Taxation and the Adoption of the Whiskey Excise," *William and Mary Quarterly* 3rd ser. 25, no. 1 (1968): 58–84; Jeffrey A. Davis, "Guarding the Republican Interest: The Western Pennsylvania Democratic Societies and the Excise Tax," *Pennsylvania History* 67, no. 1 (2000): 43–62; Elkins and McKitrick, *The Age of Federalism*, 461–88; Slaughter, "Tax Man," 566–91.

18. Kohn, "The Washington Administration's Decision," 568–69.

19. Kohn, "The Washington Administration's Decision," 569–73; Gordon S. Wood, "Conspiracy and the Paranoid Style: Causality and Deceit in the Eighteenth Century," *The William and Mary Quarterly* 39, no. 3 (1982): 401–41.

20. Elkins and McKitrick, *The Age of Federalism*, 468, 470.

21. Edling, *A Revolution in Favor of Government*, 213–16.

22. Max M. Edling, *Perfecting the Union: National and State Authority in the US Constitution* (New York: Oxford University Press, 2021), 10–15, 135–36.

23. Hugh Henry Brackenridge, *Incidents of the Insurrection in the Western Parts of Pennsylvania, in the Year 1794* (Philadelphia: John M'Culloch, 1795), I, 36.

24. Brackenridge, *Incidents of the Insurrection*, I, 38.

25. William Findley, *History of the Insurrection in the Four Western Counties of Pennsylvania: In the Year 1794; and an Historical Review of the Previous Situation of the Country* (Philadelphia: Samuel Harrison Smith, 1796), 49–50.

26. Findley, *History of the Insurrection*, 42; Alexander Hamilton to George Washington, August 5, 1794, Founders Online, https://founders.archives.gov/documents.

27. Findley, *History of the Insurrection*, 44–45.

28. Findley, *History of the Insurrection*, 48–49.

29. Findley, *History of the Insurrection*, 53.

30. Saul Cornell, *A Well Regulated Militia: The Founding Fathers and the Origins of Gun Control in America* (New York: Oxford University Press, 2006), 73–74, 76, 82, 85; Saul Cornell, "Beyond the Myth of Consensus: The Struggle to Define the Right to Bear Arms in the Early Republic," in *Beyond the Founders: New Approaches to the Political History of the Early American Republic*, eds. Jeffrey L. Pasley, Andrew

W. Robertson, and David Waldstreicher (Durham: University of North Carolina Press, 2004), 256–57. Influential eighteenth-century legal commentator St. George Tucker argued the constitutional case for the right to resist the federal government relying upon Article 1, section 8 and the Second and Tenth Amendments; Cornell, *A Well Regulated Militia*, 73–74, 102–04. A natural law right to revolution was the legacy of the American Revolution that the 1786 Shays' Rebellion in Massachusetts and the 1787 Carlisle riot in Pennsylvania relied upon. See Richard H. Kohn, *Eagle and Sword: The Federalists and the Creation of the Military Establishment in America, 1783–1802* (New York: Free Press, 1975).

31. Bouton, *Taming Democracy*, 232, 235; Hugh Marie Brackenridge, *History of the Western Insurrection in Western Pennsylvania, Commonly Called the Whiskey Insurrection, 1794* (Pittsburgh, 1859), 47, 82; Hogeland, *The Whiskey Rebellion*, 117–23, 152; Leland D. Baldwin, *Whiskey Rebels: The Story of a Frontier Uprising* (Pittsburgh: University of Pittsburgh Press, 1939), 118, 154; Slaughter, *The Whiskey Rebellion*, 178–79; Kenneth Owen, *Political Community in Revolutionary Pennsylvania, 1774–1800* (Oxford: Oxford University Press, 2018), 137–45.

32. Coxe later served as Hamilton's revenue commissioner during the rebellion.

33. "A Pennsylvanian," *Pennsylvania Gazette*, February 20, 1788; Stephen P. Halbrook and David P. Kopel, "Tench Coxe and the Right to Keep and Bear Arms," *William and Mary Bill of Rights Journal* 7, no. 2 (1999): 363; Cornell, "Beyond the Myth of Consensus," 261. David Thomas Konig, "Arms and the Man: What Did the Right to Keep Arms Mean in the Early Republic," *Law and History Review* 25, no. 1 (2007): 180–181, 183.

34. U. S. Constitution, Article 1, section 8. Pennsylvania Constitution of 1790, Article 6, section 2.

35. Cornell, "Beyond the Myth of Consensus," 259, 262.

36. Saul Cornell, "Mobs, Militias, and Magistrates: Popular Constitutionalism and the Whiskey Rebellion," *Chicago-Kent Law Review*, 81, no. 3 (2006): 894; Cornell, *A Well Regulated Militia*, 74, 76.

37. Cornell, "Mobs, Militias, and Magistrates," 896; Cornell, *A Well Regulated Militia*, 76. The radical aspect of the militia broke out in a 1787 riot in Carlisle in which local militia freed from jail anti-Federalists who had rioted over a Federalist celebration of Pennsylvania's ratification of the Constitution. Their spokesman William Petrikin's vision was one of a populist militia enforcing direct democracy, an ideology which the Carlisle riot exemplified and which the radical wing of the Whiskey Rebellion would emulate; Saul Cornell, *The Other Founders: Anti-Federalism and the Dissenting Tradition in America, 1788–1828* (Chapel Hill: University of North Caroline Press, 1999),108, 115; Cornell, *A Well Regulated Militia*, 55–58, 64, 80–81.

38. Cornell, "Mobs, Militias, and Magistrates," 890.

39. Cornell, "Beyond the Myth of Consensus," 263–65.

40. Cornell, *A Well Regulated Militia*, 66; David P. Currie, "The Constitution in Congress: Substantive Issues in the First Congress, 1789–1791," *The University of Chicago Law Review* 61, no. 3 (1994): 813–16. The government had in 1790 proposed military reform—a plan provided by Secretary of War Henry Knox—which would have organized a national militia under the control of the federal government.

41. Peter S. Onuf, *The Origins of the Federal Republic: Jurisdictional Controversies in the United States, 1775–1787* (Philadelphia: University of Pennsylvania Press, 1983), 65–66.

42. Onuf, *The Origins of the Federal Republic*, 66–67.

43. Onuf, *The Origins of the Federal Republic*, 72.

44. Robert C. Lieberman and Suzanne Mettler, *Four Threats: The Recurring Crises of American Democracy* (New York: St. Martin's Press, 2020); Nicholas Casey, "Making Political Forecasts, and Wincing All the While," *New York Times*, Sunday, November 17, 2019, https://www.nytimes.com; Elkins and McKitrick, 476–77, 482.

45. Sonia Mittal and Barry R. Weingast, "Self-Enforcing Constitutions: With an Application to Democratic Stability in America's First Century," *Journal of Law, Economics, and Organization* 29, no. 2 (2013): 278–302.

46. Owen, *Political Community in Revolutionary Pennsylvania*, 138–42.

47. See here, Larry D. Kramer, *The People Themselves: Popular Constitutionalism and Judicial Review* (Oxford: Oxford University Press, 2004); Christian G. Fritz, *American Sovereigns: The People and America's Constitutional Tradition Before the Civil War* (Cambridge: Cambridge University Press, 2008); Robert W. T. Martin, *Government by Dissent: Protest, Resistance, and Radical Democratic Thought in the Early American Republic* (New York: New York University Press, 2013); Cornell, *A Well Regulated Militia.*

48. Russell J. Ferguson, *Early Western Pennsylvania Politics* (Pittsburgh: University of Pittsburgh Press, 1938), 62, 64, 73–74, 92; Sharp, *American Politics in the Early Republic*, 97–98.

49. Sharp, *American Politics in the Early Republic*, 93–100.

50. James Roger Sharp, "The Whiskey Rebellion and the Question of Representation," in *The Whiskey Rebellion: Past and Present Perspectives*, ed., Steven R. Boyd (Westport, CT: Greenwood Press, 1985), 119-20.

51. Saul Cornell, "Aristocracy Assailed: The Ideology of Backcountry Anti-Federalism," *Journal of American History* 76, no. 4 (1990): 1172.

52. "An Indian Treaty," *Pennsylvania Archives,* Second Series, eds. John B. Linn and William H. Egle (Harrisburg, PA: Clarence M. Busch, 1896), IV, 458–63; *Pittsburgh Gazette*, August 23, 1794; Brackenridge, *Incidents of the Insurrection*, II, 6–7.

53. Slaughter, *The Whiskey Rebellion*, 206.

54. Slaughter, *The Whiskey Rebellion*, 218.

55. Slaughter, *The Whiskey Rebellion*, 219, 277n33.

56. Findley, *History of the Insurrection*, 295, 305.

57. Findley, 305.

58. James Wilson to George Washington, August 4, 1794, *Pennsylvania Archives*, Second Series, IV, 70. To mount a federal army, a Supreme Court justice had to certify that the conditions for implementation of the Militia Act (1792) had been met.

59. Findley, *History of the Insurrection*, 318.

60. William Bradford to George Washington, August 5, 1794, Founders Online, https://founders.archives.gov/documents.

61. Edmund Randolph to George Washington, August 5, 1794, in Francis Wharton, *State Trials of the United States during the Administrations of Washington and*

Adams, with References Historical and Professional (New York: B. Franklin, 1849), 156–58. Randolph was secretary of state from 1794 to1795. He had served earlier as Washington's attorney general.

62. Thomas Mifflin to George Washington, August 5, 1794, in Francis Wharton, *State Trials of the United States during the Administrations of Washington and Adams, with References Historical and Professional* (New York: B. Franklin, 1849), 144; Thomas Mifflin to George Washington, August 12, 1794, *Pennsylvania Archives*, Second Series, IV, 130; Edmund Randolph to Thomas Mifflin, August 7, 1794, *Pennsylvania Archives*, Second Series, IV, 96–104.

63. Edmund Randolph to Thomas Mifflin, August 30, 1794, in Wharton, *State Trials of the United States*, 154.

64. "Instructions to General Lee," October 20, 1794, communicated by Alexander Hamilton as from George Washington, https://founders.archives.gov/documents; Brackenridge, *Incidents of the Insurrection*, II, 65–67.

65. Brackenridge, *Incidents of the Insurrection*, II, 66. Peters was the chief judicial official accompanying the militia; he served with Supreme Court Justice William Paterson as presiding judge of the Whiskey Rebellion trials in which one Supreme Court justice presided with the district judge.

66. Brackenridge, *Incidents of the Insurrection*, I, 61; II, 78; II, 80.

67. Alexander Hamilton to George Washington, September 2, 1794, *Pennsylvania Archives*, Second Series, IV, 242–43, 248.

68. Charles Nisbet was the first Principal of Dickinson College. Charles Nisbet to Alexander Addison, January 13, 1795, Alexander Addison Papers, 1786–1803, DAR. 1925.06, Darlington Collection, University of Pittsburgh.

69. Charles Nisbet to Alexander Addison, February 20, 1795, Addison Papers.

70. Brackenridge, *Incidents of the Insurrection*, II, 63.

71. William S. Lofquist, "Justice on the Western Frontier: The Death Penalty in Pre-Industrial Pittsburgh, 1754–1840," *Pennsylvania History: A Journal of Mid-Atlantic Studies* 85, no. 4 (2018): 571.

72. According to Wythe Holt, the grand jury indicted twenty-four out of the thirty-four bills for treason presented (or 73%), of which ten stood trial since of those indicted thirteen had fled and one fell under the amnesty. Two of these ten (or 20%) were convicted. The grand jury refused to indict four rebels for misprision of treason and five rebels for misdemeanor. Two rebels were indicted for felony, twenty-six for misdemeanor, and two for misprision of treason. Only two of these were tried and convicted. Holt's review shows fifty-two indictments: twenty-four for treason, two for felony, and twenty-six for misdemeanors (all the misdemeanors were speech related). Wythe Holt, "The Whiskey Rebellion of 1794: A Democratic Working-Class Insurrection," http://colonial seminar.uga.edu/whiskeyrebellion-6 (2004), 74–81; Wythe Holt, "The Federal Whiskey Rebellion Cases of 1795 and the Rise of the National Security State," unpublished manuscript, 2010, generously made available by the author.

73. William Rawle to Alexander Addison, August 15, 1795, *Pennsylvania Archives*, Second Series, IV, 450.

74. Albert Gallatin to Hannah Gallatin, May 12, 1795, Gallatin Papers, New York Historical Society (Nhi).

75. Albert Gallatin to John Badollet, May 20, 1795, Gallatin Papers, NHi.

76. Extracts from "Captain Porter's Narrative," in Brackenridge, *History of the Western Insurrection*, 331.

77. Albert Gallatin to Hannah Gallatin, June 1, 1795, *The Documentary History of the Supreme Court of the United States, 1789–1800*, Maeva Marcus, ed. (New York: Columbia University Press, 2004), VI, 53.

78. Albert Gallatin to Hannah Gallatin, May 18–19, 1795, Gallatin Papers, NHi.

79. Holt, "Federal Whiskey," chapter V.

80. Albert Gallatin refers to two men named Miller, Thomas and William, who were involved in the rebellion and indicate Thomas was about to be tried, but William, who was indicted, had fled. Albert Gallatin to Thomas Clare, May 30, 1795, Gallatin Papers, NHi.

81. Albert Gallatin to Hannah Gallatin, June 1, 1795, in Marcus, VI, 53.

82. Albert Gallatin to Hannah Gallatin, June 1, 1795, in Marcus, VI, 53.

83. Holt, "Federal Whiskey," chapter V, 67, 11–12.

84. Alexander Dallas, *Reports of Cases Ruled and Adjudged in the Several Courts of the United States, and of Pennsylvania, Held at the Seat of the Federal Government* (Philadelphia: Aurora Office, 1790–1807).

85. Dallas, *Reports of Cases Ruled*, II, 350.

86. Alexander Addison's September 1795 grand jury charge described the Federalist context in which the trials addressed individual rights. Alexander Addison, *Reports of Cases in the County Courts of the Fifth Circuit, and in the High Court of Errors and Appeals of the State of Pennsylvania, and Charges to Grand Juries of Those Courts* (Washington, DC: John Colerick, 1800), 156–57, 159–60.

87. Albert Gallatin to John Badollet, May 20, 1795, Gallatin Papers, NHi; William Paterson, bench notes, United States vs. Philson and Husband, see note 72.

88. *U. S. v. Mitchell*; Dallas, *Reports of Cases Ruled*, II, 348–57. Paterson's bench notes are as follows: *U. S. v. Robert Porter*, May 18, 1795, on deposit Senator John Heinz History Center, Pittsburgh Regional History Center, in association with the Smithsonian Institution, MFF2739. 1795; *United States v. John Barnet*, May 29, 1795, Autograph Manuscript, Gilder Lehrman Institute of American History, GLC01114; *United States v. Miller*, June 1, 1795, William Paterson Papers. Court Cases, 1765–1802; 2.B. Federal Court Cases, File 119, William Paterson College; *United States v. Philson and Husband*, June 3, 1795, William Paterson Papers, Court Cases, 1765–1802; 2.B, Federal Court Cases, File 120, William Paterson College.

89. Slaughter, *The Whiskey Rebellion*, 179.

90. Slaughter, *The Whiskey Rebellion*, 179–80; Leland D. Baldwin, *Whiskey Rebels: The Story of a Frontier Uprising* (Pittsburgh: University of Pittsburgh Press, 1939), 124.

91. Dallas, *Reports of Cases Ruled*, II, 349.

92. Dallas, *Reports of Cases Ruled*, II, 349.

93. Dallas, *Reports of Cases Ruled*, II, 350.

94. Dallas, *Reports of Cases Ruled*, II, 352.

95. Dallas, *Reports of Cases Ruled*, II, 353.
96. Dallas, *Reports of Cases Ruled*, II, 354.
97. Dallas, *Reports of Cases Ruled*, II, 354–355.
98. Dallas, *Reports of Cases Ruled*, II, 356.
99. Slaughter, *The Whiskey Rebellion*, 178–179; Bouton, *Taming Democracy*, 232–35; Brackenridge, *History of the Western Insurrection*, 44–47; Hogeland, *The Whiskey* Rebellion, 117–23, 152; Baldwin, *Whiskey* Rebels, 118, 154.
100. Konig, "Arms and the Man," 181, 183.
101. Militia Act, May 8, 1792, Providing Federal Standards for the Organization of the Militia, sec. IV.
102. Dallas, *Reports of Cases Ruled*, II, 349.
103. *U. S. v. Robert Porter*, May 18, 1795, Senator John Heinz History Center, Pittsburgh Regional History Center, in association with the Smithsonian Institution, MFF2739, 1795.
104. Dallas, *Reports of Cases Ruled*, II, 349.
105. Dallas, *Reports of Cases Ruled*, II, 353–54.
106. Chapin claims William Bradford was "the first to bring in the English doctrine of constructive war" to Washington as the president debated invoking the Militia Act to move troops against the rebels. See Bradley Chapin, *The American Law of Treason: Revolutionary and Early National Origins* (Seattle: University of Washington Press, 1964), 86. Constructive treason—succinctly described by Chapin—was the means by which the Crown added new treasons to the statue of Edward III to undermine its restrictions: "Any attempt to modify public policy by force amounted to treason . . . any attempt to prevent the application of a statute was not riot, but treason"; Chapin, *The American Law of Treason*, 3; William Bradford to George Washington, August [5], 1794, Founders Online, https://founders.archives.gov/documents.
107. William Bradford to Elias Boudinot, August 1, 1794, Wallace Papers, II, Historical Society of Pennsylvania (HSP).
108. Dallas, *Reports of Cases Ruled*, II, 350, 353.
109. Dallas, *Reports of Cases Ruled*, II, 350–51.
110. Defense counsel admitted Mitchell might have been guilty of some crime but not treason and called attention to Bradford's admission, which they had "laid down in all the books, which have been cited," that conspiracy was not treason; Dallas, *Reports of Cases Ruled*, II, 351.
111. Dallas, *Reports of Cases Ruled*, II, 351.
112. Dallas, *Reports of Cases Ruled*, II, 350.
113. Dallas, *Reports of Cases Ruled*, II, 355.
114. Dallas, *Reports of Cases Ruled*, II, 355; Thomas P. Slaughter, "'The King of Crimes': Early American Treason Law, 1787–1860," in *Launching the 'Extended Republic': The Federalist Era*, eds. Ronald Hoffman and Peter Albert (Charlottesville: University of Virginia, 1996), 94.
115. William Blackstone, *Commentaries on the Laws of England*, 13th ed. (London: A Strahan, 1800), IV, 75, 82; Matthew Hale, *The History of the Pleas of the Crown* (London: E. and R. Nutt and R. Gosling, 1736), I, 80, 84, 151.

116. Willard Hurst contends the only historical evidence of the intention behind the two-witness requirement was James Madison's note that Dr. Franklin was behind that "amendment" as "prosecutions were generally virulent; and perjury too easily made use of against innocence." Willard Hurst, "Treason in the United States: III, Under the Constitution," *Harvard Law Review* 58, no. 6 (1945): 844.

117. Dallas, *Reports of Cases Ruled*, II, 349–50, 353.

118. Dallas, *Reports of Cases Ruled*, II, 356. Rawle had argued for the prosecution, in addition, that acts at other sites and at other times were sufficient "corroborative demonstrations of that *mala mens*" necessary to crimes that carried a death penalty; Dallas, *Reports of Cases Ruled*, II, 350; James Willard Hurst, "Treason in the United States: I, Treason, Down to the Constitution," *Harvard Law Review* 58, no. 2 (1944): 243; James Willard Hurst, *The Law of Treason in the United States: Collected Essays* (Westport, CT: Greenwood Publishing Company, 1971), 80–81.

119. Dallas, *Reports of Cases Ruled*, II, 355–56.

120. Dallas, II, *Reports of Cases Ruled*, 350–51.

121. Dallas, II, *Reports of Cases Ruled*, 351.

122. The *Vigol* treason trial, the only other trial for treason that was reported by Dallas, involved an attack against excise collector Benjamin Well's house; Dallas, *Reports of Cases Ruled* (1790–1807), II, 346–48.

123. The misdemeanor case, *Philson and Husband*, was an anomaly as it had ten prosecution witnesses and twenty defense witnesses. Paterson's bench notes take up sixteen manuscript pages in *Porter*, seventeen in *Miller*, thirty in *Barnet* (including the judge's charge to the jury and defense and prosecution arguments), and thirty-two in *Philson and Husband*. Except for *Barnet*, the notes do not include counsels' opening and closing arguments.

124. John E. O'Connor, *William Paterson: Lawyer and Statesman, 1745–1806* (New Brunswick, NJ: Rutgers University Press, 1979), 203, 224, 233–36; Linda Myrsiades, "A Tale of a Whiskey Rebellion Judge: William Paterson, Grand Jury Charges, and the Trials of the Whiskey Rebels," *The Pennsylvania Magazine of History and Biography* 140, no. 2 (2016): 129–65; Charles F. Hickox III and Andrew C. Laviano, "William Paterson," *Journal of Supreme Court History* 17, no. 1 (1922); Richard A. Ifft, "Treason in the Early Republic: The Federal Courts, Popular Protest, and Federalism During the Whiskey Rebellion," in *The Whiskey Rebellion; Past and Present Perspectives*, ed. Steven R. Boyd (Westport, CT: Greenwood Press, 1985), 165–82; Daniel D. Blinka, "'This Germ of Rottenness': Federal Trials in the New Republic, 1789–1807," *Creighton Law Review* 36, no. 2 (2003): 135–89; Thomas P. Slaughter, "'The King of Crimes': Early American Treason Law, 1787–1860," in *Launching the 'Extended Republic': The Federalist Era*, eds. Ronald Hoffman and Peter Albert (Charlottesville: University of Virginia, 1996).

125. Hugh Henry Brackenridge, "A Dissertation on the Treason Laws of the United States," *Incidents*, appendix, 41–61; Hugh Henry Brackenridge, "Treason Laws of the United States," *Law Miscellanies: Containing an Introduction to the Study of the Law, Notes on Blackstone's Commentaries, Shewing the Law of Pennsylvania from the Law of England and What Acts of Assembly Might Require to be Repealed or Modified* (Philadelphia: P. Sterne, 1814), 474–502.

126. David Paul Brown, *The Forum; or Forty Years Full Practice at the Philadelphia Bar* (Philadelphia: Robert H. Small, 1856), I, 255. Esther McFarland reveals Paterson's papers remain unavailable to the public; Esther Ann McFarland, *William Lewis, Esquire: Enlightened Statesman, Profound Lawyer, and Useful Citizen* (Darby, PA: Diane Publishing Company, 2012), iii–iv; personal correspondence with the estate.

127. *Respublica v. Chapman* was the only American case before the ratification of the Constitution that answered who owed allegiance; it held that the party who received protection from a government owed allegiance to it; Dallas, *Reports of Cases Ruled*, I, 53, 57–59; Carlton Larson, "The Forgotten Constitutional Law of Treason and the Enemy Combatant Problem," *University of Pennsylvania Law Review* 154, no. 4 (2006): 881–82. As attorney general of Pennsylvania at the time of the *Chapman* decision, William Bradford did not hold with Chief Justice McKean's argument; G. S. Rowe, *Thomas McKean: The Shaping of An American Republicanism* (Boulder: Colorado Associated University Press, 1978), 138–40.

128. Larson, "The Forgotten," 882.

129. Thomas Jefferson to Gouverneur Morris, August 16, 1793, Founders Online, https://founders.archives.gov/documents; *Henfield*'s *Case*, Whart. St. Tr. 49 Circuit Court, D. Pennsylvania (1793), 85–89.; 11 F. Cas. 1099 No. 6360.

130. Hugh Henry Brackenridge, *Law Miscellanies*, 500.

131. William Blackstone, *Commentaries on the Laws of England*, 15th ed., 4 vols. (London: A. Strahan, 1809), I, 366.

132. Hale, *The History*, I, 59. According to Hale, as a subject received protection from his sovereign, he was "bound by his allegiance to be true and faithful" to him and his laws; Larson, "The Forgotten," 876.

133. Blackstone, *Commentaries*, I, 368.

134. Blackstone, *Commentaries*, I, 369.

135. Blackstone, *Commentaries*, I, 369, 453; Brackenridge, *Law Miscellanies*, 406.

136. Brackenridge, *Law Miscellanies*, 407–08.

137. George P. Fletcher, "Ambivalence about Treason (Law, Loyalty, and Treason: How Can the Law Regulate Loyalty Without Imperiling It?)," *North Carolina Law Review* 82, no. 5 (2004): 1619.

138. Brackenridge, *Law Miscellanies*, 295.

139. Brackenridge, *Law Miscellanies*, 412–14, 480, 483.

140. Brackenridge, *Law Miscellanies*, 485.

141. Brackenridge, *Law Miscellanies*, 490, 493–94.

142. Brackenridge, *Law Miscellanies*, 404, 414, 500; Brackenridge, *Incidents*, I, 369–70; Blackstone, *Commentaries*, I, 369.

143. R. G. McCloskey ed., *The Works of James Wilson*, (Cambridge, MA: Belnap Press, 1967), II, 663.

144. The preamble of 25 Edw. III (the Treason Act of 1351, the English statutory correction to inventive common law) limited the "divers pains of treason" that had previously been "ordained by statutes, in as much that there was no man which did know how he ought to behave himself, to do, speak, or say, for doubt of such pains." Brackenridge, *Law Miscellanies*, 475n.

145. Brackenridge, *Law Miscellanies,* 494–95.

146. Alexander Addison, "Necessity of Submission to the Excise Laws," in *Reports of Cases in the County Courts of the Fifth Circuit, and in the High Court of Errors and Appeals of the State of Pennsylvania* (Philadelphia: John Colerick, 1800), 100–12; Addison, "Remarks on the Late Insurrection," in *Reports*, 113–29; Alexander Hamilton to George Washington, August 5, 1794, *Pennsylvania Archives,* Second Series, IV, 71–78; U.S. Commission's Report, September 24, 1794, *Pennsylvania Archives*, Second Series, IV, 293–302.

147. Brackenridge, *Law Miscellanies*, 495, 497; Michael Foster, *A Report of Some Proceedings on the Commission for the Trial of the Rebels in the Year 1746, in the County of Surry, and of Other Crown Cases* (London: E. and R. Brooke, 1792), 218; Hale, *The History*, I, 144–46.

148. Brackenridge, *Law Miscellanies*, 494. Wilson had argued similarly that assembling in a warlike manner (with commanders, banners, in great numbers in "continuance together") was a levying of war but only so long as it was "an actual insurrection or rebellion." Otherwise, the conduct was no more than a great riot. If distinguishing between a riot and treason was too fine a line, he would resolve "on the side of the inferiour crime"; McCloskey, II, 667–68.

149. Brackenridge, *Law Miscellanies*, 494.

150. As Wilson would hold, a private quarrel as a motive, a particular party as an object, a specific nuisance which affected "in point of interest, the parties who assemble," none of these was a levying of war but a felony or trespass. Insurrection had to accomplish an end that was general, to have a public nature, and "to alter the established law, or to render it ineffectual." McCloskey, II, 668.

151. Brackenridge, *Law Miscellanies*, 494–95.

152. Brackenridge, *Law Miscellanies*, 494.

153. Brackenridge, *Law Miscellanies*, 498–99.

154. Ed White, ed., *Modern Chivalry* (Indianapolis, IN: Hackett Publishing Company, Inc., 2009), 382.

155. Brackenridge, *Law Miscellanies*, 495.

156. Claude M. Newlin, *The Life and Writings of Hugh Henry Brackenridge* (Mamaroneck, NY: Paul P. Appel, 1971), 268.

157. Blackstone, *Commentaries*, IV, 75.

158. Brackenridge, *Law Miscellanies*, 474, 494, 501.

159. Brackenridge, *Law Miscellanies*, 492.

160. Brackenridge, *Law Miscellanies*, 491, 496.

161. Brackenridge, *Law Miscellanies*, 491. Pennsylvania appointed Brackenridge to a panel of state Supreme Court justices in 1807 to report on the use of English common law and English statutes as they affected Pennsylvania law. G. S. Rowe, *Embattled Bench: The Pennsylvania Supreme Court and the Forging of a Democratic Society, 1684–1809* (Newark: University of Delaware Press, 1994), 282; Newlin, *The Life*, 282–86; Lawrence Friedman, *A History of American Law*, 3rd ed. (New York: Simon and Schuster, 2005), 68–69; William E. Nelson, *Americanization of the Common Law: The Impact of Legal Change on Massachusetts Society, 1760*–1830 (Cambridge, MA: Harvard University Press), 8–10.

162. In the Whiskey Rebellion trials, there was greater interplay of English constructivism and American law than legal historians have recognized; Slaughter, "King," 60–62, 70–71, 74–75, 81.

163. Myrsiades, "A Tale," 142–45.

164. Myrsiades, "A Tale," 144.

165. In a play on public police (the safety and welfare of the people), Peters positioned federal courts in a prosecutorial role and ensured that national interests superseded local interests. Such presumptions were assumed by Federalists to be necessary to the common weal in practice, as in principle; Myrsiades, "A Tale," 146.

166. Myrsiades, "A Tale," 147–48, 151–52.

167. Myrsiades, "A Tale," 152.

168. Brackenridge, *Law Miscellanies*, 196.

169. Brackenridge, *Law Miscellanies*, 491, 497–98.

170. *Fries*, 908; *Case of Fries*, 1799. Circuit Court, District of Pennsylvania. 9 F. Cas. 826; 1799 U.S. App. Lexis 35; 3 Dall. 515; Thomas Carpenter, *The Two Trials of John Fries, on an Indictment for Treason; Together with a Brief Report of the Trials of Several Other Persons, for Treason and Insurrection, in the Counties of Bucks, Northampton and Montgomery, in the Circuit Court of the United States* (Philadelphia: William W. Woodward, 1800); Paul Douglas Newman, *Fries's Rebellion: The Enduring Struggle for the American Revolution* (Philadelphia: University of Pennsylvania press, 2004); Robert H. Churchill, "Popular Nullification, Fries' Rebellion, and the Waning of Radical Republicanism, 1798–1801," *Pennsylvania History* 67, no. 1 (2000): 105–40; G. E. Connor, "The Politics of Insurrection: A Comparative Analysis of the Shays,' Whiskey, and Fries' Rebellions," *Social Science Journal* 29, no. 3 (1992): 259–81; Jane Shaffer Elsmere, "The Trials of John Fries," *The Pennsylvania Magazine of History and Biography* 103, no. 4 (1979): 437–39; Stephen B. Presser, "A Tale of Two Judges: Richard Peters, Samuel Chase, and the Broken Promise of Federalist Jurisprudence," *Northwestern University Law Review* 73, no. 1 (1978): 86–89.

171. As an aside, Paterson mentored Burr in the law and there was some suspicion that if Paterson left the court Burr would replace him; Roger G. Kennedy, *Burr, Hamilton, and Jefferson: A Study in Character* (New York: Oxford University Press, 2000), 350.

172. Robert A. Ferguson's study of treason trials positions the *Burr* trial as the first truly high-profile case the new nation faced. He considers its ideological importance in the public sphere more important than the law of the matter, that is, as a question of public justice. Robert A. Ferguson, *The Trial in American Life* (Chicago: University of Chicago Press, 2007), 82.

173. Thomas Jefferson to James Madison, January 30, 1787, Founders Online, https://founders.archives.gov/documents; Ferguson, *The Trial*, 97.

174. *United States v. Burr.* Case No. 14,693. Circuit Court, District of Virginia. 25 F. Cas. 55 August 31, 1807.

175. *United States v. Burr*, 11–12, 14.

176. *United States v. Burr*, 25–26.

177. *United States v. Burr*, 26; Judge George Jeffreys (1645–1689), the notorious English hanging judge, presided over the infamous "Bloody Assizes" of 1685. R. Kent Newmyer, *The Treason Trial of Aaron Burr: Law, Politics, and the Character Wars of the New Nation* (Cambridge: Cambridge University Press, 2012), 109, 158–59.

178. In examining *Mitchell*, Marshall opened a new ground of dispute, arguing that the indictment was "not specifically stated" in the law report. He contended that "the indictment must give notice of the offence; that the accused is only bound to answer the particular charge which the indictment contains, and that the overt act is laid to that particular charge." A legal doctrine that says otherwise, Marshall claimed, "contradicts every idea" he ever had about indictments, "since it admits that one case may be stated, and a very different case may be proved"; *United States v. Burr*, 25, 27; Newmyer, *The Treason Trial*, 154–66; Slaughter, "King," 109–18.

179. *United States v. Burr*, 27.

180. Brackenridge, *Law Miscellanies*, 501–02.

181. Slaughter, "King," 118.

182. Joseph J. Ellis, *His Excellency: George Washington* (New York: Vintage, 2004), 22–23, 224.

183. John L. Brooke, "Consent, Civil Society, and the Public Sphere in the Age of Revolution and the Early American Republic," in *Beyond the Founders: New Approaches to the Political History of the Early American Republic*, eds. Jeffrey L. Pasley, Andrew W. Robertson, and David Waldstreicher (Chapel Hill: University of North Carolina Press, 2004), 224–26, 228, 236; Jonathan Curran, "Examining Public Opinion during the Whiskey Rebellion," *Journal of the American Revolution* (September 7, 2021), 1–11, https://allthingsliberty.com.

184. Reeve Huston, "Rethinking the Origins of Partisan Democracy in the United States, 1795–1840," in *Practicing Democracy: Popular Politics in the United States from the Constitution to the Civil War*, eds. Daniel Peart and Adam I. P. Smith (Charlottesville: University of Virginia Press, 2015), 49–51, 64. Gordon S. Wood, "The Significance of the Early Republic," *Journal of the Early Republic* 8, no. 1 (1988): 1–20.

185. Huston, "Rethinking," 52–57.

186. Huston, "Rethinking," 61–65. Alan Taylor, *Liberty Men and Great Proprietors: The Revolutionary Settlement on the Main Frontier, 1760–1820* (Chapel Hill: University of North Carolina Press, 1990); Woody Holton, *Unruly Americans and the Origins of the Constitution* (New York: Hill and Wang, 2007); Bouton, *Taming Democracy*; Owen, *Political Community*.

187. Jeffrey A. Davis, "The Whiskey Rebellion and the Demise of the Democratic-Republican Societies of Pennsylvania," *Topic: A Journal of the Liberal Arts* 45 (1994): 22, 26–27, 35.

188. Edling, *A Revolution in Favor of Government*, 216.

189. Matthew Schoenbachler, "Republicanism in the Age of Democratic Revolution: The Democratic-Republican Societies of the 1790s," *Journal of the Early Republic* 18, no. 2 (1998): 261; Colleen A. Sheehan, "Madison v. Hamilton: The Battle over Republicanism and the Role of Public Opinion," *American Political Science Review* 98, no. 3 (2004): 405–24.

Chapter 5

Sangrado v. the Cloven Foot

The Libel Trial of Benjamin Rush v. William Cobbett, 1799

"Sangrado" (Benjamin Rush) and the "Cloven Foot" (William Cobbett)

—Trial transcript, T. Carpenter, *A Report of an Action for a Libel Brought by Dr. Benjamin Rush against William Cobbett*

Rush v. Cobbett is an ideal trial to examine the intersections of law, medicine, the press, and religion as they informed the trial strategies and roles of Benjamin Rush and William Cobbett, the plaintiff and the defendant in the trial. Rush was a leading Republican in Philadelphia and a signer of the Declaration of Independence, which made him a prime target for a Federalist journalist like Cobbett, for whom Rush was a figure who posed a danger to the health of the city as a medical man and to the health of the body politic as a political figure. Cobbett's preferred mode of attack against Rush's heroic bleeding practices was satire, a weapon he used to ridicule Rush relentlessly and which left him open to a libel charge by his victim. Rush's response was to file a civil action against the journalist, filing the case before the prestigious Pennsylvania Supreme Court—Edward Shippen, Jasper Yeates, and Thomas Smith sitting en banc.[1]

William Cobbett, newly emigrated from England, found himself drawn into a doctors' war over the treatment of yellow fever during the epidemic of 1797. Having established a newspaper, *Porcupine's Gazette*, in Philadelphia that year, Cobbett joined the American John Fenno, publisher of another Federalist paper, *Gazette of the United States*, to ridicule not merely Benjamin Rush's system of bloodletting but Rush's attempts at "puffing," a form of quackery or self-advertisement. Cobbett added a series of satiric letters about a tavern keeper turned bleeder, which clearly mocked Rush, and then compared him to an infamous fictional bleeder, the Spanish physician Sangrado in Alain Rene Le Sage's satirical novel *The Adventures of Gil Blas of Santillane*. Cobbett's accusation that Rush slew more patients than Samson slew Philistines had more bite than perhaps Cobbett intended, as it led Rush to charge him and Fenno with libel in October 1797, although Rush later dropped the charges against the American publisher.[2]

The critical political events of the last decade of the eighteenth century—Jay's Treaty with England of 1795, secret negotiations with the revolutionary government in France in 1797–1798 (the XYZ Affair),[3] the Alien and Sedition Acts of 1798, and the yellow fever epidemics of 1793 and 1797—were all implicated in the trial. *Rush v. Cobbett* occurred just at the cusp of the presidential election of 1800 and at the acme of a frenzied decade that produced the development of political parties, a partisan press, and political consolidation of the new republic. The trial reflected the debate between Anglophiles and Francophiles emanating from efforts to drag America into the war declared by France against England in 1793. It raised questions about an emerging free enterprise medical marketplace whose malpractice issues came to a boil with the turn of the century, and it pitted liberty of the press against the privacy interests of individuals. At the same time, American law was still beholden to English common law, a particular problem for the Pennsylvania Supreme Court, which had to address popular outrage against its adherence to the English law on libel, an issue it would try in the Rush case.[4]

The case was, finally, a stellar example of the oratorical eloquence to which late eighteenth-century lawyers subscribed, expressing the shift the nation was experiencing from the evangelism of the Second Great Awakening (1790 to the mid-nineteenth century) to a secular culture of civic jeremiad and the political development of an American national identity. In the clash between individual reputation and the free press, a rash of libel suits clogged Philadelphia courts that concerned legal figures, politicians, and the public tendency to fuel feuds and duels and to lead to mob actions, undermining the efficacy of the legal system and public confidence in it. The liberty of the press was threatened every time a publisher was taken to court for assailing government officials or private reputations, giving rise to unpopular prosecutions aimed by Federalists at the Republican press.

Called for trial on December 13, 1799,[5] Rush's prosecution of Cobbett was tried under the nisi prius system whereby the Supreme Court tried selected criminal and civil cases as the first trier of fact while it still acted as an appeals court for errors from the lower courts. *Rush v. Cobbett* was thus tried before a court in which a clear distinction between review and trial functions, criminal and civil law, and issues of law and fact had not yet evolved.[6] A transcript of sixty-seven pages was taken in shorthand by an independent court reporter T. Carpenter presumably assigned to the trial by the printer W.

W. Woodward, who announced publication of the transcript within days of the trial.[7] Transcripts of scandalous trials like *Rush v. Cobbett* were rare enough—they largely appeared with more sustained and extensive newspaper trial coverage after 1800[8]—and a trial taken down by a court reporter who attributed the work as his own was the rarest of all.[9] Trials in the seventeenth and eighteenth centuries had been recorded by clergymen as exemplars (conversion or execution narratives, for example) and in the nineteenth century by printers for popular consumption, but an official transcript was not a common practice until court reporters began to be assigned by legislatures.[10] Massachusetts did so in 1804, but Pennsylvania delayed until 1845.[11] The present transcript thus presents an uncommon opportunity to access an important eighteenth-century trial that preserves the judge's charge to the jury, the evidence, some witness testimony, and legal arguments by prosecution and defense counsel, making it possible to examine the trial in detail.[12]

YELLOW FEVER

The trial was inseparable from the event that precipitated it—the yellow fever epidemic—in that the epidemic instigated Cobbett's attack on Rush and the trial cast the epidemic as a central character both in the disintegration of the medical profession and as a test for freedom of the press. Absent from Philadelphia for a twenty-eight-year period,[13] yellow fever reappeared in 1793 and again in 1797 to challenge the culture and structure of the medical profession. Until the end of the century, and even beyond, there was little clarity in how or whether medicine would be effectively regulated,[14] other than by voluntary controls and a promise of licensing that did not take hold until the next century.[15]

Divisions among physicians over unproven medical treatments, lack of control over the proliferation of untrained practitioners, and little scientific understanding of the cause of yellow fever left patients at the mercy of happenstance. When the epidemic hit Philadelphia in 1793, all those with means to move into the countryside left the city. The seat of municipal, state, and federal government in the 1790s, Philadelphia was left bereft and was forced to rely on a volunteer government. Surrounding towns and distant cities refused Philadelphia's products and refugees, essentially isolating the infected city from the rest of the country. Trapped residents were unable to sustain themselves as businesses ceased operating, jobs became scarce, and foodstuffs were impossible to find.[16] Within the city limits, Cobbett reported, Governor Mifflin's proclamation required suspending a yellow flag from any house suspected of infection.[17] People were dragged from their homes, in some cases tossed out by their relatives, and transported to the "stinking and infected" fever hospital, begging "the Almighty to preserve [them] from the clutches of the heroes of the yellow flag."[18]

Whereas doctors with experience in the fevers of the West Indies, among them the notable Dr. Jean Deveze who organized the Bush Hill fever hospital, maintained a conservative treatment regimen, Rush proclaimed an aggressive purging and bleeding treatment adopted by large numbers of physicians influenced by his prominence in the Philadelphia medical establishment. The treatment was deservedly controverted and attracted much commentary as it combined the deleterious effects of heavy doses of mercury or calomel to purge, ipecac to vomit, profuse sweating, blisters (or cupping), and laudanum to subdue the effects of vomiting and purging, and extreme bleeding. The treatment was guaranteed to debilitate patients even more than the fever itself. In one letter in 1794, Rush acknowledged taking blood "*twelve* times in *six* days; taking at least 140 ounces of blood—sixty of which [the patient] lost in four & twenty hours, by five bleedings."[19] Even Rush's colleague Dr. Griffitts admitted that "the use of the lancet [was] . . . much dreaded by our physicians."[20] Troubled by those who called a "clamour against me . . . to *drum me out of the city*,"[21] Rush offered a reward of fifty guineas to any who might produce evidence against him and rejected the heresy of compromise, which he considered "a criminal compact between physicians."[22] The dilemma, he contended, was like a Mohametan and a Jew trying to worship the Supreme Being in the same temple.

As a satirist, Cobbett's strategy in attacking Rush was to caricature him. His most resounding blow was his association of Rush with Sangrado, who first appeared in Tobias Smollett's popular English translation of Le Sage's novel in 1749.[23] The use of Sangrado to skewer Rush did not occur in a vacuum. The figure had a history in English sources from at least 1742 when Henry Fielding referred in *Joseph Andrews* to a doctor Sangrado who "used his patients as a vintner doth his wine-vessels, by letting out their blood, and filling them up with water."[24] He was followed by a "disciple of Sangrado" who treated the title character in Smollett's *Peregrine Pickle* (1751) and "scarce left a drop of blood in [his] body."[25]

Cobbett opined after the trial, "It is well known, that every eminent physician in Philadelphia, Kuhn, Wistar, Stevens, Hodge, Monges, Currie, etc. etc. totally disapproved" of bleeding, setting aside the medical witnesses (Doctors James Mease, William Dewees, and John Redman Coxe) that Rush described as having volunteered to testify at the trial.[26] Cobbett also denied that in calling Rush a Sangrado, he had called him a quack.[27] In a flurry of fallacious logic, he argued that Sangrado did not proclaim in the marketplace (the sign of a quack) as Rush did; if Sangrado was no quack, calling Rush a Sangrado was not to call him a quack, which made this no slander (the oral counterpart to libel). Nonetheless, he would accept damages if his use of the term was unjust.[28] The truth of a slander, after all, constituted a standard of proof in common law that could be argued in one's defense. To pass the test, Cobbett announced, he had only to prove Rush bore a resemblance to the fictional figure in his "*person*," "*general character*," or his "*medical opinions, practice, and fame*."[29] It was enough, Cobbett represented, that Sangrado was called "the Hippocrates of Spain"[30] while Rush was called "the Hippocrates of Pennsylvania"; but Rush also shared the arrogance of the Spaniard, his certainty with regard to rational medical knowledge, and his lack of concern for clinical experience and scientific proof.[31] Cobbett's construction of Le Sage's bleeder-quack was, in sum, more than a simple assault on Rush. Having inspired a generation of writers, Sangrado provided the gadfly journalist with a culturally resonant stalking horse that Rush would find profoundly disturbing.

THE LAW

Malpractice Law

Rush's prosecution of Cobbett was a libel case based on an accusation of medical malpractice. As the body of law that informed malpractice, English common law was dominated by "assumptions about the nature of the doctor-patient relationship,"[32] many of which were culturally bound to customs and traditions. Medicine was, after all, made up of religious, political, and cultural components, a mix of morality and virtue, community values, and partisan loyalties, as much as it was art, science, or commercial enterprise. At the same time, under common law, medical malpractice was based on a claim for damages for a civil wrong, a breach of duty that covered negligence and want of skill. Blackstone's *Commentaries*[33] cited harm due to neglect or unskillful treatment without force as the standard for liability. But once one voluntarily placed oneself in a physician's care, it was difficult to claim force.[34] As Kenneth De Ville puts it, "The physician's liability and responsibility for his patient emanated not from a commercial contractual relationship agreement but from the affirmative act of entering into the doctor-patient relationship."[35] On the physician's end, false accusations of malpractice could constitute defamation, oral or written, done to one's person or reputation rather than to real or personal property.[36]

In actual cases of malpractice, the most frequent charge was failure to act, that is, the physician "did not do that he should have done," so that he "defaulted in the discharge of some customary duty incident to a public calling."[37] But where good people disagreed, he was not responsible for errors, so long as he had the necessary knowledge and the errors were those any prudent man might have committed. Liability occurred where he lacked "reasonable skill and diligence"[38] and yet undertook a duty, in effect warranting "his special preparation for it."[39] Here, as one legal source said, an implied contract based on common law would apply such that offering one's service to the public implied a contract that one possessed "the necessary skill and experience ordinarily possessed by those who practiced 'the same art of science.'"[40]

Still, since medical principles, theories, and practices varied from physician to physician, it was difficult to speak convincingly of an ordinary standard of care.[41] "Ordinary" did not mean the best standard of care available, which was what graduates of medical schools rather than itinerant physicians or rural practitioners offered.[42] Nor care that was outside the scope of a common calling.[43] Not naming oneself a creature of some common calling could obviate one's responsibility, a tactic adopted by those who identified themselves as quacks or empirics. Added complications arose from conditions where there were few physicians or surgeons and where extreme differences existed due to physician inexperience, geography, competition from untrained practitioners, and differences of medical theory.[44] Surgeons, in particular, would become scarce in rural areas if negligence standards required more than the ordinary care available in that area, that is, "the inexperienced and the unlearned attend to the surgery in their way, or it is not attended to at all."[45] In urban areas where more medical care and medical education were available, for example, doctors could be held to a higher "common practice standard."[46]

Physicians argued the patient was expected to choose a provider of good judgment and the failure to do so ought "not to be visited upon the head of the man who has done his best endeavor in his service."[47] Patients thus bore a share of responsibility. Since freedom of choice left patients open to the predatory behavior of quacks, caveat emptor became the prevailing principle. As Rush told his students, it was the patient's responsibility should competition and predation on the part of practitioners lead to a bad choice,[48] ensuring that patients paid the full cost should they choose to employ or contract with an empiric, that is, a practitioner relying on his own experiences.

By these standards, until 1800 a patient would have to prove, first, "affirmatively a duty of care owed by the defendant and a breach of that duty, resulting in damage."[49] Second, that the patient had not been delinquent and contributed to his own illness, thereby breaching his duty to the doctor. As medical treatment required a consistency of care that could be interfered with by multiple hands, a patient who engaged another physician was liable to the charge that he had deserted his doctor's treatments.[50] As Rush lectured his students, "Nothing but a strong constitution can save [a patient] from being injured or destroyed by the hands of two physicians, who are influenced in their practice by opposing theories in medicine, or who are personally hostile to each other."[51]

Anticipating a powerful legal defense based on a patient's contributory negligence, Rush covered himself by arguing that obedience to the physician's prescriptions should be "prompt, strict, and universal"; a "failure in any one of these particulars may be the loss of a link which may render the whole chain of a physician's plan of cure useless or hurtful."[52] A patient might recover by not following his doctor's advice, pointing to the physician's error. But for Rush, the general public, and the courts, patient noncompliance and not physician incompetence was the default rationale in considering physician liability. Once the patient consented to the injurious or deadly treatment, the law presumed a waiver of liability or at the very least shared responsibility. Under an assumed physician-patient contract, both parties had agreed to a treatment; the patient not only accepted some risk by virtue of the agreement, but he had only himself to blame for entering into the agreement. Such a standard could only have assisted Rush in his case against Cobbett, for the latter's burden of proof in a buyer-beware culture, together with the unprovable link of care to catastrophe, was sufficient to sink any third-party malpractice argument Cobbett might launch.

Libel Law and the Press

As a journalist, Cobbett exemplified the plight of the partisans in his profession from John Peter Zenger in 1735 to Eleazer Oswald in the 1780s and such Sedition Act targets as James Thomson Callender and Thomas Cooper. In many ways, the press had succumbed to the same "contagion of liberty" that afflicted the American Revolution, a contagion that demanded freedoms for the press that would prove unsustainable. The fever of freedom that raged around the press would destabilize not only the public support the press sought but the consensus the republic so critically needed to survive as a new nation; it fanned party politics, breaches of the peace, and foreign influence and inflamed abuses of power and destruction of reputation. Supporters of a free press contended that a man would survive attacks on his reputation, but that suppression of the press would lead to the loss of general liberty.[53] Proponents of individual privacy and social order, on the contrary, held that without determined enforcement by the legal system, press freedom linked to party politics and personal libels would lead to almost unthinkable risks to public peace.

The debate over libel law centered in America on limits of free speech and a free press; civil libel could control assaults on private reputation to protect privacy and seditious libel could be used in public life to absolve the state and its officials from scurrilous scrutiny of its actions and conduct.[54] This debate was critical to establishing order and peace in political discourse, the lives of public men, and the affairs of government in a nation newly established and threatened in its very legitimacy, so that a good public opinion of the government could maintain the state. The threat of assaults on personal reputation, of inciting the public to riot, and of disruptive partisan political parties, on the one hand, and the important role the press played in protecting free speech, providing a free flow of information, and exposing chicanery, on the other, became the touchstones of American libel law.

Those accused of libel in America were protected under civil procedures essentially adopted in the states as a carryover from colonial law as the accused could introduce a justification of truth as a defense or offer a justification by virtue of a "privileged occasion" where the comments were made.[55] In effect, "the truth could be no libel," as both truth and privilege were considered absolute justifications if successful.[56] Blackstone contributed, notably, that as a free press was essential to a free society, there ought to be "no *previous* constraints upon publication."[57] Moreover, the press was strengthened if, having abused its responsibility to use publication wisely, it was thereafter censured. Blackstone's contribution to libel law was that freedom of the press entailed no prior restraint on publication, but that criticism of the government or public officials was still criminally liable, limiting press liberty.[58] He extended the constraint to a libel that would "set a man in a ridiculous light . . . and thereby diminish his reputation,"[59] and thus his livelihood, a common law justification Ingersol argued in the trial.

The passage in 1798 of the Sedition Act added statutory law to the mix, setting the stage for the Rush trial and codifying the law that would inform *Rush v. Cobbett.* The Sedition Act targeted any person who shall write, publish, or assist "knowingly and willingly" in writing or publishing "any false, scandalous and malicious writing or writings" against the government, Congress, or the president "with intent to defame . . . or to bring them . . . into contempt or disrepute; or to excite against them . . . the hatred of the good people of the United States, or to stir up sedition within the United States."[60] Public peace was the central concern of the act, which presumed a limited right to discuss public persons. Like the Pennsylvania Constitution of 1790, and unlike Blackstone, the act included the principles of a truth defense and an enhanced role for the jury while it added intent and malice as critical aspects of the proscribed conduct. According to the act's chief architect, Robert Goodloe Harper (in an ironic twist, Cobbett's lead attorney in the Rush trial), conviction could only follow from a publication that was false, malicious, and printed with criminal intent.[61] But prosecuting falsehood left every speech act at risk, as truth often appeared untrue and deception was often convincing.[62] Moreover, truth was treated in the Sedition Act as a question of fact, while the kind of truths that were being bargained over in trials were more aptly described as thoughts, ideas, interpretations, and opinions and thus unlikely to be demonstrable by means of evidence. Even more expansively, as Rawle would argue for the defense, the Pennsylvania Constitution[63] allowed the press to exercise the rights granted by state law to investigate matters of public interest[64] and the federal Constitution protected liberty of the press.

Cobbett and the Law

Cobbett's trial took place a full two and half years after charges were filed. The delay was much to Rush's benefit and left Cobbett to deal with a tangle of other legal actions. His legal troubles ranged from prominent figures like the journalist Mathew Carey to the Spanish minister to the United States Don Carlos Martinez Yrujo, Pennsylvania Supreme Court chief justice Thomas McKean, and President John Adams. In an earlier Rush case, Cobbett had already failed to remove his trial to the federal circuit court, was fined on a conviction for libel, appealed for a new trial, faced an action by Rush to recover the fine, and filed a petition to avoid payment.[65]

In a remarkable act of jurisprudential arrogance, Justice McKean filed charges in 1797 to take Cobbett before the grand jury for libeling Spanish minister D'Yrujo—soon to become McKean's son-in-law—going to the extreme of stepping down from the bench to testify against Cobbett and then returning to charge the jury.[66] He admitted he had interfered in the case by binding over Cobbett to ensure future good behavior and appealed to the jury to do its part by returning a true bill.[67] The grand jury failed to heed his advice and returned a bill of ignoramus, dismissing the charges against Cobbett and thereby preventing his being taken before a petit, or trial, jury. Undeterred, McKean held Cobbett in contempt for violating a peace bond pledging good behavior during the course of the grand jury hearings.[68] Defending his peremptory use of a peace bond, McKean took the position that free will was protected by permitting the publication of a piece and only punishing the press after publishing it.[69] Equally, he promoted registering complaints with the courts so that citizens would have a means of redress through the law, which alone offered fairness and justice. There should thus be no need to accuse through the press, particularly in Philadelphia where for years past, McKean avowed, such scurrility had raged that "libeling has become a national crime [which] distinguishes us not only from all the states around us, but from the whole civilized world."[70]

The Supreme Court's insistence on using a peace bond approach to silence Cobbett meant that the accused, in advance of breaking the law, had to guarantee a surety that could be forfeited, ensuring he would not commit a particular prohibited act. It was a strategy used on the smallest provocation to require a defendant to assume a weighty financial burden and a constraint on his freedom, even if he had already been acquitted of the charges in a case. Indeed, a party need not be charged nor need he be given an opportunity to defend himself before the imposition of the peace bond, recalling the excesses of English rule in the colonies and breaking with common law proscriptions against prior restraint.[71] The fact that prior restraint was not explicitly resorted to in the 1799 Rush case—in spite of what appears to have been Rush's original intent by suggesting nothing be spoken on his behalf in the press—suggests that the Supreme Court by that time had exceeded the limits of the public's patience in pursuing Cobbett.[72]

In response to the restraint on his conduct, Cobbett asked in *Respublica v. Cobbett* (1798) that as "he was an alien, a subject of the king of Great Britain"[73] and as the Judicial Act of 1789 gave the federal circuit court authority over civil cases involving aliens, his case ought to be moved to a federal court. Justice McKean's decision, however, affirmed the state's jurisdiction on the grounds that the Judicial Act "did not extend to actions brought against aliens by a state" and that the recognizance, albeit a civil suit, that is, a contract suit, "was taken to prevent criminal action by the defendant [and] . . . for no other purpose."[74] Cobbett's own counsel had resisted his declaring himself "in open court, a subject of the King of Great Britain," which would not only offend the court but which, Cobbett acknowledged, "would inevitably tend to render me odious in the eyes of the people of America."[75] His lawyer at the time, Mr. Thomas, rose to speak in a trembling voice to present the petition:[76]

> For some time he did not make himself heard. There was a great talking all round the bar; Levi, the lawyer, was reading a long formal paper to the Judges, and the Judges were laughing over the chit-chat of the day. Amidst the noisy mirth that surrounded him, there stood poor Thomas, with his papers in his hands, like a culprit at school, just as the boys are breaking up. . . . The moment the sound of the word *Cobbett* struck the ear of M'Kean, he turned towards the bar, and having learnt the subject of the petition, began to storm like a madman. A dead silence ensued. The little scrubby lawyers . . . crouched down for fear, just like a brood of poultry, when the kite [McKean][77] is prepared to pounce in amongst them; whilst hapless Thomas, who stood up piping like a straggled chicken, seemed already to feel the talons of the judicial bird of prey. . . . M'Kean did, indeed, grin most horribly, and I could very distinctly hear, *"insolent scoundrel!"—"damned aristocrat!"—"damned Englishman!"* etc. etc. from the mouths of the sovereign people.[78]

Cobbett compared the legal argument in the hearing to "Pulchinello and the Devil"[79] and the chief justice to a "showman" on "a wire"; McKean ended "the farce by declaring . . . *that the petition of William Cobbett should not be granted.*"[80]

CHANGES IN THE COURTROOM

In the background of *Rush v. Cobbett*, the judicial apparatus was shifting its treatment of libel. On the cusp of Republican victories in electing a governor and a president, the Republican response to Federalist prosecutions of seditious libel was to move cases from the federal to the state venue, from criminal to civil cases, and from a focus on political expression to personal reputation, both public and private.[81] Such a tack meant that the Republican prosecution of Cobbett could be framed not only as a question of defending reputation (rather than attacking the press),[82] but as a way of serving the public good by ensuring that the best men would remain in public life. In procedural terms, it meant that the Yrujo case against Cobbett, prosecuted as a criminal case, would be matched in 1797 with Rush's filing of a civil case against Cobbett in the same state court. Not only were Cobbett's petitions to remove both his cases to a federal court denied, but Rush's triumph two years later would avenge Yrujo's loss in his case and justify the Rush case as a Republican response to Federalist sedition trials.[83]

As in *Respublica v. Oswald* (1788), those accused of libel were still in the position of representing themselves despite access to counsel. The residual "accused speaks" model tempted William Lewis, who prosecuted Oswald, to argue the necessity for the accused to speak, asserting that Oswald was not, as some complained, compelled to convict himself by his testimony but might be able "by his own oath to purge and acquit himself, in spite of all the testimony, which can possibly be produced against him."[84] Alexander Dallas, William Duane's preference for counsel in his 1800 sedition case,[85] had in fact recommended that his client adopt an "accused speaks" strategy as well, on the grounds that extenuation was best presented to advantage by the accused rather than counsel.[86] Some defendants still felt they had no choice but to represent themselves (the accused in *U. S. v. Cooper*, 1800, for example)[87] because they considered their counsel manacled or gagged in court. Others, like Cobbett, wished they had spoken on their own behalf.

But times were changing from full-blown altercation-style trials where the undefined roles of the judge, counsel, and the jury led to a disconcerting jockeying over power in the courtroom. Coming off a period when judicial authority seemed to dominate the courts, judges could no longer routinely direct jury verdicts and assume the functions of witness, prosecutor, protector of the accused, nor could they easily replace counsel who raised objections. With full development of an adversarial system, the judge was restricted to questions of law, leaving the facts of the case to the jury.[88] Judges continued to lose influence over juries as counsel gained in importance but could apply rules of evidence to prevent counsel from unduly influencing jury verdicts.[89] At the same time, rules of evidence gave defense counsel the ability to challenge witnesses and proof, insist upon corroboration of testimony, and protect the accused from self-incrimination. The burden of proof shifted to the prosecution as standards of proof became established, including probable cause, exclusion of evidence, and credibility tests. Counsel could open a case and address closing arguments to the jury rather than merely examine or cross-examine witnesses, and judges ceased interrogating witnesses.[90] In toto, the form of the modern trial process had begun to solidify. A structure for presenting a case had developed to bring order to the court and fix due process as a norm. As the century ended, meaningful representation gave the accused the opportunity to be represented by a trained advocate and the plaintiff, in a criminal trial, to be represented by a public prosecutor.[91]

Beyond a changing legal process, *Rush v. Cobbett* was situated within the history and traditions of the Pennsylvania Supreme Court. The court was ensconced in the west wing of the Pennsylvania State House,[92] later to be known as Independence Hall, just across the hallway from Independence Chamber where the Second Continental Congress delivered the Declaration of Independence. Having signed the declaration that separated the colonies from England, both Rush and McKean were shining beacons for the jury. Known as a workshop for liberty,[93] the building's western corner was the site of the ratification of the Bill of Rights in 1791, George Washington's inauguration in 1793, his Farewell Address in 1797, and John Adams's inauguration in 1797.[94] In sum, *Rush v. Cobbett* would be tried in the very building that was the site of the origins of the nation,[95] the historical significance of which could not have escaped those involved in the trial.

It was thus no coincidence that the performance space in which the trial played out resonated with the prosecution's chosen theme: America as a chosen land, Americans as a chosen people, the testing and redemption of such a people, and the promise of republicanism as a hope for the future of America and its cultural exceptionalism. Rush's application to move the case to the court was a calculated move. Of the civil cases heard in that space, only select ones were chosen and "on a strictly nonlegal basis."[96] Just as Washington had moved his property case to the Supreme Court in 1786, assuming it would prove more sympathetic to the father of the country,[97] Rush's standing in the city would ensure that his case would be one of those likely to be heard. The choice of the prestigious Supreme Court as the trier of fact for a civil case was strategic in another sense. Under the nisi prius system, the justices oversaw trials and appeals,[98] and they could try both civil and criminal cases. In the Rush case, that would result in an award for both exemplary and compensatory damages,[99] that is, both civil and criminal damages.

Rush also had the advantage of his association with two of the court's prior members. His younger brother, Jacob Rush, had served on the court from

1784 to 1791,[100] and McKean (chief justice from 1777 to 1799) had benefited politically from Benjamin Rush's support in 1788 during the fight for ratification of the US Constitution.[101] The Constitution was ratified in the same month that the publisher Eleazer Oswald filed an impeachment proceeding with the Pennsylvania Assembly against McKean and two members of his court: Jacob Rush and William Atlee.[102] As Oswald considered that Benjamin Rush had instigated a court case against him in 1788 to stymie his opposition to the Constitution,[103] Rush was doubly endeared to the court, putting him on the right side of the press controversy and aligning him politically with a chief justice who had essentially controlled the court for twenty-two years. Justice Shippen in particular found good reason to be sympathetic to Rush as he had ambitions to fill McKean's seat as chief justice.[104] Indeed, Shippen's handling of the case avenged McKean for Cobbett's attacks on him, and on December 17, following a verdict for Rush three days earlier, Shippen was appointed chief justice.

A big part of the court's dilemma as it related to *Rush v. Cobbett* was the reputation the court had engendered under Chief Justice McKean on the issue of libel law. The more power the court aggregated to itself, the more the court's problematic treatment of publishers of libel mattered.[105] By 1799, many Pennsylvanians believed the high court had become undemocratic and antiegalitarian.[106] This was partly the product of McKean's high-handedness, which influenced the role the other justices played, and partly the result of an increased sense of entitlement by the public in criticizing the court. The public would have to be won over if the court was to exercise itself as a respected institution defending the public interest under newly elected Governor McKean's Republican administration in 1800.[107]

Rush v. Cobbett was thus tried before a court that was in a transitional period, weaning itself from McKean's decades-long reign and the court's reputation for abusing its powers. The case offered the prospect of mediating the court's attacks on the press and its relationship with the citizenry. In fact, the Rush case was a good test for the court's jurisprudence, since the very issues that defined the court after the revolution—libel, a free press, federal and state jurisdiction, republican values, and political philosophy—were the very issues raised in the Rush case. In this sense, *Rush v. Cobbett* came at a critical time in the history of the court.

Facing the replacement of the chief justice after his extensive tenure and anticipating significant reforms should Jefferson win the presidential election, the court was caught in an interstitial period where much was demanded in terms of the definition and use of its power. Indeed, one could argue that the court's sensitivity to the need to resolve its questioned authority[108] might have tempted it to split the difference in the Rush case by applying common law libel (which favored government, public men, and public order) in a way that privileged a local hero, privacy of the individual, and republicanism (state law) over federalism (federal law) and that preferred republican ideology (a native Americanism) over federalist ideology (influenced by the English).

THE TRIAL

Following a two-year delay, Justice Edward Shippen convened a three-judge court that included Jasper Yeates and Thomas Smith to try *Rush v. Cobbett*.[109] Cobbett attributed the delay to McKean's continuing interference: "The base and corrupt Judge contrived the means of postponing the cause seven times . . . till, at last, he found one [jury] from which he was sure of a verdict."[110] Rush's counsel was accused of being at the center of the delay as it hoped to keep Cobbett on good behavior by postponing the trial as well as using a struck jury (whereby each side alternately struck off a juror) to ensure a favorable hearing.[111] Their hopes regarding Cobbett were soon dashed as he continued to publish attacks against Rush and McKean. In a form of Russian roulette, court terms passed one after another without the trial being called.[112] The conditions for the trial to go forward, Cobbett complained, only clicked into place when a jury favorable to Rush was empaneled; of the seven men on the jury list "we thought fit to be trusted on the trial," all were struck by Rush's counsel.[113]

Six lawyers alternately argued the two sides of the case in the following order: plaintiff's counsel opened (Joseph Hopkinson) and closed (Jared Ingersol); defense counsel argued in the second (William Rawle) and the third (Robert Goodloe Harper) positions; plaintiff's counsel (Moses Levy) appeared fourth; and defense counsel (Edward Tilghman) fifth. This mixed order of presentation reflected the earlier form of court proceeding, the altercation trial,[114] in which the efforts of the judge, the victim, and the accused were poorly separated, indeed overlapped. Any idea of dividing well-delineated responsibilities in a systematic presentation to create a coherent argument proved problematic in *Rush v. Cobbett*. Hopkinson and Rawle (opening for each side) and Tilghman and Ingersol (closing for each side) did not, for example, introduce, on the one hand, or conclude, on the other, by covering the range of arguments for their position or tying them together. Neither did Levy and Harper isolate for themselves a discrete role, whether to clarify the evidence, build proof, argue the law, or undermine the other side's argument. The jury, as a result, would have found it difficult to follow the arguments. Differentiating defense and prosecution positions would have been particularly difficult as the law was not clear and conflicting interpretations were possible. If a clear theme were to emerge in the trial, it needed to be repeated over and again, be uninterrupted, and be opposed forcefully to alternative arguments; it needed to fit comfortably into the jury's perspective. With alternating arguments, the prosecution and defense sidetracked each other and stepped on each other's storyline. Interrupted by the defense and itself interrupting defense counsel's momentum, the prosecution still had a discursive advantage in beginning and ending the course of arguments, which allowed it to command the jury's attention. The first words (the initial framing of the case, for a primacy effect) and the last words (the final and concluding statement, for a recency effect) the jury would hear about the case were those of the prosecution.

As John H. Langbein puts it, the altercation trial was a form of spontaneous bickering—reminiscent of the chaos Cobbett reported in the Yrujo case—"A formless or wandering quality that resembles ordinary discourse, a conversation of sorts, lacking [a] crisp division into prosecution and defense cases."[115] Judge and jury questioned witnesses and commented on the trial, while counsel freely addressed the jury throughout the trial. Judges served as advocates for the accused, who were expected to testify on their own behalf; victims were expected to gather evidence and witnesses and to pursue private prosecution of cases at their own time and expense.[116] Vestiges of the altercation trial were joined in *Rush v. Cobbett* to the "combat effect" of a developing adversarial system in which rivalry and partisanship among counsel to gain the ear of the jury competed to distort the facts, undermine witnesses, and win the argument. The process not only tested the jury's mettle as it tried to separate defense and prosecution arguments, making a truth defense based on the facts of the case difficult to argue successfully, but the defense failed to capitalize on essential attributes of the system: undermining the prosecution's case, distracting the prosecution, and posing an alternative theory of the crime.

The trial opened with Rush's lead attorney Hopkinson, a fiery young lawyer and nephew of McKean trying only his second big case.[117] Hopkinson's passionate speech made it immediately clear that a struck jury was not Cobbett's only problem. He became the referent for each of the other five pleaders (he was referenced, countered, or endorsed by each of them in turn) and inspired a rowdy reception among trial watchers by burying questions of fact and law in themes that catered to popular prejudice and hometown preferences.[118] In his opening, Hopkinson waived his responsibility to stick to the "usual" protocol of an "ordinary" libel trial. Taking liberties, his framing of the trial effectively excused the prosecution from sticking to the charges and presenting evidence to support them.[119] The choice was inspired, for the trial was to become a tale of competing stories aimed at persuading the jury of a higher truth than that told by the facts. Indicating the low regard in which libel suits were held, Hopkinson aimed to elevate the stakes in the trial to a test of the moral order itself, demeaning ordinary cases of slander that congested the dockets of the courts and distinguishing them from the case presently before the jury. The appeal to the exceptional nature of the Rush trial clearly resonated with Judge Shippen whose charge to the jury expressed his irritation that "offences of this kind have for some time past too much abounded in our city," urging the jury that "it seems high time to restrain them."[120]

Cobbett called the role played by "the zealous Hopkinson" a "rare sport"[121] and expressed surprise at his depiction of Rush as one who "*in the service of his country . . . has added a fresh and blooming laurel to the head of American genius*"; he questioned why Hopkinson did not produce a laurel sprig to "delight their eyes" or, indeed, recollect Mark Antony's "judicious display of a piece of blotted parchment."[122] Cobbett contended his own version would have told a tale of the death of an ambitious Caesar (Rush) cut down at his height whose blood now flowed through wounds Brutus (Cobbett) had inflicted, a nice touch considering Rush's practice of heroic bleeding. According to defense counsel Tilghman, Hopkinson's Caesar-laden theme, was intended to electrify the jury and distract it from noticing that the argument was "foreign to the question at present."[123] Levy, by comparison, lauded the approach. His colleague's zeal, he represented, might have "carried him into a state of effervescence, for which he is blamed by our opponents" but even the most moderate among them "who is warmly attached to reputation and character . . . could refrain a warmth of expression at seeing a worthy, valuable citizen so lavishly abused without provocation";[124] the intended comparison to Caesar could not have been clearer.

The prosecution strategy initially organized itself around two questions: First, did Rush's conduct during the calamity reinforce the charges against Cobbett or did it extenuate Cobbett's actions? Second, what inducement did Cobbett have for attacking Rush: was his intent in attacking Rush's character malicious and politically motivated, thereby aggravating the charges, or was it intended to inform the public, thereby extenuating his actions? Here, the mixed order of presentation and the differing argumentative styles of prosecution counsel undermined the plan, which, although it was periodically revisited, could not be sustained coherently throughout the trial. On the other hand, the prosecution had some success in appealing to the jury's self-interest, addressing the public's love-hate relationship with the press, and vilifying Cobbett.

The prosecution had more success in pursuing a political story and a story of character, narratives that characterized the parties to the suit in oppositional roles: Cobbett as an antihero who capitalized on the uncertainty of public experiences to create anxiety and Rush as the kind of hero the public needed to resolve contradictions. These constructions raised deeply troubling historical themes that marginalized Cobbett morally and politically. In the complex political terrain of negotiations like those of Jay's Treaty and the

XYZ Affair, Cobbett was seen as a figure "unfriendly to our government, a man ignorant of his true *situation* in this country and of the *kind of value or use* that has been put upon him."[125] Cobbett recalled the old corrupt order and had become a dangerous weapon in the hands of a foreign power. In the tale of character, Cobbett became an alien interloper and a violator of family honor, a figure of satanic impulses. At the domestic level, the story of character began by asking whether "the virtue of the injured" had not become the injurer's defense, a response to the defense argument that Rush's virtue was such that Cobbett's attacks could have no effect on his reputation. The prosecution queried whether this was not like calling "the daughter of spotless virtue and discretion . . . a prostitute."[126] It thereafter transformed the question to an archetypal struggle between the angelic acts of a good shepherd and divine physician and those of the "cloven foot."[127]

The prosecution's strategy with the jurors was to frame them as republicans and citizens and thereby to create empathy with one special Philadelphia republican, Benjamin Rush, and to instill resistance to its enemy, the alien Cobbett. Raising the red herring that Cobbett would avenge himself on jurors should they fail to deliver a verdict for him, the prosecution counted on reverse psychology as well as the jury's chauvinism. The pathetic appeal of an old man and his American family at the hands of an English army-trained ruffian should be enough to ignite both their patriotic fervor and their desire to come to the aid of their country. What was asked was small enough weighed against the prospects for society should the jury lack the courage to embrace its responsibility. Failure to punish Cobbett would undermine the court system and threaten the peace; citizens without recourse to public justice would revert to a private justice that would rend the very bonds of society.[128]

To make this line of reasoning work, the prosecution had, first, to succeed in convincing the jury that Cobbett represented just the kind of threat it warned against and, second, that bringing him down would not destabilize its freedoms. Cobbett was thus represented in imagery that spoke to assassinating the honor of one of the nation's great men (Brutus to Rush's Caesar). The prosecution spoke of his polluting the land like infesting slime (contaminating the city as a secondary epidemic), running to ground his helpless prey (a predator on the hunt), and subverting the foundations of a great national institution (undermining liberty of the press). Such depictions constituted a metaphorical level of struggle to reinforce the idea of the trial as no ordinary case and justified language that might otherwise have been regarded as actionable libel to which the jury might justifiably take exception.

Once the prosecution had opposed Cobbett to Rush as an inferior creature from a foreign culture who posed a heightened threat to the city, it then expanded its characterization of Cobbett to make the case that he represented an irremediable danger that implicated a larger body of meaning. Thus, the prosecution conceptualized Cobbett as an abuser of the press who stood for all abusers of the press. He stood for an entire pack of libelers whom he epitomized, a phenomenon among libelers in a country plagued by them. By the same argument, the prosecution captured in Cobbett an Englishman who desired to reverse Britain's defeat in the American Revolution, a move that would defuse any residual pro-English sentiments lingering within the minds of potential holdout jurors. Holdouts risked being outed as antirepublican agents, spies from within conspiring to reenslave the nation. The very sickness of the city during the fever epidemic argued against the interests of those who would make it sicker. Those who would destabilize the city's confidence in those with the ability to cure it, those informers still suffering from postcolonial anxiety over separation from the home country, would be exposed.

In the last of its appeals to the jury, the prosecution's most delicate task was to thread the needle on freedom of the press. The politics of the partisan press had not merely to be suppressed, it had to be rejected. Hopkinson inoculated his case against party motives by, first, acknowledging that all political action was attributable to such motives. He then refuted the implied charge that he was himself guilty of such a bias, neither denying nor admitting that his own politics were opposed to those of Cobbett; he stood, rather, on the grounds of conscientious independence. On the one hand, Hopkinson argued that Cobbett's politics, indeed his political character, was open to question, and, on the other, that the prosecution stood above the fray. With the ongoing alien and sedition trials against Republican journalists (and the present case sizing up as a Republican-style alien and sedition prosecution), the irony of Cobbett's situation cannot have escaped Rush's counsel. With political sentiment gravitating from a Federalist to a Republican disposition and appreciating that turnabout was only fair play, the jury was likely amenable to punishing a Federalist journalist to even the score, so long as it was not forced to admit openly to doing so. The prosecution thus argued that the best defense of the press was to punish all abusers equally. The jury should honor the press when it operated within the proper bounds of liberty, not when it used its liberty as a political shield to hide behind. Where the press failed to act as part of a public stock of information, where it was guilty of untruths, of malice, and of attacks on personal reputation, the press generally should have its legal rights constrained. The court (clogged with libels), the city (rife with scurrility), and the country (in which libels had become a national scandal) would all benefit from the courage to restrain such a press, whatever one's party affiliation.

As for Rush's standing in the face of press attacks, he would need the cover of privacy and family to inoculate him against those aspects of libel that left public men and controversies open to public commentary and that assigned to men of the press certain rights to hold figures of high station up to public scrutiny. To make this case, the prosecution capitalized on character and reputation as forms of property to be protected under the law. Character assassination was as good as an attack on one's livelihood and one's legacy; an honorable man like Rush could be reduced to penury and his family to ignominy. With Rush portrayed as taking on the suffering of the people, the jury was asked to take on Rush's suffering as their own, supposing themselves libeled and called upon to bring the libeler to judgment: "My character—my professional and moral character attacked with the venom and art of a daemon—my daily bread about to be taken from me—the subsistence for my family in danger of being lost to me—a head covered with grey hairs—fortune gone in paper money."[129] The prosecution trial plan thus played out as a tribute to a sacrificed hero.[130]

The prosecution strategized as well that ultimately an individual good (such as the right of a private man to his privacy) might best be understood within the context of the public welfare (as a collective right in a time of public crisis). The trial was not only a question of a civil dispute in which one man's reputation or a second man's right to express a view on a matter of public concern was in jeopardy. The case, the prosecution contended, was as much a public as a private prosecution, as much a criminal as a civil case because a threat to social order was at issue. Recognizing that the privacy argument might not be enough to give Rush the verdict he needed, the prosecution had to cover the risk to collective rights as well. Here, common law came into play. As common law implied, it would not be enough to reward an injured party, to make good a harm done, or to ensure the enjoyment of a right denied. The public peace once breached must also be set right, and the state must be satisfied that no hue and cry had been raised that would call forth private revenge or mob action.

In this scene, the young republic was itself at risk: its courts' ability to protect rights of reputation and property were tested, its ability to govern was undermined, and the means of patrolling abuse of government (the liberty of its press) was called into question. International unrest, an uncivil contest of party politics in preparation for a presidential election year, a threatened foreign war, and an epidemic that ravaged the population of the nation's capital were all implicated. These were threats to the foundation of the country and to the kind of nation to which the jury wished to belong. Only prosecution of the press would protect it. Only punishment of offenders would legitimize the court. Only a jury called to arms would ensure the safety of the streets and the public peace. The government would not then fall into contempt, nor the court into ridicule. The guilty would not go free, and the country would not deny its citizens the justice they demanded.

These were the public protections that outweighed private considerations. They were sealed in lines of argument that extolled the virtues of the republic and expanded upon the responsibility of its citizen jurors amid the noisy clamor of partisan attacks and riots. They were served by rhetoric that exploited themes of dreadful days and just retribution, a wilderness of disease and death, and the heightened oppositionality of an elevated saint and a downcast Satan. Cutting through the confusing mélange of prosecution and defense addresses in a stew of sometimes indistinguishable stories, the jury would come down on the side of overarching themes that resonated with religious sermons and patriotic rhetoric nourishing a developing myth of American exceptionalism. For all its disparate appeals, the prosecution reached the jury with a message that resonated with the times and caught Cobbett's team off guard.

The defense team had difficulty arriving at a coherent argument, partly because it had no clear line of attack. It was, for example, ambivalent about casting Rush as a threat to the public, even if Cobbett's writings read like a malpractice trial by press. Cobbett's case was thereby vulnerable to the prosecution argument that Rush was an innocent victim who stood in for the divine physician Himself. Cobbett's counsel made two other bad moves: it decided not to replay the scandal as a truth defense by arguing the facts, and it failed to make an aggressive case for press freedom, compromised by Cobbett's denial that the American press was a free press.[131] In addition, they were reluctant to challenge the prosecution's contention that Cobbett was an alien journalist as it would have called attention to the suspicion that Cobbett was an English spy.

Rather, the defense couched Cobbett as a member of the fourth estate with a protected status under the law guarding the public trust and coming to the defense of an endangered public. In this role, Cobbett might inoculate himself against the mischief of which he had been accused and at least mitigate the charge of malice. The defense counsel presented the free market of ideas as Cobbett's venue, a public space where he could caution his readers on an issue of public controversy and invoke the public welfare. It strategized that where the public was split and physicians divided, where all had the right to speak their piece, Cobbett had the right to add his voice by way of raising an alarm. When the entire medical profession and public were divided in their opinions, who was the greater fearmonger? Was it Cobbett or the warring physicians? Why, the defense argued, should he above all others be denied his opinion, unless to suppress the public's right to be informed and to choose freely in an open arena?

This move into the marketplace of ideas compensated for Cobbett's refusal of a liberty of the press defense and avoided the risk of public disapproval that attacking a great man, a local son, entailed. Having dismissed attacking Rush, the best possible scenario was to concede the ground of Rush's benevolence and altruism and to sidestep the contest of opposites into which the prosecution was maneuvering it. With support for the press waning and the courts trying the public's patience—clogged as they were with a backlog of noisome libel cases—the better course appeared to be admitting Rush's good faith and intent and acknowledging Cobbett's ignorance of alternative medical treatments. If the defense had introduced Rush's intemperate language, his feuds with other physicians, his sons' feuds,[132] and his disruptive role in the wartime court-martial of William Shippen (director general of the Continental Army Hospitals, a son of Philadelphia, and a cousin of presiding justice Edward Shippen),[133] it would also have to defend Cobbett's disputative conduct.[134] Rather than fight a battle it was unlikely to win, the defense resolved to take on Rush's medical treatment. It stressed the novel experimental nature of his treatment for yellow fever, the great number of deaths associated with the epidemic, the dissension among physicians, and the inconsistency of treatments for the disease. At best, such a move would displace blame and raise doubts about the prosecution's view of Rush even as it deflected assaults against Cobbett. At worst, it would only demonstrate that Rush was never at much risk from Cobbett's attacks given the prevailing devastation of the city. They argued that Cobbett might have been a popular journalist, but his ability to destroy Rush's system and his reputation did not, in this environment, pose a credible threat. Elevating Rush's importance as a public figure, the defense concluded, could only diminish the threat Cobbett was presumed to have posed.

THE TRIAL CONCLUDED

A defense foray early in the trial had advised the jury that it must "possess no prejudices no opinions—no prepossessions" and that it must hold the two men "on equal grounds." In vain, Rawle had pleaded that Cobbett was entitled to fair treatment and due process: "Let him have every censure he deserves, and yet, I repeat, both stand upon equal ground before you. Cobbett puts himself upon the issue, and you are to decide according to the evidence, and thus only."[135] Tilghman's closing argument took up the theme that equal standing before the law applied to aliens as well as to citizens so that the jury ought to receive the case "in the language of the law 'like blank paper,' and receive such impressions only as law and evidence must make." Cobbett was thereby to be treated no worse than "an *American* standing in his place."[136]

However well meant, Tilghman's closing address to the jury was a pedantic reading of the litany of issues before the court. He made the argument that although Cobbett's coarse expressions were highly improper, he never acted out of malice or criminal intent; yet, the prosecution characterized him as litigious, noxious, and cloven-footed.[137] Cobbett had a right to attack Rush's politics, just as he had a right to write against Rush's medical system, if not his person.[138] Thus, Cobbett's ridicule was "surely the test of truth,"[139] not murder by malice, and was no more than Rush's own intemperate attacks against doctors "who had the misfortune to differ with him in practice."[140] Addressing the issue of damages, Tilghman contended that other doctors posed a greater threat to Rush's livelihood than Cobbett, and none could say what presumed harm occurred or from whom. How, in fact, could one prove a negative, that is, a loss of business? In conclusion, Tilghman's laundry list reduced to one wrong: Cobbett was liable for contempt as he published "from the moment the suit commenced,"[141] when he ought not to. Although "everything ought to come before a Jury, who should not have their passions raised, or be prepossessed in favor of either party,"[142] Tilghman appealed, the jury ought not to ruin the man.

Ingersol's closing admonition to the jury countered that the law must be determinate to act as a deterrent. He warned the jury not to be naïve in holding too high an opinion of any man, for if damages were not assigned no one would fear the law and complaints would "be obtained in another, and most fatal way."[143] He called on the jury to act the part of a deus ex machina, returning the court to a natural, universal law that would defeat wickedness, outrage, and malignancy. Ingersol sounded a cry that could have been used by divines in their yellow fever sermons in calling on the heavens at the highest tribunal to reap the whirlwind as "Virtue, bleeding at every pore, calls for justice on her despoiler."[144] The jury, on whose decision hung the character of the country and the respectability of the government, was entrusted with retribution ("THE SCOURGERS OF VICE") and with vindication of the injured. On the legal front, Hopkinson had already demanded the jury exceed legal doctrine and accept the burden of religious and secular law, of nature and society; on the domestic side, he had summoned the jury to restore a father's legacy of reputation and economic well-being to his family, to finish the work Rush had set out to do as citizen, physician, moral guardian, and private prosecutor in culling the ranks of the wicked. The prosecution asked the jury, in sum, to render a verdict that would complete the nation-building begun by the revolution, that is, to act parens patriae on behalf of republicanism to save the nation. The stakes the prosecution case presented could not have been higher.

Justice Shippen delivered his charge to the jury on the second day of the trial, December 14, careful to distinguish the American from the English jury and to affirm the continued authority of the old-style trial. Thus, the jury might judge both law and the fact, but "under the direction of the court";[145] the court must not supersede the jury on the facts but may direct them on the law and narrow their role in determining damages. Cobbett, he held, could as easily have been tried in the present court by criminal indictment as by civil action, while Cobbett's publications were "certainly libelous"[146] and admittedly false—so that they could not be justified by a truth defense—leaving little to the jury's imagination in disposing of the facts. In addition, since malice depended upon personal intent the defendant had to bear the burden of proof, a burden, in his view, his defense had not successfully borne.

On the most serious (and presumably the most republican) issues—the public peace, health, and "lives of our fellow citizens"[147]—Shippen cast the case as a threat to private reputation and breach of the peace, not as a question of liberty of the press. Cobbett's conduct, in this regard, impeded a citizen's access to the courts and risked recourse to "duels, Murders, and perhaps to Assassinations."[148] Framed in this way, the "principal subject of consideration" was the issue of damages, that is, to inflict punishment capable of curing so endemic a social disease. Here, Shippen implied a role for the jury comparable to that Rush assumed as a physician in the fever epidemic—purging the body politic of an uncontrolled evil. In this light, he instructed the jury that it possessed a power whose exercise would have to be "outrageously disproportionate" and shocking to the conscience before any court would intervene.[149]

Under these instructions, the jury took a mere two hours to convict Cobbett and assign an unprecedented fine of $5,000. As Cobbett described the writ, it demanded payment greater than all the fines assessed in all such cases put together. Spectators in the gallery and in the environs of the courthouse broke out into loud cheers, which, Cobbett noted, included the press.[150] Embittered by the jury verdict against him, Cobbett had Tilghman file immediately for a new trial on the grounds of excessive damages, which the court unanimously rejected. Four days after the trial, he expressed his fear that "they will come here and seize my body. Blessed be God, the villains cannot seize my soul. . . . If I should be put to death, I should only share the fate of Roberts and Carlisle [executed for treason in the revolution]."[151] Tilghman advised him to flee the writ, which he refused to do. For all his protestations, Cobbett took leave of America for England when he heard that the case for the Yrujo recognizance (which he called "Old McKean versus Peter Porcupine") would be brought in June 1800.[152]

THE JUDGE AND THE JURY

Although Hopkinson had warned jurors, Cobbett had threatened them.[153] Cobbett considered them no more than sycophantic subjects under the influence of a judge who designed to puff up their pride "to embolden them to gratify [him] and [his] private wishes, at the expense of justice."[154] As for Justice Shippen, Cobbett accused him of having forgotten his oath to sum up the evidence fairly in his zeal to assist the plaintiff and in hope of higher office.[155] Shippen compounded Cobbett's misgivings by misrepresenting the defense counsel's position on the "libelous" publications, claiming his counsel had "repeatedly acknowledged" the falsity of Cobbett's claims against Rush.[156] Thereafter, the judge telegraphed his intention to certify the jury's verdict "provided they laid on damages enough."[157] The judge's instructions on excessive damages gave "cheering encouragement" to the jury, which, Cobbett mused, could easily have come from the French revolutionary Robespierre or, more pointedly, from a Pennsylvania law book.[158] Whereas a British judge would have been stoned to death for applying such a standard, he argued, a Philadelphia jury would sit before such a judge "submissively as a penitent does to his father confessor."[159]

Justice Shippen's courtroom management complimented his charge to the jury in guiding the jury verdict.[160] Cobbett complained especially of the difficulty his counsel Rawle and Tilghman had in being heard over the cries of observers in the court. The public had been admitted to an open area in the courtroom where they stood packed in rows that overflowed to the outside of the building. The jury sat in boxes to the right and left of the room near the justices' bench. When defense counsel tried "to repel the abominable aspersions which were cast on his character and conduct," the crowd hissed and cursed at them from the gallery and around the courthouse. Although he was not in the courtroom, Cobbett remarked upon "this most scandalous behavior," shocked to discover that it was not met with "any reproof from the Court." He took Shippen's conduct to mean he refused to control the court where the defense was involved,[161] whereupon he wrote to his friend and counsel Tilghman, "I hear that the rascally sovereign people hissed you while you were pleading on my behalf; you, undoubtedly, understood this as a very high compliment . . . [from] such base miscreants."[162]

The Rush camp found the judge more accommodating. With the close of a jury charge attuned to the crowd, people in the gallery and the area of the courthouse—Cobbett called them the "herd"—broke into applause.[163] Again, when the verdict was delivered "the joy of the malignant wretches broke out into *loud and repeated acclamations*," Cobbett reported.[164] Whereas the partiality of the crowd and an influential judge had a significant effect on the jury, the prosecution's command and control of the trial argument was a more likely candidate for having persuaded the jury. For one thing, jurors tended to be less successfully controlled by judges when it came to controversial cases, particularly political ones.[165] As in English courts, judges could refuse to accept verdicts, return juries with additional instructions, or probe the rationale for their decisions,[166] but such practices had progressively fallen out of favor by the end of the eighteenth century. Indeed, as counsel's greater importance accrued over the eighteenth century, juries gained an even greater freedom to avoid judge-directed verdicts[167] and to downvalue or upgrade a crime.[168] The prosecution team in Cobbett's case had, in fact, made a direct appeal to jurors, reminding them that if any one of them could be libeled or be called a libeler, if anything, true or false, could be called a libel, then no one was safe.[169] Only members of the community, and not a judge, would be sensible of the suffering experienced at the hands of a libeler. Who, after all, was best situated to determine public sentiment, if not a representative of the local public? The jury's two-hour deliberation and the excessive damages awarded spoke convincingly to the appeal of the prosecution's argument.

The jury's verdict reflected the shifting political tide that would punish the Federalists and bring in a Republican administration in the 1800 elections. Cobbett complained that many more Republicans were, in fact, part of the jury pool, and since a struck jury process enhanced the prospect of a stacked jury, the likelihood was that Cobbett's jury was weighted in favor of Rush. The public preference for free exercise of speech could have helped Cobbett whereas the prospect that a new administration might be a Republican one would not have helped him, even if public attitudes about the court and political figures were largely negative. In any case, the public figure in question in this instance was a Republican. If the public objected to the Alien and Sedition Acts as they were directed against a Republican press, here was an opportunity for a Republican jury to turn the same acts against a Federalist.

With the court under attack as an elitist institution, the Cobbett case had the potential to redeem the court, which would profit from being seen as a purveyor of Republican justice.[170] Equally, the delay in trying the case until December 1799 aided the Republican argument. Charges had been filed in 1797 at the height of contentious debate over passage of the Alien and Sedition Acts, but the exposure in 1798 of the XYZ Affair had blown over and the presidential elections of 1800 were looming. Cobbett's decided advantage during the Federalist period going into the trial was thus diminished. Federalists were now seen as risking a breach of the peace or a war with France, accusations that positioned them as self-interested parties who took their pleasure at the expense of the public's welfare. With themes of patriotism taking center stage, Republican jurors were likely to embrace a nativist, defiantly patriotic love of America and reject Europeans of any type. In this way, the jury could celebrate prosecution themes of American independence without being linked to a transatlantic Francophile revolutionary perspective. The jury was freed to arrive at a Republican verdict if it so chose.

CONCLUSION

Several events of consequence attended the end of the century *Rush v. Cobbett* trial. First, it signaled the true end of an era when George Washington died on the last day of the trial at the hands of a team of physicians that included Dr. Elisha Dick, a student of Benjamin Rush. The irony could not have been more striking. Cobbett could hardly contain himself, offering in print "that their treatment of the deceased was in precise conformity to *the practice of* Rush."[171] He estimated, based on the physicians' report, that the sixty-eight-year-old Washington must have been bled of nine pints of blood, a debilitating amount even for a man of Washington's physical prowess. Rush's reputation was undermined as well by his history with Washington dating back to the Revolutionary War. He had become involved in the Conway cabal, a group of officers that included General Thomas Conway and General Horatio Gates, among others, that challenged Washington's fitness to lead the Continental Army.[172] Rush had leaked a comment to the effect that it was only by the grace of God that Washington and his weak counselors did not lose the war, and he then injudiciously encouraged his correspondent, Patrick Henry, to destroy his letter but make the contents public.[173]

The trial of William Cobbett expressed in many ways the benefits of the cult of personality that many of the founding figures enjoyed and which Rush capitalized on in casting himself as an honorable man victimized by seditious and psychological assault. A development in the law whereby the refinements of late-century high rhetoric displaced legalistic technicalities in the courtroom also benefited him. The turn of the century oversaw the death of legal holdovers like the older altercation style of trial and the localism attached to independent juries. It saw a growing professionalization of counsel and a concomitant rise of rules of evidence to which the court was increasingly beholden. The colonial jury in which ordinary citizens asserted jury nullification, manipulation of the law, and broad discretion over both facts and the law had declined and so had antipathy to appointed judges.[174]

The democratic changes associated with reform in the courtroom aligned with changes in the legal picture overall as the nation shored up the project of establishing a federal republic. Discretion in the postwar judiciary was curbed in tandem with the development of a federal judiciary. At the same time, states jealously protected themselves against federal authority overtaking the jurisdiction of state courts. Legislatures took on more substantial drafting of statutes to reform or undercut the importance of common law and to reflect the partisan concerns of the two political parties, with every state struggling with problems in its judiciary. Meanwhile, institutions of legal education, law reports of court cases, and legal treatises began to proliferate to create a legal profession that could keep up with the country's expansion.[175]

The trial of John Joyce and Peter Mathias, taken up in the next chapter, illustrates the continuation of just such developments in the context of a growing concern with urban crime as the country grew and cities became a new economic focus for commerce. Democracy became more a matter of street politics and riots than the questions of honor and reputation, character and libel that characterized *Rush v. Cobbett*. And the nation transferred power in an end-of-century change of administrations that brought Jefferson to the presidency and the end of the early republic as it transitioned into an era of Jacksonian politics.

NOTES

1. Debra J. Poul and Wendy L. Waller, "The Pennsylvania Project: The Pennsylvania Supreme Court Perspectives from Within," *Villanova Law Review* 23, no. 5–6 (1977): 1044–47; Edwin C. Surrency, "The Development of the Appellate Function: The Pennsylvania Experience," *The American Journal of Legal History* 20, no. 3 (1976): 175, 181, 1813–85.

2. Mary Elizabeth Clark, *Peter Porcupine in America: The Career of William Cobbett, 1792–1800* (Philadelphia: PhD diss., University of Pennsylvania, 1939), 146–47; David A. Wilson, ed., *Peter Porcupine in America: Pamphlets on Republicanism and Revolution* (Ithaca, NY: Cornell University Press); James Grande, John Stevenson, and Richard Thomas, eds., *The Opinions of William Cobbett* (New York: Routledge, 2013).

3. XYZ stood for the names of the French diplomats who were involved in the negotiations.

4. G. S. Rowe, *Embattled Bench: The Pennsylvania Supreme Court and the Forging of a Democratic Society, 1684–1809* (Newark: University of Delaware Press, 1994), 239–40.

5. *Gazette of the United States*, October 3, 1797; *Porcupine's Gazette*, October 5, 1797.

6. Renee Lettow Lerner, "The Transformation of the American Civil Trial: The Silent Judge," *William and Mary Law Review* 42, no. 1 (2000): 213. Before and after the American Revolution the number of cases removed to the state Supreme Court for trial was quite small and required the involvement of a cost that exceeded over $100 initially, by 1806 over $500, linked to the value of the property in dispute. The choice of cases was largely on a nonlegal basis. Restriction of the court's trial function began during the first decades of the nineteenth century; civil trials ended fully in 1834. Rowe, *Embattled Bench*, 28–29, 31, 35, 129, 202, 290; Surrency, "The Development of the Appellate Function," 175, 181, 183–85.

7. *Philadelphia Gazette and Universal Daily Advertiser*, December 20, 1799.

8. Morris L. Cohen and Sharon Hamby O'Connor, *A Guide to the Early Reports of the Supreme Court of the United States* (Littleton, CO: Rothman & Co., 1995), 31.

9. Alexander J. Dallas, *Reports of Cases Ruled and Adjudged in the Courts of Pennsylvania, Before and Since the Revolution*, 4 vols. (Philadelphia: [T. Bradford; Aurora; Ormrod; Fry and Kammerer] 1790–1807), an abbreviated set of trial reports for the Pennsylvania Supreme Court, was one of the earliest collections; Rowe, *Embattled Bench*, 203–04; Erwin C. Surrency, "Law Reports in the United States," *The American Journal of Legal History* 25, no. 1 (1981): 50–58.

10. Cohen and O'Connor, *A Guide*, 14–16, 29.

11. Surrency, "The Development," 55–56.

12. T. Carpenter, *A Report of an Action for a Libel Brought by Dr. Benjamin Rush against William Cobbett in the Supreme Court of Pennsylvania, December Term, 1799, for Certain Defamatory Publications in a Newspaper Entitled Porcupine's Gazette* (Philadelphia: W.W. Woodward, 1800). The transcript provides evidence of attacks on Rush from Cobbett's *Porcupine's Gazette*, truncated examination of two witnesses, and a deposition from a third. The prosecution's arguments were disproportionately longer (thirty-six pages) than that of the defense (twenty pages).

13. Yellow fever epidemics occurred in Philadelphia in 1648, 1699, 1741, 1747, 1749, 1762, 1765, 1793, 1797, 1798, and 1799; John Duffy, *Epidemics in Colonial America* (Baton Rouge: Louisiana State University Press, 1953).

14. Duffy, *Epidemics*, 24.

15. Duffy, *Epidemics*, 27.

16. *Minutes of the Proceedings of the Committee, Appointed on the 14th September, 1793, by the Citizens of Philadelphia, the Northern Liberties, and the District of Southwark, To Attend to and Alleviate the Sufferings of the Afflicted with the Malignant Fever Prevalent in the City and Its Vicinity, 1848* (Philadelphia: City of Philadelphia, 1848).

17. *Porcupine's Gazette*, August 24, 1797; William Cobbett, *Porcupine's Works; Containing Various Writings and Selections, Exhibiting a Faithful Picture of the United States of America* (London: Cobbett and Morgan, 1801), VII, 41–42.

18. *Porcupine's Gazette*, August 26, 1797.

19. "Extracts of Letters from Dr. Rush and Others, on the Subject of the Yellow Fever," College of Physicians of Philadelphia Library, handwritten manuscript 10a175, 167; September 18, 1794. An average adult body contains ten pints of blood (160 ounces); Rush's bleeding method took 140 ounces in six days.

20. Benjamin Rush, *An Account of the Bilious Remitting Yellow Fever, as It Appeared in the City of Philadelphia, in the Year 1793* (Philadelphia: Thomas Dobson, 1794), 190.

21. Rush, *An Account*, 164.

22. Rush, *An Account*, 246.

23. Alain Rene Le Sage, *The Adventures of Gil Blas of Santillane*, trans. T. Smollett, 2 vols. (London: J. Walker, 1809).

24. Henry Fielding, *The Adventures of Joseph Andrews, and His Friend Mr. Abraham Adams* (London, 1793), II, 4.

25. Tobias George Smollet, *The Adventures of Peregrine Pickle. In Which are Included, Memoirs of a Lady of Quality* (London, 1794).

26. *Rush-Light* III, March 15, 1800; *Rush-Light* IV, March 31, 1800; *Porcupine's Gazette*, January 13, 1800; Cobbett, *Porcupine's Works*, XII, 140, 307–43, 370.

27. *Rush-Light* III, March 15, 1800; Cobbett, *Porcupine's Works*, XI, 313–14.

28. *Rush-Light* III, March 15, 1800; Cobbett, *Porcupine's Works*, XI, 314.

29. *Rush-Light* III, March 15, 1800; Cobbett, *Porcupine's Works* XI, 316–17.

30. *Rush-Light* III, March 15, 1800; Cobbett, *Porcupine's Works*, XI, 318.

31. Le Sage, *The Adventures*, 56–59, 65.

32. Kenneth Allen De Ville, *Medical Malpractice in Nineteenth Century America: Origins and Legacy* (New York: New York University Press, 1990), 156–57.

33. Blackstone was published in England in 1765 and appeared in its first American edition in 1771–1772; William Blackstone, *Commentaries on the Laws of England. In Four Books*, 6th ed., 4 vols. (London: T. Cadell, 1774).

34. The applicable doctrine, trespass in case, reflects negligence, nonfeasance, and the absence of force; Morton J. Horwitz, *The Transformation of American Law, 1780–1860* (Cambridge, MA: Harvard University Press., 1977), 89.

35. It was not until the mid-nineteenth century that the law moved away from "*status-based* responsibilities growing out of a physician's role as a public servant to *contract-based* responsibilities emanating from bilateral agreements"; De Ville, 162. Supported by community standards and implied obligations, contracts left patients at a disadvantage as they were not equal bargainers with doctors and could not freely consent to medical treatment with knowledge equal to that of the physician. De Ville, 162–163, 185.

36. De Ville, *Medical Malpractice*, 156–69.

37. Wex Malone, *Essays on Torts* (Baton Rouge: Louisiana State University Press, 1986), 18–19.

38. John J. Elwell, *A Medico-Legal Treatise on Medical Malpractice and Medical Evidence* (New York: John S. Voorhis, 1860), 29–30.

39. Malone, *Essays*, 20.

40. Elwell, *A Medico-Legal Treatise*, 21–22.

41. De Ville, *Medical Malpractice*, 21.

42. See *Braunberger v. Cleis* (1864); such conditions continued to influence the legal standard of care well into the nineteenth century; *Medical and Surgical Reporter*, 1865, 555–58, 569–73. See Milo A. McClelland, *Civil Malpractice: A Treatise on Surgical Jurisprudence* (New York: Hurd and Houghton, 1877), 127–45.

43. Malone, *Essays*, 20; Elwell, *A Medico-Legal Treatise*, 22.

44. Elwell, *A Medico-Legal Treatise*, 19–35.

45. Elwell, *A Medico-Legal Treatise*, 22, 27.

46. Elwell, *A Medico-Legal Treatise*, 23.

47. Elwell, *A Medico-Legal Treatise*, 29.

48. Benjamin Rush, *Sixteen Introductory Lectures to Courses of Lectures Upon the Institutes and Practice of Medicine, With a Syllabus of the Latter* (Philadelphia: Bradford and Innskeep, 1811), lecture 14, 318–59.

49. Malone, *Essays*, 21, 26.

50. Elwell, *A Medico-Legal Treatise*, 29–32.

51. Rush, "On the Duties of Patients to their Physicians," *Lectures*, lecture 14, 326.

52. Rush, *Lectures*, lecture 14, 324.

53. Stanley Nider Katz, "Introduction," in *A Brief Narrative of the Case and Trial of John Peter Zenger, Printer of the New York Weekly Journal*, ed. Stanley Nider Katz (Cambridge, MA: Harvard University Press, 1963), 11–12.

54. Norman L. Rosenberg, *Protecting the Best Men: An Interpretive History of the Law of Libel* (Chapel Hill: University of North Carolina Press, 1986), 12.

55. Rosenberg, *Protecting the Best Men*, 6.

56. Rosenberg, *Protecting the Best Men*, 78.

57. Blackstone, *Commentaries*, IV, 151–52.

58. Rosenberg, *Protecting the Best Men*, 54, 69.

59. Blackstone, *Commentaries*, III, 125; Carpenter, *A Report*, 59.

60. Sedition Act, 1798, Section 3.

61. Rosenberg, *Protecting the Best Men*, 87.

62. Jeffery A. Smith, *Printers and Press Freedom: The Ideology of Early American Journalism* (New York: Oxford University Press, 1988), 32.

63. Pennsylvania Constitution, Section 3, article 9.

64. Carpenter, *A Report*, 25.

65. Cobbett- Yrujo cases occurred in 1797, 1798, 1800, 1817, and 1819; Davis and North, who put up the bond for Cobbett in the original case, faced cases for payment of the bond in 1801, 1804, and 1805. Cases related to the Rush trial occurred in 1798, 1799, 1800, and 1801. Cobbett faced charges in civil and criminal cases in federal, state, and a mayor's court, including a petition to the state legislature; his cases ranged from libel, forfeiture of a peace bond (recognizance), application for removal to a federal court, recovery of a fine, and application for a new trial.

66. The Yrujo case was filed as a federal criminal action on August 8, 1797. It was not completely resolved until 1819 when Cobbett finally dropped all efforts to contest it; Clark, *Peter Porcupine in America*, 115–22; Cobbett's longhand petition to the Pennsylvania House of Representatives is on deposit at the Historical Society of Pennsylvania. William Cobbett, *The Republican Judge: or the American Liberty of the Press, as Exhibited, Explained, and Exposed, in the Base and Partial Prosecution of William Cobbett, for a Pretended Libel against the King of Spain and his Embassador, before the Supreme Court of Pennsylvania* (London: J. Wright, 1798).

67. Rowe, *Embattled Bench*, 229, 239.

68. Cobbett's *Republican Judge* addresses Cobbett's issues with the American judiciary and the press. That the grand jury refused to indict in a case where the chief justice had become personally involved and judicially overinvested—as prosecutor, witness, and judge—gave Cobbett ammunition to claim persecution by and corruption of republican government in Pennsylvania.

69. Cobbett, *Republican,* 44.

70. Cobbett, *Republican,* 45.

71. Rosenberg, *Protecting the Best Men*, 18–19, 94–96, 106–07; Markus Dirk Dubber, "'The Power to Govern Men and Things': Patriarchal Origins of the Police Power in American Law," *Buffalo Law Review* 52 (2004): 1325–28; Paul Lermack, "Bonds

and Criminal Justice in Colonial Philadelphia," *The Pennsylvania Magazine of History and Biography* 100, no. 2 (1976): 173–90; Robert Force, "Decriminalization of Breach of Peace Statutes: A Nonpenal Approach to Order Maintenance," *Tulane Law Review* 46 (1972): 367–412; "Note: Peace and Behavior Bonds—Summary Punishment for Uncommitted Offenses," *Virginia Law Review* 52, no. 5 (1966): 914–33; Glanville Williams, "Preventative Justice and the Rule of Law," *The Modern Law Review* 16, no. 4 (1953): 417–27.

72. Rowe, *Embattled Bench*, 252.

73. Dallas, *Reports of Cases Ruled*, III, 476.

74. Dallas, *Reports of Cases Ruled*, III, 474; *Rush-Light* IV, March 31, 1800; Cobbett, *Porcupine's Works*, XI, 360, 362. Cobbett's petition was dismissed because damages could not, as with property, be calculated at more than $500 and therefore the case did not qualify as required under federal law; Burton Alva Konkle, *Joseph Hopkinson, 1770–1842: Jurist, Scholar, Inspirer of the Arts* (Philadelphia: University of Pennsylvania Press, 1981), 60; Clark, *Peter Porcupine in America*, 148.

75. *Rush-Light* IV, 31 March 1800; Cobbett, *Porcupine's Works*, XI, 358.

76. Cobbett, *Porcupine's Works*, XI, 358, 367.

77. A kite is a large hawk-like bird of prey.

78. *Rush-Light* IV, 31 March 1800; Cobbett, *Porcupine's Works*, XI, 360–61.

79. Cobbett, *Porcupine's Works*, XI, 362.

80. Cobbett, *Porcupine's Works*, XI, 362.

81. Rosenberg, *Protecting the Best Men*, 93–94, 96.

82. Rosenberg, *Protecting the Best Men*, 108.

83. Rosenberg, 94–96. The Republican position opposing the Sedition Act, while Pennsylvania Republicans prosecuted Cobbett, led Cobbett's counsel Harper to claim rank partisanship in the trial: "I wish to interpose this law between the freedoms of discussion and the overbearing sway of that tyrannical spirit, by which a certain political party in this country, is activated;" Robert Goodloe Harper, in *Annals of Congress*, 6th Congr., 2nd session, 940, in vol. 10, January 1801. See Rosenberg, 102–3.

84. Republica v. Oswald (1788); Dallas, *Reports of Cases Ruled*, I, 328.

85. A Republican editor, Duane's newspaper was the *Aurora General Advertiser*.

86. James Morton Smith, "The Aurora and the Alien and Sedition Laws, Part II: The Editorship of William Duane," *Pennsylvania Magazine of History and Biography* 77, no. 2 (1953): 146–47.

87. Smith, "Aurora," 146.

88. William E. Nelson, "Emerging Notions of Modern Criminal Law in the Revolutionary Era: An Historical Perspective," *New York University Law Review* 42, no. 3 (1967): 450–82; William E. Nelson, *Americanization of the Common Law: The Impact of Legal Change on Massachusetts Society, 1760–1830* (Cambridge, MA: Harvard University Press, 1975).

89. Lerner, "The Transformation," 203, 208, 220.

90. Nelson, "Emerging," 450, 462, 469, 472–73; Nelson, *Americanization*, 175–76.

91. Barbara Shapiro, *'Beyond Reasonable Doubt' and 'Probable Cause': Historical Perspectives on the Anglo-American Law of Evidence* (Berkeley: University of California Press, 1991), 180.

92. Richard Webster, *Philadelphia Preserved: Catalog of the Historic American Buildings Survey* (Philadelphia: Temple University Press, 1976), 78; Rowe confirms the Supreme Court met in the west wing on the first floor; Rowe, *Embattled Bench*, 102.

93. Charlene Mires, *Independence Hall in American Memory* (Philadelphia: University of Pennsylvania Press, 2002), 20.

94. Webster, *Philadelphia Preserved*, 79.

95. For the ten years (1790–1800) that Philadelphia served as capital of the United States, the Pennsylvania Supreme Court was sandwiched between the US Supreme Court in the east building (Philadelphia City Hall), where the US Circuit Court for the Eastern District of Pennsylvania also sat, and the US Congress in the west building (Congress Hall), where the Philadelphia County Court sat; Webster, *Philadelphia Preserved*, 78–79.

96. Surrency, "The Development of the Appellate Function," 183.

97. Rowe, *Embattled Bench*, 190.

98. Lerner, "The Transformation," 213.

99. *Rush-Light* IV, March 31, 1800; Cobbett, *Porcupine's Works*, XI, 380.

100. In 1791, Jacob Rush was commissioned president of the Third Circuit, seated in Reading, and in 1806 president of the Philadelphia Circuit. Unlike his brother, Justice Rush was a strict Federalist with a strong penchant for maintaining social order; Louis Richards, "Hon. Jacob Rush of the Pennsylvania Judiciary," *The Pennsylvania Magazine of History and Biography* 39, no. 1 (1915): 66.

101. July 9, 1788, letter to Elias Boudinot in *Letters of Benjamin Rush*, ed. L. H. Butterfield (Princeton, NJ: Princeton University Press, 1951), I, 473.

102. Rowe, *Embattled Bench*, 194–97.

103. Rosenberg, *Protecting the Best Men*, 62.

104. Rowe, *Embattled Bench*, 202, 232, 276. At least four other candidates were considered: Benjamin Chew, a former chief justice, Jasper Yeates, Moses Levy, and James Ross.

105. Rowe, *Embattled Bench*, 77, 179, 194, 201, 206.

106. Rowe, *Embattled Bench*, 242.

107. G. S. Rowe, "Judicial Tyrant and Vox Populi: Pennsylvanians View Their State Supreme Court, 1777–1799," *Pennsylvania Magazine of History and Biography* 118, no. 1 (1994): 34, 37; Rowe, *Embattled Bench*, 244–246.

108. Rowe, *Embattled Bench*, 244–45.

109. Linda Myrsiades, *Law and Medicine in Revolutionary America: Dissecting the Rush v. Cobbett Trial* (Bethlehem, PA: Lehigh University Press, 2012).

110. *Rush-Light* IV, March 31, 1800; Cobbett, *Porcupine's Works*, XI, 365; George Spater, *William Cobbett: The Poor Man's Friend,* Vol 1. (Cambridge, MA: Cambridge University Press, 1982), 269, n51.

111. William Cobbett, *Letters from William Cobbett to Edward Thornton Written in the Years 1797 to 1800*, ed. G. D. H. Cole (London: Oxford University Press, 1937), xxi.

112. *Rush-Light* IV, March 31, 1800; Cobbett, *Porcupine's Works,* XI, 365; the sessions referred to were September 1798, December 1798, March 1799, September 1799.

113. *Rush-Light* IV, March 31, 1800; Cobbett, *Porcupine's Works*, XII, 365–66.

114. The question in an altercation trial was largely one of "what really happened, and did the accused really do it," whereas the adversarial trial focused on "whether defence counsel had succeeded in raising sufficient doubt about the strength of the prosecution case"; Sanjeez Anand, "The Origins, Early History and Evolution of the English Criminal Trial Jury," *The Alberta Law Review* 43, no. 2 (2005): 427–28. The adversarial trial did not take hold until late in the eighteenth century. John H. Langbein, *The Origins of Adversary Criminal Trial* (Oxford: Oxford University Press, 2003), 10–66.

115. Langbein, *The Origins*, 259.

116. Langbein, *The Origins*, 1, 313, 332, 339; Stephan Landsman, "The Rise of the Contentious Spirit: Adversary Procedure in Eighteenth Century England," *Cornell Law Review* 75, no. 3 (1990): 487, 502–03; Anand, "The Origins," 407–32.

117. Konkle, *Joseph Hopkinson*, 85–94. Hopkinson acted for the defense in the famous Fries' Rebellion trial (1799), in which Rawle, as district attorney, and Ingersol acted for the prosecution.

118. Serving as Rush's counsel both before and after the trial, Brockholst Livingston wrote several revealing letters to Rush that suggest the verdict reached in Philadelphia might have been unlikely had the trial occurred either in federal court (as Cobbett would have preferred) or in New York (to which Cobbett removed shortly before the trial began). Rush Manuscript, Historical Society of Pennsylvania, vol. 29, letters 85 (June 4, 1800) and 87 (May 30, 1801).

119. Carpenter, *A Report*, 8.

120. Carpenter, *A Report*, 2.

121. *Rush-Light* I, February 15, 1800; Cobbett, *Porcupine's Works*, XI, 239.

122. *Rush-Light* I, February 15, 1800, Cobbett, *Porcupine's Works*, XI, 239–340.

123. Carpenter, *A Report*, 49.

124. Carpenter, *A Report*, 38.

125. Carpenter, *A Report*, 10.

126. Carpenter, *A Report*, 13.

127. Carpenter, *A Report*, 48, 60, 62.

128. Carpenter, *A Report*, 63.

129. Carpenter, *A Report*, 63.

130. Carpenter, *A Report*, 39.

131. Cobbett took the position that the American press was not as free as the English press—the Grub street press of which he felt himself a proud example.

132. *Rush v. Cobbett* takes place coextensive with a long history of physician feuds in which Rush was involved; Linda Myrsiades, *Medical Culture in Revolutionary America: Feuds, Duels, and a Court Martial* (Madison, NJ: Fairleigh Dickinson University Press, 2009), 77–115.

133. Myrsiades, *Medical Culture*, 116–77. Carl A. L. Binger, *Revolutionary Doctor: Benjamin Rush, 1746–1813* (New York: Norton, 1966), 132–39; Butterfield,

Letters of Benjamin Rush, II, 1197–1208; Nathan Goodman, *Benjamin Rush: Physician and Citizen, 1746–1813* (Philadelphia: University of Pennsylvania Press, 1934), 107–27; Harlow Giles Unger, *Dr. Benjamin Rush: The Founding Father Who Healed a Wounded Nation* (New York: Hachette Book Group, 2018).

134. Cobbett had a reputation for feuding as well; Mathew Carey, *Plumb Pudding for the Humane, Chaste, Valiant, Enlightened Peter Porcupine by His Obliged Friend Mathew Carey*, 2nd ed. (Philadelphia: Mathew Carey, 1799); Mathew Carey, *The Porcupiniad: A Hudibrastic Poem in Three Cantos Addressed to William Cobbett* (Philadelphia: Matthew Carey, 1799); Mathew Carey, *Mathew Carey: Autobiography* (Brooklyn, NY: Research Classics, [1837] 1942).

135. Carpenter, *A Report*, 25.

136. Carpenter, *A Report*, 47–48.

137. Carpenter, *A Report*, 50.

138. Carpenter, *A Report*, 52.

139. Carpenter, *A Report*, 51.

140. Carpenter, *A Report*, 55.

141. Carpenter, *A Report*, 54.

142. Carpenter, *A Report*, 54.

143. Carpenter, *A Report*, 66.

144. Carpenter, *A Report*, 20.

145. Carpenter, *A Report*, 1.

146. Carpenter, *A Report*, 1.

147. Carpenter, *A Report*, 2.

148. Carpenter, *A Report*, 2.

149. Carpenter, *A Report*, 2.

150. *Rush-Light* IV, March 31, 1800; Cobbett, *Porcupine's Works*, XI, 383.

151. December 18, 1799, letter to Edward Tilghman, Historical Society of Pennsylvania, file no. PHI 2129.

152. April 25, 1800, letter to Edward Thornton; Cobbett, *Letters*, 86–87.

153. Carpenter, *A Report*, 10.

154. *Rush-Light* III, March 15, 1800; Cobbett, *Porcupine's Works*, XI, 371.

155. Cobbett, *Porcupine's Works*, 376.

156. Carpenter, *A Report*, 1.

157. *Rush-Light* III, March 15, 1800; Cobbett, *Porcupine's Works*, XI, 376.

158. Cobbett, *Porcupine's Works*, XI, 376.

159. Cobbett, *Porcupine's Works*, XI, 373–74, 377.

160. In the transcript of the trial, Carpenter did not provide evidence of Shippen's management of the court.

161. *Rush-Light* IV, March 31, 1800, Cobbett, *Porcupine's Works*, XI, n374.

162. December 30, 1799, letter to Edward Tilghman, Historical Society of Pennsylvania, file no. PHI 2129.

163. Cobbett, *Porcupine's Works*, XI, 383.

164. Cobbett, *Porcupine's Works*, XI, n383.

165. Langbein, *The Origins*, 331–32.

166. Langbein, *The Origins*, 336.

167. The Pennsylvania Constitution of 1790 endowed juries with "the right to determine the law and the facts" (Article IX, Section 7), giving it powers that rivaled those of the judge. Where a judge's direction was in line with the jury's verdict, it was likely that they were both part of the same political community.

168. Langbein, *The Origins*, 6, 58.

169. If it was a satire, it could not be strictly true; if merely an opinion, it could not be proved true; if it was false, it could provoke a breach of the peace even if it was free speech; if true and proved true, it risked undermining confidence in a public person or governing body, damage to the polity, and the threat of retribution.

170. The court was being tested in *Rush v. Cobbett* because of its long-standing feud with Cobbett and its inability to make its charges stick in the Yrujo case. It became popular to disapprove publicly of the high court, leading to the impeachment in 1804 of all three of those who had sat on the bench in the Rush case—Shippen, Yeates, and Smith. Rowe, *Embattled Court,* 167, 169, 172, 240–243, 252, 264–268, 271.

171. *Porcupine's Gazette*, January 13, 1800; Cobbett, *Porcupine's Works,* XII, 146–47.

172. Mark Edward Lender, *Cabal! The Plot against George Washington* (Yardley, PA: Westholme Publishing, 2019).

173. Benjamin Rush to John Adams, October 21, 1777; Benjamin Rush to Patrick Henry, January 12, 1778, Rush, *Letters*, I, 161, 183.

174. Shannon C. Stimson, *The American Revolution in the Law: Anglo-American Jurisprudence Before John Marshall* (Princeton, NJ: Princeton University Press, 1990), 48–49, 53, 60, 62–63.

175. Gordon S. Wood, *Empire of Liberty: A History of the Early Republic, 1789–1815* (New York: Oxford University Press, 2009), 408–18, 425; G. Edward White, *Law in American History, Volume I: From the Colonial Years Through the Civil War* (New York: Oxford University Press, 2012), 279–91; Lawrence M. Friedman, *A History of American Law*, 3rd ed. (New York: Simon & Shuster, 2005), 79–104, 226–48.

Chapter 6

"I *will* a tale unfold"

The Murder Trial of John Joyce and Peter Matthias, 1808

I *will* a tale unfold, whose lightest word/ *Shall* harrow up thy soul.

—Toby Scratch'em, *The Tickler*, March 16, 1808

In Philadelphia's Black Horse Alley on Friday, December 18, 1807, thieves robbed and murdered Mrs. Sarah Cross, a fifty-year-old widowed white shopkeeper.[1] Authorities apprehended two suspects, African American laborers John Joyce and Peter Matthias. As reported in *American State Trials*, the court indicted Joyce "with being the actual perpetrator of the crime and Matthias with being present aiding and abetting and assisting in it."[2] In February 1808, both were tried in a jury trial in the oyer and terminer, or criminal, Court of the City and County of Philadelphia. At their arraignments, the prisoners pleaded not guilty. The court convicted the defendants of first-degree murder. In a confession dictated before his execution, Matthias proclaimed his innocence in the hope of receiving a pardon and was supported in his claim by Joyce's own confession. Authorities hanged the two men March 14, 1808, before some twenty thousand to twenty-five thousand persons.[3]

Joyce had determined his murder plan before meeting Matthias. He proposed they seek out a Mr. Kennedy, on the pretense that he owed Joyce wages. A reluctant Matthias nonetheless accompanied Joyce on the promise of sharing his wages. On the way, Joyce collected items necessary to the crime and persuaded Matthias to stop several times to drink some gin. Finding Kennedy not at home, Joyce suggested they visit Mrs. Cross's shop, to which Matthias initially agreed but soon departed, leaving Joyce alone with the victim. During this interval, Joyce killed the shopkeeper. Before Matthias returned, a young girl (Anne Messinger) entered the shop, whom Joyce prevented from leaving. Matthias, upon his return, tried to free the girl to no avail and thereafter assisted Joyce in carrying out some goods. Escaping from Joyce's grip as they left the shop, the girl cried out an alarm as the two men fled unobserved. Neighbors rushed to the site to discover Mrs. Cross dead, strangled, and wounded by a knife.[4]

Though recorded in newspaper accounts, a trial report, execution confessions, sermons, addresses, and a popular crime narrative, making it one of the most well-documented interracial crimes of the early nineteenth century, the Joyce-Matthias case has received scant attention in scholarly studies. Without a court reporter or official trial record, study of the crime and trial of Joyce and Matthias depends upon original material reported in pamphlets or, taken from minutes of the trial, notes "indebted to a friend," and public press accounts.[5] Both Peter Matthias and John Joyce dictated execution confessions transcribed by the Reverend Richard Allen, a member of the Black elite and founder of the first truly independent African American church in America, Bethel African Methodist Episcopal Church. Together with the confessions (sworn by the accused, and signed with their marks), Allen published his addresses to the public and people of color, notes on the execution, a newspaper account of the trial, and Chief Justice William Tilghman's sentencing statement, as well as the amanuensis's own notes.[6]

The narrative and newspaper accounts capitalized on the sensational aspects of the crime, catering to the prurient interests of their readers. The confessions and the execution sermons, to the contrary, must be assessed in terms of a narrative tradition into which they fit, both of which fulfilled religious and racial needs. Transcribed by a second hand and intended to teach their readers a moral lesson, the confessions reveal crucial testimony about the crime, although their evidentiary value is limited. Reports of the court proceedings, by contrast, reflect respect for the need to provide a reliable record. They tend to be relatively straightforward accounts comparable to reports of other contemporary trials in their factual accuracy. They lack, however, the legal expertise expressed in cases collected in early law reports by such figures as Alexander Addison and Alexander Dallas.[7]

The paucity of legal sources from the period has led to an imperfect understanding about the legal treatment of Black defendants. Those who study such issues cannot automatically assume that courts and judges robotically used the law to discriminate racially or that racial constructions or prejudice that seeped into the courtroom wholly infected the legal system. It is, rather, an important task to explore the complex interfaces of cultural and legal racial consciousness and to examine the complications of the legal experience in the courtroom. As Paul Finkelman says, the cases that arose in the wake of the 1780 Gradual Abolition Act reflected a "deeply complicated" legal experience with race and slavery.[8]

The experience that surrounded the trial is itself an important indicator of where the Black community of Philadelphia was situated in 1808. One clear motif is the leadership of the Black elite of Philadelphia, a sign of a growing Black middle class and an indicium of the advent of the Black church and Black abolitionism. Concomitant with those developments, Black print culture and political activity within the community sponsored discourse that historian Richard S. Newman identifies as "debates over black identity in the Atlantic world." What we find in Philadelphia is a world in which slavery seemed to be under assault (in 1808 the United States prohibited transatlantic slave trade into the country on the heels of the first experiments in gradual emancipation—1780–1804) at the same time that northern states cut back on Black voting rights and racially subjugating codes surged. The American Revolution was still in the forefront of peoples' minds, as were the sixty to one hundred thousand slaves who fled from slavery during the war as well as the thousands who were manumitted in the early 1800s. Even so, slavery doubled by the end of the early republic. The Joyce-Matthias trial took place in a complex and turbulent time for the Black community of the city.[9]

CONTEXT

Joyce, the twenty-four-year-old instigator of the crimes perpetrated against Mrs. Cross, was born a slave. In his confession, he referred to his parents as "piously inclined," although he admitted to depraved morals and did not belong "to any religious society."[10] Given the conventions of the confession genre and the preferences of Reverend Allen, it is unlikely the emphasis on morality that infuses Joyce's confession necessarily represented his sentiments. Joyce fled his mistress, joined the US Navy at fifteen, and sailed for seven years, possibly hoping, like many fleeing slaves, that he would gain his freedom as compensation for his service. Interrupting his life on the sea for a stint in the household of a Washington, DC, physician, he married and had two children, had two more by another woman, and returned to sea once again with the navy. Joyce was like one-quarter of the young Black males in Philadelphia who made a living at sea until a decline in wages and a collapse of commerce resulting from President Jefferson's Embargo Act of 1807 depressed maritime labor.[11]

In 1806, at twenty-two, Joyce arrived in Philadelphia. He worked a variety of jobs often held by those who wished to improve themselves: coachman, driver, waiter, and stable hand. He moved among a variety of residences for a year and half, never longer than two or three months in one place, residing in the households of white employers and later boarding with a Black woman, Margaret Tucker. Joyce had a criminal history and admitted to several thefts, including one in Washington, DC, where stealing a horse prompted him to move to Philadelphia, and as a coachman in Lancaster, Pennsylvania, where he lost his job for stealing a watch. "Toby Scratch'em" in *The Tickler*, a satirical Philadelphia newspaper, avowed that on two occasions when Joyce was a servant, he robbed his master and that Scratch'em was aware of other such circumstances.[12]

Twenty-six-year-old Peter Matthias was Joyce's sidekick and clearly a follower. His father was a freeman and his family pious, although Peter "paid but little attention" to their advice. Matthias claimed he had gained his freedom upon the death of his master when his mistress gave him "six years credit" on an opportunity to purchase his freedom for $200. Over the next few years, on his own admission, he would pay only part of the price. Matthias arrived in Delaware where he remained for several months in 1806 building a garden for one employer, and then working for two brothers before he, too, took to the water. He made commercial trips between Delaware and Philadelphia and settled in Philadelphia about the same time as Joyce. He worked at menial labor on the wharves picking apart old rope but also played a violin at dances and taverns. Peripatetic like Joyce, but with no criminal history, Matthias moved among several residences for a year before the murder of Mrs. Cross, including the rental of a room from "a man of color, named Pompey."[13] At the time of the crime, he lived with Hester Cook, a likely, if unindicted, accomplice to the theft after the fact.

Both Joyce and Matthias resided at one time or another in Cedar Ward, which was bounded by Fourth and Eighth Streets and by Cedar and Fitzwater and touched on the Southwark and Moyamensing wards. Some fourteen blocks long and two blocks wide, it included Matthias's home at Fifth below Small Street from which he and Joyce made their way to Mrs. Cross's shop on Blackhorse Alley. Cedar Ward was on the southern edge of the city and by 1811 housed a working-class population of predominantly Black laborers, although it included a spectrum of African Americans ranging from the city's poorest inhabitants to the wealthiest Black community elites in the city. The area included Black-founded churches and benevolent, educational, and cultural institutions.[14]

Racial segregation was already established in Philadelphia by the first decade of the eighteenth century as white residents moved from the Cedar Ward area to occupy more comfortable homes in the center of the city. They left behind what they considered a ghetto with high crime rates, low land values, and few services; indeed, the Cedar Ward area accommodated activities they characterized as immoral—drunkenness, prostitution, and gambling. At the same time, Black residents retreated from the center of the city to the outskirts at Cedar Ward, a move accompanied by downward social mobility, crowded conditions, and epidemic diseases. The geographical shift suggested for whites an escape from the moral suasion and social control of white social and legal norms, yet another kind of spatial disconnect signaling distance between the two populations that compounded the sense of difference associated with the Black poor.[15] There was little interaction between Cedar Ward on the city's periphery and Center City's Middle Ward (the location of Letitia Court, the area of the crime) where wealthy white homes dominated, and the area bustled with commerce.[16] The neighboring wards of Southwark and Cedar were areas where parties dealing in stolen goods could be kept anonymous and the ownership of property obscured. In terms of their location and the distribution of manual and nonmanual occupations, poor Black neighborhoods were geographically and socially peripheral—by space and by class—which reinforced a sense of strangerhood.[17]

Matthias and Joyce were caught up in significant events across the end of the eighteenth and the beginning of the nineteenth centuries that affected the condition of African Americans in Philadelphia, how they would be perceived by the city's white majority, and the state of their legal rights. From 1780 to 1815, great numbers of manumitted, self-emancipated, and fugitive slaves migrated from rural Pennsylvania, New Jersey, and Delaware, from the slave states, and from the slave revolt in Santo Domingo (Haiti). Joyce and Matthias belonged to the very subgroup of young ex-slave males that white society most feared would become a dependent class of the poor or a criminal class that would prey on better-off residents of the city. Pennsylvania's 1780 Gradual Abolition of Slavery Act did not, in the process of gradual emancipation, fully eliminate slavery until sixty-seven years after it became law, leading to substantial ambiguity surrounding the legal status of Philadelphia's Black population.[18] Insofar as Joyce and Matthias's manumission was both incomplete and suspect (Matthias's by his failure to complete an agreement to buy his freedom and Joyce's by fleeing from servitude), their status as free men was clearly tenuous. The same was true for Pennsylvania slaves whose delayed freedom largely meant continuation of the status quo for people of color and their newly born and left the population spread across a range of statuses related to their freedom.[19] In the courts, to the contrary, the act changed the status of free Blacks and slaves as it granted them the legal right to have their offenses and crimes "enquired of, adjudged, corrected and punished in like manner as the offences and crimes of the other inhabitants of this state."[20] They thereby had the right to the same criminal processes and courts as all others who were tried, with the exception that slaves could not testify against freemen.

More encompassing legal questions loomed, however, including how to render the legally invisible (slaves) visible (free persons) and in doing so how to render them equal (with the same rights as whites). Moreover, there were two realms (civil and criminal), three conditions (slave, partially free, and freed), and several laws (including the promise of the Declaration of Independence and the realities of state and US constitutions and statutes related to emancipation and judicial reform) that had to be navigated. The transition created anomalies such that moving from enslavement led to criminalizing Black conduct and ensuring civil invisibility. The emancipated population would thus be relieved of being noncitizens while being disallowed from becoming citizens.[21]

The experience of Black people caught up in the criminal justice system in Pennsylvania in the course of gradual emancipation was conditioned by a history in which Blacks, slave or free, had been subjected from 1700 to 1780 to the summary justice of "Negro Tryals" that took place in courts before two justices and six freeholders of the neighborhood.[22] Black people were subjected to separate statutes or to separate punishments in general statutes for such crimes as arson, debauchery, hunting, regulation of carters, and curfews, allowing courts to impose heavier penalties for Black than for white offenders.[23] Nor did they have the same rights in court as white defendants; they had no right to counsel, nor could they question their accusers.[24]

The advent of the 1780 act, compounded by large-scale migration and concern for petty theft of property, aggravated public perceptions of Black crime and led to a dramatic increase from 1784 to 1830 of accusations against Blacks for disorderly conduct and disturbing the peace.[25] Charges against Black people were not as frequently quashed or reduced; accused Blacks were more likely to be convicted, sentenced, and serve longer sentences; and Black defendants were less likely to be freed on bond.[26] Because Black defendants were disproportionately accused of petty crimes, they found themselves subjected in greater numbers to the summary treatment of magistrate or justice of the peace courts. Some magistrates, accused of being "trading justices," lived by exacting costly legal fees and victimizing vulnerable defendants who came before them. Abusive magistrates sent defendants to prison even when grand juries refused to charge them; they encouraged whites to sue Blacks, collected court fees for frivolous crimes, and filled the prison with those who could not raise money for their release.[27] What Jeannine Marie De Lombard calls "racial criminalization" was institutionalized by legislation establishing the first prison in 1790. It resulted in a Black population of over 40 percent of the prisoners in Walnut Street Prison between 1810 and 1816, well beyond their 10 percent portion of the population, and a conviction rate of 80 percent of Blacks who went to jury trial between 1780 and 1800.[28]

Gradual emancipation was followed by penal reform, an ongoing change in Pennsylvania law that by 1794 restricted capital punishment to murder in the first degree.[29] As a result, the question of guilt or innocence in Pennsylvania for a Black person accused of a hanging offense became both less confusing (through legislation clarifying the law) and increasingly complicated (as racial perceptions became exacerbated).[30] The state thereafter faced a shift in perceptions that would create turmoil few had anticipated.[31] It would result in a legal condition described by Joanne Pope Melish as racialized "strangerhood," objectified like chattel and yet held accountable as subjects in legal matters.[32] In many ways, white society simply transferred assumptions about slaves to free Blacks so that their estrangement made them an object of persistent harassment and debasement under the presumption that they were an inferior and distinct class of people.[33] In this anomalous condition, free Blacks were both free and not free. They possessed legal rights in courts but lacked civil rights in society, rendering their substantive claims without much merit.[34]

Into this mix, racial perceptions in the public sphere helped to shape Black criminal and civil rights through published crime narratives, execution sermons, and execution confessions operating in a space in which vernacular legal discourse took place. Print culture from newspapers (*The Tickler*) to pamphlets (*The Fate of Murderers: A Faithful Narrative of the Murder of Mrs. Sarah Cross*) allowed for anonymous authorship and invited a wider public. This undermined the authority of traditional ways of thinking about the law and made it a matter of public discussion as popular storying reinvented how the law was perceived. The vernacular infected the legal culture of rules and regulations like a form of judicial shorthand. The execution confession, for example, served as self-incrimination and legitimization of a trial's verdict and sentencing, whereas sermons and petitions for pardon challenged evidence and argued innocence. Such interplay had a confounding effect on the varying degrees of certainty and completeness of public and legal narratives. On the one hand, trials offered competing witnesses and evidence, and defense and prosecution counsel told competing stories. Here, trials contributed to ambiguity rather than certainty. Guilt might have been proved but it was not divinely revealed. Gallows literature, by contrast, provided providential certainty, inserting itself into the courtroom through the common man jury and through judges like Tilghman who reverted to its language.[35]

In print culture, publicly useful exemplars—like tales of Black crime that spread through newspaper accounts, popular crime narratives, and execution sermons and confessions—were intended to act as a deterrent.[36] They framed well-attended trials and executions as a spectacle in which God could see all: the hidden would be revealed and murder would out, like the blood of Abel crying for vengeance against his brother Cain.[37] Biblical constructs linked blackness to the mark of Cain, imagery that Reverend Allen employed in addressing the execution of Joyce and Matthias to remind the public that once the "mark was set upon Cain" he could find no refuge, no pardon: "As to the murderer, no sacrifice must be offered to God." Especially in the

"Courts of Judicature . . . Darkness or Solitude, Art or Confederacy, Flight or concealment, afford not protection" to shedders of blood.[38] In this iconic narrative, the blackness of one's sin signified the Father's curse upon the son who sinned and was blackened. It became the mark of one's social position and character, signaling that Blacks inhabited a lower rung on the chain of being and that Black crime was a sign of revolt against one's place in that order.[39] Allen's address cited the fearsome words of Noah (whoever "sheds man's blood, by man shall his blood be shed") and of Moses ("The land cannot be cleansed of the blood that is shed therein, but by the blood of him that shed it") embraced in the commentary of William Blackstone as a cornerstone of common law. Divine vengeance, said Allen, must set an example and "fearfully punish the man, who shed the blood of his fellow man," for "the eye of god is upon thee!" and all "secret crimes shall be dragged to light."[40] Once Joyce and Matthias were charged with a crime, society anticipated they would confess. Sentenced to execution, they would be seen to be accountable to Noah's law.

Execution confessions, initially informed by fears of the blackness of sin and divine retribution, followed suit. But a more salutary effect appeared, instilling personhood in Black defendants. In the face of the political, social, and carceral constructions under which the accused struggled, confessions offered details speaking to their individuality: birthplace, their family and associates, where and if they worshipped, employment history, social conduct, criminal acts committed, and their repentance. A peculiar dynamic attended the assumption of personhood, both in the legal and the public sphere. Passing through the legal system authorized the subject status of the accused who was entitled in that space to take advantage of rights that entailed legal personhood. Thereafter, even though people of color were civilly dead, affirmation of personhood legitimized the condemned in the public world of execution literature. Such humanization gave those who confessed an agency and a voice, reinforcing the legal personhood accused Blacks enjoyed in the courtroom. Unavailable in the summary legal proceedings to which slaves were historically subject, the enhanced interactivity of the public and legal spheres and the trends it stimulated—racializing criminality, humanizing the condemned, and assuming legal personhood—laid down the parameters that would frame the Joyce and Matthias trial.[41]

The downside of such interactivity was evident in the 1798 trial of Charles M'Manus et al., a case that exemplified the threat offered by the public notoriety of a crime.[42] A "remarkable" and bloody capital case, the crime committed by M'Manus and others involved a conspiracy that resulted in shooting and axing to death one of the heirs of an estate in an attempt by an in-law to enjoy the whole inheritance with his wife. This resulted in the execution of the two principals (the party who committed the murder and the party who initiated it). Tales told of the atrocity of the crime might "freeze every particle of your blood," the defense counsel warned the *M'Manus* jury, so that its members ought not to expiate one murder by committing another, which would be no less than "judicial murder."[43] Judge John Joseph Henry admonished jurors that "we must divest ourselves of all prejudices we may have imbibed from stories told out of doors," an acknowledgement that jurors were already inflamed by tales told in the public sphere.[44] Judge Tilghman's challenge in the Joyce and Matthias trial to protect the presumed hermetic seal of the courtroom and exorcise external and extralegal considerations from their inquiry was like Judge Henry's "zeal for [the] truth."[45]

The treatment of Black defendants in the courtroom—where Blacks could not serve on juries—could not realistically escape racial perceptions within the community and the interactivity of the public and legal spheres. But trials depended just as much on how officials applied the law under a predetermined racial hierarchy characterized by differential enforcement of the law. Judges, after all, had discretion to determine who had rights, what those rights were, and to control access to those rights through judicial interpretation. Even as Pennsylvania courts repeatedly ruled against unequal access to justice, and the state stood virtually alone in the Western world in granting legal rights to Black people, Pennsylvania found that the gradualness of the Abolition Act was an impediment to evenhanded execution of equal justice[46] and that the slow pace affected cases like the Joyce-Matthias trial.[47] Liberty and equality were similarly entwined in *Respublica v. Blackmore* (1797) where the defense successfully argued for the liberty rights of fugitive slaves and tied them to equality.[48] *Chisholm v. Georgia* (1793) cited the promise "which every free government makes to every free citizen of equal justice and protection," a promise reprised by *Marbury v. Madison* (1803), which affirmed "the right of every individual to claim the protection of the laws."[49] In practice, however, the rights guaranteed by the government only included limited natural rights protected through regular judicial procedures, even if gradual emancipation considered Black defendants persons before the law with the same rights in trials as white defendants.[50] Neither were civil rights included for black defendants; nor did state constitutions prohibit courts from deciding that individual rights were not protected.[51] Still, the principles of equitable treatment and impartiality that Judge Tilghman, a preeminent jurist, would apply in the Joyce and Matthias trial were considered judicially sufficient to ensure due process and equal protection.

The starting point for the Joyce and Matthias trial was thus that regular procedures protected Black defendants, under common law, from arbitrary and unreasonable laws and, under natural law, according to reason.[52] Such protection—statutorily enforced for Pennsylvania free Blacks and slaves through the Abolition Act—meant that Black defendants would be held legally accountable for their criminal acts with the same procedural rights as whites in trials, a notable matter in a state where slavery was still legal.[53] A floor for equality was nonetheless a low bar, meaning that the law applied in courtrooms could vary widely even if it did provide a general standard of equality and due process. How the law varied is the subject of the following treatment of the Joyce and Matthias trial.

THE TRIAL

The murder trial of John Joyce and Peter Matthias began on Tuesday, February 15, 1808. In one description of the scene it was stated that "the adjoining streets and State House yard were all day crowded with people, such appeared to be the curiosity to see the prisoners and hear the trial."[54] Chief Justice William Tilghman of the Pennsylvania Supreme Court presided, Walter Franklin, who would became Pennsylvania attorney general the following year, prosecuted, and two counsel appointed by the court, Richard Rush and Nicholas Biddle, advocated for the defense.[55] At the time of the trial, Biddle was a mere twenty-two years of age and Rush twenty-eight. The trial report referred to them as "members of the bar just of legal age," both having studied law for three years with William Lewis, an eminent Philadelphia lawyer respected for his defense strategies in abolition and treason trials.[56]As novice lawyers, even their connection to Lewis would have been insufficient in a trial that attracted such intense interest. Appointment of counsel was practiced on a court by court, judge by judge basis since neither statutory nor common law required counsel for criminal defendants.[57] The appointment of Rush and Biddle to represent the defendants was likely a function of Judge Tilghman's court management in response to the notoriety afforded the case.[58]

Having Chief Justice Tilghman at the helm of the trial was no small matter. For comparison, the equally sensational M'Manus trial just ten years earlier had been tried by a president judge of the district, indicating that Tilghman's presence reinforced the public importance of the case and emboldened the prosecution.[59] Tilghman had been appointed chief justice just two years before the trial, coincidental with the passage of the state's Judiciary Reform Act of 1806, so that he was operating under judicial reform new to him.[60] That Joyce and Matthias would become the only two men executed for murder out of a Philadelphia jail since 1790 represented another test for the chief justice.[61] Still, Tilghman was no newcomer to criminal cases. He had been chief justice of the US Third Circuit Court from 1801 to 1802, served in 1805 on Pennsylvania's first judicial circuit, and as chief justice would annually preside over Philadelphia's criminal court. Tilghman was known as a jurist meticulously attentive to the law and respected for his ability to remain outside of politics. Notably, he infrequently exercised judicial discretion from the bench and did not rely overly on legal authorities in his opinions. Peers considered him severe though impartial with the guilty, thorough, and principled.[62]

A slaveowner, Tilghman was concerned lest his impartiality as a jurist be brought into question.[63] In fact, a later decision in a slave case (*Wright, alias Hall v. Deacon, 1819*) would become notorious in legal circles. There, Tilghman ruled that a writ of *de homine replegiando* (to redeem the body taken) could not be used where a habeas corpus had failed to secure the liberty of a slave. His ruling undermined a compromise on property rights that underpinned Pennsylvania's Abolition Act. In 1820, passage of an act to prevent kidnapping was intended to correct that ruling and thereby to prevent forcible kidnapping and rendition of free and fugitive slaves.[64] Apart from his status as a slaveowner, Tilghman was otherwise much like other justices in his willingness to release slaves who had not been properly registered under Pennsylvania's gradual emancipation law.[65] He was not so amenable with fugitives, a position that might well have affected his predisposition to exercise his discretionary powers in the Joyce and Matthias trial, as they were self-emancipated.

The Joyce and Matthias trial depended upon witness testimony and circumstantial evidence. The trial report cited three witnesses by name. The first, Samuel Mather, a passerby, saw the prisoners in Blackhorse Alley before the murder "standing not far from deceased's house; Joyce [whom he knew] had a stick in his hand; thought he had some criminal purpose in view." A second named witness, John Jones, saw Matthias before the murder with a stick "which was found in the house after the murder."[66] The third named witness, Anne Messinger (described in one newspaper as "a child . . . a little girl"), was fourteen years old by her testimony. She alone claimed to have seen the murder (in the dark and through a keyhole) which, she testified, was committed by Joyce.[67] Other unnamed witnesses testified to events after the murder and to the condition of the body.

According to one crime narrative, Sarah Cross's murder was met by a rush to judgment in which, upon the discovery of the crime, a coroner was sent for and a jury inquest assembled in the presence of an "immense number of persons." Without hesitation, it rendered its finding: "The evidence was as clear and conclusive as the recent evidence is on the trial; conviction was carried to every mind, and a verdict of wilful murder awarded." A party of five to six constables and citizens reportedly set out in search of the accused, on the grounds that Joyce and Matthias had been seen in the area before the murder and based on what the girl witnessed. The party took instruction from a man of color, "by name Barnes (since dead)," who directed the pursuers to the Southwark area where he was sure the two suspects could be found.[68] Witnesses testified they saw the prisoners at Matthias's house after the crime as they "counted and displayed the booty they had brought off." The witnesses offered that the prisoners, when caught, had a piece of rope; that several stolen articles were found on Matthias; and that he confessed to being at the house of the deceased the previous evening.[69] Newspaper accounts, the execution confessions, and a crime narrative revealed several complicating factors. First, the parties who claimed to have seen the stolen goods displayed were presumably implicated in receiving stolen property. Second, the property, when recovered, was much greater than what had been taken from the shop. Third, the recovered goods were in the possession of the party at whose home Matthias was found. Matthias's involvement, it could be argued, was as a member of a ring of thieves who received stolen property rather than as a willful party to a premeditated murder.

Witnesses

The most astonishing fact of the trial was its reliance on the principal witness, young Anne Messinger, who "gave her testimony with striking distinctiveness and precision."[70] The judge at sentencing referred to her as a beacon of light cutting through the darkness of sin:

> In vain did you flatter yourselves that you were covered by the darkness of night. Before that God with whom there is no light the bloody deed appeared in full day! And in the course of his Providence, the eyes of an innocent little child were directed towards you, while you thought yourselves in perfect security.[71]

Of her credibility, he added, "Her simple, artless story carried conviction to the minds not only of the respectable jury, who condemned you, but of the court, and the numerous audience who attended your trial. You are guilty beyond a doubt."[72]

Characterized on one hand as a young girl more mature than her years and, on the other, as an innocent little child, the witness gained the sympathy and affection of the court, the jury, and the crowd. This dynamic offset inherent contradictions in her testimony and played into popular stereotypes of innocence uncovering evil. Whereas common law required two witnesses to a capital crime, she was the sole witness to what transpired inside the shop during the theft and murder, enhancing the criticality of her evidence. Moreover, Anne's usefulness as a witness depended upon the legal value given to the sworn testimony of women and children. Common law not only classed women and children among those (like slaves, felons, spouses, and interested parties) likely to lie or unable to appreciate the importance of swearing an oath,[73] but it prohibited those with a greater than average temptation to lie from taking an oath.[74] This protected truthful evidence and signified the primacy of God's judgment, which—where the death penalty was involved—was the only judgment that society, if not the law, felt justified condemnation.

Beyond questions of law and charisma, Anne Messinger was a problematic witness regarding the facts of the case. What she actually saw and how much light there was to see it by was questionable. The girl testified she had gone to the shop for licorice and arrived at about 7:00 p.m. The shutters were closed. She stood outside in the dark and, looking through a keyhole into a dim room lit by candle, claimed to see "Joyce, shaking Mrs. Cross by the neck."[75] As the door was unlocked, she pushed it open and entered. Joyce, holding a rope "which appeared to be tied round the [victim's] neck," dropped Mrs. Cross to lock the door.[76] The girl testified she thought Mrs. Cross was dead on the floor. Matthias, she claimed, was in the room. At issue was how she could have seen the murder through the keyhole and why she would have entered the shop if she had just seen a murder. Why she did not cry out and flee, as she would upon exiting the scene when she pulled free of Joyce, was never challenged.[77]

As the case involved a capital crime and since a child's evidence was not, under common law, the best evidence but merely the best available, there was a clear need for corroboration by a second witness. But the two-witness rule cut two ways. Blackstone represented that condemning a person to death on the word of one witness "was fatal to liberty," but he also advised that crimes existed whose very nature "excludes the possibility" of having more than one witness.[78] Judge Tilghman did not invoke a two-witness rule and he made it clear at sentencing that he was not predisposed to doubt the guilt of either prisoner; he regarded her evidence as "providential." Since sworn witnesses were presumed truthful, contesting the girl's evidence would have framed a white witness as a perjurer and exposed her to "beliefs in divine retribution for falsehoods under oath."[79] On the defense side, counsel did not challenge her testimony, likely because the attempt would not have sat well with the jury.

In terms of evidence on behalf of the accused, the most common use of defense witnesses was to testify to one's character and reputation, but there were serious drawbacks constraining what witnesses the defense could present. As indicated in his execution confession, Matthias could have called on several possible witnesses: Hester Cook, Mrs. Stores, Charles Fisher, Mr. Raybould, John Dolin, Mary Lee, and Caroline Cedars. Some had hired Matthias to play the violin (Jenny Miller, Mrs. Jordan, Peggy Tucker), and others could testify about events related to the crime (Hester Cook, Cyrus Porter, Peggy Tucker, Rebecca Brunswick). Most prominently, Hester Cook and Peggy Tucker were identified in Matthias's execution confession as possible alibi witnesses for they had told watchmen who came for Matthias that he was elsewhere at the time of the crime; Tucker ran a house in the Cedar Ward where dancing and drinking took place and Cook was living with Matthias. In addition, Cook had procured brandy with money received from the crime, had taken possession of stolen goods, and aided the fleeing suspects. She could easily have been the unnamed prosecution witness who claimed to see Joyce and Matthias display their booty after the crime, leaving her open to the accusation that she was trading a criminal charge for her testimony or perjuring herself. As for other witnesses, Joyce had solicited two of them for sex. Another was implicated in the crime itself, having hidden Matthias and the booty on the night of the murder. Finally, the bulk of potential witnesses for the accused resided in the neighborhood to which he had fled, an area associated with lower-class crime, which made their testimony less attractive as a means of offsetting that of Anne Messinger, the "little girl of Mr. Salade" and a neighbor of the victim.[80]

The Defendants

As for the prisoners, the trial report noted they "offered no testimony."[81] They were not exceptional in that regard as it was uncommon for defendants to testify.[82] The reasons were manifold. Whereas the Abolition Act prohibited the testimony of slaves against freemen (which suggested that free Blacks could testify against whites), under statutory law Black defendants could not uniformly testify until 1885 and, even then, not under oath. Furthermore, Joyce and Matthias were in the same anomalous position as other Black defendants under gradual emancipation—their legal status was compromised.[83] Joyce's criminal history constituted yet another impediment as it undermined his credibility,[84] while Matthias, as an accomplice, was a problematic candidate. John H. Langbein explains that in a reward system, accomplices often perjured themselves in exchange for not being prosecuted or out of anger or revenge. Having traded his testimony against another to advantage himself[85] he would, in any case, have been a compromised witness. A general rationale for not testifying lay in the protection against self-incrimination, a liability for defendants in that they then served as an "information resource" against themselves.[86] Defendants were better off—given the opportunity—to have counsel represent their case.

Whether and how a defendant testified was ultimately controlled under common law by Judge Tilghman.[87] First, the judge used his discretion when he allowed hearsay testimony that Matthias had confessed to being at the home of the deceased on the night of the crime.[88] He could have invoked a provision in the 1794 Better Preventing of Crimes Act[89] that allowed for a court confession by the accused. In the 1798 *M'Manus* case,[90] for example, the signed confession of one of the principals was read in court and addressed by the judge in his charge to the jury under the terms of the 1794 Crimes Act. Although Tilghman was familiar with confessions from his experience with slave cases (where the only testimony accused slaves could offer in capital cases was a confession), Tilghman did not offer such an option nor did the defense propose it. The prosecution, for its part, could have used Matthias's confession to shore up weaknesses in its case against Joyce (the lesser competency of a young witness, circumstantial evidence—the rope, the stick, the stolen goods—and the lack of a second witness), a common practice with weak evidence or when the accused might be acquitted. Still, like the second-witness standard in a capital case, an accomplice's testimony required corroboration either by a person of credit or "pregnant circumstances" (the functional equivalent of a second witness).[91] The defense could offer neither on Matthias's behalf.

Whereas his testimony would have been open to doubt, there were aspects of common law on accomplices that could have worked to the benefit of Peter Matthias. Common law specified that for a "second" to be punished for murder, the two together must commit an unlawful act whose "probable consequence might be bloodshed"; to constitute "murder in them all," common law required malice aforethought (a conspiracy with intent).[92] Similarly, the 1794 Crimes Act provided that an accomplice to murder should be an abettor or counselor of the crime. In his execution confession, Matthias claimed that he did not participate in tandem with Joyce in an unlawful act that could lead to bloodshed, nor did he counsel, premeditate, or conspire in the murder. In mitigation, he offered that he had been enticed by Joyce to accompany him to the shop and that he made several unsuccessful attempts to escape Joyce's company. Having no idea Joyce intended to commit a murder, once they got to the shop, Matthias departed. He returned only after the murder and took part in the robbery under coercion. He and Joyce argued when Matthias tried to free the girl, and he threatened to expose Joyce if questioned by the authorities. Matthias's conduct was thereby mitigated in his confession by his lack of knowledge of and his resistance to Joyce's crime. In the confession, Joyce controlled events and kept Matthias in the dark. He committed the murder in Matthias's absence, and he entangled Matthias in the theft after the murder.

Precedent existed in Pennsylvania case law that an accessory was not implicated if his actions were not intended to be part of a crime and his will did not concur with that of the principal. Matthias, it could be argued, had no bad intent and was merely the dupe of the principal. Matthias's inexperienced defense counsel (who, following Blackstone, carried the burden "to take away or mitigate" guilt) did to their credit argue mitigation in claiming that the evidence did not support malice and premeditation; their argument was less convincing since it was applied equally to Joyce. On the issue of malice, as well, several Pennsylvania cases supported Matthias. *Pennsylvania v. Honeyman* (1793) required clear and malicious intent which "imports wickedness . . . cuts off excuses" and indicates "a heart regardless of social duty, and fatally bent on mischief." In other words, "a voluntary cruel act." In *Pennsylvania v. Bell* (1793), malice, a necessary element of first-degree murder, was implied in every killing for which justification was not proved, so that, as in *Pennsylvania v. M'Fall* (1794) and *Pennsylvania v. Lewis* (1796), a killing lacking "plain marks of a deliberate design," that is, lacking express malice, was not murder.[93] Malice, by this argument, was not present in the case facts as they related to Matthias.

On these facts, the trial jury could have found Matthias was not proved guilty. As argued in *M'Manus*, the evidence relied upon, particularly in a capital crime, must not "lose itself in doubt, conjecture and uncertainty." Judge Henry agreed that probable presumption (the circumstantial standard applied by Tilghman) must be minutely scrutinized as "sometimes uncertain and fallible." Rather, he charged the jury, in a capital case defendants should be judged by the violent presumption standard, which "necessarily concludes to the establishment of the fact at the same time that it excludes all and every other way of accounting for it."[94]

To the contrary, the defense in the Joyce and Matthias trial accepted the evidence as it stood, without challenging Tilghman's application of probable presumption. The evidence was, however, open to challenge. Though the victim's throat showed "a cut three inches in length," and the victim presented as "wounded and bruised on the head with a stick, or perhaps some sharp instrument," no knife or sharp instrument was ever found.[95] There was no evidence that a stick discovered inside the shop was used in the crime or that it belonged to the accused. A rope found with the accused was not convincingly linked to the defendants. Rather, upon comparison it was said to have "appeared" to be the "counterpart" of the rope around the victim's neck.[96] Other than the girl, witnesses could only place Matthias in the area before the murder and no witness could swear to have seen him aid or abet in the murder. His purported admission that he was at the shop was hearsay. There was thus no "necessarily" conclusive physical evidence or corroborated eyewitness testimony to the murder, nor any directly linked to Matthias. To Matthias's detriment, he was convicted not only by circumstantial evidence but by the lower probable presumption standard. As for reasonable doubt (the prevailing standard in a capital case) and as for the more ancient presumption of innocence, neither was argued by the defense; nor were they raised by the prosecution or the judge.[97] Measured by the contemporary standard of the jury's moral certitude, informed conscience, or fully satisfied belief that the accused was guilty, reasonable doubt reflected Blackstone's ratio—based in Abraham's admonition in Genesis—"that it is better that ten guilty persons escape, than that one innocent suffer." Recognized in *M'Manus*, the principle was not acknowledged in the Joyce and Matthias trial.[98] The unlikely prospect of a court confession remained the only possibility that Matthias's innocence could be introduced in the trial.

It is worth noting that Matthias's innocence was supported in Joyce's execution confession—transcribed, witnessed, sworn, and signed with a mark as a dying declaration—where he absolved Matthias of the murder, though not the theft. It is notable that in supporting Matthias, Joyce spoke against his own interest, enhancing his credibility. Joyce had, in addition, made several incriminating admissions: he admitted a prior criminal history, that he had fortified himself with gin before the murder, that he collected the necessary weapons and conceived the plan beforehand, and that he had a sudden urge to kill Mrs. Cross. Having demonstrated the malicious, premediated, and unprovoked disposition to kill, which is necessary to a first-degree murder conviction, Joyce's admissions on Matthias's behalf were persuasive in two ways. First, Joyce profited in no other way than to purge himself of his sins in preparation for his own execution. He offered that it "laid heavy on his mind: he had murdered that Old lady, and was the cause of the death of that innocent man [Matthias]."[99] Second, his admissions credibly supported that Matthias did not commit murder (the charge in the indictment against Joyce). They supported as well that Matthias had no prior knowledge, nor did he aid, abet, or assist in the murder (the charge in the indictment against Matthias) so that the charge against Matthias might reasonably be reduced to that of a noncapital crime.

First-degree murder—described in the 1794 Crimes Act as "willful, deliberate, or premeditated killing" or murder in the commission or attempt "to perpetrate any arson, rape, robbery or burglary"—clearly applied in Joyce's case.[100] As Judge Alexander Addison found in *Pennsylvania v. Bell*, premeditation (gathering up the stick and the rope) and a design of mischief in the commission of an unlawful and unusually cruel act constituted a perfect recipe for murder in the first degree.[101] To cover a lack of direct, positive evidence of intent, moreover, Blackstone allowed that an evil design be "evidenced by external circumstances discovering that inward intention," a legal nicety that proved critical in using the weapons Joyce had gathered to convict him. Second-degree murder was the identified charge in the 1794 Crimes Act for "all other kinds of murder" than that which was intentional or premeditated, which carried a punishment of confinement for not less than five and no more than eighteen years. The statute offered Matthias an olive branch in its preamble: "Whereas the several offenses which are included under the general denomination of murder, differ so greatly from each other in the degree of their atrociousness," it proclaimed, "it is unjust to invoke them in the same punishment." Matthias was thereby a candidate for a lesser sentence than Joyce. Indeed, defense counsel would in its closing argument to the jury argue that, regarding the murder, second degree was all the evidence would support, pointing to room in the law for a noncapital verdict for Matthias, as well as reason to hope for a pardon.[102]

The fairness of the Joyce-Matthias trial depended in no small measure upon its impressionable defense counsel. Rush and Biddle chose not to have the accused testify, not to call defense witnesses, and not to cross-examine prosecution witnesses, which cut deeply into a proper defense for the accused. Their case thereby amounted to a presentation "with embarrassment and regret, as the weight and clearness of the testimony against [the accused] constrained [defense counsel] to acknowledge the criminality of the prisoners." Rush, speaking for one and a half hours, and Biddle for forty-five minutes, mounted an argument that admitted the crime and urged amelioration of the severity of the sentence. They focused on showing that the accused did not meet the requirement under Pennsylvania law for murder in the first degree and its consequent death penalty. The accused, they argued, had not fixed upon a "previously formed design," so that the criminal act lacked malice or premeditation. A newspaper account noted that if counsel had based their case on an appeal to the human heart, forensic eloquence, and legal knowledge, the verdict would have been moderated. The account nonetheless expressed the same certainty as the coroner's inquest in declaring there was "no loop [in this crime] upon which to hang a doubt." Biddle and Rush, for all their youth, were competent counsel, but law and humanity guarded the route to compassion: "The Angel of Mercy hid her face in the bosom of Pity" and resigned herself to justice.[103]

The trial report noted "the prisoners had no testimony to impeach [the prosecution case]," so that the evidence provided by state prosecutor Franklin seemed complete. The prosecution merely contested defense counsel's plea for mitigation; it "replied to, and obviated the objections to his interpretation of the law of Pennsylvania." It then reprised the evidence with a view to demonstrate "the fullest proof" of willful, deliberate, premeditated intent to murder. It declared that unprovoked killing was the "most atrocious form" of murder, adverting to the language of the 1794 criminal reform statute, and demanded the death penalty.[104] Whereas the indictment distinguished the crimes of the two accused, Franklin's final statement did not, much to the detriment of Matthias. Matthias would have been better served had his trial followed the precedent of *M'Manus* and been separated from that of Joyce. Indeed, in *M'Manus*, which centered on whether an accused could be convicted as a principal where the evidence only proved him an accessory, the state conducted three separate trials for seven defendants and delivered four different verdicts, admitting that "in the consideration of law their offences are quite different."[105] This distinction was apparently lost on Tilghman; moreover, unlike the white, mostly alien, defendants in *M'Manus*, Joyce and Matthias were Black.

THE TRIAL CONCLUDED

Chief Justice Tilghman turned the case over to the jury, informing them that they could declare the crime murder in the first degree if they thought, as he did, the facts proved the crime. Under statutory law, he advised, predetermination did not require "that a scheme should have been concerted long antecedent" to a murder, only that the intent be "perfect, complete" even if it was formed "only a minute before." Indeed, "judicial authority" had given such meaning to the 1794 reform statute, referring to the *M'Fall* precedent in which the design that demonstrated predetermination need not be "long forward."[106] Tilghman did not share with the jury the other applicable provisions in the 1794 law: that the two men could be treated differently and that a killing that was not "willful, deliberate or premeditated" allowed for a second-degree murder verdict. As for mercy, it was not, in his view, within the jury's province to extend it to the prisoners, by which he meant granting or not granting mercy was the judge's prerogative.

The jury returned with the verdict—murder in the first degree for both prisoners—within minutes of retiring, a not-uncommon practice as juries often delivered a verdict directly from the box upon the conclusion of a trial. Crowds "whose curiosity was not to be restrained" had rushed into the courtroom, intruding upon "the seats within the enclosure appropriated to the bar and the jurors." No racial animus was expressed, according to one newspaper, which observed, "To the honor of the Men of Colour, be it said, that though they attended in crowds the trial of these wretches, not one of them was to be seen in the Court-house on Saturday."[107] The account failed to note that the excitement of the white crowd was itself a sign of racial consciousness, if not racism.

Sentencing took place at noon, Saturday, February 19, 1808, four days after the trial opened. Tilghman's sentencing statement was his most extended commentary on the case. In it, he highlighted that "after an impartial trial" the accused were convicted of the only crime punishable by death. Attended by "the most aggravating circumstances," the crime was not committed in the heat of passion but "without pity or remorse" and with no other motive than depriving a poor woman of the little property she had. Tilghman found both defendants "guilty beyond a doubt," their guilt sealed by innocent testimony that exposed their dark deed. Addressing himself to members of the Black community who attended the sentencing, he made clear that injury was not merely to an old woman, but that it extended to society in general and to "the people of your own colour in particular," for whom this crime must serve as an example. Declaring that both defendants should be hanged, the judge admonished them to fully confess their crime, repent, pray for forgiveness, and seek the mercy of God.[108]

In his statement Judge Tilghman acknowledged such legal considerations as provocation, aggravated circumstances, predetermination, doubt, and lack of remorse. He did not consider, either here or in the trial, the risk of relying for his chief witness on a child, the importance of the second-witness rule in a capital crime, the prospect of inadequate counsel, differing degrees of guilt, the possibility of separate trials, more rigorous evidentiary standards, or a more liberal use of the judge's powers of discretion. In one view, Tilghman did what a competent judge of his times might do. For example, President Judge Jacob Rush of the Philadelphia District rendered a comparable ruling in the Richard Smith trial of 1816. He endorsed a verdict on much the same set of facts that informed Tilghman's charge and sentencing statements: the aggravated nature of Smith's crime, its willful deliberateness, the lack or provocation or passion, the short time to frame the design, and the flight of the accused. Applied to a white defendant in the Smith case, the Joyce and Matthias verdict had stood the test of time; it was still good law eight years later.

In another view, Tilghman did not have the ability to affect aspects of the law that constrained the accused's defense; he had no control over the lesser competency attributed to Black or female witnesses or the lack of Black jurors. Equally, public perceptions of Black inferiority and sinfulness, and juror preferences for a white victim over Black defendants or for the credibility of white witnesses were outside his control. Still, if there was any room for discretion on the relative guilt of the accomplice or the justification for a second witness, Chief Justice Tilghman never exercised it. His mental disposition was in line with the 1793 Fugitive Slave Act (which he rigorously upheld in his slave cases) where free Blacks were subject to ex parte proceedings and had no right to be heard or to defend themselves so that they could be renditioned without access to legal process. His jurisprudence contrasted with that of judges more sympathetic to Black defendants and with that of courts where defendants without counsel profited from judges assisting them on the law.[109]

Tilghman's approach was that of a status quo, law-and-order judge with a penchant for expressing in his sentencing statement moral perceptions typical of the public sphere. The chief justice produced a moral lesson, a crime story, a sentimental tale, a sermon, and a legal sentence all in one. He delivered a narrative of a secret crime hidden in the dark and seen through a keyhole, as if through a glass darkly, so that half of the statement could as easily have appeared in an execution sermon by Reverend Allen. Providence, revelation, confession, and repentance played roles in rendering judgment in a battle between innocence and guilt, good and evil, light and dark, negotiating the suspense of being detected and the victory of the right. Facing the first opportunity in his judicial life to pass a sentence of death, Tilghman was like Judge Rush, who noted that the nation's penal practice "accords with the voice of religion, which is the voice of God." Tilghman's "stern dignity," one newspaper reported, "was lost in the sensibility of the man and the piety of the Christian." Another newspaper found he "shed a tear" and "choacked [*sic*] in the poignancy of his feelings."[110]

The rarity of a murder trial and the interracial and aggravated nature of the crime as Tilghman represented them were undeniable to people at the sentencing as they reflected the intense public scrutiny and the response of the immense crowds that would gather at the hanging. Christian sensibility, public interest, and fear of an interracial incident competed in Tilghman's statement with a scenario of remorseless, undoubted criminality. Cold-blooded determination to assault one of society's most vulnerable souls and the atrociousness of "an offense of the blackest dye" constituted a tale in which "awful judgment" alone could right the wrong done and expose that which had been "covered by the darkness of night." An evocation of sinfulness hidden and virtue transgressed, Tilghman's narrative linked the skin color of the accused indelibly to the "blackness" of their crime and to the brutality of the beast.[111] The normalization of racial criminalization was, in Tilghman's rendering, taken for granted; its recalibration of fairness and impartiality was itself assumed as normative, indeed societally and divinely justified.

Officials read the warrant for execution to the prisoners nine days later, on Sunday, February 28; the execution was set for Monday, March 14, at noon. "Clergymen of several denominations" visited the condemned, including Reverend Allen who called the visit "the first enquiry" into the minds of the pious: "*How did they seem prepared?*" Admonished to repent their sins and recognize their lost condition, Matthias was especially distraught while Joyce "professed to have attained from a merciful God . . . a lively hope of acceptance."[112]

At ten o'clock on the morning of the execution, the condemned emerged from the prison accompanied by Allen and four other clergymen singing hymns. The condemned expressed gratitude for the kindnesses shown them by the keepers of the prison and others, "freely forgave all," and confirmed their confessions with "hopes of happiness beyond the grave." A Methodist preacher, a Black preacher, and the coroner addressed those assembled. Reverend Allen remarked that the accused faced not merely the sentence of the law, "but that more awful one which roars in thunder '*The soul that sinneth, it shall die.*'"[113]

In a last-minute attempt at a reprieve for Matthias sometime before the execution, the mayor of Philadelphia had visited Joyce and "closely interrogated him as to . . . whether Peter was present when he committed the murder." Twice, Joyce answered that Matthias was indeed present. Once the mayor withdrew, Joyce exclaimed, "Lord! forgive me for it; for he is an innocent man." On the gallows itself, in "the atoning blood of Christ," Joyce made his final affirmation of Matthias's innocence, to no avail. Matthias reaffirmed his innocence to the sheriff and coroner the night before the execution only to be faced on the gallows with warnings from the attending clergy "of the danger of covering his crimes with falsehood" and entreaties "to implore mercy" from Him "before whose bar he must shortly stand." In response, Matthias fell upon his knees, whereupon the Lord "smiled upon him." Until the end, Matthias continued to proclaim his innocence.[114]

Execution statements like Matthias's carried a presumption of truthfulness similar to a positive oath, for, as in *Pennsylvania v. Lewis* (1796), "every motive to falsehood is silenced,"[115] which lends additional support to the argument that Mattias was telling the truth about his role. The legal world commonly found execution statements useful, as, by convention, the convicted party tended to publicly confirm the fairness of a trial—certifying that justice had been done—and acted as a deterrent for other criminals. In the shadow of the gallows, the convicted party often offered the statement in the hope of heavenly forgiveness. The execution statements of two notorious Black criminals, Abraham Johnstone in 1797 and Joseph Mountain in 1790, both allowed that their trials were fair, an obligatory declaration if they were to have any hope of a pardon.[116] Johnstone, however, was in the anomalous situation of claiming a fair trial that was not just, so that, like Matthias, he contested his death sentence.[117] Johnstone's statement was unique in that it provided a rare instance of a Black person explicitly attacking the judicial system in asserting his innocence, contending the evidence was so vague that the verdict could only have been reached by perjury. As with Matthias, he might have been found guilty, but the verdict was the result of a legal system that was basically flawed, however fair in appearance.

CONCLUSION

The Joyce-Matthias case produced more questions than answers. Was their criminal conviction a function of racism in the jury, a slave-owning judge, inexperienced counsel, the atrociousness of the crime, a lack of due process, fairness, or equal treatment under the law, harsh and disproportionate laws, or harsh punishment under the laws? Were the defendants denied equal protection in the courtroom because they were Black? Were they convicted based on oppressive customs, racial prejudice, partial laws? Comparing the bias they faced to that of William Cobbett, in both trials the defendants were the public face of a larger, more intractable problem. The politics of Cobbett's case played out in debate in the public sphere, so that partisan and reputational issues were fully aired. Joyce and Matthias, by contrast, dealt with unconscious racism that ran silent and deep and with the kind of animus capable of instigating interracial violence. Sociologically distinct, each trial roiled a jury that delivered a technically correct although deeply flawed emotional verdict.

It is clear the accused had reason in the Joyce and Matthias trial to challenge whether officials applied the law in its fullest and fairest sense. For example, although life itself was at stake and the higher, more rigorous standard of violent presumption was more appropriate in a capital case, the trial used the lower standard for circumstantial evidence, probable presumption. Matthias was not, furthermore, tried separately as an accomplice on the charge on which he was indicted (aiding and abetting), but was convicted on the charge (first-degree murder) on which Joyce was indicted and convicted. Neither a presumption of innocence nor the reasonable doubt standard was argued in determining his guilt, judicial standards commonly applied in criminal cases at the time and well understood by the presiding judge.[118]

How the Black community responded to the verdict is one way to gauge whether the trial was considered fair in its own times. Here we find a range of interpretations. Tilghman had adverted in his sentencing statement to "the people of your own colour, in particular," who, having been rendered "objects of public disgust and suspicion" by Joyce's and Matthias's crimes, "view [the defendants] conduct with horror." A crime narrative referred to "clergymen of [Matthias's] own colour" who strongly urged Matthias to accept that hope of a pardon was a "fallacy." As for the Black community itself, despite the presence of a vast mixed-race crowd at the execution, none of the press accounts reported demonstrations or protests.[119]

Gary B. Nash, in his study of Philadelphia's Black community does not mention support for Joyce and Matthias among African American clergy and the Black elites. Rather, he notes that James Forten, Absalom Jones, and Richard Allen used the case to found the Society for the Suppression of Vice and Immorality with the aim of suppressing the kind of vice that white groups could use to argue "that African people were inherently immoral and hence unfit for freedom."[120] De Lombard observes that Allen published "the first black-edited gallows pamphlet" to denounce "a pernicious racial" tendency to crime.[121] Compared to middle-class Blacks and industrious Black laborers, Joyce and Matthias were, for Allen, useful examples of bad associates, lust, and drunkenness.

Richard S. Newman in his study of Richard Allen disagrees. Allen apparently believed, Newman represents, that Matthias's "role in the crime was murky and subject to dispute," that he was "a wronged man, guilty . . . of bad luck or lack of piety—or both." The accused had made poor choices, but an oppressive environment narrowed their opportunities and enslaved them as much as their own immorality. Allen's message to the white community was that moral failures affected Blacks and whites alike and that Blacks had no desire to harm whites, a view that typified his preaching. Newman refers here to Allen's "double consciousness," an assimilationist "warring of one's African and American selves."[122] Samuel Otter is alone in holding that Allen "was unwilling or unable to disclose" that some Black clergy believed Matthias was not involved in the murder and that the authorities should review the evidence and spare him. Allen's position was, in this view, a protest against "the intransigence of the system that has judged Peter Matthias" and a reminder of the collective oppression of slavery that was ultimately responsible for the accused's crimes.[123]

In truth, leaders of the African American community had their eyes on a larger prize, which led them to distance themselves from the condemned men. The abolitionist movement had achieved a great victory in 1808, abolition of the transatlantic slave trade. Excluded from arguing in courtrooms and legislatures, African Americans contributed to that achievement in their sermons, narratives, and speeches as voices in the larger moral struggle against racial oppression. To protect their standing in this struggle, to establish an independent Black church, schools for Black youth, and a vibrant Black middle class, leaders like Allen focused on assimilation.[124] At the very core of Allen's plea for equality, liberty, and identity was the argument that Black Americans had a stake in a homeland built with their tears and labor and that morally they deserved an American identity. Adopting Joyce and Matthias as a cause would mean defending the Black community's least defensible members, those defined by their crimes. Such empathy risked undermining the moderate Black community's identification with white values and high moral standing, which they considered crucial in a white-defined world if they were to fight effectively for racial justice. Defending Joyce and Matthias would have played into white perceptions of Blacks as racially alien, lower-class disruptors who threatened to reverse the social order and whose crimes (murder—which effected replacement of the white body—and property crime—the removal of white wealth) required exorcising rituals like executions.[125] Black leaders chose to expound a moral narrative of repentance and redemption that treated Joyce and Matthias as deterrents for people of color.

Nineteenth-century trials of accused Blacks like John Joyce and Peter Matthias never lived up fully to what Pennsylvania's 1780 Abolition Act and 1790 Constitution promised, nor did they redress the inequities of a gradual emancipation process that spanned seven decades and left many in legal limbo. While equal legal rights for African Americans in Pennsylvania occurred while slavery was still legal in the state and when Pennsylvania stood alone in granting Blacks such equality, the law was still an imperfect tool. For Joyce, the legal process might have been fair and the verdict appropriate, but for Peter Matthias a fair process was not enough to address his claim of innocence. The trial may well have delivered fairness and impartiality in appointing counsel for the accused, procedural regularity, and judicial due process, a significant advance in justice for a people yet to be recognized as citizens with full civil rights. But if ambiguity characterized the status of Black defendants, it shrouded the courtroom as well in complexities that never truly cut through the kind of discrimination that Blacks accused of crime endured. That the verdicts and sentences were not just and equitable in present-day terms should not surprise anyone, but neither should the fact that they went largely unchallenged by contemporaries both in the Black community and among abolitionists.[126]

NOTES

1. Published in its original form as "Law, Culture, and Race: The 1808 Murder Trial of John Joyce and Peter Matthias," *Pennsylvania History: A Journal of Mid-Atlantic Studies* 86, no. 2 (2019): 155–96.

2. "The Trial of John Joyce and Peter Mathias for the Murder of Sarah Cross, Philadelphia, Pennsylvania, 1808," in *American State Trials*, ed. John D. Lawson, vol. 7 (St. Louis, MO: F. H. Thomas Law Book Co., 1917), 746.

3. *Petersburg Intelligencer*, March 22, 1808; *L'Oracle and Daily Advertiser*, March 18, 1808.

4. John Joyce, *Confession of John Joyce, Alias Davis* (Philadelphia: Bethel Church, 1808), 14–15; Peter Matthias, *Confession of Peter Matthias, alias Mathews* (Philadelphia: Bethel Church, 1808), 31–34. *American State Trials* spells Matthias's name "Mathias."

5. *Poulson's American Daily Advertiser*, February 22, 1808. The trial report and relevant material published in *American State Trials* is based on Matthias, *Confession*.

6. Joyce, *Confession of John Joyce*, 12–16; Matthias, *Confession of Peter Matthias*, 30–35.

7. Alexander Addison, *Reports of Cases in the County Courts of the Fifth Circuit, and in the High Court of Errors and Appeals of the State of Pennsylvania, and Charges to Grand Juries of Those Courts* (Washington, PA: John Colerick, 1800); Alexander Dallas, *Reports of Cases Ruled and Adjudged in the Several Courts of the United States and of Pennsylvania, Held at the Seat of the Federal Government*, vol. 4 (Philadelphia: Aurora Office, 1807).

8. Paul Finkelman, "Human Liberty, Property in Human Beings, and the Pennsylvania Supreme Court," *Duquesne Law Review* 53, no. 2 (2015): 456.

9. Richard S. Newman, *Freedom's Prophet: Bishop Ricard Allen, the AME Church, and the Black Founding Fathers* (New York University Press, 2008), 4–5. See

Richard S. Newman and Roy E. Finkenbine, "Black Founders in the New Republic: Introduction," *William and Mary Quarterly*, 3rd series, 64, no. 1 (2007): 83–94; Gary B. Nash, *Forging Freedom: The Formation of Philadelphia's Black Community, 1720–1840* (Cambridge, MA: Harvard University Press, 1988); Gary B. Nash and Jean R. Soderlund, *Freedom by Degrees: Emancipation in Pennsylvania and Its Aftermath* (New York: Oxford University Press, 1991); Samuel Otter, *Philadelphia Stories: America's Literature of Race and Freedom* (Oxford: Oxford University Press, 2010); Thomas E. Will, "Liberalism, Republicanism, and Philadelphia's Black Elite in the Early Republic: The Social Thought of Absalom Jones and Richard Allen," *Pennsylvania History* 69, no. 4 (2002): 558–76; Julie Winch, *Philadelphia's Black Elite: Activism, Accommodation, and the Struggle for Autonomy* (Philadelphia: Temple University Press, 1988); Shane White, "'It Was a Proud Day': African Americans, Festivals, and Parades in the North, 1741–1834," *Journal of American History* 81, no. 1 (1994): 13–50; Sharon V. Salinger, "Spaces, Inside and Outside, in Eighteenth-Century Philadelphia," *Journal of Interdisciplinary History* 26, no. 1 (1995): 1–31; Emma Jones Lapsansky, *Neighborhoods in Transition: William Penn's Dream and Urban Reality* (New York: Garland, 1994).

10. Joyce, *Confession of John Joyce*, 12.

11. Nash, *Forging Freedom*, 145–46.

12. *The Tickler*, March 16, 1808.

13. Matthias, *Confession of Peter Matthias*, 30–31.

14. Lapsansky, *Neighborhoods in Transition*, 74–76, 78; Newman, *Freedom's Prophet*, 221–22.

15. Steven Wilf, *Law's Imagined Republic: Popular Politics and Criminal Justice in Revolutionary America* (Cambridge: Cambridge University Press, 2010), 67–68.

16. Salinger, "Spaces," 8, 14, 26–27, 30–31; Lapsansky, *Neighborhoods in Transition*, 72, 75, 78–79, 84.

17. Salinger, "Spaces," 26; Joanne Pope Melish, *Disowning Slavery: Gradual Emancipation and "Race" in New England, 1780–1860* (Ithaca, NY: Cornell University Press, 1998), 204, 206.

18. Nash, *Forging Freedom*, 63, 65, 66, 72–73, 135–37.

19. Melish, *Disowning Slavery*, 84; Jeannine Marie De Lombard, *In the Shadow of the Gallows: Race, Crime, and American Civic Identity* (Philadelphia: University of Pennsylvania Press, 2012), 64–66; Lois E. Horton, "From Class to Race in Early America: Northern Post-Emancipation Racial Reconstruction," in *Race in the Early Republic: Racial Consciousness and Nation-Building in the Early Republic*, eds. Michael A. Morrison and James Brewer Stewart (Lanham, MD: Rowman & Littlefield, 2002), 63–64.

20. Section 7, "An Act for the Gradual Abolition of Slavery," 1780, in *Statutes at Large of Pennsylvania from 1682–1801*, eds. James T. Mitchell and Henry Flanders, vol. 10 (1904), 67–73; Leslie Patrick-Stamp, "Numbers That Are Not New: African Americans in the Country's First Prison, 1790–1835," *Pennsylvania Magazine of History and Biography* 119, nos. 1–2 (1995): 98; G. S. Rowe, "Black Offenders, Criminal Courts, and Philadelphia Society in the Late Eighteenth-Century," *Journal of Social*

History 22, no. 4 (1989): 686; Stanley I. Kutler, "Pennsylvania Courts, the Abolition Act, and Negro Rights," *Pennsylvania History* 30, no. 1 (1963): 15.

21. De Lombard, *In the Shadow*, 64–67.

22. Jack D. Marietta and G. S. Rowe, *Troubled Experiment: Crime and Justice in Pennsylvania, 1682–1800* (Philadelphia: University of Pennsylvania Press, 2006), 31–32, 246, 248; Rowe, "Black Offenders," 686; Patrick-Stamp, "Numbers," 99; Nash, *Forging Freedom*, 35.

23. Statutes specific to Blacks were passed in 1700, 1705, and 1725; statutes that distinguished Black from white punishments were passed in 1721, 1750, 1759, 1769, and 1770; Patrick-Stamp, "Numbers," 99n7.

24. Marietta and Rowe, *Troubled Experiment*, 20, 31–32, 246, 248. As a further context, Jen Manion's work on carceral ideology helps us reevaluate a late eighteenth-century revision of the penal code that "disguised its violence under the rubric of humanitarianism" and which those subject to unjust laws resisted. When crime rates rose, punishment reset the hierarchy through claims of "enlightened justice" that sorted and segregated people, as she says, by their differences of "crime, class, and gender, race, and age" to enforce submission and to domesticate prisoners by their being "raced, classed, and gendered." This process determined which people would be punished, manipulating social norms. The penitentiary thereby became one of several institutions (the workhouse, hospitals, asylums) that allowed "elite white men" to position themselves at the center of American identity. Jen Manion, *Liberty's Prisoners: Carceral Culture in Early America* (Philadelphia: University of Pennsylvania Press, 2015), 1–5.

25. De Lombard, *In the Shadow*, 66. Winch, *Philadelphia's Black Elite*; White, "'It Was a Proud Day,'" 13–50; Otter, *Philadelphia Stories*, 131–38, 73–88; Nash, *Forging Freedom*, 217–27.

26. Nash, *Forging Freedom*, 73, 76, 135, 145, 161, 163; Rowe, "Black Offenders," 694.

27. Marietta and Rowe, *Troubled Experiment*, 226.

28. De Lombard, *In the Shadow*, 66; Patrick-Stamp, "Numbers," 99–04, 124; Rowe, "Black Offenders," 385–86, 702–05. Marietta and Rowe, *Troubled Experiment*, 20, 31–32, 229, 231–32, 237–44, 246, 248–49, 252–53, 255, 260; Nash, *Forging Freedom*, 157–58.

29. "An Act Amending the Penal Laws of the State," 1786, *Statutes at Large of Pennsylvania*, vol. 7 (1900), 280–90; Marietta and Rowe, *Troubled Experiment*, 210–16. Pennsylvania passed reform bills in 1786, 1790, and 1794.

30. Marietta and Rowe, *Troubled Experiment*, 226, 246–62; Rowe, "Black Offenders," 705; Nash, *Forging Freedom*, 227, 250; Allen Steinberg, "'The Spirit of Litigation': Private Prosecution and Criminal Justice in Nineteenth-Century Philadelphia," *Journal of Social History* 20, no. 2 (1986): 231–49.

31. Nash and Soderlund, *Freedom by Degrees*, 137–55; Melish, *Disowning Slavery*, 84–118; James Brewer Stewart, "Modernizing 'Difference': The Political Meaning of Color in the Free States, 1776–1840," in *Race in the Early Republic*, eds. Michael A. Morrison and James Brewer Stewart (Lanham, MD: Rowman & Littlefield, 2002), 113–34; Horton, "From Class to Race," 55–74; Joanne Pope Melish,

"The 'Condition' Debate and Racial Discourse in the Antebellum North," in *Race in the Early Republic*, eds. Michael A. Morrison and James Brewer Stewart (Lanham, MD: Rowman & Littlefield, 2002), 75–94; David R. Roediger, "The Pursuit of Whiteness: Property, Terror, and Expansion, 1790–1860," in *Race in the Early Republic*, eds. Michael A. Morrison and James Brewer Stewart (Lanham, MD: Rowman & Littlefield, 2002) 5–26.

32. Melish, "'Condition' Debate," 77, 82; Melish, *Disowning Slavery*, 3, 25, 76–79, 81; Kunal M. Parker, "Making Blacks Foreigners: The Legal Construction of Former Slaves in Post-Revolutionary Massachusetts," *Utah Law Review* 2001, 75, no. 1 (2001): 117–19.

33. Melish, *Disowning Slavery*, 2; Nash, *Forging Freedom*, 73; Parker, "Making Blacks Foreigners," 119. African Americans' ambiguous status was compounded by their nonforeign, noncitizen status under An Act to Establish a Uniform Rule of Naturalization, 1790, 1 Stat. 103; 1 Stat. 414; De Lombard, *In the Shadow*, 159. Christopher Malone, "Rethinking the End of Black Voting Rights in Antebellum Pennsylvania: Racial Ascriptivism, Partisanship and Political Development in the Keystone State," *Pennsylvania History* 72, no. 4 (2005): 466–68, 494; Devon W. Carbado, "Legal Borderlands: Law and the Construction of American Borders," *American Quarterly* 57, no. 3 (2005): 643–45; Melvin I. Urofsky, *Dissent and the Supreme Court: Its Role in the Court's History and the Nation's Constitutional Dialogue* (New York: Vintage, 2015), 70.

34. Melish, *Disowning Slavery*, 87–89.

35. Wilf, *Law's Imagined Republic*, 8–10, 59, 63, 71–72, 76–77; Saul Cornell, *The Other Founders: Anti-Federalism and the Dissenting Tradition in America, 1788–1828* (Chapel Hill: University of North Carolina Press, 1999), 76, 91–92; Karen Halttunen, *Murder Most Foul: The Killer and the Gothic Imagination* (Cambridge, MA: Harvard University Press, 1998), 97–100.

36. Richard Slotkin, "Narratives of Negro Crime in New England, 1675–1800," *American Quarterly* 25, no. 1 (1973): 3–31; Ronald A. Bosco, "Early American Gallows Literature: An Annotated Checklist," *Resources for American Literary Study* 8, no.1 (1978): 85–105; Daniel E. Williams, *Pillars of Salt: An Anthology of Early American Criminal Narratives* (Madison, WI: Madison House, 1993); Daniel A. Cohen, *Pillars of Salt, Monuments of Grace: New England Crime Literature and the Origins of American Popular Culture, 1674–1860* (Oxford: Oxford University Press, 1993).

37. Halttunen, *Murder Most Foul*, 93.

38. Matthias, *Confession of Peter Matthias*, 21–22.

39. Williams, *Pillars of Salt*, 53. On biblical racism understood by an ex-slave in 1787, see Quobna Ottobah Cugoano, *Thoughts and Sentiments on the Evil of Slavery* (New York: Penguin Books, [1787]1999), 28–40.

40. William Blackstone, *Commentaries on the Laws of England*, 4 vols., 15th ed. (London: A Strahan, 1809), IV:194; Matthias, *Confession of Peter Matthias*, 21–22.

41. De Lombard, *In the Shadow*, 6, 9–10, 18, 28–32, 38, 40.

42. *A Correct Account of the Trials of Charles M'Manus, John Hauer, Elizabeth Hauer, Patrick Donagan, Francis Cox, and Others* (Harrisburg: John Wyeth, 1798).

43. *M'Manus*, 97.
44. *M'Manus*, 154.
45. *M'Manus*, 154.
46. Rodney D. Coates, "Law and the Cultural Production of Race and Racialized Systems of Oppression: Early Court Cases," *American Behavioral Scientist* 47, no. 3 (2003): 348–49, 345. Unprepared to ensure that Black people had rights like those of other inhabitants, the state was faced with large numbers of cases to be litigated from 1786 to 1861. Black peoples' rights have been described by different parties as those of essential justice, legal emancipation, entitlements, legal status, fundamental rights, natural rights, civil rights, criminal rights, constitutional rights, rights of equal treatment, and liberty rights. Finkelman, "Human Liberty," 455–56, 467–81.
47. As Joanne Melish argues, equal treatment demands by Black people threatened "the stability of whiteness" so that Black defendants' "enacting their freedom as an entitlement"—a means of triggering the link between liberty and equality—met with stronger claims for Black people to adapt to white expectations of them. So long as perceptions of "innate [Black] inferiority" prevailed, Black people would not win full equality. Melish, *Disowning Slavery*, 161, 238.
48. *Respublica v. Blackmore* 2 Yeates 234; 1797 PA. Lexis 26. Richard S. Newman, *The Transformation of American Abolitionism: Fighting Slavery in the Early Republic* (Chapel Hill: University of North Carolina Press, 2001), 77, 80; John Marquez Lundin, "The Law of Equality before Equality Was Law," *Syracuse Law Review* 49, no. 4 (1999): 1179; Melish, *Disowning Slavery*, 87–88.
49. Chisholm v. Georgia 2 US (2 Dall.) 419 (1793); Marbury v. Madison 5 US (1 Cranch) 137 (1803); Phillip A. Hamburger, "Equality and Diversity: The Eighteenth-Century Debate about Equal Protection and Equal Civil Rights," *Supreme Court Review* (1992): 377n209, 378; Lundin, "The Law of Equality," 1156, 1176.
50. Lundin, "The Law of Equality," 1181; "Developments in the Law: Race and the Criminal Process: II. The Limits of Racial Equality: The Fourteenth Amendment and the Criminal Justice System," *Harvard Law Review* 101, no. 7 (1988): 1480.
51. Hamburger, "Equality and Diversity," 376; Lundin, "The Law of Equality," 1139, 1140, 1175; "Developments in the Law," 1480–1481. The 1790 Pennsylvania state constitution declared in Article 9, sec. 1, all men were born equally free with "certain inherent and indefeasible rights," a reference to natural rights; section 11 held that "all courts shall be open, and every man . . . shall have remedy by the due course of law," a reference to legal rights.
52. Lundin, "The Law of Equality," 1139–42, 1148, 1175.
53. Finkelman, "Human Liberty," 466; Hamburger, "Equality and Diversity," 373–74, 376, 387.
54. "Trial of John Joyce and Peter Mathias for the Murder of Sarah Cross, Philadelphia, Pennsylvania, 1808," in John D. Lawson, ed., *American State Trials*, vol. 7 (St. Louis: F. H. Thomas Law Book Co., 1917), 746.
55. William Tilghman was chief justice of the Pennsylvania Supreme Court from 1806 to 1827. Walter Franklin was attorney general from 1809 through 1810 and then appointed president judge of the Second Judicial District. John Golder, *Life of the Honourable William Tilghman, Late Chief Justice of the State of Pennsylvania*

(Philadelphia: Thomas Town, 1829); G. S. Rowe, *Embattled Bench: The Pennsylvania Supreme Court and the Forging of a Democratic Society, 1684–1809* (Newark: University of Delaware Press, 1994), 266–78, 282–86, 289, 338n15; G. S. Rowe, *Thomas McKean: The Shaping of an American Republicanism* (Boulder: Colorado Associated University Press, 1978), 369, 471n15.

56. "Trial of Joyce and Mathias," 745; Esther Ann McFarland, *William Lewis, Esquire: Enlightened Statesman, Profound Lawyer, and Useful Citizen* (Darby, PA: Diane Publishing Company, 2012), 10–11, 13–14, 22–25, 75–77, 82–83; William Primrose, "Biography of William Lewis," *Pennsylvania Magazine of History and Biography* 20, no. 1 (1896): 30–40. Nicholas Biddle became a Pennsylvania legislator in 1809, a state senator in 1814, and president of the Second Bank of the United States in 1822. Richard Rush, Benjamin Rush's son, became attorney general of Pennsylvania in 1811, US attorney general from 1814–1817, and secretary of the treasury from 1825–1829.

57. John H. Langbein, *The Origins of Adversary Criminal Trial* (Oxford: Oxford University Press, 2003), 48; J. M. Beattie, *Crime and the Courts in England, 1660–1800* (Oxford: Clarendon Press, 1986), 73, 167–69, 176; Rowe, "Black Offenders." Law reports of murder trials from 1783 to 1816 show defense counsel in ten cases (in two cases they were appointed; each received two counsel). In two other cases defendants had three counsel; in two cases they had two counsel; and in two cases they had one counsel.

58. The US Constitution (the Sixth Amendment), the Pennsylvania Constitution (sec. 9), and the Judiciary Act of 1789 (sec. 35) allowed assistance of counsel, extended by the Emancipation Act, sec. 7, to "Negroes and Mulattoes, as well slaves and servants as freemen." The Judiciary Act affirmed that the right depended in practice on "the rules of the said courts respectively [which] shall be permitted to manage and conduct causes therein."

59. *M'Manus*; Kutler, "Pennsylvania Courts," 18–26; Newman, *Transformation*, 81–83; Rowe, *Embattled Bench*, 276–86. 57.

60. Rowe, *Embattled Bench*, 276–78.

61. Patrick-Stamp, "Numbers," 124.

62. Golder, *Life of the Honourable William Tilghman*, 27–36, 46.

63. Rowe, *Embattled Bench*, 283; Golder, *Life of the Honourable William Tilghman*, 58, 61–62; Newman, *Transformation*, 81–83. *Commonwealth, Ex. Rel. Negro Lewis v. Holloway* 6 Binney 213 (1814). Finkelman, "Human Liberty," 471; *Marchand v. Negro Peggy* 2 Serg. & Rawle, 18, 19 (1815); Finkelman's review of twenty-six slave cases shows twelve from 1789–1809, eight from 1814 to 1825, and six from 1837 to 1855; Finkleman, 467–82.

64. *Wright alias Hall v. Deacon*, 5 Serg. & Rawle 62 (1819); Nash and Soderlund, *Freedom by Degrees*, 200; Finkelman, "Human Liberty," 476; Thomas D. Morris, *Free Men All: The Personal Liberty Laws of the North, 1780–1861* (Union, NJ: The Lawbook Exchange, 2001), 24–29, 42–46; Pennsylvania, An Act to Prevent Kidnapping, 1820, 1826; US Fugitive Slave Act of 1793, 1 Stat. 302; US Constitution, art. 4, sec. 2.

65. Finkelman, "Human Liberty," 471–72; Wilson v. Belinda, 3 Serg. & Rawle 396 (1817).

66. "Trial of Joyce and Mathias," 747–48.

67. *The Tickler*, March 16, 1808; *Democratic Press* (Philadelphia), February 20, 1808.

68. *Fate of Murderers*, 5, 7–8.

69. "Trial of Joyce and Mathias," 748.

70. *The Tickler*, March 16, 1808; Joyce, *Confession of John Joyce*, 7.

71. "Trial of Joyce and Mathias," 750.

72. "Trial of Joyce and Mathias," 750.

73. The hierarchy of testimony has the freeborn valued over freedmen, men of estate over their inferiors, particularly the poor, men over women and children, and Christians over the nonreligious. Barbara J. Shapiro, *"Beyond Reasonable Doubt" and "Probable Cause"* (Berkeley: University of California Press, 1991), 117, 138, 187–88, 196–97, 202; George Fisher, "The Jury's Rise as Lie Detector," *Yale Law Journal* 107 no. 3 (1997): 589–90; James Forman Jr., "Juries and Race in the Nineteenth Century," *Yale Law Journal* 113, no. 4 (2004): 897–913.

74. Fisher, "The Jury's Rise," 589–90, 624–25, 645, 657.

75. "Trial of Joyce and Mathias," 747–48. One witness saw Matthias before the murder "a little before dark"; a second saw them both on that evening. Joyce and Matthias noted the dim light and found it difficult to see in the shop; Matthias, *Confession of Peter Matthias*, 32–33; Joyce, *Confession of John Joyce*, 15.

76. "Trial of Joyce and Mathias," 747.

77. Matthias, *Confession of Peter Matthias*, 32–33; Joyce, *Confession of John Joyce*, 15.

78. Blackstone, *Commentaries*, IV, 357.

79. Fisher, "The Jury's Rise," 657; Shapiro, *"Beyond Reasonable Doubt,"* 18–25; Langbein, *The Origins*, 33, 261–66; Anthony A. Morano, "A Reexamination of the Development of the Reasonable Doubt Rule," *Boston University Law Review* 55, no. 507 (1975): 516–19.

80. Matthias, *Confession of Peter Matthias*, 34–35; "Trial of Joyce and Mathias," 748; *The Tickler*, March 16, 1808.

81. "Trial of Joyce and Mathias," 748.

82. Prosecution witnesses usually testified under oath. Whereas defendants sometimes testified, in Pennsylvania criminal trials they could not give sworn testimony until late in the nineteenth century. Although defense witnesses could by 1702 have testified under oath, in 1780 only 18 percent of cases even used defense witnesses. Defense witnesses whose competency could be challenged were not usually presented. This pattern skewered the proceedings to favor the prosecution. Fisher, "The Jury's Rise," 649, 668n441.

83. Finkelman, "Human Liberty," 466. Many slaves joined American forces with the hope that it would lead to freedom or otherwise legitimize their status.

84. Fisher, "The Jury's Rise," 597–98, 662–65; Howard Bodenhorn, "Criminal Sentencing in 19th-Century Pennsylvania," *Explorations in Economic History* 46, no. 3 (2009): 295.

85. Langbein, *The Origins*, 148–58. In *M'Manus* the judge held that the defendant's testimony ought not to be used to incriminate those against whom he testified; *M'Manus*, 154. The reward system in England was abolished in 1818.

86. Until the second half of the eighteenth century, the accused was expected to defend himself without protection against self-incrimination. Langbein, *The Origins*, 34, 48, 61, 280–84.

87. Beattie, *Crime and the Courts*, 342–43.

88. "Trial of Joyce and Mathias," 748.

89. An Act for the Better Preventing of Crimes, and for Abolishing the Punishment of Death in Certain Cases," 1794, *The Statutes at Large of Pennsylvania from 1682 to 1801*, vol. 15 1794–1797 (Harrisburg, PA: C. P. Aughinbaugh, 1911), 174–81.

90. *M'Manus*, 66–69, 154.

91. Pregnant circumstances were those "as to [the jury] shall seem convincing," tied to the belief that whereas witnesses might lie, circumstances cannot. Blackstone, *Commentaries*, IV, 342; Langbein, *The Origins*, 203–11; Fisher, "The Jury's Rise," 644; Matthew Hale, *The History of the Pleas of the Crown* (London: E. and R. Nutt and R. Gosling, 1736), II, 289; Blackstone, *Commentaries*, III, 371; Morris, "Slaves," 1217; Shapiro, *"Beyond Reasonable Doubt,"* 217–20.

92. Blackstone, *Commentaries*, IV, 200.

93. *M'Manus*, 99–101; Blackstone, *Commentaries*, IV, 192–93, 199, 201; *Pennsylvania v. Honeyman* (1793); Addison, *Reports of Cases*, 149, 161, 256, 283; *Pennsylvania v. Bell* (1793); *Pennsylvania v. M'Fall* (1794); *Pennsylvania v. Lewis* (1796). James Wilson, *The Works of James Wilson*, ed. R. G. McClosky (Cambridge: Belknap Press, 1967), II, 276.

94. Fisher, "The Jury's Rise," 643; *M'Manus*, 100, 156.

95. *Fate of Murderers*, 6; "Trial of Joyce and Mathias," 748.

96. Witnesses testified a stick had been seen in their possession before the crime but differed on which man had it. "Trial of Joyce and Mathias," 747–48.

97. Blackstone, *Commentaries*, IV, 358; Langbein, *The Origins*, 261–62; Alexander Volokh, "n Guilty Men," *University of Pennsylvania Law Review* 146, no. 2 (1997): 173; Daniel Epps, "The Consequence of Error in Criminal Justice," *Harvard Law Review* 128, no. 4 (2015): 1067–89.

98. Shapiro, *"Beyond Reasonable Doubt,"* 20–21. Abraham's admonition appeared in Gen. 18:23–32 on the destruction of Sodom. *M'Manus* cited it as "better the guilty flee justice than the innocent suffer" (156). Blackstone, *Commentaries*, IV, 358; Hale, *The History*, II, 289.

99. Joyce, *Confession of John Joyce*, 16.

100. The 1794 act mirrored Blackstone's common law language, excluding killing by passion or provocation and defining malice aforethought as "any evil design in general." *Respublica v. Mulatto Bob* (1795); Dallas, *Reports of Cases Ruled*, IV, 145–47.

101. *Pennsylvania v. Bell* (1793); President Judge Alexander Addison analyzed the common law on murder extensively; Addison, *Reports of Cases*, 160–164; Wilson, *The Works of James Wilson*, II, 275–76.

102. Blackstone, *Commentaries*, IV, 192–93, 199; "An Act for the Better Preventing of Crimes" (1794), 174; "Trial of Joyce and Mathias," 748.

103. "Trial of Joyce and Mathias," 748; *Democratic Press*, February 20, 1808.

104. "Trial of Joyce and Mathias," 748–49; *Democratic Press*, February 20, 1808; *Fate of Murderers*, 12.

105. A decade-old precedent, *M'Manus*, saw seven defendants accused, three separate trials held, and four different verdicts delivered (first-degree murder; assault and battery with intent to kill; discharge; and the issuance of peace bonds).

106. "Trial of Joyce and Mathias," 749; *Pennsylvania v. M'Fall* (1794); Addison, *Reports of Cases*, 257. Tilghman's reference to judicial authority under the 1794 statute would have included *Pennsylvania v. M'Fall* (1794), in Addison, *Reports of Cases*, 255–57; *Respublica v. Mulatto Bob* (1795), in Dallas, *Reports of Cases Ruled*, IV:145–47; *Pennsylvania v. Lewis* (1796), in Addison, *Reports of Cases*, 279–83; and *Commonwealth v. O'Hara* (1797), referenced in John H. Lawson ed., "The Trial of Richard Smith for the Murder of John Carson, Philadelphia, 1816," in *American State Trials* (St. Louis, MO: F. H. Thomas Law Book Co., 1917), V, 719.

107. *Fate of Murderers*, 14; *Poulson's American Daily Advertiser*, February 22, 1808. The *Democratic Press* reported it took the Joyce and Matthias jury ten minutes to deliver the verdict; February 20, 1808. The rationale for quick verdicts was enhanced by the practice of refusing food and drink to jurors while they were deliberating to hasten the course of justice and prevent interested parties influencing a verdict; Langbein, *The Origins*, 22–23.

108. "Trial of Joyce and Mathias," 749–50.

109. Forman, "Juries and Race," 900; Newman, *Transformation*, 60–86; Linda Myrsiades, "Legal Practice and Pragmatics in the Law: The 1821 Trials of John Reed, 'Fugitive Slave,'" *Pennsylvania Magazine of History and Biography* 138, no. 3 (2014): 310–13; Beattie, *Crime and the Courts*, 342–43.

110. "Trial of Joyce and Matthias," 750; "The Trial of Richard Smith" (1816), 724. Jacob Rush served on the Pennsylvania Supreme Court from 1784–1790 and was president judge of the Philadelphia District Court from 1806–1820; Louis Richards, "Hon. Jacob Rush, of the Pennsylvania Judiciary," *Pennsylvania Magazine of History and Biography* 39, no.1 (1915): 53–68; *L'Oracle and Daily Advertiser*, February 24, 1808; *Poulson's American Daily Advertiser*, February 22, 1808.

111. "Trial of Joyce and Mathias," 749–50.

112. *L'Oracle and Daily Advertiser*, March 18, 1808; *The Tickler*, March 16, 1808 (1808 was a leap year, which explains the date and day of the execution); Matthias, *Confession*, 35; Joyce, 18.

113. *Democratic Press*, March 15, 1808; Joyce, *Confession of John Joyce*, 17.

114. Joyce, *Confession of John Joyce*, 17–18; Matthias, *Confession*, 35–36. The mayor of Philadelphia was Robert Wharton (1820–1824), a Federalist. Matthias's expectation of a pardon was not entirely unfounded in the law, as *Pennsylvania v. James Honeyman* (1793) indicated. For a crime delivered without passion or provocation but in a cool manner and upon a "poor weak man," Honeyman was pardoned on a writ of error in the indictment. The case was subsequently reversed. Addison, *Reports of Cases*, 150; Dallas, *Reports of Cases Ruled*, II, 228.

115. *Pennsylvania v. Lewis* (1796) gave dying words (in the case of a victim) the same value as positive oath; Addison, *Reports of Cases*, 282.

116. Abraham Johnstone, *The Address of Abraham Johnstone, a Black Man, Who Was Hanged at Woodbury, in the County of Glocester, and State of New Jersey, on Saturday the 8th Day of July Last* (Philadelphia: Printed for the Purchasers, 1797), 2, 4, 16, 18; Joseph Mountain, *Sketches of the Life of Joseph Mountain, a Negro, Who was Executed at New-Haven on the 20th Day of October, 1790, for a Rape* (New Haven, CT: T. S. Green, 1790), 18; Donna Denise Hunter, "Dead Men Talking: Africans and the Law in New England's Eighteenth-Century Execution Sermons and Crime Narratives" (PhD diss. University of California, Berkeley, 2000), 164–223, DA3001879; Donna Denise Hunter, "Race, Law and Innocence: Executing Black Men in the Eighteenth Century," *New Perspectives on Capital Punishment* 20 (2000): 71–97; Joseph Mountain, "Petition to the General Assembly of the State of Connecticut," *The Connecticut State Archives Crimes and Misdemeanors*, 2nd ser., 1671–1820, IV, 131a; Williams, *Pillars of Salt*, 51–55, 288–307.

117. Johnstone declared that his trial was impartial, candid, and decided by a jury of peers who were good and worthy, lived the truth, and were clear of all doubts and scruples. De Lombard, *In the Shadow*, 119–28, 142–64, 155–61; Hunter, "Dead Men Talking," 164–79.

118. Beattie, *Crime and the Courts*, 341.

119. "Trial of Joyce and Matthias," 749–50; *Fate of Murderers*, 18; Matthias, *Confession*, 35; *Democratic Press*, March 15, 1808, *L'Oracle and Daily Advertiser*, March 18, 1808, *Petersburg Intelligencer*, March 22, 1808.

120. Nash, *Forging Freedom*, 134, 221.

121. De Lombard, *In the Shadow*, 143.

122. Newman, *Freedom's Prophet*, 149–51, 200–01.

123. Otter, *Philadelphia Stories*, 32, 36, 39–40, 46. Of collateral interest to the Joyce and Matthias trial, Absalom Jones and Richard Allen, *A Narrative of the Proceedings of the Black People, During the Late Awful Calamity in Philadelphia, in the Year 1793* (Philadelphia: William W. Woodward, 1794), discussed in Otter, *Philadelphia Stories*, 29, 40–46; Newman, *Freedom's Prophet*, 96–98; Nash, *Forging Freedom*, 122–25.

124. Newman, *Transformation*, 86–96; Nash, *Forging Freedom*, 195–202; Newman, *Freedom's Prophet*, 149–50.

125. Slotkin, "Narratives of Negro Crime," 4, 26, 28; Melish, *Disowning Slavery*, 163–209.

126. One notes here Susan Branson's work detailing difference in treatment, with one form of justice for those who disappear in the historical record and another for those linked to the world of white male property holders. Her work demonstrates that studies have failed to examine the alternatives available for women who challenged norms and "occupied a middle ground that has been largely unexplored for this economically volatile era." In the present study, Matthias stands for those who challenged norms and who, like Branson's subjects, are memorialized in subsequent discourse

through documents like execution statements that frame them as notorious. As Branson makes clear, it is critical to reevaluate "the unique experiences and survival strategies," the gender and class implications, of those subject to society's criminal justice system. Susan Branson, *Dangerous to Know: Women, Crime, and Notoriety in the Early Republic* (Philadelphia: University of Pennsylvania press, 2008), 138–39.

Conclusion

This book has examined the law in many of its guises—military law, common law, natural law, indigenous law, criminal, civil, local, state, federal, constitutional, and statutory—and considered cases (1783–1808) that extend across twenty-five years of the new republic. It does not pretend to present a seamless history of trials across that period, to argue that the trials it studies are a representative sample of types of trials, or that they present a history of how trials developed—although, in truth, they have provided something of that history. What this study has undertaken is to treat exceptional, even scandalous, trials that explored issues critical to their times. What has proved important is that they have either not been previously studied or in some cases not been properly or thoroughly studied. I contend they deserve to be examined intensively and have done so using newly available and rescuing material from oblivion to better understand our early legal history.

Detailing the uniqueness of court cases without forcing them into the procrustean bed of a particular thematic narrative, the study engages selective cases that punctuate the early republic to display crucial moments in the history of law, but it is also conscious of how cases interface to comment on each other and how the law progresses over time. For our purposes, the task has been to stay close to the ground (exploring local knowledge as Clifford Geertz would have it), access the interpretations of our subjects, isolate the elements of the trials and their relationships, detail practices through thick description, and construct an explanatory reading.[1]

Having studied, with one exception, Pennsylvania trials, it is important to ask to what extent these trials reflect the larger legal culture of the United States. The issues Pennsylvania faced in the trials represented here were undeniably critical issues for the nation as a whole. Military law during the revolution, the only case in the study that occurred outside of Pennsylvania, was clearly a shared concern for all the states, possibly the first legal issue they would mutually face. Regarding the other five cases, there are persuasive reasons for considering them relevant to the rest of the country.

The acquisition of western land was central to setting boundaries between states and to the needs of an expanding nation. The implications of working out the demands of constitutional government and how the country would govern itself, how the federal government was to pay the costs of its recent war or finance a national government without taxing its subjects were not issues only for the whiskey rebels. It was clear in the Whiskey Rebellion that Pennsylvania was chosen by the Washington administration as an "experiment" to send a message to any other state whose western territory was prepared to rebel. As for the terrors of urban crime, they had clearly come to plague large cities throughout the Union as much as they were felt in the bustling city of Philadelphia. Philadelphia, moreover, served as a focal point from the moment of the country's inception in the Declaration of Independence. As capital of the nation for the critical decade following ratification of the Constitution, 1790 to 1800, it was home to the nation's executive, legislative, and judicial branches. As a city targeted by the migration of fugitive slaves from the South, by debt-ridden rural Pennsylvanians, by gradually emancipated Pennsylvania slaves, and by European immigrants, Philadelphia's explosive growth and its crime rate epitomized much of what was already happening or would happen elsewhere in the country. So, too, Philadelphia was a critical center for litigiousness related to partisan politics and personal libel in the new nation. Moreover, it was the site where the Alien and Sedition Acts were passed by Congress and where signature prosecutions of the press—of Eleazer Oswald, William Cobbett, and Thomas Cooper—were held. By this argument, the trials treated in this work were not merely landmarks in the history of Pennsylvania, but they stand up to scrutiny as exemplars of events that appeared throughout the United States.

This is not, of course, the whole story, for regional differences, particularly over slavery, split the country. Pennsylvania was uniquely identified by its Quaker origins as a colony and a developed middle-class Black community in Philadelphia. Its egalitarianism and accommodation of capitalism severed it from its southern neighbors.[2] Pennsylvania, according to Robert H. Churchill, fully expressed the complex nature of the North's antislavery activism, both as a borderland area and as a contested region.[3] As the first northern state that fugitives from the eastern coast slave states would reach, the state of Pennsylvania provided the perfect crucible for state laws that aimed to defy fugitive slave laws.

The approach of this book thus leaves us faced with the question of commonality across the states. To begin, by 1763 England's dominance in North America, as G. Edward White tells it, had expanded to Anglicize American law, including "the entire land mass of the eastern North American continent, stretching from Canada to Florida."[4] But that was only half of the story. While a shared legal culture developed from adherence to English common law and applicable English statutes, distinctive patterns of social and economic organization and laws adapted to local conditions affected the colonies differentially as means of self-governance.[5] Sufficient mutuality was, however, forged by common grievances against the British to unite them in support of the revolution.[6] Moreover, creating and living under the Articles of Confederation and the Constitution helped to overcome regional differences; the states were mutually responsible for the identity of a nation shaped by mutual agreement around a set of accepted ideas. They might have created separate constitutions by 1780, but they mutually swore allegiance to a common republic and subscribed to a common constitution by 1787.[7]

William E. Nelson's extensive work on common law in colonial America up to the war concludes that Americans were so deeply attached to the liberty "provided by common law and localist constitutionalism" that they not only rebelled to defend them but maintained them "well into the nineteenth century."[8] Robert G. Parkinson's study of "common cause" follows suit, arguing that the phrase became a call to arms like that which characterized great struggles from the English Civil War to wars against American Indians and the French Revolution.[9] By 1774, the phrase was "shorthand" for the idea that an attack on one was an attack on all. Even where pursuing the war fractured such commonality, Parkinson represents, shared marketplace experiences and the public discourse of liberty returned Americans to one common cause.[10]

As for Pennsylvania, in its relative self-governance under the British it was as much like Virginia and South Carolina as it was the New England states. Nelson argues that the Crown allowed diverse colonies the freedom to accept the elements of the law that fit their conditions, which brought them together to create "a common legal culture." Indeed, the legal profession "became a glue that could hold together the diverse people of all thirteen colonies." Lawyers could thereby practice across different colonial jurisdictions sharing education, language, and concepts,[11] so that Pennsylvania's Anglicized legal experience resembled that of other colonies from the 1760s.[12] Equally, Pennsylvania was similar to other regions of the country in its history of Indian troubles, land rushes, agrarian rebellions, debt crises, intercolonial struggles over its borders, and the struggle between states' rights and federalism. In some ways, it was a state whose struggles were more intense as it sat precariously between several states with claims on what it considered its territory (Connecticut, Maryland, Virginia, West Virginia, Kentucky, and Ohio). It fought extended wars with the eastern Indian nations (the Delaware, Iroquois, and Shawnee), and was at the center of the Seven Years War and the major land treaties of the eighteenth century.[13] Clearly it was central to the issues related to western migration, land acquisition, and resolution of fluid boundaries that were so essential to the early development of the new nation.

While Pennsylvania's history was indicative of the law and history that the states held in common, and while there were considerable commonalities among the states, the present work does not contend that Pennsylvania's legal culture stood for the legal culture of the early republic in the United States as a whole. As Woody Holton argues, the model historians often rely upon imposes a northern perspective that did not make sense for the South. Indeed, Virginia's concern with transatlantic debt, class relationships, and the importation of slaves as reasons for supporting the struggle against Britain was not shared with their northern counterparts. Virginia's "gentleman revolutionaries" had simply found their interests were better served by adopting a broader American identity even if it meant banding together with those with whom they had differences.[14] The general picture, in other words, was more nuanced than has usually been appreciated. There were considerable inconsistencies among southern states in terms of legal culture, common law, and localism as well as significant differences related to the degree, and sometimes the lack, of support for slavery,[15] even as the southern states shared a common ideology of slavery that distinguished them from the Republican egalitarianism of the North. And it was clear that the plantation culture that characterized Virginia, the Carolinas, Georgia, and Maryland stood in stark contrast to northern manufacturing and domestic trade.[16] It was no surprise, as a result, that by the late 1790s, with the emergence of sectional differences based on a southern states' rights philosophy that protected slavery, the South opposed itself to centralized government in the new nation.[17]

In toto, nonetheless, the trials presented in the present study were critical events in the legal history and legal culture of Pennsylvania over the period of the early republic as well as exemplars for a crucial transitional period in the history of American law in the new nation. In considering Pennsylvania's position in the early republic, this study claims the commonalities in law and culture Pennsylvania shared with other states were meaningful. Thomas Jefferson apparently agreed in expressing his opinion about the different character of the North and South, allowing that Pennsylvania was the place where the two "seem to meet and blend and to form a people free from the extremes of vice and virtue."[18]

NOTES

1. Clifford Geertz, *The Interpretation of Culture: Selected Essays* (New York: Basic Books, 1973), 3–30; Clifford Geertz, *Local Knowledge: Further Essays in Interpretive Anthropology* (New York: Basic Books, 1985), 187–95, 205; Anthony G. Amsterdam and Jerome Bruner, *Minding the Law: How Courts Rely on Storytelling, and*

How Their Stories Change the Ways We Understand the Law—and Ourselves (Cambridge, MA: Harvard University Press, 2000), 229–30.

2. William M. Offutt Jr., *Of 'Good Laws' & 'Good Men': Law and Society in the Delaware Valley, 1680–1710* (Urbana: University of Illinois Press, 1995); William M. Offutt Jr., "The Limits of Authority: Courts, Ethnicity, and Gender in the Middle Colonies, 1670–1710," in *The Many Legalities of Early America*, eds. Christopher Tomlins and Bruce H. Mann (Chapel Hill: University of North Carolina Press, 2001), 357–87; Richard S. Newman, *The Transformation of American Abolitionism: Fighting Slavery in the Early Republic* (Chapel Hill: University of North Carolina Press, 2002); Andrew Shankman, *Crucible of American Democracy: The Struggle to Fuse Egalitarianism & Capitalism in Jeffersonian Pennsylvania* (Lawrence: University Press of Kansas, 2004).

3. Robert H. Churchill, *The Underground Railroad and the Geography of Violence in Antebellum America* (New York: Cambridge University Press, 2020), 9; Gary B. Nash, *Forging Freedom: The Formation of Philadelphia's Black Community, 1720–1840* (Cambridge, MA: Harvard University Press, 1988); Gary B. Nash and Jean R. Sonderlund, *Freedom by Degrees: Emancipation in Pennsylvania and its Aftermath* (New York: Oxford University Press, 1991).

4. G. Edward White, *Law in American History, Volume I: From the Colonial Years Through the Civil War* (New York: Oxford University Press, 2012), 43, 46.

5. Morton J. Horwitz, *The Transformation of American Law, 1780–1860* (Cambridge, MA: Harvard University Press, 1977), 4.

6. White, *Law in American History*, 109–14.

7. White, *Law in American History*, 107–08, 148, 153.

8. Nelson cites as well the common features of a "nascent federalism," weakened religious establishment, a regulated free market, comity in labor law and the law of slavery as well as mutually embedded property, contract, and debtor-creditor law in the life of the colonies; William E. Nelson, *Common Law in Colonial America, Volume IV: Law and the Constitution on the Eve of Independence, 1735–1776* (New York: Oxford University Press, 2018), 46–63; William E. Nelson, *Common Law in Colonial America, Volume I: The Chesapeake and New England, 1607–1660* (New York: Oxford University Press, 2008); William E. Nelson, *Common Law in Colonial America, Volume II: The Middle Colonies and the Carolinas, 1660–1730* (New York: Oxford University Press, 2013); William E. Nelson, *Common Law in Colonial America, Volume III: The Chesapeake and New England, 1660–1750* (New York: Oxford University Press, 2016); William E. Nelson, *E Pluribus Unum: How the Common Law Helped Unify and Liberate Colonial America, 1607–1776* (New York: Oxford University Press, 2019).

9. Robert G. Parkinson, *The Common Cause: Creating Race and Nation in the American Revolution* (Chapel Hill: University of North Carolina Press, 2016), 4–5.

10. Parkinson, *The Common Cause* 6, 21–23, 188.

11. Nelson, *E Pluribus*, 2–5, 22, 246–47. Nelson argues "the common law constituted the basis of the legal system of every one of Britain's thirteen North American colonies"; Nelson, *Common Law*, IV, 2, 7–22.

12. White, *Law in American History*, 43, 46, n45 489–90.

13. Pennsylvania was, for example, along with Virginia and Maryland, at the center of the Treaty of 1744 with the Iroquois that essentially gave those colonies title to the Ohio Valley until the French gained control in 1754. The state's rights were impacted by the 1758 Treaty of Easton whereby the British promised to honor tribal land west of the Alleghanies—which settlers refused to honor—and the Treaty of Paris in 1763 that ended the French and Indian War, establishing a Proclamation Line that made lands west of the Appalachians again the territory of the Indian nations. The first treaty signed by the new United States with any Indian nation was signed in Pennsylvania, the Treaty of Fort Pitt in 1778. With the Treaty of Fort Stanwix in 1784, Pennsylvanians essentially took control over the land west of the Alleghanies. White, *Law in American History*, 44–45; Patrick Spero, *Frontier Country: The Politics of War in Early Pennsylvania* (Philadelphia: University of Pennsylvania Press, 2016); Peter Silver, *Our Savage Neighbors: How Indian War Transformed Early America* (New York: W. W. Norton & Company, 2008); Patrick Griffin, *American Leviathan: Empire, Nation, and Revolutionary Frontier* (New York: Hill and Wang, 2007).

14. Woody Holton, *Forced Founders: Indians, Debtors, Slaves, and the Making of the American Revolution in Virginia* (Chapel Hill: University of North Carolina Press, 1999), 209–13, 220. The conduct of the gentry was, for example, dictated by class and commerce in the struggle to best British merchant control over the economy of the commonwealth, to the extent that they had to challenge both the British government and British merchants to control the importation of new Africans in order to preserve peace on the plantation and prevent slave revolts. Holton, *Forced Founders*, xviii–xx.

15. James Campbell, "'The victim of prejudice and hasty consideration': The Slave Trial System in Richmond, Virginia, 1830–1861," *Slavery and Abolition* 26, no. 1 (2005): 72; William W. Fisher, III, "Ideology and Imagery in the Law of Slavery," in *Slavery & the Law*, ed. Paul Finkelman (Madison, WI: Madison House, 1997), 44, 53–54; Peter Westen, "Comment on Judith Schafer's 'Under the Present Mode of Trial, Improper Verdicts are Very Often Given': Criminal Procedure in the Trials of Slaves in Antebellum Louisiana," *Cardozo Law Review* 18, no. 2 (1996): 686; Louise Weinberg, "Methodological Interventions and the Slavery Cases; or, Night-Thoughts of a Legal Realist," *Maryland Law Review* 56, no. 4 (1997): 1320, 1324; William G. Thomas, III, *A Question of Freedom: The Families Who Challenged Slavery from the Nation's Founding to the Civil War* (New Haven, CT: Yale University Press, 2020); Laura Edwards, *The People and Their Peace: Legal Culture and the Transformation of Inequality in the Post-Revolutionary South* (Chapel Hill: University of North Carolina Press, 2009).

16. Gordon S. Wood, *Empire of Liberty: A History of the Early Republic, 1789–1815* (New York: Oxford University Press, 2009), 165–67.

17. James Roger Sharp, *American Politics in the Early Republic: The New Nation in Crisis* (New Haven, CT: Yale University Press, 1993), 187–88.

18. Letter, Thomas Jefferson to the Marquis de Chastellux, September 2, 1785, https://founders.archives.gov/; Wood, *Empire of Liberty*, 166.

Bibliography

A Correct Account of the Trials of Charles M'Manus, John Hauer, Elizabeth Hauer, Patrick Donagan, Francis Cox, and Others. Harrisburg, PA: John Wyeth, 1798.

Abbot, W. W. "George Washington and the Union." *Indiana Magazine of History* 84, no. 1 (1988): 88–99.

Abernathy, Thomas Perkins. *Western Lands and the American Revolution.* Richmond: University of Virginia Institute of Research in the Social Sciences, 1937.

Abrahams, Roger D. "Introduction: A Folklore Perspective." In *Riot and Revelry in Early America*, edited by William Pencak, Matthew Dennis, and Simon Peter Newman, 21–37. University Park: Penn State University Press, 2002

Achenbach, Joel. *The Grand Idea: George Washington's Potomac and the Race to the West.* New York: Simon and Schuster, 2004.

Adair, James. "Extracts," *The History of the American Indians.* In *A Selection of Some of the Most Interesting Narratives, or Outrages, Committed by the Indians in Their War with the White People.* Vol. 2., edited by Archibald Loudon. Carlisle: A. Loudon, 1808.

Addison, Alexander. *Reports of Cases in the County Courts of the Fifth Circuit, and in the High Court of Errors and Appeals of the State of Pennsylvania.* Philadelphia: John Colerick, 1800.

Adye, Payne. *A Treatise on Courts Martial. Also an Essay on Military Punishments and Rewards*, 4th ed. London: J. Murray and S. Highley, 1797.

Aleksandrov, Gleb. "Power, History, and Native-Colonial Conflicts in the Early Native American Literary Tradition (OAH 2020)." *Law and History Review* (March 2020).

Alryyes, Ala. "War at a Distance: Court-Martial Narratives in the Eighteenth Century." *Eighteenth-Century Studies* 41, no. 4 (2008): 525–42.

Amsterdam, Anthony G. and Jerome Bruner. *Minding the Law: How Courts Rely on Storytelling, and How Their Stories Change the Ways We Understand the Law—and Ourselves.* Cambridge, MA: Harvard University Press, 2000.

Anand, Sanjeez. "The Origins, Early History and Evolution of the English Criminal Trial Jury." *The Alberta Law Review* 43, no. 2 (2005): 407–32.

Anderson, James H. "Colonel William Crawford." *Ohio History Journal* 6, no. 1 (1898): 1–34.

Angell, Israel. *Diary of Colonel Israel Angell, Commanding the Second Rhode Island Continental Regiment during the American Revolution, 1778–1781*, edited by Edward Field. Providence, RI: Preston and Rounds Company, 1899.

Annals of Congress: The Debates and Proceedings in the Congress of the United States. 1789–1824. Washington, D. C.: Government printing Office, 1789–1824.

Bailey, Francis. *Narratives of a Late Expedition against the Indians; with an Account of the Barbarous Execution of Col. Crawford; and the Wonderful Escape of Dr. Knight and John Slover from Captivity, in 1782.* Philadelphia: Francis Bailey, 1783.

Baldwin, Leland D. *Whiskey Rebels: The Story of a Frontier Uprising.* Pittsburgh: University of Pittsburgh Press, 1939.

Barber, William D. "'Among the Most Techy Articles of Civil Police': Federal Taxation and the Adoption of the Whiskey Excise." *William and Mary Quarterly* 25, no. 1 (1968): 58–84.

Bartoloni-Tuazon, Kathleen. *For Fear of an Elective King: George Washington and the Presidential Title Controversy.* Ithaca, NY: Cornell University Press, 2014.

Beattie, J. M. *Crime and the Courts in England, 1660–1800.* Oxford: Clarendon Press, 1986.

Benet, S. V. *A Treatise on Military Law and the Practice of Courts-Martial.* New York: D. Van Nostrand, 1862.

Benton, Lauren. "Historical Perspectives on Legal Pluralism." *Hague Journal on the Rule of Law* 3, no. 1 (2011): 57–69.

———. *Law and Colonial Cultures: Legal Regimes in World History, 1400–1900.* Cambridge: Cambridge University Press, 2001.

Bessler, John D. *Private Prosecution in America: Its Origins, History, and Unconstitutionality in the Twenty-First Century.* Durham, NC: Carolina Academic Press, 2022.

———. "The Public Interest and the Unconstitutionality of Private Prosecutors." *Arkansas Law Review* 47, no. 3 (1994): 511–602.

Binger, Carl A. L. *Revolutionary Doctor: Benjamin Rush, 1746–1813.* New York: Norton, 1966.

Blackstone, William. *Commentaries on the Laws of England*, 15th ed., 4 vols. London: A. Strahan, 1809.

Blinka, Daniel D. "'This Germ of Rottenness': Federal Trials in the New Republic, 1789–1807." *Creighton Law Review* 36, no. 2 (2003): 135–89.

Bodenhorn, Howard. "Criminal Sentencing in 19th-Century Pennsylvania." *Explorations in Economic History* 46, no. 3 (2009): 287–98.

Bosco, Ronald A. "Early American Gallows Literature: An Annotated Checklist." *Resources for American Literary Study* 8, no. 1 (1978): 85–105.

Bothwell, Margaret Pearson. "The Astonishing Croghans." *The Western Pennsylvania Historical Magazine* 48, no. 2 (1965): 138–45.

———. "Killbuck and Killbuck Island." *Western Pennsylvania History* 44, no. 4 (1961): 343–60.

Bourdieu, Pierre. *Outline of a Theory of Practice.* Cambridge: Cambridge University Press, 1977.

Bouton, Terry. *Taming Democracy: "The People," the Founders, and the Troubled Ending of the American Revolution.* New York: Oxford University Press, 2007.

Brackenridge, Hugh Henry. "A Dissertation on the Treason Laws of the United States," in *Incidents of the Insurrection in the Western Parts of Pennsylvania, in the Year 1795*, vol, 3, appendix, 41–61. Philadelphia: John M'Culloch, 1795.

———. *Incidents of the Insurrection in the Western Parts of Pennsylvania, in the Year 1794*, 3 vols. Philadelphia: John M'Culloch, 1795.

———. "Indian Right of Soil." *Gazette Publications.* Carlisle: Alexander and Phillips, 1806.

———. *Law Miscellanies: Containing an Introduction to the Study of the Law, Notes on Blackstone's Commentaries, Shewing the Law of Pennsylvania from the Law of England and What Acts of Assembly Might Require to be Repealed or Modified.* Philadelphia: P. Sterne, 1814.

———. "Modern Chivalry." Ed White, ed. Indianapolis: Hackett Publishing Company, Inc., 2009.

———. "Observations." In *Narratives of a Late Expedition against the Indians; with an Account of the Barbarous Execution of Col. Crawford; and the Wonderful Escape of Dr. Knight and John Slover from Captivity, in 1782*, edited by Francis Bailey. Philadelphia: Francis Bailey, 1783.

———. "Thoughts on the Present Indian War." In *Incidents of the Insurrection*, edited by Daniel Marder. 1808. New Haven, CT: College & University Press, 1972.

———. "Treason Laws of the United States." In *Law Miscellanies: Containing an Introduction to the Study of the Law, Notes on Blackstone's Commentaries, Shewing the Law of Pennsylvania from the Law of England and What Acts of Assembly Might Require to be Repealed or Modified*, 474–502. Philadelphia: P. Sterne, 1814.

———. "The Trial of Mamachtaga." 1808. *Litigation* 14, no. 4 (1988): 47–50.

———. "The Trial of Mamachtaga." In *Incidents of the Insurrection*, edited by Daniel Marder. 1808. New Haven, CT: College & University Press, 1972.

———. "The Trial of Mamachtaga, a Delaware Indian, the First Person Convicted of Murder West of the Alleghany Mountains, and Hanged for His Crime." 1808. *Western Pennsylvania Historical Magazine* 1, no. 1 (1918): 27–36.

———. "The Trial of Mamachtaga, an Indian, at a Court of Oyer and Terminer for the County of Westmoreland, in the Year 1784-5." In *A Selection of Some of the Most Interesting Narratives, or Outrages, Committed by the Indians in Their War with the White People*, edited by Archibald Loudon. Carlisle: A. Loudon, 1808.

Brackenridge, Henry Marie. *History of the Western Insurrection in Western Pennsylvania, Commonly Called the Whiskey Insurrection, 1794.* Pittsburgh, 1859.

Branson, Susan. *Dangerous to Know: Women, Crime, and Notoriety in the Early Republic.* Philadelphia: University of Pennsylvania Press, 2008.

Brownson, James L. *The Life and Times of Senator James Ross*. Washington, PA: The Observer Job Rooms, 1910.

Bray, Chris. *Court Martial: How Military Justice Has Shaped America from the Revolution to 9/11 and Beyond.* New York: W. W. Norton & Co., 2016.

Brooke, John L. "Consent, Civil Society, and the Public Sphere in the Age of Revolution and the Early American Republic." In *Beyond the Founders: New Approaches to the Political History of the Early American Republic*, edited by Jeffrey L. Pasley, Andrew W. Robertson, and David Waldstreicher, 207–50. Chapel Hill: University of North Carolina Press, 2004.

Brown, David Paul. *The Forum; or Forty Years Full Practice at the Philadelphia Bar.* Philadelphia: R. H. Small, 1856.

Bushnell, Amy Turner. "Indigenous America and the Limits of the Atlantic World, 1493-1825." In *Atlantic History: A Critical Appraisal*, edited by Jack P. Greene and Philip D. Morgan, 191–221. New York: Oxford University Press, 2008.

Bushnell, Amy Turner and Jack P. Greene. "Peripheries, Centers, and the Construction of Early Modern American Empires." In *Negotiated Empires: Centers and Peripheries in the Americas, 1500–1820*, edited by Christine Daniels and Michael V. Kennedy, 1–4. London: Taylor and Francis Group, 2002.

Butterfield, C. W., ed. *The Washington-Crawford Letters, Being the Correspondence between George Washington and William Crawford, from 1767 to 1781, Concerning Western Lands.* Cincinnati, OH: Robert Clarke & Co., 1877.

Butterfield, L. H., ed. *Letters of Benjamin Rush*, 2 vols. Princeton, NJ: Princeton University Press, 1951.

Cable, Robert L., ed. "Law About Trial of Indians (1793)." In *The Statutes at Large of Pennsylvania, vol. 1, 1682–1700* chapter 73, 64–65. Harrisburg, PA: Legislative Reference Bureau, 2001.

Camenzind, Krista. "Violence, Race, and the Paxton Boys." In *Friends and Enemies in Penn's Woods*, edited by William A. Pencak and Daniel K. Richter, eds., 201–20. University Park: The Pennsylvania State University Press, 2004.

Campbell, James. "'The victim of prejudice and hasty consideration': The Slave Trial System in Richmond, Virginia, 1830–1861." *Slavery and Abolition* 26, no. 1 (2005): 71–91.

Capoccia, Giovanni and R. Daniel Kelemen. "The Study of Critical Junctures: Theory, Narrative, and Counterfactuals in Historical Institutionalism." *World Politics* 59 no. 3 (2007): 341–69.

Capoccia, Giovanni and Daniel Ziblatt. "The Historical Turn in Democratization Studies: A New Research Agenda for Europe and Beyond." *Comparative Political Studies* 43, nos. 8/9 (2010): 931–68.

Carbado, Devon W. "Racial Naturalization." *American Quarterly* 57, no. 3 (2005): 633–58.

Carey, Mathew. *Mathew Carey: Autobiography.* 1837. Brooklyn, NY: Research Classics, 1942.

———. *Plumb Pudding for the Humane, Chaste, Valiant, Enlightened Peter Porcupine by His Obliged Friend Mathew Carey*, 2nd ed. Philadelphia: Mathew Carey, 1799.

———. *The Porcupiniad: A Hudibrastic Poem in Three Cantos Addressed to William Cobbett.* Philadelphia: Matthew Carey, 1799.

Carpenter, Thomas. *A Report of an Action for a Libel Brought by Dr. Benjamin Rush against William Cobbett in the Supreme Court of Pennsylvania, December Term,*

1799, for Certain Defamatory Publications in a Newspaper Entitled Porcupine's Gazette. Philadelphia: W.W. Woodward, 1800.

———. *The Two Trials of John Fries, on an Indictment for Treason; Together with a Brief Report of the Trials of Several Other Persons, for Treason and Insurrection, in the Counties of Bucks, Northampton and Montgomery, in the Circuit Court of the United States.* Philadelphia: William W. Woodward, 1800.

Carter, Katlyn Marie. "Denouncing Secrecy and Defining Democracy in the Early American Republic." *Journal of the Early Republic* 40, no. 3 (2020): 409–33.

Casey, Nicholas. "Making Political Forecasts, and Wincing All the While." *New York Times*, November 17, 2019, https://www.nytimes.com.

Cavafy, C. P. "Ithaka." In *The Canon: The Original One Hundred and Fifty-Four Poems by C. P. Cavafy*, translated by Stratis Haviaras, 90–93. Washington, DC: Center for Hellenic Studies, 2007.

Chamberlain, Ava. "The Execution of Moses Paul: A Story of Crime and Contact in Eighteenth-Century Connecticut." *The New England Quarterly* 77, no. 3 (2004): 414–50.

Chapin, Bradley. *The American Law of Treason: Revolutionary and Early National Origins.* Seattle: University of Washington Press, 1964.

Chervinsky, Lindsay M. *The Cabinet: George Washington and the Creation of an American Institution.* Cambridge, MA: Belnap Press, 2020.

Christensen, Grant and Melissa L. Tatum, eds. *Reading American Indian Law: Foundational Principles*. Cambridge: Cambridge University Press, 2020.

Churchill, Robert H. "Popular Nullification, Fries' Rebellion, and the Waning of Radical Republicanism, 1798-1801." *Pennsylvania History* 67, no. 1 (2000): 105–40.

———. *The Underground Railroad and the Geography of Violence in Antebellum America.* New York: Cambridge University Press, 2020.

Clark, Mary Elizabeth. "Peter Porcupine in America: The Career of William Cobbett, 1792–1800." PhD diss., University of Pennsylvania, 1939.

Coates, Rodney D. "Law and the Cultural Production of Race and Racialized Systems of Oppression: Early Court Cases." *American Behavioral Scientist* 47, no. 3 (2003): 329–51.

Cobbett, William. *Letters from William Cobbett to Edward Thornton Written in the Years 1797 to 1800*, edited by G. D. H. Cole. London: Oxford University Press, 1937.

———. *Porcupine's Works; Containing Various Writings and Selections, Exhibiting a Faithful Picture of the United States of America*, 12 vols. London: Cobbett and Morgan, 1801.

———. *The Republican Judge: or the American Liberty of the Press, as Exhibited, Explained, and Exposed, in the Base and Partial Prosecution of William Cobbett, for a Pretended Libel against the King of Spain and his Embassador, before the Supreme Court of Pennsylvania.* London: J. Wright, 1798.

Cohen, Daniel A. *Pillars of Salt, Monuments of Grace: New England Crime Literature and the Origins of American Popular Culture, 1674–1860.* Oxford: Oxford University Press, 1993.

Cohen, Dov and Joe Vandello. "Social Norms, Social Meaning, and the Economic Analysis of Law: Meanings of Violence." *Journal of Legal Studies* 27, no. 2 (1988): 567–84.

Cohen, Morris L. and Sharon Hamby O'Connor. *A Guide to the Early Reports of the Supreme Court of the United States.* Littleton: Rothman & Co., 1995.

Connor, G. E. "The Politics of Insurrection: A Comparative Analysis of the Shays,' Whiskey, and Fries' Rebellions." *Social Science Journal* 29, no. 3 (1992): 259–81.

Constable, Marianne. *The Law of the Other: The Mixed Jury and Changing Conceptions of Citizenship, Law, and Knowledge.* Chicago: The University of Chicago Press, 1994.

Cook, Roy Bird. *Washington's Western Lands.* Strasburg, VA: Shenandoah Publishing Inc., 1930.

Cornell, Saul. "Aristocracy Assailed: The Ideology of Backcountry Anti-Federalism." *Journal of American History* 76, no. 4 (1990): 1148–72.

———. "Beyond the Myth of Consensus: The Struggle to Define the Right to Bear Arms in the Early Republic." In *Beyond the Founders: New Approaches to the Political History of the Early American Republic*, edited by Jeffrey L. Pasley, Andrew W. Robertson and David Waldstreicher, 251–73. Durham: University of North Carolina Press, 2004.

———. "Mobs, Militias, and Magistrates: Popular Constitutionalism and the Whiskey Rebellion." *Chicago-Kent Law Review*, 81, no. 3 (2006): 883–903.

———. *The Other Founders: Anti-Federalism and the Dissenting Tradition in America, 1788–1828.* Chapel Hill: University of North Caroline Press, 1999.

———. *A Well Regulated Militia: The Founding Fathers and the Origins of Gun Control in America.* New York: Oxford University Press, 2006.

Countryman, Edward. "The Problem of the Early American Crowds." *Journal of American Studies* 7, no. 1 (1973): 77–90.

Crumrine, Boyd, ed. *The Boundary Controversy between Pennsylvania and Virginia, 1748–1785: Minute Book of the Virginia Court Held at Fort Dunmore (Pittsburgh) for the District of West Augusta, 1775–1776*. One of four papers from The Annals of the Carnegie Museum.

Crumrine, Boyd and Franklin Ellis. *History of Washington County, Pennsylvania, with Biographical Sketches of Many of its Pioneers and Prominent Men.* Philadelphia: H. L. Everts & Co., 1882.

Crytzer, Brady J. "Frontier Justice: The Trial and Execution of Mamachtaga." *Westmoreland History* 20, no. 2 (2015): 4–9.

Cugoano, Quobna Ottobah. *Thoughts and Sentiments on the Evil of Slavery.* 1787. New York: Penguin Books, 1999.

Curran, Jonathan. "Examining Public Opinion during the Whiskey Rebellion." *Journal of the American Revolution* (September 7, 2021), 1–11, https://allthingsliberty.com.

Currie, David P. "The Constitution in Congress: Substantive Issues in the First Congress, 1789–1791." *The University of Chicago Law Review* 61, no. 3 (1994): 775–865.

Dahlinger, Charles W. "The Last Days of Fort Pitt." *Western Pennsylvania Historical Magazine* 5, no. 2 (1922): 99–107.

Dallas, Alexander J. *Reports of Cases Ruled and Adjudged in the Courts of Pennsylvania, Before and Since the Revolution*, 4 vols. Philadelphia: [T. Bradford; Aurora; Ormrod; Fry and Kammerer] 1790–1807.

Danforth, Samuel. *The Woeful Effects of Drunkenness, a Sermon Preached at Bristol, Octob. 12. 1709. When Two Indians, Josias and Joseph, Were Executed for Murther, Occasioned by the Drunkenness both of the Murthering & Murthered Parties.* Boston: B. Green, 1710.

Davis, Jeffrey A. "Guarding the Republican Interest: The Western Pennsylvania Democratic Societies and the Excise Tax." *Pennsylvania History* 67, no. 1 (2000): 43–62.

———. "The Whiskey Rebellion and the Demise of the Democratic-Republican Societies of Pennsylvania." *Topic: A Journal of the Liberal Arts* 45 (1994): 22–38.

De Lombard, Jeannine Marie. *In the Shadow of the Gallows: Race, Crime, and American Civic Identity.* Philadelphia: University of Pennsylvania Press, 2012.

De Vattel, Emmerich. *The Law of Nations; or Principles of the Law of Nature, Applied to the Conduct and Affairs of Nations and Sovereigns*, Joseph Chitty, ed., 1834. Cambridge: Cambridge University Press, 2011.

De Ville, Kenneth Allen. *Medical Malpractice in Nineteenth Century America: Origins and Legacy.* New York: New York University Press, 1990.

Diamond, Larry. "Facing Up to Democratic Recession." In *Democracy in Decline*, edited by Larry Diamond, Marc F. Plattner, and Condoleezza Rice, 98–118. Baltimore, MD: Johns Hopkins University Press, 2015.

Dubber, Markus Dirk. "'The Power to Govern Men and Things': Patriarchal Origins of the Police Power in American Law." *Buffalo Law Review* 52 (2004): 1277–1345.

Duffy, John. *Epidemics in Colonial America.* Baton Rouge: Louisiana State University Press, 1953.

Duke, Robert D. and Howard S. Vogel. "The Constitution and the Standing Army: Another Problem of Court-Martial Jurisdiction." *Vanderbilt Law Review* 13, no. 2 (1960): 435–60.

Eames, Steven. *Rustic Warriors: Warfare and the Provincial Soldier on the New England Border, 1689–1748.* New York: New York University Press, 2011.

Edling, Max M. *A Hercules in the Cradle: War, Money, and the American State, 1783–1867.* Chicago: University of Chicago Press, 2014.

———. *Perfecting the Union: National and State Authority in the U. S. Constitution.* New York: Oxford University Press, 2021.

———. *A Revolution in Favor of Government: Origins of the U. S. Constitution and the Making of the American State.* New York: Oxford University Press, 2003.

Edwards, Laura. *The People and Their Peace: Legal Culture and the Transformation of Inequality in the Post-Revolutionary South.* Chapel Hill: University of North Carolina Press, 2009.

Egle, William Henry, ed. *Notes and Queries: Historical, Biographical and Genealogical: Relating Chiefly to Interior Pennsylvania.* Harrisburg, PA: Harrisburg Publishing Company, 1893.

Elkins, Stanley and Eric McKitrick. *The Age of Federalism: The Early American Republic, 1788–1800.* New York: Oxford University Press, 1993.

Ellickson, Robert C. *Order Without Law: How Neighbors Settle Disputes.* Cambridge, MA: Harvard University Press, 1991.

Ellis, Joseph J. *American Dialogue: The Founders and Us.* New York: Vintage Books, 2018.

———. *His Excellency, George Washington.* New York: Vintage Books, 2004.

Elsmere, Jane Shaffer. "The Trials of John Fries." *The Pennsylvania Magazine of History and Biography* 103, no. 4 (1979): 432–45.

Elwell, John J. *A Medico-Legal Treatise on Medical Malpractice and Medical Evidence.* New York: John S. Voorhis, 1860.

Epps, Daniel. "The Consequence of Error in Criminal Justice." *Harvard Law Review* 128, no. 4 (2015): 1067–89.

Everest, Allan S. *Moses Hazen and the Canadian Refugees in the American Revolution.* Syracuse, NY: Syracuse University Press, 1976.

Fennell, Dorothy Elaine. "From Rebelliousness to Insurrection: A Social History of the Whiskey Rebellion, 1765–1802." PhD diss., University of Pittsburgh, 1981.

Ferguson, Robert A. *The Trial in American Life.* Chicago: University of Chicago Press, 2007.

Ferguson, Russell J. *Early Western Pennsylvania Politics.* Pittsburgh: University of Pittsburgh Press, 1938.

Fielding, Henry. 1742. *The Adventures of Joseph Andrews, and His Friend Mr. Abraham Adams.* London, 1793.

Findley, William. *History of the Insurrection in the Four Western Counties of Pennsylvania: In the Year 1794; and an Historical Review of the Previous Situation of the Country.* Philadelphia: Samuel Harrison Smith, 1796.

Finkelman, Paul. "Human Liberty, Property in Human Beings, and the Pennsylvania Supreme Court." *Duquesne Law Review* 53, no. 2 (2015): 453–82.

Fisher, George. "The Jury's Rise as Lie Detector." *Yale Law Journal* 107, no. 3 (1997): 575–713.

Fisher, William W., III. "Ideology and Imagery in the Law of Slavery." In *Slavery & the Law*, edited by Paul Finkelman, 43–86. Indianapolis, IN: Madison House, 1997.

Fitzpatrick, John C., ed. *The Writings of George Washington from the Original Manuscript Sources, 1745–1799*, 39 vols. Washington, DC: U. S. Printing Office, 1932.

Fletcher, George P. "Ambivalence about Treason (Law, Loyalty, and Treason: How Can the Law Regulate Loyalty Without Imperiling It?)." *North Carolina Law Review* 82, no. 5 (2004): 1611–28.

Force, Robert. "Decriminalization of Breach of Peace Statutes: A Nonpenal Approach to Order Maintenance." *Tulane Law Review* 46 (1972): 367–412.

Forman, James Jr. "Juries and Race in the Nineteenth Century." *Yale Law Journal* 113, no. 4 (2004): 895–938.

Foster, Michael. *A Report of Some Proceedings on the Commission for the Trial of the Rebels in the Year 1746, in the County of Surry, and of Other Crown Cases.* London: E. and R. Brooke, 1792.

Fox, Francis S. "Pennsylvania's Revolutionary Militia Law: The Statute that Transformed the State." *Pennsylvania History: A Journal of Mid-Atlantic Studies* 80, no. 2 (2013): 204–14

Franklin, Benjamin. "A Narrative of the Late Massacres in Lancaster County, of a Number of Indians." *The Papers of Benjamin Franklin*, Vol. 2, edited by Leonard W. Labaree, 42–69. New Haven, CT: Yale University Press, 1967.

Fratcher, William F. "History of the Judge Advocate General's Corps, United States Army." *Military Law Review* 4 (1959): 89–122.

Friedenberg, David M. *Life, Liberty and the Pursuit of Land: The Plunder of Early America.* New York: Prometheus, 1992.

Friedman, Lawrence M. 1973. *A History of American Law.* New York: Simon and Schuster, 2005.

Fritz, Christian G. *American Sovereigns: The People and America's Constitutional Tradition Before the Civil War.* Cambridge: Cambridge University Press, 2008.

Fukuyama, Francis. "Why is Democracy Performing so Poorly?" In *Democracy in Decline*, edited by Larry Diamond, Marc F. Plattner, and Condoleezza Rice, 11–24. Baltimore, MD: Johns Hopkins University Press, 2015.

Geertz, Clifford. *The Interpretation of Culture: Selected Essays.* New York: Basic Books, 1973.

———. *Local Knowledge: Further Essays in Interpretive Anthropology.* New York: Basic Books, 1985.

Gilbert, Arthur N. "Military and Civilian Justice in Eighteenth-Century England: An Assessment." *Journal of British Studies* 17, no. 2 (1978): 41–65.

Gilje, Paul A. *The Road to Mobocracy: Popular Disorder in New York City, 1763–1834.* Durham: University of North Carolina Press, 1987.

Gittler, Josephine. "Expanding the Role of the Victim in a Criminal Action: An Overview of Issues and Problems." *Pepperdine Law Review* 11, no. 5 (1984): 117–82.

Golder, John. *Life of the Honourable William Tilghman, Late Chief Justice of the State of Pennsylvania.* Philadelphia: Thomas Town, 1829.

Goodman, Nathan. *Benjamin Rush: Physician and Citizen, 1746–1813.* Philadelphia: University of Pennsylvania Press, 1934.

Government Printing Office. *Business Methods in the War Department: Report of the Board Appointed in Compliance with the Request of the Senate Select Committee to Investigate the Methods of Business in the Executive Departments.* Washington, DC: Government Printing Office.

Gramsci, Antonio. *Selections from Cultural Writings*, translated by William Boelhower. Cambridge, MA: Harvard University Press, 1985.

Grande, James, John Stevenson, and Richard Thomas, eds. *The Opinions of William Cobbett.* New York: Routledge, 2013.

Grandjean, Katherine. "'Our Fellow-Creatures & our Fellow-Christians': Race and Religion in Eighteenth-Century Narratives of Indian Culture." *American Quarterly* 62, no. 4 (2010): 925–50.

Greene, Jack P. *The Constitutional Origins of the American Revolution.* Cambridge: Cambridge University Press, 2011.

Griffin, Patrick. *American Leviathan: Empire, Nation, and Revolutionary Frontier.* New York: Hill and Wang, 2007.
Grotius, Hugo. *The Most Excellent Hugo Grotius, His Three Books Treating of the Rights of War and Peace*, translated by William Evats. London: M. W. for Thomas Basset and Ralph Smith, 1682.
Gudridge, Patrick O. "Ely, Black, Grotius & Vattel." *University of Miami Law Review* 50, no. 1 (1995): 81–106.
Hagedorn, Nancy L. "'A Friend to Go Between Them': The Interpreter as Cultural Broker During Anglo-Iroquois Councils, 1740–70." *Ethnohistory* 35, no. 1 (1988): 60–80.
Halbrook, Stephen P. and David P. Kopel. "Tench Coxe and the Right to Keep and Bear Arms." *William and Mary Bill of Rights Journal* 7, no. 2 (1999): 347–99.
Hale, Matthew. *The History of the Pleas of the Crown*, 2 vols. London: E. and R. Nutt and R. Gosling, 1736.
Hall, Kermit L., Peter Hoffer, David Bodenhamer, and Allen Steinberg. "Allen Steinberg's The Transformation of Criminal Justice in Philadelphia: 1800–1880: A Symposium." *Pennsylvania History* 59, no. 2 (1992): 145–69.
Halttunen, Karen. *Murder Most Foul: The Killer and the Gothic Imagination.* Cambridge, MA: Harvard University Press, 1998.
Hamburger, Phillip A. "Equality and Diversity: The Eighteenth-Century Debate about Equal Protection and Equal Civil Rights." *Supreme Court Review* (1992): 295–392.
Harley, David. "Honour and Property: The Structure of Professional Disputes in Eighteenth-Century English Medicine." In *The Medical Enlightenment of the Eighteenth Century*, edited by Andrew Cunningham and Roger French, 138–64. Cambridge: Cambridge University Press, 1990.
Harper, R. Eugene. *The Transformation of Western Pennsylvania, 1770–1800.* Pittsburgh: University of Pittsburgh Press, 1991.
Harper, Steven C. "Delawares and Pennsylvanians After the Walking Purchase." In *Friends and Enemies in Penn's Woods: Indians, Colonists, and the Racial Construction of Pennsylvania*, edited by William A. Pencak and Daniel K. Richter,167–79. University Park: Pennsylvania State University Press, 2004.
Harris, Todd C. "George Washington" A Revolutionary Approach to Leadership." *Leadership & Organization Development Journal* 39, no. 8 (2018): 995–1009.
Harvard Law Note. "Developments in the Law: Race and the Criminal Process: II. The Limits of Racial Equality: The Fourteenth Amendment and the Criminal Justice System." *Harvard Law Review* 101, no. 7 (1988): 1472–1641.
Hein, David. "George Washington and the Patience of Power." *Modern Age* 57, no. 4 (2015): 35–43.
Heller, Francis H. "Military Law in the Continental Army." *University of Kansas Law Review* 25, no. 3 (1977): 353–60.
Hening, William Waller. *The Statutes at Large; Being a Collection of all the Laws of Virginia, from the First Session of the Legislature, in the Year 1619*, Vol. 6. Richmond, VA: George Cochran, 1822.
Hermes, Katherine. "'Justice Will Be Done Us': Algonquin Demands for Reciprocity in the Courts of European Settlers." In *The Many Legalities of Early America*, edited

by Christopher Tomlins and Bruce H. Mann, 123–49. Chapel Hill: University of North Carolina Press, 2001.

Hickox, Charles F. III, and Andrew C. Laviano. "William Paterson." *Journal of Supreme Court History* 17, no. 1 (1992): 53–61.

Hillman, Benjamin J. *Executive Journals of the Council of Colonial Virginia (June 20, 1754–May 3, 1775)*, Vol. 6. Richmond, VA: Virginia State Library, 1966.

Hofstadter, Richard. *The Paranoid Style in American Politics and Other Essays.* New York: Vintage, 1964.

Hogeland, William. *Autumn of the Black Snake: George Washington, Mad Anthony Wayne, and the Invasion that Opened the West.* New York: Farrar, Straus and Giroux, 2017.

———. *The Whiskey Rebellion: George Washington, Alexander Hamilton, and the Frontier Rebels who Challenged America's Newfound Sovereignty.* New York: Simon and Schuster, 2006.

Holleman, J. F. "Trouble-Cases and Trouble-Less Cases in the Study of Customary Law and Legal Reform." *Law and Society Review* 7, no. 4 (1973): 585–610.

Holt, Wythe. "The Federal Whiskey Rebellion Cases of 1795 and the Rise of the National Security State." Unpublished manuscript, 2010.

———. "The Whiskey Rebellion of 1794: A Democratic Working-Class Insurrection." 2004. http://colonial seminar.uga.edu/whiskeyrebellion-6.

Holton, Woody. *Forced Founders: Indians, Debtors, Slaves, and the Making of the American Revolution in Virginia.* Chapel Hill: University of North Carolina Press, 1999.

———. *Unruly Americans and the Origins of the Constitution.* New York: Hill and Wang, 2007.

Hope, Ian C. *A Scientific Way of War: Antebellum Military Science, West Point, and the Origins of American Military Thought.* Lincoln: University of Nebraska Press, 2015.

Horton, Lois E. "From Class to Race in Early America: Northern Post-Emancipation Racial Reconstruction." In *Race in the Early Republic: Racial Consciousness and Nation-Building in the Early Republic*, edited by Michael A. Morrison and James Brewer Stewart, 55–74. Lanham, MD: Rowman and Littlefield, 2002.

Horwitz, Morton J. *The Transformation of American Law, 1780–1860.* Cambridge, MA: Harvard University Press, 1977.

Hulbert, Archer Butler. *Washington and the West, being George Washington's Diary of September, 1784, Kept During his Journey into the Ohio Basin in the Interest of a Commercial Union Between the Great Lakes and the Potomac River.* New York: Century Co., 1905.

Hunter, Donna Denise. "Dead Men Talking: Africans and the Law in New England's Eighteenth-Century Execution Sermons and Crime Narratives." PhD diss., University of California, Berkeley, 2000.

———. "Race, Law and Innocence: Executing Black Men in the Eighteenth Century." *Studies in Law, Politics, and Society* 20 (2000): 71–97.

Hurst, James Willard. *The Law of Treason in the United States: Collected Essays.* Westport, CT: Greenwood Publishing Company, 1971.

———. "Treason in the United States: I, Treason, Down to the Constitution." *Harvard Law Review* 58, no. 2 (1944): 226–72.

Huston, Charles. *An Essay on the History and Nature of Original Titles to Land in the Province and State of Pennsylvania.* Philadelphia: T. & J. W. Johnson, 1849.

Huston, Reeve. "Rethinking the Origins of Partisan Democracy in the United States, 1795–1840." In *Practicing Democracy: Popular Politics in the United States from the Constitution to the Civil War*, edited by Daniel Peart and Adam I. P. Smith, 46–71. Charlottesville: University of Virginia Press, 2015.

Ifft, Richard A. "Treason in the Early Republic: The Federal Courts, Popular Protest, and Federalism During the Whiskey Rebellion." In *The Whiskey Rebellion; Past and Present Perspectives*, edited by Steven R. Boyd, 165–82. Westport, CT: Greenwood Press, 1985.

Imagination, Collectif. "From Whiskey Rebellion to Donald Trump and the Question of Power: An Interview with Isaac Ariail Reed." *Sociaini Studia* 13, no. 4 (2017): 99–104.

Irvin, Benjamin H. *Clothed in Robes of Sovereignty: The Continental Congress and the People out of Doors.* New York: Oxford University Press, 2011.

Jackson, Donald and Dorothy Twohig, eds. *The Diaries of George Washington, Volume IV, 1784–June 1786.* Charlottesville: University Press of Virginia, 1978.

Jensen, Merrill. "The Creation of the National Domain, 1781–1784." *The Mississippi Valley Historical Review* 26, no. 3 (1939): 323–42.

Johnstone, Abraham. *The Address of Abraham Johnstone, a Black Man, Who Was Hanged at Woodbury, in the County of Glocester, and State of New Jersey, on Saturday the 8th Day of July Last.* Philadelphia: Printed for the Purchasers, 1797.

Jones, Absalom and Richard Allen. *A Narrative of the Proceedings of the Black People, During the Late Awful Calamity in Philadelphia, in the Year 1793.* Philadelphia: William W. Woodward, 1794.

Jones, Keith Marshall, III. "John Laurance and the Role of Military Justice at Valley Forge." *Pennsylvania Magazine of History and Biography* 141, no. 1 (2017): 7–29.

Joyce, John. *Confession of John Joyce, Alias Davis.* Philadelphia: Bethel Church, 1808.

Katz, Stanley Nider. "Introduction." In *A Brief Narrative of the Case and Trial of John Peter Zenger, Printer of the New York Weekly Journal*, edited by Stanley Nider Katz, 1–35. Cambridge, MA: Harvard University Press, 1963.

Kawashima, Yashuhide. "Forced Conformity: Puritan Criminal Justice and Indians." *Kansas Law* Review 25, no. 3 (1977): 361–74.

———. "Forest Diplomats: The Role of Interpreters in Indian-White Relations on the Early American Frontier." *American Indian Quarterly* 13, no. 1 (1989): 1–14.

———. *Puritan Justice and the Indian: White Man's Law in Massachusetts, 1630–1763.* Middletown, CT: Wesleyan University Press, 1986.

Kennedy, Roger G. *Burr, Hamilton, and Jefferson: A Study in Character.* New York: Oxford University Press, 2000.

Kennedy, Vans. *Practical Remarks on the Proceedings of General Courts Martial.* London: A Strahan, 1825.

Klein, Rachel N. "Ordering the Backcountry: The South Carolina Regulation." *William and Mary Quarterly* 38, no. 4 (1981): 661–80.

Knapp, Aaron T. "From Empire to Law: Customs Collection in the American Founding." *Law & Social Inquiry* 43, no. 2 (2018): 554–84.

Knouff, Gregory T. "Whiteness and Warfare on a Revolutionary Frontier." In *Friends and Enemies in Penn's Woods*, edited by William A. Pencak and Daniel K. Richter, 238–57. University Park: The Pennsylvania State University Press, 2004.

Kohn, Richard H. *Eagle and Sword: The Federalists and the Creation of the Military Establishment in America, 1783–1802.* New York: The Free Press, 1975.

———. "The Washington Administration's Decision to Crush the Whiskey Rebellion." *Journal of American History* 59, no. 3 (1972): 567–84.

Konig, David Thomas. "Arms and the Man: What Did the Right to Keep Arms Mean in the Early Republic." *Law and History Review* 25, no. 1 (2007): 177–86.

Konkle, Burton A. *George Bryan and the Constitution.* Philadelphia: W. J. Campbell, 1932.

———. *Joseph Hopkinson, 1770–1842: Jurist, Scholar, Inspirer of the Arts.* Philadelphia: University of Pennsylvania Press, 1981.

———. *The Life and Times of Thomas Smith, 1745–1809.* Philadelphia: Campion & Company, 1904.

Kozuskanich, Nathan R. "Pennsylvania, the Militia, and the Second Amendment." *The Pennsylvania Magazine of History and Biography* 133, no. 2 (2009): 119–47.

Kramer, Larry D. *The People Themselves: Popular Constitutionalism and Judicial Review.* New York: Oxford University Press, 2004.

Kutler, Stanley I. "Pennsylvania Courts, the Abolition Act, and Negro Rights." *Pennsylvania History* 30, no. 1 (1963): 14–27.

Landsman, Stephan. "The Rise of the Contentious Spirit: Adversary Procedure in Eighteenth Century England." *Cornell Law Review* 75, no. 3 (1990): 497–609.

Langbein, John H. *The Origins of Adversary Criminal Trial.* Oxford: Oxford University Press, 2003.

Lantzer, Jason S. "Washington as Cincinnatus: A Model of Leadership." In *George Washington, Foundation of Presidential Leadership and Character*, edited by Ethan Fishman, William D. Peterson, and Mark J. Rozell, 33–51. Westport, CT: Praeger, 2001.

Lapsansky, Emma Jones. *Neighborhoods in Transition: William Penn's Dream and Urban Reality.* New York: Garland, 1994.

Larson, Carlton. "The Forgotten Constitutional Law of Treason and the Enemy Combatant Problem." *University of Pennsylvania Law Review* 154, no. 4 (2006): 863–926.

Laub, C. H. "Revolutionary Virginia and the Crown Lands (1775–1783)." *The William and Mary Quarterly* 11, no. 4 (1931): 304–14.

Laws of the Commonwealth of Pennsylvania, May 24, 1781–September 3, 1790, Vol. 2. Philadelphia: John Bioren, 1810.

Le Sage, Alain Rene. *The Adventures of Gil Blas of Santillane*, 2 vols. Translated by T. Smollett. London: J. Walker, 1809.

Lender, Mark Edward. *Cabal! The Plot against George Washington.* Yardley, PA: Westholme Publishing, 2019.

Lermack, Paul. "Bonds and Criminal Justice in Colonial Philadelphia." *The Pennsylvania Magazine of History and Biography* 100, no. 2 (1976): 173–190.

Lerner, Renee Lettow. "The Transformation of the American Civil Trial: The Silent Judge." *William and Mary Law Review* 42, no. 1 (2000): 195–264.

Levitsky, Steven and Daniel Ziblatt. *How Democracies Die.* New York: Crown, 2018.

Levitsky, Steven and Lucan Way. "The Myth of Democratic Recession." *Journal of Democracy* 26, no. 1 (2015): 45–58.

Lieberman, Robert C., Suzanne Mettler, Thomas B. Pepinsky, Kenneth M. Roberts, and Richard Valelly. "The Trump Presidency and American Democracy: A Historical and Comparative Analysis." *Perspectives on Politics* 17, no. 2 (2019): 470–79.

Llewellyn, Karl N. and E. A. Hoebel. *The Cheyenne Way: Conflict and Case Law in Primitive Jurisprudence.* Norman: University of Oklahoma Press, 1941.

Lofquist, William S. "Justice on the Western Frontier: The Death Penalty in Pre-Industrial Pittsburgh, 1754–1840." *Pennsylvania History: A Journal of Mid-Atlantic Studies* 85, no. 4 (2018): 556–93.

———. "State Killings in the Steel City: The History of the Death Penalty in Pittsburgh," accessed September 1, 2023, https://state-killings-in-the-steel-city.org/2018/01/09/mamachtaga/.

Lundin, John Marquez. "The Law of Equality before Equality Was Law." *Syracuse Law Review* 49, no. 4 (1999): 1137–90.

Lurie, Jonathan. *Military Justice in America: The U.S. Court of Appeals for the Armed Forces, 1775–1980.* Lawrence: University Press of Kansas, 2001.

Macomb, Alexander. *A Treatise on Martial Law, and Courts-Martial; as Practised in the United States of America.* Charleston, SC: J. Hoff, 1809.

Maier, Pauline. "Popular Uprisings and Civil Authority in Eighteenth-Century America." *William and Mary Quarterly* 27, no. 1 (1970): 3–35.

———. 1972. *From Resistance to Revolution: Colonial Radicals and the Development of American Opposition to Britain, 1765–1776.* New York: W. W. Norton and Company, 1992.

Malone, Christopher. "Rethinking the End of Black Voting Rights in Antebellum Pennsylvania: Racial Ascriptivism, Partisanship and Political Development in the Keystone State." *Pennsylvania History: A Journal of Mid-Atlantic Studies* 72, no. 4 (2005): 466–504.

Malone, Wex. *Essays on Torts.* Baton Rouge: Louisiana State University Press, 1986.

Mancall, Peter C. *Deadly Medicine: Indians and Alcohol in Early America.* Ithaca, NY: Cornell University Press, 1995.

Manion, Jen. *Liberty's Prisoners: Carceral Culture in Early America.* Philadelphia: University of Pennsylvania Press, 2015.

Marcus, Maeva, ed. *The Documentary History of the Supreme Court of the United States, 1789–1800*, vol. 6. New York: Columbia University Press.

Marder, Daniel. *Hugh Henry Brackenridge.* New York: Twayne Publishers, Inc., 1967.

Martin, James Kirby and Mark Edward Lender. *"A Respectable Army": The Military Origins of the Republic, 1763–1789.* Hoboken, NJ: Wiley Blackwell, 2015.

Martin, Robert W. T. *Government by Dissent: Protest, Resistance, and Radical Democratic Thought in the Early American Republic.* New York: New York University Press, 2013.

Matthias, Peter. *Confession of Peter Matthias, alias Mathews.* Philadelphia: Bethel Church, 1808.

Maurer, Maurer. "Military Justice Under General Washington." *Military Affairs* 28, no. 1 (1964): 8–16.

McBurney, Christian M. *George Washington's Nemesis: The Outrageous Treason and Unfair Court-Martial of Major General Charles Lee During the Revolutionary War.* El Dorado Hills, CA: Savas Beatie, 2020.

McClelland, Milo A. *Civil Malpractice: A Treatise on Surgical Jurisprudence.* New York: Hurd and Houghton, 1877.

McDonald, Forrest. "Presidential Character: The Example of George Washington." *Perspectives on Political Science* 26, no. 3 (1997): 134–39.

McFarland, Esther Ann. *William Lewis, Esquire: Enlightened Statesman, Profound Lawyer, and Useful Citizen.* Darby, PA: Diane Publishing Company, 2012.

McGloskey, R. G., ed. *The Works of James Wilson*, 2 vols. Cambridge, MA: Belnap Press, 1967.

Melish, Joanne Pope. "The 'Condition' Debate and Racial Discourse in the Antebellum North." In *Race in the Early Republic*: *Racial Consciousness and Nation-Building in the Early Republic*, edited by Michael A. Morrison and James Brewer Stewart, 75–94. Lanham, MD: Rowman and Littlefield, 2002.

Melish, Joanne Pope. *Disowning Slavery: Gradual Emancipation and "Race" in New England, 1780–1860.* Ithaca, NY: Cornell University Press, 1998.

Melton, Ada Pecos. "Indigenous Justice Systems and Tribal Society." *Judicature* 79, no. 3 (1995): 126–33.

Mettler, Suzanne and Robert C. Lieberman. *Four Threats: The Recurring Crises of American Democracy.* New York: St. Martin's Press, 2020.

Minutes of the Proceedings of the Committee, Appointed on the 14th September, 1793, by the Citizens of Philadelphia, the Northern Liberties, and the District of Southwark, To Attend to and Alleviate the Sufferings of the Afflicted with the Malignant Fever Prevalent in the City and Its Vicinity, 1848. Philadelphia: City of Philadelphia, 1848.

Mires, Charlene. *Independence Hall in American Memory.* Philadelphia: University of Pennsylvania Press, 2002.

Mitchell, James T. and Henry Flanders, eds. *Statutes at Large of Pennsylvania from 1682–1801*, Vols. 9–10. Harrisburg, PA: State Printer, 1896–1909.

Mittal, Sonia and Barry R. Weingast. "Self-Enforcing Constitutions: With an Application to Democratic Stability in America's First Century." *Journal of Law, Economics, and Organization* 29, no. 2 (2013): 278–302.

Moore, R. Walton. "George Washington as a Judge and His Attitude Towards Courts and Lawyers." *American Bar Association Journal* 18, no. 3 (1932): 151–55.

Morano, Anthony A. "A Reexamination of the Development of the Reasonable Doubt Rule." *Boston University Law Review* 55, no. 4 (1975): 507–29.

Morris, Sue. *Blogspot* (blog). *The Historical Dilettante: Pittsburgh's Lost Islands.* historicaldilettante.blogspot.com/2016/05/things-that-arent-there-any-more.html.

Morris, Thomas D. *Free Men All: The Personal Liberty Laws of the North, 1780–1861.* Union, NJ: The Lawbook Exchange, 2001.

———. "Slaves and the Rule of Evidence in Criminal Trials." *Chicago-Kent Law Review* 68, no. 3 (1993): 1209–40.

Mountain, Joseph. "Petition to the General Assembly of the State of Connecticut." *The Connecticut State Archives Crimes and Misdemeanors*, 2nd ser., 1671–1820, IV, 131a.

———. *Sketches of the Life of Joseph Mountain, a Negro, Who was Executed at New-Haven on the 20th Day of October, 1790, for a Rape.* New Haven, CT: T. S. Green, 1790.

Myers, Albert Cook. *Narrative of Early Pennsylvania, West New Jersey, and Delaware, 1630–1701.* New York: Charles Scribner's Sons, 1912.

Myrsiades, Linda. "Law, Culture, and Race: The 1808 Murder Trial of John Joyce and Peter Matthias." *Pennsylvania History: A Journal of Mid-Atlantic Studies* 86, no. 2 (2019): 155–94.

———. *Law and Medicine in Revolutionary America: Dissecting the Rush v. Cobbett Trial.* Bethlehem, PA: Lehigh University Press, 2012.

———. "Legal Practice and Pragmatics in the Law: The 1821 Trials of John Reed, 'Fugitive Slave.'" *Pennsylvania Magazine of History and Biography* 138, no. 3 (2014): 305–38.

———. *Medical Culture in Revolutionary America: Feuds, Duels, and a Court-Martial.* Madison, NJ: Fairleigh Dickinson University Press, 2009.

———. "A Tale of a Whiskey Rebellion Judge: William Paterson, Grand Jury Charges, and the Trials of the Whiskey Rebels." *The Pennsylvania Magazine of History and Biography* 140, no. 2 (2016): 129–65.

Nash, Gary B. *Forging Freedom: The Formation of Philadelphia's Black Community, 1720–1840.* Cambridge, MA: Harvard University Press, 1988.

Nash, Gary B. and Jean R. Soderlund. *Freedom by Degrees: Emancipation in Pennsylvania and Its Aftermath.* New York: Oxford University Press, 1991.

Neagles, James C. *Summer Soldiers: A Survey and Index of Revolutionary War Courts-Martial.* Salt Lake City, UT: Ancestry Incorporated, 1986.

Nelson, William E. *Americanization of the Common Law: The Impact of Legal Change on Massachusetts Society, 1760–1830.* Cambridge, MA: Harvard University Press, 1975.

———. *Common Law in Colonial America, Volume I: The Chesapeake and New England, 1607–1660.* New York: Oxford University Press, 2008.

———. *Common Law in Colonial America, Volume II: The Middle Colonies and the Carolinas, 1660–1730.* New York: Oxford University Press, 2013.

———. *Common Law in Colonial America, Volume III: The Chesapeake and New England, 1660–1750.* New York: Oxford University Press, 2016.

———. *Common Law in Colonial America, Volume IV: Law and the Constitution on the Eve of Independence, 1735–1776.* New York: Oxford University Press, 2018.

———. *E Pluribus Unum: How the Common Law Helped Unify and Liberate Colonial America, 1607–1776.* New York: Oxford University Press, 2019.

———. "Emerging Notions of Modern Criminal Law in the Revolutionary Era: An Historical Perspective." *New York University Law Review* 42, no. 3 (1967): 450–83.

Newlin, Claude Milton. *The Life and Writings of Hugh Henry Brackenridge.* Princeton, NJ: Princeton University Press, 1932.

Newman, Paul Douglas. "The 'Four Nations of Indians Upon the Susquehanna': Mid-Atlantic Murder, Diplomacy, and Political Identity, 1717–1723." *Pennsylvania History: A Journal of Mid-Atlantic Studies* 88, no. 3 (2021): 287–318.

———. *Fries's Rebellion: The Enduring Struggle for the American Revolution.* Philadelphia: University of Pennsylvania Press, 2004.

Newman, Richard S. and Roy E. Finkenbine. "Black Founders in the New Republic: Introduction." *William and Mary Quarterly* 64, no. 1 (2007): 83–94.

———. *Freedom's Prophet: Bishop Ricard Allen, the AME Church, and the Black Founding Fathers.* New York University Press, 2008.

———. *The Transformation of American Abolitionism: Fighting Slavery in the Early Republic.* Chapel Hill: University of North Carolina Press, 2002.

Newmyer, R. Kent. *The Treason Trial of Aaron Burr: Law, Politics, and the Character Wars of the New Nation.* Cambridge: Cambridge University Press, 2012.

Nicholson, Bradley J. "Courts in the Legion Army: American Military Law in the Early Republic: 1792–1796." *Military Law Review* 144 (1994): 77–109.

Nordham, George Washington. *George Washington and the Law.* Chicago: Adams Press, 1982.

"Note: Peace and Behavior Bonds—Summary Punishment for Uncommitted Offenses." *Virginia Law Review* 52, no. 5 (1966): 914–33.

O'Connor, John E. *William Paterson: Lawyer and Statesman, 1745–1806.* New Brunswick, NJ: Rutgers University Press, 1979.

Offutt, William M. Jr. "The Limits of Authority: Courts, Ethnicity, and Gender in the Middle Colonies, 1670–1710." In *The Many Legalities of Early America*, edited by Christopher Tomlins and Bruce H. Mann, 357–87. Chapel Hill: University of North Carolina Press, 2001.

———. *Of 'Good Laws' & 'Good Men': Law and Society in the Delaware Valley, 1680–1710.* Urbana: University of Illinois Press, 1995.

Onuf, Peter S. *The Origins of the Federal Republic: Jurisdictional Controversies in the United States, 1775-1787.* Philadelphia: University of Pennsylvania Press, 1983.

Otter, Samuel. *Philadelphia Stories: America's Literature of Race and Freedom.* New York: Oxford University Press, 2010.

Owen, Kenneth. *Political Community in Revolutionary Pennsylvania, 1774–1800.* Oxford: Oxford University Press, 2018.

Parker, Kunal M. "Making Blacks Foreigners: The Legal Construction of Former Slaves in Post-Revolutionary Massachusetts." *Utah Law Review* 75, no. 1 (2001): 75–124.

Parkinson, Robert G. *The Common Cause: Creating Race and Nation in the American Revolution.* Chapel Hill: University of North Carolina Press, 2016.

Patrick-Stamp, Leslie. "Numbers That Are Not New: African Americans in the Country's First Prison, 1790–1835." *Pennsylvania Magazine of History and Biography* 119, nos. 1–2 (1995): 95–128.

Pencak, William A. "Introduction: A Historical Perspective." In *Riot and Revelry in Early America*, edited by William Pencak, Matthew Dennis, and Simon P. Newman, 3–20. University Park: Penn State University Press, 2002.

———. "White Indians in Penn's City: The Loyal Sons of St. Tammany." In *Riot and Revelry in Early America*, edited by William Pencak, Matthew Dennis, and Simon P. Newman, 179–205. University Park: Penn State University Press, 2002.

Pencak, William A. and Daniel K. Richter, eds. *Friends and Enemies in Penns Woods: Indians, Colonists, and the Racial Construction of Pennsylvania.* University Park: Pennsylvania State University Press, 2004.

Philips, Verne D. J. "The American Military Court of Inquiry." *The Military History of Texas and the Southwest* 14, no. 1 (1978): 45–52.

Porter, David. "Washington v. Anarchy: A Prelude to the Whiskey Rebellion." *Topic: A Journal of the Liberal Arts* 45 (1994): 11–17.

Potter, John E. "The Pennsylvania and Virginia Boundary Dispute." *The Pennsylvania Magazine of History and Biography* 38, no. 4 (1914): 407–26.

Poul, Debra J. and Wendy L. Waller. "The Pennsylvania Project: The Pennsylvania Supreme Court Perspectives from Within." *Villanova Law Review* 23, nos. 5–6 (1977–1978): 1041–94.

Presser, Stephen B. "A Tale of Two Judges: Richard Peters, Samuel Chase, and the Broken Promise of Federalist Jurisprudence." *Northwestern University Law Review* 73, no. 1 (1978): 26–111.

Primrose, William. "Biography of William Lewis." *Pennsylvania Magazine of History and Biography* 20, no. 1 (1896): 30–40.

Rao, Gautham. "The New Historiography of the Early Federal Government: Institutions, Contexts, and the Imperial State." *The William and Mary Quarterly* 77, no. 1 (2020): 97–128.

———. *National Duties: Custom Houses and the Making of the American State.* Chicago: University of Chicago Press, 2016.

Reid, A. B. "Early Courts, Judges, and Lawyers of Alleghany County." *Western Pennsylvania Historical Magazine* 5, no. 3 (1922): 185–202.

Rhys, Isaac. *The Transformation of Virginia, 1740–1790.* Durham: University of North Carolina Press, 1999.

Richards, Louis. "Hon. Jacob Rush, of the Pennsylvania Judiciary." *Pennsylvania Magazine of History and Biography* 39, no. 1 (1915): 53–68.

Roediger, David R. "The Pursuit of Whiteness: Property, Terror, and Expansion, 1790–1860." In *Race in the Early Republic: Racial Consciousness and Nation-Building in the Early Republic*, edited by Michael A. Morrison and James Brewer Stewart, 5–26. Lanham, MD: Rowman & Littlefield, 2002.

Roney, Jessica Choppin. "1776, Viewed from the West." *Journal of the Early Republic* 37, no. 4 (2017): 655–700.

Rosenberg, Norman L. *Protecting the Best Men: An Interpretive History of the Law of Libel.* Chapel Hill: University of North Carolina Press, 1986.

Rowe, G. S. "Black Offenders, Criminal Courts, and Philadelphia Society in the Late Eighteenth-Century." *Journal of Social History* 22, no. 4 (1989): 685–712.

———. "Crime and its Resolution in 18th Century Cumberland County." *Cumberland County History* 3, no. 1 (1986): 22–26.

———. *Embattled Bench: The Pennsylvania Supreme Court and the Forging of a Democratic Society, 1684-1809.* Newark: University of Delaware Press, 1994.

———. "Judicial Tyrant and Vox Populi: Pennsylvanians View Their State Supreme Court, 1777-1799." *Pennsylvania Magazine of History and Biography* 118, nos. 1–2 (1994): 33–62.

———. *Thomas McKean: The Shaping of an American Republicanism.* Boulder: University of Colorado Press, 1978.

Rowe, G. S. and Jack D. Marietta. *Troubled Experiment: Crime and Justice in Pennsylvania, 1682-1800.* Philadelphia: University of Pennsylvania Press, 2006.

Rush, Benjamin. *An Account of the Bilious Remitting Yellow Fever, as It Appeared in the City of Philadelphia, in the Year 1793.* Philadelphia: Thomas Dobson, 1794.

———. *Sixteen Introductory Lectures to Courses of Lectures Upon the Institutes and Practice of Medicine, With a Syllabus of the Latter.* Philadelphia: Bradford and Innskeep, 1811.

Salinger, Sharon V. "Spaces, Inside and Outside, in Eighteenth-Century Philadelphia." *Journal of Interdisciplinary History* 26, no. 1 (1995): 1–31.

Schenawolf, Harry. "General Moses Hazen of the Infernals: Ruthless and Fierce, He Was Just the Man Washington Needed." *Revolutionary War Journal* (July 16, 2019): 1–59. www.revolutionarywarjournal.com/.

Schlueter, David A. "The Court-Martial: A Historical Survey." *Military Law Review* 87 (1980): 129–66.

Schmidt, Michael S. and Maggie Haberman. "Trump Weighed Insurrection Act Against Protests." *New York Times*, June 26, 2021, https://www.nytimes.com.

Schoenbachler, Matthew. "Republicanism in the Age of Democratic Revolution: The Democratic-Republican Societies of the 1790s." *Journal of the Early Republic* 18, no. 2 (1998): 237–61.

Schwartz, Barry. "Social Change and Collective Memory: The Democratization of George Washington." *American Sociological Review* 56, no. 2 (1991): 221–36.

Schwartz, Warren F., Keith Baxter, and David Ryan. "The Duel: Can these Gentlemen be Acting Efficiently." *Journal of Legal Studies* 13 (1884): 321–55.

Shankman, Andrew. *Crucible of American Democracy: The Struggle to Fuse Egalitarianism & Capitalism in Jeffersonian Pennsylvania.* Lawrence: University Press of Kansas, 2004.

Shapiro, Barbara. *'Beyond Reasonable Doubt' and 'Probable Cause': Historical Perspectives on the Anglo-American Law of Evidence.* Berkeley: University of California Press, 1991.

Sharp, James Roger. *American Politics in the Early Republic: The New Nation in Crisis.* New Haven: Yale University Press, 1993.

———. "The Whiskey Rebellion and the Question of Representation." In *The Whiskey Rebellion: Past and Present Perspectives*, edited by Steven R. Boyd, 119–34. Westport, CT: Greenwood Press, 1985.

Sheehan, Colleen A. "Madison v. Hamilton: The Battle over Republicanism and the Role of Public Opinion." *American Political Science Review* 98, no. 3 (2004): 405–24.

Shenk, Morris N. "Crimes and Punishments in Provincial Cumberland County." *Cumberland County History* 18, no. 1 (2001): 10–14.

Shogan, Colleen J. "George Washington: Can Aristotle Recapture What his Countrymen Have Forgotten?" In *George Washington, Foundation of Presidential Leadership and Character*, edited by Ethan Fishman, William D. Peterson, and Mark J. Rozell, 53–69. Westport, CT: Praeger, 2001.

Shurkin, Michael. *The Evolution of U. S. Military Policy From the Constitution to the Present, Volume I: The Old Regime: The Army, Militia, and Volunteers From Colonial Times to the Spanish-American War.* Santa Monica, CA: Rand Corporation, 2020.

Silver, Peter. *Our Savage Neighbors: How Indian War Transformed Early America.* New York: W. W. Norton & Company, 2008.

Slaughter, Thomas P. "'The King of Crimes': Early American Treason Law, 1787–1860." In *Launching the 'Extended Republic': The Federalist Era*, edited by Ronald Hoffman and Peter Albert, 54–135. Charlottesville: University of Virginia, 1996.

———. "The Tax Man Cometh: Ideological Opposition to Internal Taxes, 1760-1790." *William and Mary Quarterly* 41, no. 4 (1984): 566–91.

———. *The Whiskey Rebellion: Frontier Epilogue to the American Revolution.* New York: Oxford University Press, 1986.

Slotkin, Richard. "Narratives of Negro Crime in New England, 1675–1800." *American Quarterly* 25, no. 1 (1973): 3–31.

Smith, James Morton. "The Aurora and the Alien and Sedition Laws, Part II: The Editorship of William Duane." *Pennsylvania Magazine of History and Biography* 77, no. 2 (1953): 123–55.

Smith, Jeffery A. *Printers and Press Freedom: The Ideology of Early American Journalism.* New York: Oxford University Press, 1988.

Smolenski, John. "The Death of Sawantaeny and the Problem of Justice on the Frontier." In *Friends and Enemies in Penn's Woods*, edited by William A. Pencak and Daniel K. Richter, 104–28. University Park: The Pennsylvania State University Press, 2004.

———. *Friends and Strangers: The Making of a Creole Culture in Colonial Pennsylvania.* Philadelphia: University of Pennsylvania Press, 2010.

Smollet, Tobias George. 1751. *The Adventures of Peregrine Pickle. In Which are Included, Memoirs of a Lady of Quality.* London: 1794.

Spater, George. *William Cobbett: The Poor Man's Friend*, Vol 1. Cambridge: Cambridge University Press, 1982.

Spero, Patrick. *Frontier Country: The Politics of War in Early Pennsylvania.* Philadelphia: University of Pennsylvania Press, 2016.

Stansfield, George James. "A History of the Judge Advocate General's Department United States Army." *Military Affairs* 9, no. 3 (1945): 219–37.

Steinberg, Allen. "'The Spirit of Litigation': Private Prosecution and Criminal Justice in Nineteenth-Century Philadelphia." *Journal of Social History* 20, no. 2 (1986): 231–249.

———. *The Transformation of Criminal Justice, 1800-1880.* Chapel Hill: The University of North Carolina Press, 1989.

Steppler, G. A. "British Military Law, Discipline, and the Conduct of Regimental Courts Martial in the Later Eighteenth Century." *The English Historical Review* 102, no. 405 (1987): 859–86.

Stewart, James Brewer. "Modernizing 'Difference': The Political Meaning of Color in the Free States, 1776–1840." In *Race in the Early Republic: Racial Consciousness and Nation-Building in the Early Republic*, edited by Michael A. Morrison and James Brewer Stewart, 113–34. Lanham, MD: Rowman & Littlefield, 2002.

Stimson, Shannon C. *The American Revolution in the Law: Anglo-American Jurisprudence Before John Marshall.* Princeton: Princeton University Press, 1990.

Surrency, Edwin C. "The Development of the Appellate Function: The Pennsylvania Experience." *The American Journal of Legal History* 20, no. 3 (1976): 173–91.

———. "Law Reports in the United States." *The American Journal of Legal History* 25, no. 1 (1981): 48–66.

Taylor, Alan. "Land and Liberty on the Post-Revolutionary Frontier." In *Devising Liberty: Preserving and Creating Freedom in the New American Republic*, edited by David Thomas Konig, 81–108. Stanford, CA: Stanford University Press, 1995.

———. *Liberty Men and Great Proprietors: The Revolutionary Settlement on the Main Frontier, 1760–1820*. Chapel Hill: University of North Carolina Press, 1990.

Thomas, William G. III. *A Question of Freedom: The Families Who Challenged Slavery from the Nation's Founding to the Civil War.* New Haven, CT: Yale University Press, 2020.

Thompson, E. P. "The Moral Economy of the English Crowd in the Eighteenth Century." *Past and Present* 50 (1971): 76–136.

Thompson, Norman. "Before we had Wings." *The Reporter* 26 (1999): 55–63.

Tovy, Tal. "Militia or Regular Army? The Debate on the Character of the American Army during the Revolution." *European Journal of American Studies* (2010). https://journals.openedition.org/ejas/7814.

"Trial of John Joyce and Peter Mathias for the Murder of Sarah Cross, Philadelphia, Pennsylvania, 1808." In *American State Trials*, Vol. 7, edited by John D. Lawson, St. Louis, MO: F. H. Thomas Law Book Co., 1917.

"Trial of Richard Smith for the Murder of John Carson, Philadelphia, 1816." In *American State Trials*, Vol. 5., edited by John H. Lawson. St. Louis, MO: F. H. Thomas Law Book Co., 1917.

Turley, Jonathan. "Tribunals and Tribulations: The Antithetical Elements of Military Governance in a Madisonian Democracy." *George Washington Law Review* 70, no. 4 (2002): 649–734.

Twining, William. "Two Works of Karl Llewellyn-II." *The Modern Law Review* 31, no. 2 (1968): 165–82.

Tytler, Alexander Fraser. *An Essay on Military Law, and the Practice of Courts Martial.* Edinburgh: Murray & Cochrane, 1800.

Unger, Harlow Giles. *Dr. Benjamin Rush: The Founding Father Who Healed a Wounded Nation.* New York: Hachette Book Group, 2018.

Urofsky, Melvin I. *Dissent and the Supreme Court: Its Role in the Court's History and the Nation's Constitutional Dialogue.* New York: Vintage, 2015.

Urwin, Gregory J. W. "'The Army of the Constitution': The Military, American Values, and the Early Republic." *Foreign Policy Research Institute Footnotes* (March 9, 2012): 3.

U.S. Government Printing Office. *The Army Lawyer: A History of the Judge Advocate Generals Corps, 1775–1795.* Washington, DC: U.S. Government Printing Office, 1975.

Van der Linden, Saunder. Costas Panagopoulos, Flavio Azevedo, and John T. Jost. "The Paranoid Style in American Politics Revisited: An Ideological Asymmetry in Conspiratorial Thinking." *Political Psychology* 42, no. 1 (2021): 23–51.

Verdun-Jones, Simon. "The Jurisprudence of Karl Llewellyn." *Dalhousie Law Journal* 1, no. 3 (1973–1974): 441–81.

Volokh, Alexander. "n Guilty Men." *University of Pennsylvania Law Review* 146, no. 2 (1997): 173–216.

Von Steuben, Friedrich Wilhelm. *A Letter on the Subject of an Established Militia and Military Arrangements: Addressed to the Inhabitants of the United States.* New York: J. McLean and Co., 1784.

———. *Regulations for the Order and Discipline of the Troops of the United States.* Philadelphia: Styner and Cist, 1779.

Waddell, Louis M. "Justice, Retribution, and the Case of John Toby." In *Friends and Enemies in Penn's Woods*, edited by William A. Pencak and Daniel K. Richter, 129–43. University Park: The Pennsylvania State University Press, 2004.

Walters, Mark D. "The Judicial Recognition of Indigenous Legal Traditions: *Connolly v. Woolrich at 150.*" *Review of Constitutional Studies* 22, no. 3 (2017): 347–77.

———. "*Mohegan Indians v. Connecticut* (1705–1773) and the Legal Status of Aboriginal Customary Laws and Government in British North America." *Osgood Hall Law Journal* 33, no. 4 (1995): 785–829.

Ward, Harry M. *George Washington's Enforcers: Policing the Continental Army.* Carbondale: Southern Illinois University Press, 2006.

Webster, Richard. *Philadelphia Preserved: Catalog of the Historic American Buildings Survey.* Philadelphia: Temple University Press, 1976.

Weinberg, Louise. "Methodological Interventions and the Slavery Cases; or, Night-Thoughts of a Legal Realist." *Maryland Law Review* 56, no. 4 (1997): 1316–70.

Westen, Peter. "Comment on Judith Schafer's 'Under the Present Mode of Trial, Improper Verdicts are Very Often Given': Criminal Procedure in the Trials of Slaves in Antebellum Louisiana." *Cardozo Law Review* 18, no. 2 (1996): 679–87.

Wharton, Francis. *State Trials of the United States during the Administrations of Washington and Adams, with References Historical and Professional.* New York: B. Franklin, 1849.

White, Ed, ed. *Hugh Henry Brackenridge: Modern Chivalry*. Indianapolis, IN: Hackett Publishing Company, Inc., 2009.

White, G. Edward. *Law in American History, Volume I: From the Colonial Years Through the Civil War.* New York: Oxford University Press, 2012.

White, J. W. F. "The Judiciary of Allegheny County." *Pennsylvania Magazine of History and Biography* 7, no. 2 (1883): 143–93.

White, Shane. "'It Was a Proud Day': African Americans, Festivals, and Parades in the North, 1741–1834." *Journal of American History* 81, no. 1 (1994): 13–50.

Wiener, Frederick Bernays. "Courts-Martial and the Bill of Rights: The Original Practice I." *Harvard Law Review* 72, no. 1 (1958): 1–49.

Wilf, Steven. "The First Republican Revival: Virtue, Judging, and Rhetoric in the Early Republic." *Connecticut Law Review* 32, nos. 4–5 (2000): 1675–98.

———. *Law's Imagined Republic: Popular Politics and Criminal Justice in Revolutionary America*. Cambridge: Cambridge University Press, 2010.

Wilkinson, Norman. *Land Policy and Speculation in Pennsylvania, 1779–1800: A Test of the New Democracy.* 1958. New York: Arno Press, 1979.

Will, Thomas E. "Liberalism, Republicanism, and Philadelphia's Black Elite in the Early Republic: The Social Thought of Absalom Jones and Richard Allen." *Pennsylvania History* 69, no. 4 (2002): 558–76.

Williams, Daniel E. *Pillars of Salt: An Anthology of Early American Criminal Narratives.* Madison, WI: Madison House, 1993.

Williams, Glanville. "Preventative Justice and the Rule of Law." *The Modern Law Review* 16, no. 4 (1953): 417–27.

Wills, Garry. *Cincinnatus: George Washington and the Enlightenment.* Garden City, NY: Doubleday, 1984.

Wilson, David A., ed. *Peter Porcupine in America: Pamphlets on Republicanism and Revolution.* Ithaca, NY: Cornell University Press.

Winch, Julie. *Philadelphia's Black Elite: Activism, Accommodation, and the Struggle for Autonomy.* Philadelphia: Temple University Press, 1988.

Winthrop, William. *Military Law and Precedents.* 1896. Washington, D.C.: U.S. Government Printing Office, 1920.

Wood, Gordon S. "Conspiracy and the Paranoid Style: Causality and Deceit in the Eighteenth Century." *The William and Mary Quarterly* 39, no. 3 (1982): 401–41.

———. *Empire of Liberty: A History of the Early Republic, 1789–1815.* New York: Oxford University Press, 2009.

———. "The Greatness of George Washington." *Virginia Quarterly Review* 68 (1992): 189–207.

———. "A Note on Mobs in the American Revolution." *William and Mary Quarterly* 23, no. 4 (1966): 635–42.

———. *The Radicalism of the American Revolution.* 1992. New York: Vintage Books, 1993.

———. "The Significance of the Early Republic." *Journal of the Early Republic* 8, no. 1 (1988): 1–20.

Index

About the Author

Linda Myrsiades is Professor Emerita from West Chester University. She received her PhD from Indiana University. Her specialties include the study of law and literature and interdisciplinary studies. She has been awarded National Endowment and PA Council for the Humanities grants that include a Research Fellowship (Harvard University) and Humanities Seminars and Institutes (Haverford College; Indiana University; Columbia University School of Medicine), as well as a State System Higher Education Research Grant (Temple Law School). Her publications include such books as *Law and Medicine in Revolutionary America: Dissecting the Rush v. Cobbett Trial, 1799*; *Medical Culture in Revolutionary America: Feuds, Duels, and a Court Martial*; and *Splitting the Baby: A Cultural Study of Abortion in Literature and Law, Rhetoric and Cartoon.*

www.ingramcontent.com/pod-product-compliance
Ingram Content Group UK Ltd.
Pitfield, Milton Keynes, MK11 3LW, UK
UKHW040857081026
15587UKWH00016B/750